en in Print 1

Printing History and Culture

Volume 2

Series Editors
Caroline Archer-Parré, Malcolm Dick and John Hinks

Women in Print 1
Design and Identities

Artemis Alexiou and Rose Roberto (eds)

PETER LANG
Oxford • Bern • Berlin • Bruxelles • New York • Wien

Bibliographic information published by Die Deutsche Nationalbibliothek.
Die Deutsche Nationalbibliothek lists this publication in the Deutsche
Nationalbibliografie; detailed bibliographic data is available on the Internet at
http://dnb.d-nb.de.

A catalogue record for this book is available from the British Library.

Library of Congress Cataloging-in-Publication Data

Names: Alexiou, Artemis, 1981- editor | Roberto, Rose, 1972- editor.
Title: Women in print : design and identities / Artemis Alexiou, Rose
   Roberto [editors].
Other titles: Title appears on item as: Women in print. 1
Description: Oxford ; New York : Peter Lang Publishing, [2022] | Series:
   Printing history and culture, 2504-4915 ; volume no. 2 | Includes
   bibliographical references and index.
Identifiers: LCCN 2022028542 (print) | LCCN 2022028543 (ebook) | ISBN
   9781789979787 (paperback) | ISBN 9781800798427 (ebook) | ISBN
   9781800798434 (epub)
Subjects: LCSH: Women in the book industries and trade--Europe--History. |
   Women printers--Europe--History. | Women publishers--Europe--History. |
   LCGFT: Essays.
Classification: LCC Z291.3 .W658 2022 (print) | LCC Z291.3 (ebook) | DDC
   381/.45002082094--dc23/eng/20220615
LC record available at https://lccn.loc.gov/2022028542
LC ebook record available at https://lccn.loc.gov/2022028543

Cover image: Elizabeth C. Yeats (right), Beatrice Cassidy (middle) and Esther Ryan (left) at
the printing room in 1904 (photograph from the Dun Emer press album, part of the Cuala
Press Archive MS11535). Image courtesy of the Board of Trinity College, Dublin.
Cover design by Brian Melville for Peter Lang Ltd.

ISSN 2504-4915
ISBN 978-1-78997-978-7 (print)
ISBN 978-1-80079-842-7 (ePDF)
ISBN 978-1-80079-843-4 (ePub)

© Peter Lang Group AG 2022

Published by Peter Lang Ltd, International Academic Publishers,
Oxford, United Kingdom
oxford@peterlang.com, www.peterlang.com

Artemis Alexiou and Rose Roberto have asserted their right under the Copyright, Designs
and Patents Act, 1988, to be identified as Editors of this Work.

All rights reserved.
All parts of this publication are protected by copyright.
Any utilisation outside the strict limits of the copyright law, without the permission of the
publisher, is forbidden and liable to prosecution. This applies in particular to reproductions,
translations, microfilming, and storage and processing in electronic retrieval systems.

This publication has been peer reviewed.

Contents

List of Figures   vii

List of Tables   xiii

Acknowledgements   xv

ARTEMIS ALEXIOU AND ROSE ROBERTO
Introduction   1

ROSA SMURRA
1 Women's Contribution to Manuscript Textbook Production in Thirteenth- and Fourteenth-Century Bologna   9

REESE ALEXANDRA IRWIN
2 Elizabeth Newbery, Publisher and Bookseller, 1780–1821: A Case Study from the Women's Print History Project   33

HANNAH LYONS
3 Letitia Byrne (1779–1849) and the 'Prejudice Against Employing Women as Engravers'   57

DIANNE ROMAN
4 The *Olive Branch* and Female Compositors, Writers and Editors, 1836–57   85

PATRICIA THOMAS
5 'Choice Type' and 'Elegant Founts': Advertising in Elizabeth Heard's Truro Printing Office   111

ERIKA LEDERMAN
6 *Examples of Art Workmanship*: The Victoria and Albert Museum's Educational Publishing Initiative and Its Female Institutional Photographer — 141

ARTEMIS ALEXIOU
7 Late Nineteenth-Century Periodical Texts and Paratexts: The *Women's Penny Paper/Woman's Herald* (1888–92) — 167

ANGELA GRIFFITH
8 Elizabeth Corbet Yeats: Dun Emer and Cuala Presses and Irish 'Art Printing', 1903–40 — 195

ANIL AYKAN BARNBROOK
9 Suffragettes: Radical Design in Action, 1903–30 — 219

ABBEY REES-HALES
10 'The Woman Thoroughly Dominates': Lene Schneider-Kainer (1885–1971) and Weimar Lesbian Erotica — 245

JESSICA GLASER
11 Beatrice Warde, May Lamberton Becker and 'Books Across the Sea' — 273

Notes on Contributors — 295

Index — 299

Figures

Figure 1.1. *Digestum vetus cum glossa ordinaria* (handwritten), c. thirteenth century © Universitätsbibliothek, Basel, C I 1, f. 9v, <www.e-codices.ch>, accessed 14 April 2020. 11

Figure 1.2. *Digestum vetus cum glossa ordinaria* (printed), 1468 © Bayerische Staatsbibliothek, Munich, <https://daten.digitale-sammlungen.de/>, accessed 19 April 2020. 27

Figure 2.1. *The New Game of Human Life, with Rules for Playing: Being the Most Agreeable & Rational Recreation Ever Invented for Youth of Both Sexes,* John Wallis, 1790 © Victoria and Albert Museum, London. 43

Figure 2.2. James Cook and John Rickman, eds, *Journal of Captain Cook's Last Voyage to the Pacific Ocean, on Discovery* (London: E. Newbury, 1781). Image courtesy of the University of British Columbia Library Digitization Centre. 54

Figure 3.1. *Plympton*, Letitia Byrne (etcher) and Joseph Farington (painter), *Memoirs of the Life of Sir Joshua Reynolds: With Some Observations on His Talents and Character,* Joseph Farington, 1819, London: T. Cadell and W. Davies, frontispiece. Image courtesy of the Victoria and Albert Museum, London. 58

Figure 3.2. *Donnington Castle Taken from a Field Adjoining the Road to East Ilsley from Newbury,* William and Letitia Byrne (etchers) and J.M.W Turner (painter), 1805. Image courtesy of Yale Center for British Art. 68

Figure 3.3.	*Roche Rocks* (graphite on thin paper), Joseph Farington [n.d.]. Image courtesy of Yale Center for British Art.	74
Figure 3.4.	*Roche Rocks* (etching), Letitia Byrne, 1818. Image courtesy of the Victoria and Albert Museum, London.	75
Figure 4.1.	*Olive Branch*, 12 November 1836, frontmatter. Image courtesy of the American Antiquarian Society Collection.	91
Figure 4.2.	Clara, 'The Model Husband', *Olive Branch*, 28 June 1851. Courtesy of the American Antiquarian Society.	103
Figure 5.1.	a. Advertising poster for Tippet of Pydar Street, Heard and Sons, 1847; b. Catalogue front cover for Mr Tippet of Pydar Street, Heard and Sons, 1847. Images used with the permission of the Royal Institution of Cornwall, Courtney Library (Heard Collection).	122
Figure 5.2.	Advertisement for Heard and Sons, Heard and Sons [n.d.]. Images used with the permission of the Royal Institution of Cornwall, Courtney Library (Heard Collection).	125
Figure 5.3.	a. Advertisement for L. I. Pouchée; b. Advertisement using Pouchée types, *The West Briton and Cornwall Advertiser*, 13 February 1824 (details). Images used with the permission of the Royal Institution of Cornwall, Courtney Library.	128
Figure 5.4.	a. Advertising poster for T. Gerrans, Auctioneer &c, Heard and Sons, 1847; b. Advertising poster for W. Salter, Heard and Sons, 1839. Images used with the permission of the Royal Institution of Cornwall, Courtney Library (Heard Collection).	131
Figure 5.5.	a. Advertising flyer for E. Heard, printer, bookbinder, bookseller, stationer, &c, Heard and Sons 1842;	

Figures

	b. A Sketch of the Interior of the Shop of Mrs Heard and Sons Truro, c.1847. Images used with the permission of the Royal Institution of Cornwall, Courtney Library (Heard Collection).	138
Figure 6.1.	Negative No. 9088 (collodion on glass plate), Isabel Agnes Cowper © Victoria and Albert Museum, London.	153
Figure 6.2.	*The Treasure of Petrossa and Other Goldsmith's Work from Roumania: A Series of Twenty Photographs*, London: The Arundel Society for Promoting the Knowledge of Art and Bell & Daldy, 1869, title page © Victoria and Albert Museum, London.	155
Figure 6.3.	*Plate No. 6, Twelve-sided Vessel* (albumen print), Isabel Agnes Cowper, in *The Treasure of Petrossa and Other Goldsmith's Work from Roumania: A Series of Twenty Photographs*, London: The Arundel Society for Promoting the Knowledge of Art and Bell & Daldy, 1869 © Victoria and Albert Museum, London.	157
Figure 7.1.	(Left to right) a. *Women's Penny Paper*, 27 October 1888, frontmatter; b. *The British Women's Temperance Journal*, October 1888, frontmatter © British Library Board, Gale, Nineteenth-Century UK Periodicals.	169
Figure 7.2.	(Top to bottom) a. *Women's Penny Paper*, 20 March 1890, frontmatter; b. *Women's Penny Paper*, 19 July 1890, frontmatter; c. *Women's Penny Paper*, 3 January 1891, frontmatter; d. *Women's Penny Paper*, 21 February 1891, frontmatter © British Library Board, Gale, Nineteenth-Century UK Periodicals.	171
Figure 7.3.	(Top left) a. Florence Fenwick Miller, *Women's Penny Paper*, 23 February 1889, frontmatter; (top right) b. Florence Fenwick Miller (detail), *Woman's Signal*, 3 October 1895 © British Library Board, Gale,	

	Nineteenth-Century UK Periodicals; (bottom left) c. Florence Fenwick Miller, 1893 © Herbert Rose Barraud; (bottom right) d. Florence Fenwick Miller, c.1910–2 © George Deney.	179
Figure 7.4.	(Top left) a. Lady Florence Dixie, *Woman's Herald*, 12 April 1890, frontmatter © British Library Board, Gale, Nineteenth-Century UK Periodicals; (top right) b. Lady Florence Dixie, 1880; (bottom left) c. Lady Florence Dixie, 1883; (bottom right) d. Lady Florence Dixie, *Gloriana; or, The Revolution of 1900*, London: Henry and Company, 1890, frontispiece. Public domain.	181
Figure 7.5.	(Top left) a. *Women's Penny Paper*, 16 March 1889, p. 8; (top right) b. *Women's Penny Paper*, 13 July 1889, p. 12; (bottom left) c. *Women's Penny Paper*, 13 December 1890, p. 127; (bottom right) d. *Woman's Herald*, 30 May 1891, p. 512 © British Library Board, Gale, Nineteenth-Century UK Periodicals.	185
Figure 8.1.	*Specimen of 'A Broad Sheet'*, Elkin Mathews, London (Cuala Press Archive) © Estate of Jack B. Yeats, DACS London/IVARO Dublin, 2020. Image courtesy of the Board of Trinity College, Dublin.	208
Figure 8.2.	*Design for an Irish-themed Greeting Card*, Elizabeth C. Yeats (Cuala Press Archive). Image courtesy of the Board of Trinity College, Dublin.	210
Figure 8.3.	*Specimen of 'A Broadside'*, Cuala Press, Dublin (Cuala Press Archive) © Estate of Jack B. Yeats, DACS London / IVARO Dublin, 2020. Image courtesy of the Board of Trinity College, Dublin.	213
Figure 9.1.	Advertisement for *Votes for Women*. Image courtesy of Schlesinger Library, Radcliffe Institute, Harvard University.	227

Figures   xi

Figure 9.2.   *The Suffragette*, 31 July 1914, frontmatter. Public
              domain. Image courtesy of LSE Library.   237

Figure 9.3.   Front headline used as shock advertising, *Votes for
              Women*, 10 March 1911, frontmatter. Image courtesy
              of LSE Library.   239

Figure 10.1. *Untitled* (lithograph), Lene Schneider-Kainer,
              Hetärengespräche [The Dialogues of the Courtesans],
              Lucian of Samosata and Christoph Martin Wieland
              (trans), Berlin: Verlag Julius Bard, 1920. Image
              reproduced with the permission of Gesche Kainer.   246

Figure 10.2. *Untitled* (lithograph), Lene Schneider-Kainer,
              Hetärengespräche [The Dialogues of the Courtesans],
              Lucian of Samosata and Christoph Martin Wieland
              (trans), Berlin: Verlag Julius Bard, 1920. Image
              reproduced with the permission of Gesche Kainer.   248

Figure 10.3. *Untitled* (lithograph), Lene Schneider-Kainer,
              Hetärengespräche [The Dialogues of the Courtesans],
              Lucian of Samosata and Christoph Martin Wieland
              (trans), Berlin: Verlag Julius Bard, 1920. Image
              reproduced with the permission of Gesche Kainer.   265

Figure 11.1. Photograph of 'Books Across the Sea' scrapbooks,
              Outpost, April 1944, p. 4. Image courtesy of the
              Cadbury Research Library, University of
              Birmingham.   286

Tables

Table 1.1. List of women involved in the Bologna book trade. The women highlighted in semi-bold are discussed in the text. Data © Rosa Smurra, 2020; Design © Artemis Alexiou, 2022.   30

Table 3.1. A diagram of the Byrne family tree, 2020 © Hannah Lyons.   63

Acknowledgements

The series editors of *Women in Print 1* are indebted to several individuals and organizations for both contributing to and supporting the book. The chapters were originally a set of papers delivered at the University of Birmingham on 13 and 14 September 2018. Organized by the Centre for Printing History & Culture, the conference, 'Women in Print', was designed to review and reassess the contribution made by women to printing and print culture from its origins to the present day. We were convinced that the contributors deserved a wider audience and were pleased that Peter Lang was keen to publish an edited book in two volumes on the subject as part of its 'Printing History and Culture' series. Our main thanks are due to the volume editors, Dr Artemis Alexiou and Dr Rose Roberto, who oversaw this complex project from inception to completion, and all the individual contributors who were actively involved throughout this journey.

Lucy Melville, Global Publishing Director and Head of Editorial at Peter Lang, has been an enthusiastic, helpful and responsive guide and her team have efficiently and effectively guided the project through from manuscript to final product.

Dr Maureen Bell afforded valuable and detailed feedback on all the chapters during the peer-reviewing process.

Other individuals have assisted in the process. Dr Connie Wan, Dr Kate Croft and Rebecca Howson were responsible for the on-the-ground organization of the 2018 conference, without whose dedication to the project the event would not have happened. The Bibliographical Society kindly supported the conference to allow the participation of postgraduate students as both speakers and audience, and Birmingham City University generously supported the production of the book.

Women in Print 1 reflects the efforts and expertise of many people. We hope that the publication justifies their commitment and provides not only a reflection of the importance of women in print but also offers opportunities for future studies of women in the printing trade.

Caroline Archer-Parré, Malcolm Dick, John Hinks
Series Editors

ARTEMIS ALEXIOU AND ROSE ROBERTO

Introduction

Patriarchy is defined as 'a system of relationships, beliefs, and values embedded in political, social, and economic systems that structure gender inequality between men and women'.[1] Therefore, in order to understand the patriarchal societies we are born into, and have to endure throughout our lives, first we ought to understand why dichotomising society between its male and female members is unconstructive. Leslie Kaine Weisman explains: 'classifying people into opposing groups of rich/poor, white/black, young/old, straight/gay, and male/female creates a social system that justifies and supports human exploitation and white male supremacy'; this happens because 'one group is afforded power and status and the other rendered powerless and inferior'.[2] Inevitably, by default the majority of human beings on this planet are brought up in a manner that is essentially discriminatory towards anyone who may be considered as the 'Other'.[3] In historiography, this inherent bias has led to innumerable history books, including art and design history books, that have consistently excluded the achievements of anyone other than the White male heterosexual hero.[4]

1   Catherine Nash, 'Patriarchy', International Encyclopaedia of Human Geography (2020), <https://www.sciencedirect.com/science/article/pii/B9780081022955102069>, accessed 8 July 2022.
2   Laslie Kanes Weisman, *Discrimination by Design: A Feminist Critique of the Man-Made Environment* (Illinois, USA: University of Illinois, 1994), 10.
3   Simon De Beauvoir and H. M. Parshley (ed., trans.), *The Second Sex* (London, UK: Jonathan Cape, 1956).
4   For example, Elizabeth Gould (1804–81) was often unacknowledged in history of science literature as the creator of hundreds (an estimated 650 or more) lithographic plates included in her husband's, John Gould, *The Birds of Europe*, *The Birds of Australia* and *Zoology of the Voyage of the H.M.S. Beagle* (London: printed by

To address this problem, in 1971 Linda Nochlin openly called art historians, in Griselda Pollock's words, 'to reshape the processes, theories and methods through which [they] confront the historical and ideological complexity of the histories of artistic and cultural practices'.[5] In 1986, Cheryl Buckley concurred a similar problem in design history: 'women have been involved with design in a variety of ways [...]. Yet a survey of the literature of design history, theory and practice would lead one to believe otherwise. [...] These silences are not accidental [...]; rather, they are the direct consequence of specific historiographic methods'.[6] Buckley proposed that, as historians, we ought to investigate the material and ideological function of patriarchy in relation to women and design, while we critically assess why design history has habitually excluded women, so we can then write about design history in a manner that is inclusive.[7] In 1994, Martha Scotford argued that in order to write about the past in a manner that respects the diversity of voices that have existed throughout history, we ought to move beyond the hero-centred approach that has traditionally directed historiography.[8] Scotford proposed that we apply an inclusive approach to history, by investigating design activity, design roles, and response to design; writing about the 'messy history' instead of the 'neat history'.[9]

R. and J. E. Taylor, published by John Gould, 1832–7, 1840–8, and 1839–43). See: Jonathan Smith, 'Gender, Royalty, and Sexuality in John Gould's "Birds of Australia"', *Victorian Literature and Culture*, 35 (2007), 569–87.

5 Griselda Pollock, *Vision and Difference: Feminism, Femininity and the Histories of Art* (London and New York: Routledge, 2003 [1988]), xxiii. A version of Nochlin's original essay can be found here: Linda Nochlin, 'From 1971: Why Have There Been No Great Women Artists?', *ARTnews* (30 May 2015), <https://www.artnews.com/art-news/retrospective/why-have-there-been-no-great-women-artists-4201/>, accessed 8 July 2022.

6 Cheryl Buckley, 'Made in Patriarchy: Toward a Feminist Analysis of Women and Design', *Design Issues*, 3 (1986), 3. Also see: Cheryl Buckley, 'Made in Patriarchy II: Researching (or Re-Searching) Women and Design', *Design Issues*, 36 (2020), 19–29.

7 Buckley, 'Made in Patriarchy', 14.

8 Martha Scotford, 'Messy History vs Neat History: Toward an Expanded View of Women in Graphic Design', *Design Issues*, 28 (1994), 368–88.

9 Scotford, 'Messy History vs Neat History', 386, 367.

Introduction 3

Fortunately, for the last forty to fifty years, numerous scholars have made a special effort to acknowledge the contribution of women in print,[10] attempting to analyse women's involvement in design, including printing and publishing, in relation to gender, sexual division of labour, assumptions about femininity, and the hierarchy that exists across industries.[11] This collective archaeological project continues to this day, with research on women, design and/or printing history being published in different academic journals and books.[12] Building on this invaluable body of work, almost half a

10   See (this list is not exhaustive): Felicity Hunt, 'The London Trade in The Printing and Binding of Books: An Experience in Exclusion, Dilution and De-Skilling for Women Workers', *Women's Studies International Forum*, 6 (1983), 517–24; Siân Reynolds, *Britannica's Typesetters: Women Compositors in Edwardian Edinburgh* (Edinburgh: Edinburgh University Press, 1989); Ellen Mazur Thomson, 'Aims for Oblivion: The History of Women in Early American Graphic Design', *Design Issues*, 10 (1994), 27–48; F. Graeme Chalmers, 'The Early History of the Philadelphia School of Design for Women', *Journal of Design History*, 9 (1996), 237–52; Paula McDowell, *The Women of Grub Street: Press, Politics, and Gender in the London Literary Marketplace, 1678–1730*, (Oxford: Oxford University Press, 1998). DOI: 10.1093/acprof:oso/9780198183952.001.0001; Patricia L. Keats, 'Women in Printing and Publishing in California, 1850–1940', *California History*, 77 (1998), 93–7; Helen Smith, 'Printing Your Royal Father Off: Early Modern Female Stationers and the Gendering of the British Book Trades', *Text*, 15 (2003), 163–186; Michelle Elizabeth Tusan, 'Performing Work: Gender, Class, and the Printing Trade in Victorian Britain', *Journal of Women's History*, 16 (2004), 103–26; Rebecca Warren Davidson, *Unseen Hands: Women Printers, Binders and Book Designers* (Princeton: Princeton University Press, 2005); James P. Danky and Wayne A. Wiegand, eds, *Women in Print: Essays on the Print Culture of American Women from the Nineteenth and Twentieth Centuries* (Madison, Wisconsin: University of Wisconsin Press, 2006); Trysh Travis, 'The Women in Print Movement: History and Implications', *Book History*, 11 (2008), 275–300.
11   Buckley, 'Made in Patriarchy', 14.
12   See (this list is not exhaustive): Cait Coker, 'Gendered Spheres: Theorizing Space in the English Printing House', *The Seventeenth Century*, 33 (2018), 323–36; Catherine Gibson, 'Mapmaking in the Home and Printing House: Women and Cartography in Late Imperial Russia', *Journal of Historical Geography*, 67 (2020), 71–80; Christina Weyl, *Modernist Printmaking in Midcentury New York* (New Haven and London: Yale University Press, 2019); Cathleen A. Baker and Rebecca M. Chung, *Making Impressions: Women in Printing and Publishing* (Ann Arbor,

century since Nochlin's essay, this edited volume offers an inclusive historical perspective of design history, demonstrating that women have always been present and actively involved, unlike Leslie Howsam's statement that they were 'outstanding anomalies in a cultural field dominated by men'.[13]

Chapter 1 covers the scribal culture of the Mediterranean to the globalized societies created during the thirteenth and fourteenth century. From antiquity to the age of modern nation-state formation, it is clear that books were made to travel amongst and between different international communities of scholars. This chapter focuses just before the age of the printing press, establishing the presence of working women involved in the making of books, specifically based in present-day Italy, which was a centre for book production in the High Middle Ages (1000–1250). It discusses how the artisan skills and knowledge of assembling a book was consistent whether the parchment-makers, scribes, illuminators and binders were men or women. Furthermore, despite the patriarchal system in which the medieval women of Bologna operated, the manuscript industry offered women diverse opportunities to create quality illuminated manuscripts, either as members of monastic orders, or in small family-based businesses.

Chapter 2 discusses Elizabeth Newbery (1780–1821), an innovative entrepreneur who developed and published numerous illustrated books and games.[14] Records show that Newbery did not receive as much recognition

    Michigan: The Legacy Press, 2020); Maryam Fanni, Matilda Flodmark, and Sara Kaaman, *Natural Enemies of Books – A Messy History of Women in Printing and Typography* (Sheffield, UK: Occasional Papers Ltd., 2020); Briar Levit, ed., *Baseline Shift: Untold Stories of Women in Graphic Design History* (Hudson, NY: Princeton Architectural Press, 2021); Martha Scotford, 'Afterword', in Briar Levit, ed., *Baseline Shift: Untold Stories of Women in Graphic Design History* (Hudson, NY: Princeton Architectural Press, 2021), 161–3; Claire Battershill, *Women and Letterpress Printing, 1920–2020: Gendered Impressions* (Cambridge: Cambridge University Press, 2022). DOI: https://doi.org/10.1017/9781009219365; Sarah Werner, 'Working toward a Feminist Printing History', *Printing History*, 27-28 (2022), 1–12 [pre-print].

13 Leslie Howsam, 'In My View: Women in Book History', *SHARP News*, 7 (1998), 1.
14 This chapter is linked to: Kandice Sharren and Kate Moffatt, 'From Print to Process: Gender Creative- Adjacent Labour and the *Women's History Project*' in Caroline Archer-Parré and Christine Moog, eds., *Women in Print II: Production, Distribution and Consumption* (Oxford, UK: Peter Lang, 2022), 77–100.

Introduction

in comparison to other male members of her family, although she was quite accomplished within the publishing sector. The chapter highlights the complexities of the production side of book-making, bargaining over items like paper, recruiting authors and illustrators, and balancing financial accounts. Through Newbery's titles in adult and children's literature, the chapter provides examples on how inherent bias in male-dominated scholarship led to narratives that eventually underestimate Newbery's business achievements and innovations as a publisher. The chapter presents evidence of Newbery's success, including new insights discovered through the 'Women's Print History Project', while interpreting older sources on the Newbery family.

Chapter 3 covers the life and career of Letitia Byrne, an engraver whose prints were widely circulated during the late eighteenth and early nineteenth centuries. The chapter presents a focused study of artists, the circulation of their work through prints, alongside an evolving engraving trade with an apprenticeship system which provided illustrations for books as well as stand-alone copies of paintings. The author highlights the advantages of personal and professional connections between artisans and their patrons, and underscores the practical realities of living in a male-centred society, where a family's economic situation can suddenly turn upon the death of the patriarch, revealing the difficult decisions the female members had to make when assuming leadership and wage-earning roles.

Chapter 4 discusses *The Olive Branch*, a women-run business and publisher of women's literature, which offered opportunities for women as apprentice typesetters, editors and writers in a professionalized setting in Boston, US. The author explains how *The Olive Branch* prepared a generation of women for work in the quickly transforming printing trade, enabling women to gain practical experience, as well as professional and literary reputations that were often used as facilitators for entering into other areas of the ever-expanding publishing field of the period. Women writers, such as Louisa May Alcott, first published stories in *The Olive Branch*, which allowed her, like many other women in this period, to express their own creative voice.

Chapter 5 focuses on another woman-led business, owed by Elizabeth Heard, describing in detail the many fonts she employed to expand her jobbing business in Cornwall, UK. The author provides a wider contextual analysis of typographical practices as seen in the emerging field of marketing. Through newspaper advertisements and stand-alone ephemera, including advertisements designed specifically for Heard's business, the chapter provides a case study of female creativity and entrepreneurship developed in provincial England. In particular, the chapter reveals how typography can transverse from geographical peripheries to influence graphic styles in urban metropolitan centres through print and visual culture.

Chapter 6 explores the design in educational books through the lens of Agnes Cowper, who worked as the unofficial photographer of the V&A for nearly two decades. Cowper was the one who introduced the visual art collections of the South Kensington Museums, as it was then called (later the V&A), to generations of artists and art educators through a series of books incorporating new photographic technologies. The chapter reveals Cowper purposefully kept a low profile so as not to expose the museum to charges of nepotism. Unfortunately, her subterfuge was so effective that it has been a challenge for researchers to bring her name to light, and identify the numerous works she created.

Chapter 7 examines women's history through the production and graphic design of the general feminist periodical *Women's Penny Paper/Woman's Herald*, established by editor Henrietta Müller. The author describes, analyses and evaluates features of the periodical that establish the various priorities of the multiple audiences within the New Women's movement, and how the periodical sought to communicate with them on multiple levels through design, image and text. The chapter reveals that the *Women's Penny Paper/Woman's Herald*, a non-mainstream weekly periodical written, printed by, and aimed at women, employed a purposeful communication strategy in order to effectively connect with its readers.

Chapter 8 explores the production of printed images at the Dun Emer and Cuala Presses under the directorship of E. C. Yeats, showing how she implemented modern technology to replicate older craft movements, whilst bringing the work of Irish artists to the international market. The chapter reveals that E. C. Yeats approached fine printing and reproduction of imagery in a manner that was informed by the British private press, as well as the Irish revivalist aesthetic. The works she published offered a revivalist and nationalist view of Irish culture, adding to the wider effort to promote a distinctive national identity. The chapter argues E. C. Yeats achieved an unusual connection of arts and crafts, with ideology and technology.

Chapter 9 focuses on the visual language used by the Women's Social and Political Union (WSPU) in early twentieth-century England, UK. The author offers an analysis of the WSPU's branding strategy, how the suffragettes chose to publicize themselves, the controversial design methods they used, and the radical actions they took in order to 'design the protest' in their own terms. The chapter reveals that WSPU's campaign implemented creativity and dark humour as efficiently as today's protest movements that resemble contemporary design practices, such as 'shock advertising' and 'guerrilla marketing'. The author argues the design works produced by the suffragettes were of professional quality, and perhaps even placed the foundations for some of the modern advertising methods of today.

Chapter 10 analyses the illustrated works of Lene Schneider-Kainer and their challenging artistic messages that questioned notions of *bourgeois* female propriety and heteronormative values. The author reveals that European and North American women artists left behind a large body of erotic art, especially during the First World War and the Interwar period, although the vast majority of art history offers a rather 'sanitized' record of women in early twentieth-century print culture. To remedy this gap in current literature, Rees-Hales analyses thirty-two erotic and homoerotic chromolithographs included in the *Hetärengespräche des Lukian* [Lucian's Dialogues of the Courtesans] published in 1920. Putting lesbianism at the forefront of her art, the chapter reveals that Schneider-Kainer had full agency over her works, although the text accompanying the images was predominantly focused on conventionally heterosexual prostitution.

Chapter 11 focuses on Beatrice Warde, 'First Lady of Typography', and her contribution to the publishing sector through the establishment of the Anglo-American book exchange framework 'Books Across the Sea', originally founded by Warde's mother during the Second World War. This transatlantic system of book-swapping was aimed at countering existing Nazi propaganda, by offering North Americans a look into the lives of the British and *vice versa*. The author considers the circumstances, establishment and development of 'Books Across the Sea', whilst at the same time recording the numerous people and activities that had taken place to allow its success. The chapter argues that this system of book exchange offered British and U.S. readers the opportunity to develop a better cultural understanding of each other in a bid to counter the fascist propaganda of the period.

'Design is a social, economic and cultural activity',[15] and this is exactly what this volume seeks to emphasize through an examination of women as active participants and contributors in many and varied aspects of design and print culture, including the production of illustrations, typefaces, periodical layouts, photographic prints and bound volumes. In particular, the chapters discuss gender, class and sexuality, amongst other topics, expanding on the design practices of English, German, Irish, Italian and North American historical women. Furthermore, the women involved with this project bring with them a plethora of professional and personal experiences. Collectively, we come from various socio-cultural backgrounds and countries (including Canada, England, Greece, Ireland, Italy, New Zealand, Turkey, the USA, and Wales), spanning a range of age groups, working in our home or a foreign country (as faculty staff, PhD students, independent researchers, curators, librarians, designers), and living as migrants or immigrants. In this occasion, we did not have the opportunity to explore race and ethnicity, colonialism and postcolonialism, or other equally important subjects in as much depth, though we aim to do so in the near future.[16] Meanwhile, we are celebrating the fact this volume reaffirms that women, regardless of era and geography, have contributed (and continue to contribute) to print culture, through a wide variety of roles, continuously and indisputably impacting on our society's multi-layered ecology, firmly establishing their legacy in design and print history.

15 Scotford, 'Messy History vs Neat History', 386.
16 See: Rose Roberto and Selina Portera, '(Re)visualizing Indigenous and Enslaved People of Surinam During the 1700s'. [Forthcoming].

ROSA SMURRA

1 Women's Contribution to Manuscript Textbook Production in Thirteenth- and Fourteenth-Century Bologna

In the Middle Ages, Bologna was famous throughout Europe for its university whose students made up a substantial proportion of its total population at the end of the thirteenth century. Based on estimates from the years 1265 to 1269, and later in 1286, there were more than 2,000 students in Bologna, which had a population of more than 50,000 inhabitants.[1] Many businesses profited from the presence of students, including the finance, credit, clothing and hospitality sectors, and also the book trade. With its significant population of scholarly readers, the city developed into a pre-eminent centre of manuscript production south of the Alps. Textbooks on canon and Roman law were an important segment of the book business, a mass market in which thousands of texts for the law curriculum were made available to students.[2]

1   Of 2,056 students, 1,363 were foreigners: Hilde De Ridder Symoens, 'La Place de l'Université de Bologne dans la Mobilité des Étudiants Européens', in *Universitates e Università* (Bologna: Bologna University Press, 1995), 83–92; Sante Bortolami Gli Studenti delle Università Italiane: Numero, Mobilità, Distribuzione, Vita Studentesca dalle Origini al XV Secolo, in Gian Paolo Brizzi, Piero Del Negro and Andrea Romano, eds, Storia delle Università in Italia (Messina: Sicania, 2007), 65–115; Antonio Ivan Pini, 'Problemi Demografici Bolognesi del Duecento', *Atti e Memorie della Deputazione di Storia Patria per le Province di Romagna* n. s. XVII–XIX (1965–66/1967–68), 147–222.
2   Rosa Smurra, 'Manuscript Book Production and Urban Landscape: Bologna during the Thirteenth and Fourteenth Centuries', in John Hinks and Catherine Armstrong (eds), *Text and Image in the City: Manuscript, Print and Visual Culture in Urban Space* (Newcastle upon Tyne, UK: Cambridge Scholars Publishing, 2017), 81–104.

Stationers' shops were often crucial to book production.[3] Stationers served as intermediaries between the students who requested copies of textbooks and the artisans involved in their preparation.[4] The starting point for the production of university textbooks was the *exemplar*, the authentic transcript of the text to be taught. Available from accredited stationers, the *exemplar* was the model text validated by six members of a university commission (*peciarii*).[5] The complete list of *exemplaria* was displayed in the stationers' shops. These official texts were divided into parts (*pecie*), each numbered separately, generally four pages long, and distributed among the scribes, who could copy them after paying a tax, which was recorded in the Bologna University Statute Book.[6] The parts of a book would be given to the scribe one at a time, or were distributed to several scribes at once. The making of manuscript books by artisans fell into four principal areas: the manufacture of parchment, writing, illuminating and bookbinding. Parchment, created by processing and cleaning animal skin and then smoothing it to become suitable as a writing surface, was prepared in advance to allow two columns of text and margins large enough to accommodate commentary, the scribes knowing the quantity of words to be written on each line.[7] The loose pages were then put in correct order and delivered firstly to the illuminator who provided miniatures; secondly, the rubricator who was responsible for chapter headings in red ink; and finally, the bookbinder. The double column layout facilitated quick reading, allowing the absorption of an entire line of text at a single glance. In the words of archivist Armando Petrucci, the university book was not only to be read, it was to be studied and commented on. Thus, the text was divided into sections, articulated into paragraphs and ordered by titles in red and alternating red and turquoise initials. It was also linked to the commentary

---

3   Lodovico Frati, 'Gli Stazionari Bolognesi nel Medio Evo', *Archivio Storico Italiano* s. 5, 45 (1910), 380–90.
4   Franek Soetermeer, *Utrumque Ius in Peciis: Aspetti della Produzione Libraria a Bologna fra Due e Trecento*, trans. Giancarlo Errico (Milano: Giuffrè, 1997).
5   Carlo Malagola, ed., *Statuti delle Università e dei Collegi dello Studio Bolognese* (Bologna: Zanichelli, 1888), 20–1.
6   Soetermeer, *Utrumque Ius in Peciis*.
7   Giovanna Murano, *Opere Diffuse per Exemplar e Pecia* (Turnhout: Brepols, 2005).

Figure 1.1. *Digestum vetus cum glossa ordinaria* (handwritten), c. thirteenth century © Universitätsbibliothek, Basel, C I 1, f. 9v, <www.e-codices.ch>, accessed 14 April 2020.

Written in the *littera Bononiensis* (a rounded hand), it contains in the middle the *Digestum Vetus*, encompassed by Accursius' explanatory glosses.

written in the margins with letters and signs (Figure 1.1) that was both preceded and followed by indexes, and alphabetical tables of contents.[8]

This process of assembling a book prior to the age of the printing press was consistent whether the parchment-makers, scribes, illuminators and binders were men or women. Despite the patriarchal system in which medieval women operated, the manuscript industry offered them numerous possibilities for economic participation.[9] This chapter provides a brief overview of the role played by women as scribes in manuscript production since antiquity. It also offers an analysis of contracts for writing specific texts or deals of business partnerships, demonstrating the extent to which women participated in the Bolognese manuscript trade as scribes or stationers. Finally, the chapter considers the types of manuscripts produced or sold by women (for an extensive list of names see Table 1.1) for masters and students of the civil and canon law curricula. The manuscripts they produced were legal texts (i.e. textbooks for law curricula) almost always showing a challenging page layout, displaying two columns of text enclosed by commentaries (glosses).

Early Women as Scribes in Manuscript Production

There is evidence to support female scribes active during Greco-Roman antiquity and in early Christian urban communities, and that some of the earliest Christian manuscripts were probably copied by women. Many of them, as highlighted by Kim Haines-Eitzen, had a degree of literacy gained through apprenticeship or training with a tutor in the household in which they worked.[10]

---

8   Armando Petrucci, *Medioevo da Leggere. Guida allo Studio delle Testimonianze Scritte del Medioevo Italiano* (Torino: Einaudi, 1992), 23–4.

9   On Bolognese female citizenship, see Rosa Smurra, 'Cittadinanza Femminile a Bologna alla Fine del XIII Secolo il Contributo delle Fonti Fiscali', *Studi Medievali* LX (2019), 59–85.

10 Kim Haines-Eitzen, ' "Girls Trained in Beautiful Writing": Female Scribes in Roman Antiquity and Early Christianity', *Journal of Early Christian Studies* 6.4 (1998), 629–46. See also Maria Boccuzzi, 'Le Quattro Dimensioni della Scrittura Femminile nella

In the early Middle Ages female education mainly took place in religious houses, which hosted the scribal activity of its members. In centres such as the scriptoria at Chelles and Jouarre in Neustria, France, religious women copied *codices*.[11] However, the production of manuscripts was not always a neutral activity. By analysing a select corpus of 'women's manuscripts' produced in mid- and late eighth-century Karlburg and Kitzingen – monastic communities around Wurzburg and Mainz – medieval historian Felice Lifshitz identified 'the Anglo-Saxon culture province' on the Continent, uncovering the ideas of a religious life in which women could play an active role. According to Lifshitz, there was a deliberate editing of texts by these communities to eliminate traces of misogyny, and the compilations of excerpts from other writings (*florilegia*) and collections of saints' lives highlighted the public role of religious women in the Christianization of society. Female scribes thus show a feminist 'resistance' to the patriarchal ideas, embedded in the Carolingian 'reform' that affected religious women, insisting on strict enclosure of nuns and at times depriving their communities of resources. Furthermore, their manuscript production demonstrates an eighth-century initiative managed by and for women, with only occasional assistance from men in positions of power.[12]

A growing body of evidence shows that religious women were actively producing high-quality books in the later centuries, which helps to account for longstanding female participation in this trade. For example, there was remarkable activity in twelfth-century monastic book production centred

---

Tarda Antichità Greca e Romana', *Segno e Testo. International Journal of Manuscripts and Text Transmission*, 13 (2015), 165–209.

[11] Rosamond McKitterick, 'Nuns' Scriptoria in England and Francia in the Eighth Century', and 'Women and Literacy in the Early Middle Ages', in *Books, Scribes and Learning in the Frankish Kingdoms, 6th-9th Centuries* (Aldershot: Variorum, 1994); Luisa Miglio, *Governare l'Alfabeto. Donne, Scrittura e Libri nel Medioevo* (Roma: Viella, 2008). The author describes a survey aiming at identifying and describing manuscripts copied by women from the eighth century up to the fifteenth century. Luisa Miglio and Marco Palma, 'Presenze Dimenticate (VI)', *Aevum*, 86:2 (2012), 771–82.

[12] Felice Lifshitz, *Religious Women in Early Carolingian Francia: A Study of Manuscript Transmission and Monastic Culture* (New York: Fordham University Press, 2014).

in Bavaria, Germany, led by Diemut, a recluse and professional scribe. Her contributions to book production were noted at the Benedictine monastery at Wessobrunn, and her dedication to her craft led to her being recognized as a local saint.[13] Indeed, for centuries religious women were instrumental in making manuscript books. According to Patricia Stoop, who studied the case of Middle Dutch book production up to 1550, out of around 500 manuscripts some two-thirds derive from female scribes belonging to religious institutions.[14] Moreover, the fifteenth-century Observant Movement aimed at reforming religious life was responsible for substantial scribal activity. As Anne Winston-Allen who researched German- and Dutch-speaking women's communities in Belgium, Germany, Italy, the Netherlands and Switzerland demonstrated, medieval religious women not only reproduced the works of others, they were also authors of works such as devotional treatises and biographies of noteworthy religious sisters.[15]

European religious women were not the only female copyists and consumers of books; women of other faiths also engaged in manuscript copying activities in other regions of the world.[16] From the Islamic area of Fatimid Egypt in 1165, scholars Delia Cortese and Simonetta Calderini have discovered historical reports that the unnamed wife and daughter of a jurist and scholar were skilled scribes who copied, leased or sold books in that area.[17] Despite being women, their well-regarded calligraphic skills contributed to a profitable family business. Other historical research, focused on the

13 Alison I. Beach, *Women as Scribes: Book Production and Monastic Reform in Twelfth-Century Bavaria* (Cambridge: Cambridge University Press, 2004).
14 Patricia Stoop, 'From Reading to Writing: The Multiple Levels of Literacy of the Sister Scribes in the Brussels Convent of Jericho', in Virginia Blanton, Veronica O'Mara and Patricia Stoop, eds, *Nuns' Literacies in Medieval Europe: The Kansas City Dialogue*' (Turnhout: Brepols, 2015), 47–66.
15 Anne Winston-Allen, *Convent Chronicles: Women Writing about Women and Reform in the Late Middle* (University Park: Pennsylvania State University Press, 2004).
16 For biographical notes of female scribes who left their subscription in fifteenth- and sixteenth-century colophons, see Simona Gavinelli, 'Copiste: Appunti Biografici, *Mélanges de l'École Française de Rome – Moyen Âge*, 131–32 (2019), 297–310.
17 Delia Cortese and Simonetta Calderini, *Women and the Fatimids in the World of Islam*, (Edinburgh: Edinburgh University Press, 2006), 207.

period between the thirteenth and sixteenth centuries, has found unnamed Jewish women involved in the manual production of Hebrew books. These women, serving as either full-time or occasional scribes, worked from their own homes in Jewish communities.[18]

By the thirteenth century, secular female scribes began outnumbering women in religious orders engaged in manuscript production, a trade that would evolve into the university book market. Due to its proximity to the *stadium*, or university, manuscript book production by laywomen emerged to an even greater extent in Bologna, in order to meet the demand for books by scholars and their students. As the book trade grew in volume, the number of secular scribes and other book artisans increased dramatically. Although not complete, an interesting body of information about women involved in this industry has been assembled while researching Bolognese manuscript book production.[19] Records reflect family relations, properties owned, patrons served, manuscripts produced, payments received, co-workers and collaborators.

The Design of Readable Manuscript Page Layouts

The majority of works copied by women were manuscripts with challenging layouts, especially in works that were glossed, as seen in Figure 1.1. The main text in two columns of 43–48 lines is surrounded by the gloss (*glossa ordinaria*) in the marginal space; the script in gloss is smaller than the main text, requiring considerable calligraphic skill and the ability to judge what will fit appropriately. Susan L'Engle notes that in works produced in Bologna the gloss habitually displays a mirror format for verso and recto at each opening. Additionally, many manuscripts contain miniature decorations, although not all illuminations were executed

---

18   Michael Riegler and Judith R. Baskin, '"May the Writer Be Strong": Medieval Hebrew Manuscripts Copied by and for Women', *Nashim: A Journal of Jewish Women's Studies & Gender Issues*, 16 (2008), 9–28.
19   Smurra, 'Manuscript Book Production and Urban Landscape'.

in Bologna.[20] What do we know about the women who commissioned, made and sold items such as these?

Records of Women in the Bolognese Manuscript Trade

Historians have been aware of female involvement in the book production chain since the eighteenth century, when two Camaldolese monks, Mauro Sarti and Mauro Fattorini, in their magisterial biographies of medieval professors at the University of Bologna, identified three female scribes: Antonia, 1275; Allegra, 1279; and Uliana, 1286.[21] More recent studies, such as those of Francesco Filippini and Guido Zucchini, Gianfranco Orlandelli and Giovanna Murano, have further developed knowledge of books made by women in Bologna.[22] The bulk of this new information comes from the *Memoriali*, the registers of all notarial contracts concerning transactions worth 20 *lire di bolognini* [400 shillings sterling][23] or more which, from the 1260s onwards, were compiled under the supervision of the municipal authorities. As these contracts covered a

20 Susan L'Engle, 'A Zealously Annotated Liber Extra: Vich, Archivo Capitular, ms 144', in Paola Maffei and Gian Maria Varanini, eds, *Honos Alit Artes. Studi per il Settantesimo Compleanno di Mario Ascheri* (Firenze: Firenze University Press, 2014), Pt. 3, 65–72.

21 Mauro Sarti and Mauro Fattorini, *De Claris Archigymnasii Bononiensis Professoribus a Saeculo XI usque ad Saeculum XIV*, 2nd edn by Cesare Albicini and Carlo Malagola, 2 vols (Bologna: Ex Officina Regia Fratrum Merlani, 1888–1896), t. I.1, 186: 'In Bologna there was a great number of excellent scribes [...], not only men [...] but also women in case of shortage of male scribes' (my translation from Latin).

22 Francesco Filippini and Guido Zucchini, *Miniatori e Pittori a Bologna: Documenti dei secoli XIII e XIV* (Firenze: G. C. Sansoni, 1947); Gianfranco Orlandelli, *Il Libro a Bologna dal 1300 al 1330: Documenti con uno Studio su il Contratto di Scrittura nella Dottrina Notarile Bolognese* (Bologna: Zanichelli, 1959); Giovanna Murano, *Copisti a Bologna (1265–70)* (Turnhout: Brepols, 2006).

23 In the Bolognese monetary system, 12 denari (pence) = 1 soldo (shilling), 20 soldi (or 240 denari) = 1 lira (pound).

wide range of transactions, including those for writing and making books, some names of female scribes emerged.[24] While the nature of those sources does not allow the full identification of the manuscripts they produced, it does offer clues to the mode of production used by these women and limited information about their relationship with the clients who commissioned them.

Making manuscript books was a time-consuming activity, as it took many months for a scribe to complete a text. For this reason, scribes copied books only if they were formally commissioned. Legal contracts for copying books seem to have been modelled on the formula *locatio operis*, a contract for hiring work used by the leading notary Rolandino Passaggeri (d. 1300) in the *Summa totius artis notariae*, written in the 1260s. It became one of his notarial manuals used as a standard teaching text in the field.[25] The object of the *locatio operis* was the finished work, for which scribes were to provide everything needed, including the *exemplar* and parchment.[26] An example of a contract drawn up in 1268 shows that Cristiana (see Table 1.1) agreed not only to transcribe the text of the Decretals, but to also insert the small guide letters (*minora*) that assisted rubricators with painting or rendering in ink initials or running titles.[27]

The Passaggeri contract for the copying of a book differs from the *locatio operarum* elaborated in the 1220s by the notary Ranieri da Perugia (d. c.1255). Here, the funding party had to provide the *pecie* and other necessities for the scribe to complete the work (*cartas dabit ei ad scribendum*

---

24 *Memoriali* have been only partially published in the *Chartularium Studii Bononiensis. Documenti per la Storia dell'Università di Bologna dalle Origini fino al Sec. XV* (Bologna: Presso l'Istituto per la Storia dell'Università di Bologna) (henceforth ChSB).
25 For the *Instrumentum locationis operarum ad opus scripture faciendae*, see Orlandelli, *Il Libro a Bologna dal 1300 al 1330*, 9.
26 Orlandelli, *Il Libro a Bologna dal 1300 al 1330*, 16–20.
27 Franek Soetermeer, 'Un Problème Quotidien de la librairie à Bologne: "Minora" Manquants', in Bernard Durand and Laurent Mayali, eds, *Excerptiones Iuris: Studies in Honor of André Gouron* (Berkeley: Robbins Collection, 2000), 693–716.

ad sufficientiam [...] *et exemplar vel cartas*).[28] In contrast with the Passaggeri formula (*locatio operis* = finished work), it was not necessary for the funding party to negotiate with parchment-sellers or stationers, while the scribe was to provide the *pecie* and other items required to complete the work.[29] An example of such an agreement is a contract entered into by Margarita (see Table 1.1), widow of Antonio de Homodinis, and her son in 1304 who were to transcribe both text and glosses of the entire *Digestum Vetus*, at their own expense.

The nature of these legally binding contracts between parties – the funding party who paid for the work and the scribe, or other artisan, who executed it – has shed light on the involvement of women and their range of activities. These contracts benefit modern scholars because they point to complementary bodies of material, such as fiscal records for property assessment, which researchers can turn to for further information. Late thirteenth-century tax returns (*Estimi*) can be navigated more effectively with knowledge of certain women's names. Further research resulting from these sources assists in ascertaining the presence of women as taxpayers, and their wider societal role and contribution to the city's economy.[30]

According to fiscal sources such as these, which contain gender-identifying information, during the years 1296–97 women accounted for 17.5 per cent of all Bolognese taxpayers: a high percentage in comparison to tax censuses of other medieval Italian towns and cities. It is important to consider that the female contribution to direct taxation accounted for 8.65 per cent of total tax revenues. This figure highlights the role played by Bolognese women in the urban economy in which they were active in

---

28   Ranieri da Perugia, *Ars Notaria*, in Augusto Gaudenzi, ed., *Scripta Anecdota Antiquissimorum Glossatorum* (Bologna: Bibliotheca Iuridica Medii Aevi, 1892), 25–67, at 60 as to the formula.

29   Émilie Cottereau Gabillet, 'Les Contrats de Copistes en France aux XIVe et XVe Siècles et l'Influence des Formules Notariales Bolonaises', *Mélanges de l'École Française de Rome. Moyen-Age*, 119:2 (2007), 415–45.

30   Rosa Smurra, 'Fiscal Sources: the Estimi', in Sarah Rubin Blanshei, ed., *A Companion to Medieval and Renaissance Bologna* (Leiden and Boston: Brill, 2018), 42–55.

various ways, from services to individuals and families to craft activities, trade and credit.[31]

A challenge for researchers navigating these records is the legal deference to male family members that obscures the women themselves. A woman usually needed a male guardian, such as her father, brother, husband or other male guarantor, to be named in the contract in order to assume legal liability on her behalf. Thus, in 1300, Giovanni di Ardizzone vouched for Malgarita, daughter of Bartholomew. Malgarita's contract agreed to provide Friar Stefano di Matugliano a transcription of the *apparatus* of the Decretals, delivering five *pecie* (ten *folia*) each month with no other interposed works at a unit price of sixteen *soldi bol* [sixteen shillings sterling] per *quaternus*. Since the *quaternus* corresponded to two *pecie* (four *folia*), and the total price specified was six *lire bol*. [120 shillings sterling], the work amounted to seven *quaterni* and one *bifolium*. Some years later, in 1311, Malgarita, now married to Geminiano di Iacopo da Modena, made agreements on her own behalf, but needed to indicate she had her husband's consent (*suo viro consentiente*).[32] Malgarita agreed to transcribe the Decretals with the apparatus of Bernard of Parma, within ten months after the date of the contract, for an agreed price of forty-three *lire* and nine *soldi* [969 shillings sterling]. On this occasion the unit price per *quaternus* was twenty-two *soldi*; six *soldi* more than a few years earlier. This can be interpreted as is a sign of growing demand for her work.[33]

---

31 Rosa Smurra, 'Cittadinanza Femminile a Bologna'.
32 Geminiano of Modena was a member of the well-known Grasolfi family of scribes. Franek P. W. Soetermeer. 'À Propos d'une Famille de Copistes: Quelques Remarques sur la Librairie à Bologne aux XIIIe et XIVe Siècles', *Studi medievali*, 30:1 (1989), 425–78.
33 By way of example, two sheep at the end of the thirteenth century were worth twenty *soldi*: Lodovico Frati, *La Vita Privata in Bologna dal Secolo XIII al XVII* (Bologna: N. Zanichelli, 1928), 203.

Malgarita: A Case Study of Uncovering One Woman's Book Production Business

The business of Malgarita, wife of Andrea, is one of the best-known cases of this period, documented through two contracts drawn up in 1319 and 1321.[34] The 1296 tax return of Andrea and Malgarita, daughter of the late Bonfigliolo and wife of Andrea, indicates both husband and wife head the household (*domina*).[35] This tax return differs from the vast majority where, in the case of a married couple, the return lists a male head of the household. The tax declaration of Andrea and Malgarita is written in the third person plural stating they lived and continue to live (*qui habitant et habitaverunt*), and specifies which assets belong to whom, which today would be classified as 'separation of property'.[36]

Andrea and Malgarita lived in a house owned by Andrea, located in the housing development which had been established by the monastery of St Procolo between 1269 and 1274.[37] The house was situated on land owned by the monastery, and was rented annually for nineteen *soldi* and six denari. This rent was paid according to a twenty-nine-year contract, which had been in effect for a while as Andrea declared he had lived continuously in the house for a long time (*iam est longum tempus*). This home is the only property owned by Andrea. Malgarita is listed as the owner of a vineyard

---

34   Orlandelli, *Il Libro a Bologna dal 1300 al 1330*, 97, no. 256; 103, no. 287.

35   Archivio di Stato di Bologna, Comune, Ufficio dei Riformatori degli Estimi, Estimi, series II, 1296 (henceforth Estimi), Porta Procola, busta 22, S. Procolo, 23. *Fratres de penitentia* were exempt from military service, but not from direct taxation, cf. Gina Fasoli and Pietro Sella, eds, *Statuti di Bologna dell'Anno 1288*, 2 vols (Città del Vaticano: Biblioteca Apostolica Vaticana, 1937–39), vol. 2, 117.

36   On matrimonial practices in pre-modern Europe, see Philip L. Reynolds and John Witte, eds, '*To Have and to Hold*': *Marrying and Its Documentation in Western Christendom, 400–1600* (New York: Cambridge University Press, 2007).

37   Mario Fanti, 'Le Lottizzazioni Monastiche e lo Sviluppo Urbano di Bologna nel Duecento', *Atti e memorie della R. Deputazione di Storia Patria per le Province di Romagna* Ser. n.s., 28 (1977), 121–44; Francesca Bocchi, *Bologna. Il Duecento, Atlante Storico delle Città Italiane*, 2 (Bologna: Graphis, 1995), 40–1.

consisting of four-and-a-half tornature (an Italian unit of land measurement which varies by city) in Gaibola, Pizzocalvo. It had an estimated value of twenty-two *lire di bolognini* [440 shillings sterling]. She also owned a house and garden along with the land on which it was built, in Bologna, in via Torleone, which was rented for thirty-five or forty *soldi* a year and estimated at fifteen *lire di bolognini* [300 shillings sterling]. In addition, she owned a second similar house with land and an orchard in the same district, rented for twenty-five or thirty *soldi* a year and estimated at fifteen *lire di bolognini*. These properties were probably inherited by her from her father and kept in a separate estate from that of her husband. Towards the end of the tax return it indirectly reveals Malgarita's book trade activities, when Andrea declared the capital [100 shillings sterling] he had invested in raw materials and his work, which consisted of scraping animal skins and preparing them for further processing in order to become a smooth surface on which to write (*carte*). Andrea did not have his own shop but carried out his work in that of a colleague where he had invested a small amount of capital in the company.

Twenty-three years later, records show Malgarita was now widowed and continued to live in the house near St Procolo. On 7 September 1319 she signed a contract with the parchment-scraper (*abrasor cartarum*) Giovanni di Bitino for the establishment of a business for the scraping of parchment (*in arte et ministerio cartarum abrasarum*), and the purchase and sale of all kinds of necessities and whatever else was needed for the business. The business had a term of one year from the Feast of St Michael (29 September), the date on which rent payments and any other limited-term contracts usually started and finished. In the business agreement, Malgarita invested the usufruct of her shop: that is, she gave Giovanni temporary use of the shop from which to work.[38] The shop was located in the square in front of the church of St Ambrogio. Giovanni also received 118 lire [2,360 shillings sterling] in cash which he and his heirs would repay when the contract expired.

The contract further required that Giovanni remain in the shop to work for the entire year, as well as pay two apprentices (*discipuli*) or two

---

38   As usufructuary Malgarita was entitled the use of the property though she did not own the property.

servants (*famuli*) for an agreed period. While Giovanni's earnings were his alone, if he hired the two workers the gains arising from their employment would be divided equally between Malgarita and Giovanni. On 4 October 1321, however, six days after the agreement had apparently been renewed for another year, Malgarita ceded to judge Benedetto, son of the late Bartolo, all rights in a legal action against Giovanni and his son, who had not repaid the money she had invested within the time specified in the contract of 1319.[39]

These documents provide evidence of two things. Firstly, Malgarita was the usufructuary of the workshop: that is, she derived profit from it although the ownership belonged to another person. In general, when a widow was usufructuary it meant the asset had been previously owned by her husband and at his death was passed on as an inheritance to their children who retained ownership. For the duration of her life the widow could benefit from the property by letting it,[40] as happened in this case, which simply meant Giovanni used it for his work. Secondly, it can be deduced that the workshop was quite successful. Malgarita had invested a large sum in the business which was located around the ancient church of St Ambrogio where most of the Bologna book trade was concentrated, not far from the law schools.

Other Known Women in the Bolognese Manuscript Trade

The majority of known women involved in the Bologna manuscript book production were scribes. Some of them possessed significant entrepreneurial skills, as the case of Alda of Vitale (see Table 1.1) exemplifies.

On 8 May 1324, the notary Pietro di Ardizzone recorded a contract between Alda, daughter of the late Vitale di Michele, for the sale of two books to judge Giacomo di Homobono dei Tederisi, for a total cost of 260

---

39 Orlandelli, *Il Libro a Bologna dal 1300 al 1330*, 103, no. 287.
40 Fasoli and Sella, eds, *Statuti di Bologna dell'Anno 1288*, book VII, rub. 33.

lire di bolognini [5,200 shillings sterling].[41] The first was Decretals, a canon law book (*unum par Decretalium*) in parchment with text and gloss; the second book was a New Digest (civil law) with gloss, also in parchment.

The present research has not revealed any further information about Alda, but her father's 1296 tax return survives. Vitale, a house-to-house vendor of oil and cheese, declared no properties on his tax return which also shows a minimum taxable income.[42] Alda therefore came from a modest family, living in the city's peripheral area, albeit within its thirteenth-century walls.

Alda resurfaces again almost thirty years later in 1324, when she was recorded with her now deceased father's name, selling two books she transcribed – one by herself, the other partly with hired assistance. It may be inferred that Alda had a reputable business with a wide network, because not only was she a well-known scribe, but she also held valuable books in her workshop, which she had been entrusted with to sell. She also had access to the New Digest, which she had partly copied, while managing the work of other scribes and perhaps some illuminators, to decorate it.

In addition to female scribes working in Bologna during this period, records also reveal female stationers. In a contract of 2 December 1303 Mambilia, daughter of the late Mattiolo the tailor, who lived in the St Ambrogio parish, commissioned Graziadeo Alberti for a part of the Justinian Digest (*Inforciatum*) on parchment which included twelve unbound quires (*quaterni*) of text and eight glosses.[43] Mambilia commissioned both the text and the glosses consisting of twenty-four *pecie* written in a rounded hand (*littera Bononiensis*), similar to the script of the previous twelve quires (*et de meliori si poterit*).[44] Graziadeo also began work comprising the next twenty-four *pecie*, promising that the writing would be on the same high-quality parchment. Mambilia paid Graziadeo thirty-five *lire di bolognini* [700 shillings sterling] for the work.

41 Orlandelli, *Il Libro a Bologna dal 1300 al 1330*, 110, no. 315
42 Estimi, Porta Piera, b. 5a, S. Maria della Mascarella, 382: <http://www.centrofasoli.unibo.it>, accessed 24 January 2020.
43 Orlandelli, *Il Libro a Bologna dal 1300 al 1330*, 65, no. 122.
44 As expressed in Rolandino's formula mentioned above (Orlandelli, *Il Libro a Bologna dal 1300 al 1330*, 16).

Another stationer, Bolnixia, the daughter of late Bençevenis Blaxii, appears in a contract signed on 26 August 1310. Bolnixia commissioned Guidotto di Giacomo to transcribe the Guillaume Durand *Speculum iudiciale* with 'proper and good writing, equal to how he had started, and to continue similarly until its completion'.[45] The contract further states that Guidotto agreed not to accept any other work until the completion of the book, which still had four quires to copy. The agreed price amounted to twenty-three *lire di bolognini* and ten soldi [470 shillings sterling].

As in the case of Alda of Vitale, Mambilia and Bolnixia were women with entrepreneurial skills, who signed agreements to become owners of university books. These books were not intended for domestic use; they were books for the market. The women acted on their own behalf, neither had a father nor a husband assuming legal liability for them. Mambilia and Bolnixia directed the production of the manuscript, were responsible for choosing the scribes called on to perform the work and were able to pay the agreed price upon the book's delivery. It seems, therefore, that the two women carried out their activity in the context of bookshops, perhaps inherited from their father or husband.

Known Manuscript Books Produced by Women

As yet no original manuscripts produced by female Bolognese scribes, artisans and stationers have been discovered. Therefore, their materiality cannot be examined. Nevertheless, it is possible to identify some aspects of the socio-cultural context in which they lived and worked.

The available documentary evidence provides information on seventeen women active in manuscript production (see Table 1.1). Some of them, daughters or wives of professional scribes or notaries, were taught at home and were involved in the production of legal textbooks for the law curriculum. The contracts negotiated between 1268 and 1324 mainly concern

---

45   Orlandelli, *Il Libro a Bologna*, 80, no. 187.

manuscripts of the most important legal works setting out the curriculum of civil (Roman) and canon (ecclesiastical) law studies: *Digestum vetus* (Dig. 1.1. – 24.2*); Infortiatum cum tribus partes* (Dig. 24.3. – 38.17); *Digestum Novum* (Dig. 39.1. – 50.17); *Volumen*, that is, *Authenticum, Institutiones* and *Tres libri Codicis*: all textbooks of Justinian's compilations (*Corpus Juris Civilis*) used in the civil law curriculum.[46] An example of a Bolognese law manuscript can be seen in Figure 1.1. Some female scribes (Marchexana, 1270; Margarita, mother of John, 1304) respectively copied the *Digestum novum*, and *Digestum Vetus* along with the Apparatus of Accursius' gloss, a work for centuries considered to be the standard apparatus of glosses (*glossa ordinaria*). As pointed out by Alain Wijffels, 'from the late-thirteenth century until the late-sixteenth or early-seventeenth century, practically all civil law students in European universities were expected to learn texts of Justinian's compilations, literally encompassed (both in late-medieval manuscripts and early-modern imprints) by Accursius' gloss'.[47]

Among the works copied by women were books for canon law, such as *Decretum* and *Decretales*, canonical collections containing conciliar canons and papal decretals. These canon law compilations became the basis of canon law teaching across Europe and, as in the case of the *Corpus Juris Civilis*, they were surrounded by glosses. In 1300, Margarita, wife of the scribe Geminianus de Mutina (see Table 1.1), copied the text of the Decretals as well as the *glossa ordinaria*, a juridical commentary by the canon law specialist Bernard of Parma (d. 1266). In 1310 the stationer Bolnixia (see Table 1.1) sold in the ecclesiastical courts the *Speculum iudiciale* by William Durand the Elder (1230–1296), a notable textbook on medieval procedural law, including criminal procedure. During the late Middle Ages, the

---

46 Roman civil law was codified during the years 528–34 in Constantinople by order of Emperor Justinian. In the twelfth century, after reconstructing the Justinian texts, the Bolognese jurist Irnerio distributed them over fifty books.
47 Alain Wijffels, 'Accursius, Standard gloss', in Serge Dauchy, Georges Martyn, Anthony Musson, Heikki Pihlajamäki and Alain Wijffels, eds, *The Formation and Transmission of Western Legal Culture – 150 Books that Made the Law in the Age of Printing* (Cham: Springer, 2016), 24–27 (24).

Speculum became an indispensable book of reference for every European lawyer, and remained so until the first centuries of the modern era.[48]

The Bible required much time to copy. The thirteenth century saw the 'miniaturization of Bible manuscripts', a crucial transformation of the Bible from a large book used for public reading, often in many volumes, into a single volume used and owned by individuals.[49] The Bible was essential for theological study, and with the expansion of the schools (*studia*) of the mendicant orders – the Franciscans and Dominicans, and later the Servites and Carmelites – dedicated to pastoral care and preaching, a significant demand grew for new manuscripts which paralleled university programmes.[50]

Copying a Bible could take up to two years, a task that Alegra Bentivogli (see Table 1.1) accomplished in the late 1270s for a Carmelite friar, John Borgoniensis. Northern Italy, along with Paris and Southern England, contributed significantly to the production of portable Bibles, made possible in centres with well-established systems of manuscript production such as university towns. Alegra, the wife of a notary from whom she probably learned handwriting skills, is the so far known woman engaged in Bologna's Bible production. In 1296, records show Alegra had been involved in the art of writing (*in arte scribendi*) for nearly twenty years, expanding her business to include her two daughters (see Table 1.1). This record, among others, proves that in some well-established family businesses female members contributed substantially to the financial well-being of the households.[51]

48 Beatrice Pasciuta, 'Durantis, Speculum Iudiciale', in Serge Dauchy, Georges Martyn, Anthony Musson, Heikki Pihlajamäki and Alain Wijffels, eds, *The Formation and Transmission of Western Legal Culture – 150 Books that Made the Law in the Age of Printing* (Cham: Springer, 2016), 37–30. According to the author, more than eighty manuscripts of the *Speculum iudiciale* have survived, though no comprehensive inventory is yet available.

49 Chiara Ruzzier, 'The Miniaturisation of Bible Manuscripts in the Thirteenth Century: A Comparative Study', in Eyal Poleg and Laura Light, eds, *Form and Function in the Late Medieval Bible* (Leiden and Boston: Brill, 2013), 105–25.

50 William J. Courtenay, 'The Bible in Medieval Universities', in James Carleton Paget and Joachim Schaper, eds, *The New Cambridge History of the Bible. 2. From 600 to 1450*, 555–78.

51 Bolognese fiscal sources for the years 1296–97 tell us that the average estimate of female assets was of 115 *lire di bolognini* [2,300 shillings sterling]: Rosa Smurra, 'Direct

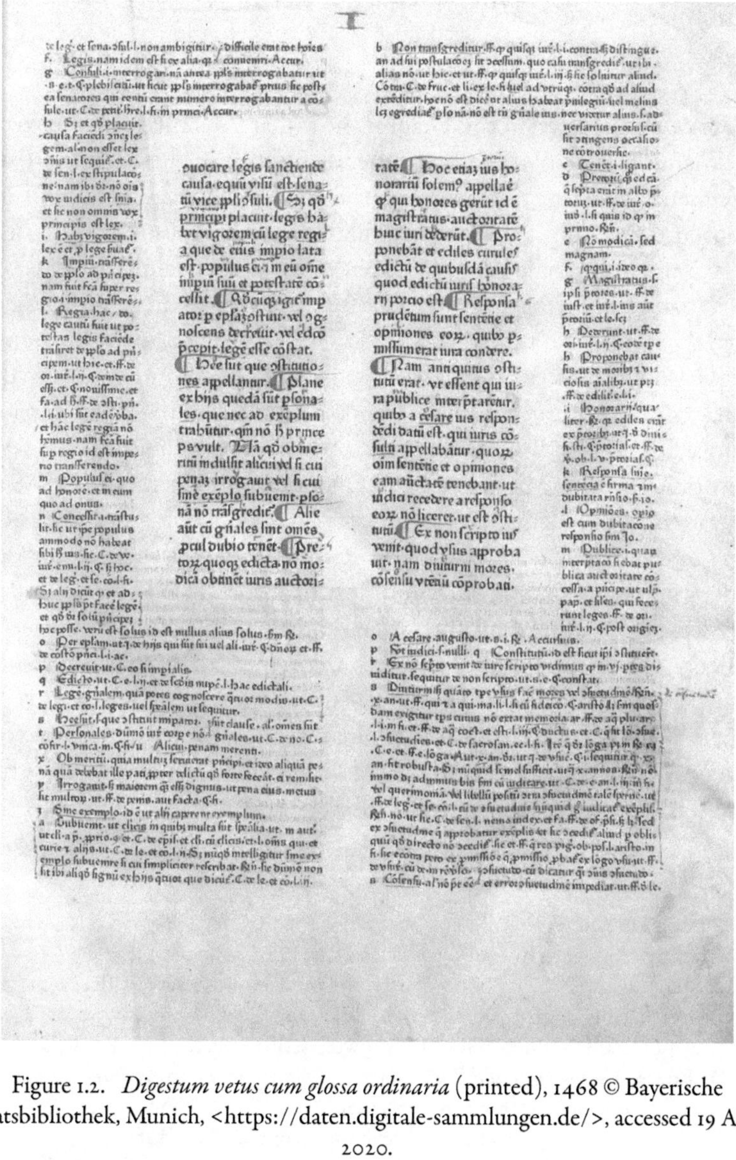

Figure 1.2. *Digestum vetus cum glossa ordinaria* (printed), 1468 © Bayerische Staatsbibliothek, Munich, <https://daten.digitale-sammlungen.de/>, accessed 19 April 2020.

Incunabula still have the same *mise en page* as medieval manuscripts. The text in the centre is surrounded by glosses in the margins.

Conclusion

All the cases discussed in this chapter show that the skills required to produce manuscript books had no gender distinctions. Although there were more men than women in the book trade, women served in various roles and progressed from apprentice to master thereby demonstrating that it was not a wholly male-dominated industry and in family owned businesses, female contributions were indisputable. An analysis of Bolognese contracts setting the terms for a manuscript's production and payment, provide valuable information about female scribes commissioned to copy legal text-books, although they do not demonstrate the exact extent of their wealth. The inclusion of Table 1.1, which chronologically lists seventeen women working in the Bologna manuscript trade between 1268 and 1324, provides the identities, dates of activity, payment history and known works of these women.[52] Many were scribes producing manuscripts with challenging layouts: two columns of text neatly enclosed by two columns of glosses. Since almost all the scribes copied manuscripts at the behest of clients, the documentary evidence offers clues to original ownership.[53] Unsurprisingly, the first users show a strong affiliation with a university or mendicant order.[54] A possible future direction for this research would be to uncover the names of clients who commissioned manuscripts from female scribes. These clients were probably students who purchased their

---

Taxation in Late Thirteenth-century Bologna: The Role of Women as Taxpayers', in *Essays in Honour of Roman Czaja* (Debrecen: Print-Art, 2020), 457–69.

[52] A study of the Parisian book trade from 1,200 to 1,500 reveals that some 1,200 people occupied that industry. No fewer than thirty women were engaged in the book trade business but only two were scribes: Richard H. Rouse and Mary A. Rouse, *Manuscripts and Their Makers. Commercial Book Producers in Medieval Paris, 1200–1500* (Turnhout: Brepols 1999).

[53] Medieval manuscripts had a long life in the secondhand market.

[54] For a social history of students who commissioned books in thirteenth-century Bologna, see Rosa Smurra, *Iohannes de Pontissara: Vescovo di Winchester (1282–1304) Studente a Bologna Professore a Modena e gli Altri Anglici suoi Compagni di Studio* (Bologna: Bononia University Press, 2012).

manuscripts in Bologna before returning to home to practise their new professions. Identifying these former university graduates, and where they lived and worked, would enable a study of the circulation and consumption of Bolognese manuscripts.

As the coexistence of manuscript and printed texts in the sixteenth-century shows, the art of manuscript copying was not abruptly supplanted by the appearance of Gutenberg's printing press in the mid-fifteenth century. Furthermore, as pointed out by Michael Clanchy, 'Instead of viewing printing as the starting point of a new age, I want to look at it as the endpoint or culmination of a millennium. Writing was of extraordinary importance in medieval culture; otherwise printing would not have been invented'.[55]

---

55   Michael Clanchy, *Looking Back from the Invention of Printing: Mothers and the Teaching of Reading in the Middle Ages* (Turnhout: Brepols, 2018), 18.

Table 1.1. List of women involved in the Bologna book trade. The women highlighted in semi-bold are discussed in the text. Data © Rosa Smurra, 2020; Design © Artemis Alexiou, 2022.

Column Headings	Source Abbreviations
Name: as given in document Occupation: types of occupation connected with book production Date: as indicated (or deducible) in document Manuscript: type of text that women were commissioned for Evidence: brief summary of the information provided in the document	ChSB VII: *Chartularium Studii Bononiensis. Documenti per la Storia dell'Università di Bologna dalle Origini fino al Sec. XV*, vol. VII (anni 1267-1268), edited by Guido Zaccagnini (Bologna: Presso l'Istituto per la Storia dell'Università di Bologna 1923). ChSB VIII: *Chartularium Studii Bononiensis. Documenti per la Storia dell'Università di Bologna dalle Origini fino al Sec. XV*, vol. VIII (anno 1268), edited by Guido Zaccagnini (Bologna: Presso l'Istituto per la storia dell'Università di Bologna, 1927). ChSB IX: Chartularium Studii Bononiensis. Documenti per la Storia dell'Università di Bologna dalle Origini fino al Sec. XV, vol. IX (anno 1986), edited by Luigi Colini-Baldeschi (Bologna: Presso l'Istituto per la storia dell'Università di Bologna). Estimi: Archivio di Stato di Bologna, Comune, Ufficio dei Riformatori degli Estimi, Estimi, series II, 1296. Filippini and Zucchini: Francesco Filippini and Guido Zucchini, *Miniatori e Pittori a Bologna: Documenti dei Secoli XIII e XIV* (Firenze: G. C. Sansoni, 1947) Orlandelli: Gianfranco Orlandelli, *Il Libro a Bologna dal 1300 al 1330: Documenti con uno Studio su il Contratto di Scrittura nella Dottrina Notarile Bolognese* (Bologna: Zanichelli, 1959). Murano: Giovanna Murano, Copisti a Bologna (1265-1270) (Turnhout: Brepols, 2006). Sarti and Fattorini: Mauro Sarti and Mauro Fattorini, *De Claris Archigymnasii Bononiensis Professo-ribus a Saeculo XI usque ad Saeculum XIV*, 2nd ed. Cesare Albicini and Carlo Malagola, 2 vols, (Bolo-gna: Ex officina regia fratrum Merlani, 1888-1896).

Name	Occupation, Date	Manuscript	Evidence	Source
Cristiana, daughter of Conradinus son of late Vitale	Scribe, 1268	Decretals (text and small guide letters)	Her father promised magister Jacob, canon at Bologna, to have Cristiana write in sixteen months, at the price of twenty-four *lire di bol*.	ChSB VIII, 95, doc. 185.
Flandina, daughter of the scribe Tebaldino from Castiglione de Regio	Scribe, 1268	*Apparatus* of Decretals	Committed to copy for Arnaldo Cerigerii in one year and half for the price of thirty-one *lire di bol*.	ChSB VII, 125, no. 239; Filippini and Zucchini, 68-69; Murano, 35, 127, 159 no. 218.
Marchexana, daughter of Benvenutus Tuschi of Borgo Pollicino	Scribe, 1270	*Digestum novum* of the Apparatus by Accursius	Promised William of Verneto to write, at the unit price of eighteen *soldi di bol*. per *quaternus*.	Murano, 35, 150 no. 182.
Donella, wife of late William	Illuminator, 1271	-	Sold a house to Lambert son of late Beccaro.	Filippini and Zucchini, 65.
Montanaria, wife of late Onestus Odofredi	Scribe, 1271	-	Agreed to work for the stationer Bencevenne Balduini for six months in the book production at the price of sixty *lire di bol*.	Filippini-Zucchini, 106, 171.
Alda, daughter of Dinigia daughter of Muçi	Scribe, 1272	*Decretum*	Promised Bernardo de Rusello that Alda will write and complete the *Decretum*.	Murano, 35.
Anthonia, daughter of Rodulphus son of late Gandulphus	Scribe, 1275	*Infortiatum cum Tribus Partibus*	Her father, scribe like her, promised Giovanni Bonabrocca that Anthonia will write, at the price of twenty-two *lire di bol*.	Sarti and Fattorini, I, 186-187; Murano, 35, 162 no. 234.
Allegra, wife of Yvanus son of late Bentivoglio	Scribe, 1279 1296	Bible	In 1279 her husband promised the Carmelite friar John Borgoniense that he would have Allegra write at the price of eighty *lire di bol*. Allegra's involvement in the book production is also witnessed in 1296.	Estimi, Porta Piera, S. Cecilia, 146; Sarti and Fattorini, I, 187; Murano, 35.
Anthonia, daughter of late John, wife of Ambroxinus son of late William of Milan	Scribe, 1286	*Apparatus* of the Decretals	Anthonia's husband promised to Libanorio of Monselice that he would have Anthonia write at the unit price of twenty-one *soldi di bol*. for each *quaternus*.	ChSB IX, 40, doc. 71; Murano, 35-36.
Uliana, daughter of Benvenutus de Faenza	Scribe, 1289	*Volumen, i. e. Authenticum, Institutiones* and *Tres libros Codicis*	Promised Alberto Odofredi to write at the price of twenty-five *lire di bol*.	Sarti and Fattorini, I, 187; Murano, 36.
Two unnamed women, daughters of Yvanus son of late Bentivoglio	Scribes, 1296	-	Involved with their mother Allegra in the book production.	Estimi, Porta Piera, S. Cecilia, 146.
Margarita, daughter of Bartholomew de Magnanis	Scribe, 1300 1311	*Apparatus* of the Decretals Decretals with the *Apparatus* of Bernardo of Parma	John son of Ardizzone committed on behalf of Margarita. For the benefit of friar Stefano of Matugliano she had to transcribe the Apparatus of the Decretals. She appears as Malgarita daughter of late Bartholomew de Magnanis and wife of Geminianus of late James de Mutina. She committed on her own account, though with her husband's consent, to transcribe the Decretals with the *Apparatus* of Bernardo of Parma, for an agreed price of forty-three *lire* and nine *soldi di bol*.	Orlandelli, 41, no. 1, 81-82, no. 192.
Mambilia, daughter of late Mathiolus taylor	Stationer, 1303	*Infortiatum* with glossa	She appointed the scribe Gratiadeo son of Albert to write at the price of thirty-five *lire di bol*.	Orlandelli, 65, no. 122.
Malgerita, mother of John, daughter of the butcher Gadi de Puçolis, and wife of late Anthony de Homodinis de Modena	Scribe, 1304	*Digestum Vetus* (text and glosses)	Margarita and her son were to transcribe at their own expense, at an agreed price of seventy-eight *lire di bol*.	Orlandelli, 67, no. 129.
Bolnixia, daughter of late Bençevenis Blaxii	Stationer, 1310	Guillame Durand's *Speculum iudiciale*	The scribe Guidotto of Giacomo committed to transcribe for Bolnisia the Guillaume Durand's *Speculum iudiciale* at an agreed price amounted to twenty-three *lire* and ten *soldi di bol*.	Orlandelli, 80, no. 187.
Malgarita, daughter of late Bonfiglolus and widow of the friar Andrew of the parish-church of St Procolo	Parchment seller, 1319 1321	-	She signed an agreement (on 7 September 1319) with a parchment scraper, John son of Bitino, for the establishment of a company for the scraping of parchment, but also for the purchase and sale of all kinds of necessities and whatever else was needed as part of the same business.	Orlandelli, 97, no. 256; 103, no. 287.
Alda, daughter of late Vitale Michaelis	Scribe, 1324	Decretals *Digestum Novum*	She sold to judge Giacomo Homobono de' Tederisi two books (Decretals and a New Digest), for a total cost of 260 *lire di bol*.	Orlandelli, 110, no. 315; Murano, Copisti a Bologna, 36.

REESE ALEXANDRA IRWIN

2 Elizabeth Newbery, Publisher and Bookseller, 1780–1821: A Case Study from the Women's Print History Project

Who was the publisher Elizabeth Newbery (c. 1780–1821)? Her surname may sound familiar, as she shares it with John Newbery (1713–67), considered the 'father of children's literature', and the man after whom the American Library Association named its annual Newbery Award for Children's Literature.[1] Yet Elizabeth, his niece-in-law, whose own publishing business spanned twenty-two years – the same length of time for which John Newbery was in business – is a relatively unknown figure in the history of eighteenth-century book publishing. Kate Ozment offers one angle from which to approach Newbery's relative obscurity: she describes how an 'early and sustained interest' in male authors such as Shakespeare has resulted in 'minute variants in Shakespeare's First Folio [being] logged, but women writers are fortunate if they have a thorough enumerative bibliography, allowing access to their works, or serious consideration of how material mediation affects textual reception'.[2] Although Ozment's discussion focuses on authorship, the same can be said of publishing. For example, men such as John Newbery and John Murray II (1778–1843) became known as publishing giants of their time, while women publishers were seen as atypical or have been disregarded.

1 Charles Welsh, *Bookseller of the Last Century* (Cambridge: Cambridge University Press, 2010); John Rowe Townsend, *Trade and Plumb-Cake For Ever, Huzza!* (Cambridge: Colt Books Ltd, 1994).
2 Kate Ozment, 'From Recovery to Restoration: Aphra Behn and Feminist Bibliography' *Early Modern Women* 13:1 (2018), 106.

In an effort to redress this pattern of 'erasure and diminishment', Professor Michelle Levy and others have embarked on the creation of *The Women's Print History Project* (WPHP), a comprehensive bibliographical database of women's contributions to print and the publishing industry during the period between 1750 and 1836.[3] Quantitative data from the project shows that much of the past portrayal of women who were atypical or uncommon, because they were publishers, printers or booksellers, is inaccurate. As of 2020, 459 records of women within the WPHP database reflect active careers in publishing, in printing, or in bookselling firms. Chapter 4 in *Women in Print Volume 2: Production, Distribution and Consumption*, written by Kandice Sharren and Kate Moffatt, details the aims, objectives and scope of the WPHP.[4] One of the women uncovered in the project, Elizabeth Newbery, is profiled in this chapter.

Newbery, in contrast with other women publishers of the period, has been given some consideration in scholarship due to her association with John Newbery. For example, John Newbery's bibliographer Sidney Roscoe paid Elizabeth Newbery some attention, but arguably as an afterthought, casting her into a passive role. This chapter serves as an extension of the 'recovery' work undertaken in the WPHP, extrapolating data from that source and others to draw out the narrative of Newbery's life and work, challenging existing, limited narratives about her in the process. It is divided into three sections: Firstly, this chapter describes the life of Elizabeth Newbery and her career using quantitative data from the WPHP and other sources. Secondly, it highlights her contributions to children's and adult literature, the latter of which is often ignored or glossed over. Finally, it challenges the traditional narrative about the nature of Elizabeth's work and her agency that still persists in the twenty-first century – downplaying her business efforts. As a case study, Elizabeth Newbery provides an enriched chronicle of one woman's involvement in the book trades, excavating the breadth and nature of her work from underneath inaccurate and scant

[3] Michelle Levy et al., 'Aims and Objectives', *The Women's Print History Project* (2020), <https://womensprinthistoryproject.com/blog/post/57>, accessed 7 December 2021.

[4] Levy et al., 'Aims and Objectives'.

representations of her, thereby aiding a better understanding of women's labour and agency in the landscape of the eighteenth century.

Newbery Legacy and the Age of Elizabeth

Elizabeth Newbery inherited her firm from her late husband, Francis Newbery (d. 1780). His 1780 will appointed her as the sole executor upon his death in January of that year. To contextualize where her firm fits within the Newbery publishing legacy, the following provides an overview of the family's history and its publishing firm(s). Scholar and writer John Rowe Townsend describes John Newbery (active from 1745 to 1767) as the 'first [to make] the publishing of children's books a substantial and successful business', whose legacy looms large over the Newbery publication lineage.[5] He is considered an innovator in the genre of children's literature, with 'diverse experimentation' that 'no other eighteenth century publisher could match'.[6] John Newbery was one of the first to promote the idea that books should amuse as well as improve their readers, reflecting a changing world entering the Age of Reason and shedding the concept of original sin.[7] Yet John Newbery did not only publish children's books. He created a range of titles and, as Townsend remarks, 'had fingers in many pies'.[8] He also had an interest in several newspapers and periodicals, and promoted patent medicines.[9] When John Newbery died in 1767, he left his publishing and literary rights (having been an author himself, as well as the publisher of others' works) to his son Francis Newbery (1743–1818)

---

[5] Townsend, *Trade and Plumb-Cake For Ever, Huzza!*, 3.
[6] Brian Anderson and Felix de Marez Oyens, *Be Merry and Wise: Origins of Children's Book Publishing in England, 1650–1850* (London: The British Library, 2006), 51.
[7] Townsend, *Trade and Plumb-Cake For Ever, Huzza!*, 3.
[8] Townsend, *Trade and Plumb-Cake For Ever, Huzza!*, xii.
[9] Ian Maxted, 'John Newbery', Oxford Dictionary of National Biography (2008), <https://doi-org.ezproxy.library.ubc.ca/10.1093/ref:odnb/19978>, accessed 22 January 2020.

and his stepson Thomas Carnan (1737–88); to his nephew, another Francis Newbery, he left a share in his newspaper interests.[10]

According to John Newbery's will, 'it seems that he had hoped the business would be carried on at his house in St Paul's Church-Yard by his son, step-son and nephew, working together for their joint interest and benefit'.[11] This hope was not realized, as John's nephew Francis set out on his own in 1767 with only the Newbery name to recommend his book publications.[12] After this break, John's son Francis and stepson Thomas frequently differentiated themselves from their cousin Francis through advertisements and imprints within their titles, often explicitly indicating that their books were:

> Printed for T. Carnan and F. Newbery, Junior, at No. 65 in St Paul's Church Yard (but not for F. Newbery, at the Corner of Ludgate-Street, who has no share in the late Mr John Newbery's Books for Children).[13]

Bibliographer and librarian M. J. P. Weedon describes a growing non-cordial relationship between John Newberry's son and stepson as well, with 'Francis Newbery junior gradually withdr[awing] from publishing to concentrate on John Newbery's patent-medicine business, in which he had inherited the sole rights'.[14] Despite Newbery and Carnan actively encouraging the public to avoid their cousin's 'paltry compilations', and even without John Newbery's publishing rights, Francis Newbery 'seems to have persevered' until his death in 1780.[15]

---

10   Sidney Roscoe, *John Newbery and His Successors* (Wormley: Five Owls Press, 1973), 20.
11   M. J. P. Weedon, 'Richard Johnson and the Successors to John Newbery', *The Library* s5-IV:1 (1949), 30–1.
12   Michelle Levy, 'Towards a History of Women's Print', *Women's Book History Symposium*, Sylvia Hotel, 15–17 August 2018 [unpublished talk]. From Francis's perspective, he was effectively disinherited as he had no legal rights to John Newbery's previous list of publications.
13   Roscoe, *John Newbery and His Successors*, 22.
14   Weedon, 'Richard Johnson and the Successors to John Newbery', 31.
15   Weedon, 'Richard Johnson and the Successors to John Newbery', 31.

In contrast to the deterioration of Newbery and Carnan's joint venture, '[t]he other branch of the family enjoyed a longer and more distinguished history'.[16] Elizabeth 'carried on and extended the business' publishing by some 520 titles over her career.[17] The firm flourished under her direction, despite her experiencing a setback between 1786 and 1787. There was a fire at her premises at No. 20 Ludgate Street, in which she lost a large portion of her stock.[18] While No. 20 underwent repairs, she operated out of No. 37 Ludgate Street, moving back to No. 20 after things were settled. She continued to publish from there until she retired in 1802.

Within five years of publishing, Elizabeth produced at least thirty-four new titles and expanded her bookselling business – as opposed to the publishing business, as historian and bibliographer Jill Shefrin notes.[19] Roscoe explains that Elizabeth 'operated a general bookshop' which stocked about 403 titles that did not bear her imprint.[20] By 1785, there is evidence that she had hired her first manager, Abraham Badcock (d. 1797).[21] After Badcock's death, Elizabeth appointed John Harris (1756–1846) as manager, and in 1802 she sold the firm to him in exchange for an annuity of £500 per year, which she collected until her death in 1821. By the time of her death, this annuity had built up to £9,500, comparable to about £1 million today. In other words, she died having amassed a considerable amount of money. Harris continued the firm until 1843, at which time it was sold to Grant and Griffith, continuing for nearly another half-century.[22]

16   Weedon, 'Richard Johnson and the Successors to John Newbery', 31.
17   This figure comes from Roscoe, *John Newbery and His Successors*. By title, Roscoe means a single work, regardless of the amount of subsequent editions it went through. To use an example, Elizabeth published at least eleven known instances of the book *A New History of England* by Richard Johnson; under the umbrella of 'title', this book would be recorded only once.
18   Weedon, 'Richard Johnson and the Successors to John Newbery', 31. '20 Ludgate Street' was written as 'At the Corner of St Paul's Church-Yard' in her imprint.
19   Jill Shefrin, 'Elizabeth Newbery', *Oxford Dictionary of National Biography* (2004), <https://doi-org.ezproxy.library.ubc.ca/10.1093/ref:odnb/63579>, accessed 20 August 2018.
20   Roscoe, *John Newbery and His Successors*, 31.
21   Shefrin, 'Elizabeth Newbery'.
22   Levy, 'Towards a History of Women's Print'.

Data on Elizabeth's Publications

Of the 520 titles Elizabeth Newbery is known to have published, Roscoe explains that 310 of these were juvenile, or children's titles, while 210 were adult titles. Of the juvenile titles, three out of four were published by Elizabeth alone, or her 'sole imprint'; of the adult titles, roughly a third were published by her alone, the others being joint ventures.[23] Despite Roscoe providing this breakdown and acknowledging Elizabeth's contributions to both children's and adult literature, demonstrating that she published titles in both broad genres, Levy finds that Elizabeth's role 'is almost always treated exclusively as a children's book publisher'.[24] Levy goes on to describe how even Shefrin, who wrote Elizabeth's *Oxford Dictionary of National Biography* entry in 2004 and who generally gives her more credit as a publisher, glosses over the [210] adult titles as 'often joint ventures', and that her participation in these ventures was 'merely financial' – though Levy begs the question, what is 'mere' about a publisher being interested in making money.[25] Roscoe goes further, stating that 'Elizabeth published books for children and young people in preference to all others'.[26] Extrapolating Roscoe's data on Elizabeth's titles, Levy provides a breakdown by percentage and category, noting that 40 per cent of Elizabeth's titles were *not* for children – a high enough ratio to merit re-examination of previous scholarship. In light of these figures, Elizabeth Newbery's reputation as a children's book publisher needs to be reassessed.

The current WPHP practice for recording data on Elizabeth Newbery extends this portrait of her as primarily a children's book publisher. In the beginning, Newbery's titles were entered into the project because of the addition of children's literature to the database in a substantial way.

---

23   Roscoe, *John Newbery and His Successors*, 29.
24   Levy, 'Towards a History of Women's Print'.
25   Shefrin, 'Elizabeth Newbery', and Roscoe, *John Newbery and His Successors*, qtd. in Levy, 'Towards a History of Women's Print'.
26   Roscoe, *John Newbery and His Successors*, 29.

Roscoe's bibliography of the Newbery family's books, for instance, was used primarily for its extensive list of children's literature, which dominates the contents of the bibliography. Only recently have some 'adult' titles published by Elizabeth Newbery been added to the database. Although this work will continue, as it stands now, gaps in the data could unintentionally perpetuate the assumption that Elizabeth Newbery's firm focused on children's literature. Mindful of this shortcoming, and in an effort to ensure that bibliographical data is accurate, thereby creating a fuller portrait of her within the WPHP, other publications by Elizabeth Newbery's firm have been flagged for entry. The goal of additional in-depth research on individuals like her in the WPHP database is to enhance its context.

Although more attention has been given to her children's publications, Elizabeth has also been criticized for publishing certain types of children's works. Roscoe asserts that her juvenile titles had a 'moral and didactic tone' at odds with John Newbery's earlier entertaining innovations, and that her 'views on education and training for life were no doubt deplorable'.[27] Roscoe's critique is a strange interpretation of the contents of a bibliography he compiled, where adult titles by Elizabeth's firm are generously represented. Additionally, Roscoe overlooks the fact that while Elizabeth Newbery did publish didactic literature, she innovated and published unique works like games, illustrated books and fun 'it' narratives like *The History of a Pin, as related by itself* (1798). Examples of these are presented in the next section.

Tools such as the WPHP aim to better equip future scholars with more accessible data on historical publishers and authors, and perhaps lead them to avoid mistakes such as characterizing historical figures based on a small selection of the works they produced. For instance, a search in the WPHP for juvenile works published by Elizabeth Newbery with the word 'moral' in the title returns fifty-one results, while the same search with the word 'amuse' in the title returns fifty-four results. At a distance, and with the data available, the balance between 'didactic' and 'fun' literature is relatively even. In fact, her publication of a range of titles for children, from didactic literature to games and playful narratives, reflects the contemporary

---

27 Roscoe, *John Newbery and His Successors*, 32.

marketplace in which she was working rather than her own 'deplorable' perspective. During this period, for instance, the moral works of Sarah Trimmer (1741–1810) and Hannah More (1745–1833) were published in great abundance. There are 191 editions of Trimmer's juvenile titles in the WPHP, and by 1800 she had more books in the Newbery catalogue than any other author. Hannah More has 162 juvenile editions in the WPHP, herself a giant of moral and religious writing.

In the context of these other writers, and publishing trends, Elizabeth Newbery's 'control [of her firm] spanned the decades in which children's books became an established branch of the publishing industry'.[28] Her diverse catalogue of books in many genres to suit children and their parents indicates strategic business plans, rather than her own inclinations. It also reflects how the genre of children's literature expanded in the eighteenth century, becoming a defined category within a profitable industry.

Publishing, Marketing and Financing

A general advertisement, included with Elizabeth Newbery's list of new titles at the back of at least one of her 1797 publications reads:

> Of E. Newbery may also be had, a catalogue of several Hundreds of instructive and amusing Books for young People, from one Penny to any Sum, which are always ready for Inspection; together with a complete Assortment of cards, on Geography, History, &c. and a variety of schemes, in the form of Games, all calculated to make the Road to Knowledge pleasant and easy. School-books, Bibles, Common Prayer Books, and every Article in the Bookselling and Stationary Branches, as usual.[29]

This advertisement indicates that the variety of Elizabeth Newbery's merchandize, ranging from amusing games to instructional books for

---

28 Shefrin, 'Elizabeth Newbery'.
29 Mary Pilkington, *The Force of Example: or, the History of Henry and Caroline: Written For The Instruction And Amusement Of Young Persons* (London: E. Newbery, 1797), 167.

children, had grown in terms of price, genre and style and number of works. The diverse options were also reflected in the physical appearance of different items, which will be discussed further in this chapter. More general descriptions of the period state that 'publishers began to devote substantial resources to a product that was marketed at children and their guardians', with 'children's books ... different in appearance, and in cost, from works published for adults'.[30] This statement holds true for Elizabeth Newbery as a publisher.

Not only did children's publications differ in appearance from works for adults, but different types of children's publications differed from each other as well. Although Elizabeth could not use John Newbery's original book list, she successfully employed some of the same marketing practices that both John Newbery and later her husband Francis had used. One tactic was to form a recognizable brand, using 'internal publisher's "puffs" [marketing titles or products inside the story of other books] to sell her wares'.[31] After her husband's passing, she also 'expanded the [firm's] bookselling business, maintaining stock from other publishers for sale in her catalogues and shop'. While stocking one's bookstore with other publishers' wares was common practice at the time, Shefrin suggests Newbery decided which stock to acquire in order to diversify her inherited portfolio and maximize her sales opportunities independently of the prior decisions of her husband.[32]

Elizabeth's publications developed a consistent and recognizable brand across differently shaped sub-genres of children's titles. *Newbery's Familiar Letter Writer* (1788), wherein her name is in the title, demonstrates how she wove brand recognition into specific products. Following John Newbery's model of packaging children's literature in entertaining or pleasing ways, she advertised a specially curated set of gift books for the Christmas season, and 'adopt[ed] the regular and extensive use of quality

---

30   M. O. Grenby, 'The Origins of Children's Literature', in M. O. Grenby and Andrea Immel, eds, *The Cambridge Companion to Children's Literature* (Cambridge: Cambridge University Press, 2009), 6.
31   Shefrin, 'Elizabeth Newbery'.
32   Shefrin, 'Elizabeth Newbery'.

copperplate engravings to embellish her children's books'.[33] It appears she used engravings and woodcuts by both Thomas Bewick (1753–1828) and his younger brother John (1760–95), the latter of whom she commissioned work from in soaring numbers.[34] Regular woodcuts and engravings gave Newbery's titles a coherent appearance in the shop, as well as a competitive edge – extensive engravings resembled early picture books for children. John Bewick's wood cuts appeared in *Tales for Youth* (1794) and *The Looking Glass for the Mind* (1794), among several other publications for Elizabeth Newbery and later John Harris.[35]

Of the games she published, one was a joint publication with John Wallis (d. 1818). Called *The New Game of Human Life, with Rules for Playing: Being the Most Agreeable & Rational Recreation Ever Invented for Youth of Both Sexes* (1790), it consisted of a printed sheet as the board for playing the game (Figure 2.1), and was housed inside a slip case.[36] Elizabeth utilized 'a savvy sense of book-marketing, and possibly financial backing' to produce this game, which according to historian Christopher Rovee evolved into the famous Milton Bradley Corporation's *Game of Life*. Despite being produced at a time of increasing competition among children's publishers, Rovee describes Wallis and Newbery's collaboration as the first of many between two London firms that both possessed a mastery of the diverse aspects of marketing and selling for children.[37]

33 Levy, 'Towards a History of Women's Print'.
34 Jenny Uglow, *Nature's Engraver: A Life of Thomas Bewick* (London: Faber and Faber Ltd, 2006), 147; 67.
35 Thomas Hugo, *The Bewick Collector: A Supplement to a Descriptive Catalogue of the Works of Thomas and John Bewick* (London: L. Reeve and Co., 1868), 234. Publishers often interchanged the terms 'wood cuts' and 'wood engravings' when discussing relief printing methods. Thomas and John Bewick were both well-known for producing highly detailed wood engravings.
36 British Library, 'The New Game of Human Life, with Rules for Playing: Being the Most Agreeable & Rational Recreation Ever Invented for Youth of Both Sexes. [A printed sheet, forming a board for playing the game, contained in a slip case.]', British Library (n.d.), <http://explore.bl.uk/BLVU1:LSCOP-ALL:BLL01001358596>, accessed 4 May 2020.
37 Rovee, 'The New Game of Human Life, 1790'.

Figure 2.1. *The New Game of Human Life, with Rules for Playing: Being the Most Agreeable & Rational Recreation Ever Invented for Youth of Both Sexes*, John Wallis, 1790 © Victoria and Albert Museum, London.

While the success of the *Game of Life* and her other children's titles are undeniable, Newbery's mastery of publishing for children has probably skewed the perception of her as a children's book publisher, despite 40 per cent of her output being adult titles about one third of which were solo ventures; the other two thirds had imprints with multiple partners. The shared titles, common at the time, were not only financially intelligent (sharing risks and costs of publishing), they also helped to disseminate her name and expand her business network.

On her own, she published the first account of the *Journal of Captain Cook's Last Voyage to the Pacific Ocean, on Discovery*, by John Rickman (1737–1818). She published the first and second editions in 1781, and a 'new' edition in 1785. Levy states that no one has considered Elizabeth's role as publisher of this important work, notable for containing the first representation of Hawaii in print created by the expedition's artist John Webber.[38] There were many abridgements and imitations of Captain Cook's voyages on the market, so her release of the first and second editions in the same year appears strategic. Consider too the second edition's title: 'the second edition, carefully revised ... and some errors in the former edition corrected'.[39]

Offering a new edition with corrections of the previous one is a marketing device, which aims to create consumer demand for the new product. This phrasing also attests to the authority of her edition over other Captain Cook narratives. The insertion of the word 'authority' distinguishes it from other, similar publications – implying that only Newbery's was the 'true' account. Title pages were the place for publishers to speak directly

---

38 Maggs Bros. Ltd, 'Journal of Captain Cook's Last Voyage to the Pacific Ocean, on Discovery; Performed in the Years 1776, 1777, 1778, 1779, and 1780. Illustrated with Cuts, and a Chart, Shewing the Tracks of the Ships Employed in this Expedition', Maggs Bros. Ltd, Rare Books & Manuscripts (2020), <https://www.maggs.com/departments/travel/all_categories/210333/>, accessed 20 January 2020.

39 British Library, 'Journal of Captain Cook's Last Voyage to the Pacific Ocean, on Discovery; Performed in the Years 1776, 1777, 1778, 1779 ... The Second Edition, Carefully Revised . . . and Some Errors in the Former Edition Corrected. [By John Rickman.]', British Library (n.d.), <http://explore.bl.uk/BLVU1:LSCOP-ALL:BLL01003098664>, accessed 30 April 2020.

to their purchasers, and Newbery's three editions of Cook's last voyage demonstrate her ability to leverage the language of authority to sell books.

Newbery was part of a large consortium of publishers to produce Hannah Glasse's (1708–70) *The Art of Cookery*. The first edition was self-published in 1747, and went through at least forty editions. It was a bestseller for at least a century after its initial production. Francis Newbery joined its long list of publishers in 1778; Elizabeth joined in 1784, and appeared in the imprint of editions in 1788 and 1796 as well. During the years her name was in the imprint, she was one of between twenty-three and twenty-five other publishers. By the time she joined this large group, *The Art of Cookery* was into at least its eighteenth edition – the edition numbers no longer being recorded on the title pages indicating it was already a successful publication.

Strangely, Roscoe points to shared ventures such as these as evidence of Elizabeth's lack of practical participation in the business side of publishing. He argues that joint publications, with more than nine and sometimes upwards of fifty names in the imprint, were 'books in the production of which Elizabeth presumably took no practical part beyond her financial backing'.[40] Imprints, like other information on a book's title page, are sources of authority, but should also be regarded with some scepticism as they could often be partial, outdated or otherwise misleading. Although they may not paint the entire picture of the financial dealings that contributed to a book's production, I would argue that Newbery's appearance in joint imprints still demonstrates active participation in the trade, and indicates an enmeshment in the industry that Roscoe does not afford her. While reasons for joining a joint venture could vary, Newbery was probably sharing the risk and cost of production of *The Art of Cookery*, and sharing the profits of the successful publication. The lack of records to better describe how Elizabeth Newbery participated in these publishing networks is unfortunate, leading to gaps in our understanding of the nuances of her business relationships, built at least in part through joint publication projects. We can, however, speculate that she was well connected to London publishing networks, and her participation in these networks enabled her to work as

---

40   Roscoe, *John Newbery and His Successors*, 29.

a trusted collaborator. She was also financially independent and had the money to fund joint ventures, and this probably afforded her continual involvement. Elizabeth Newbery was clearly an active and competitive figure in the London publishing landscape of her time and had knowledge of the market to leverage consumers towards buying her product. Furthermore, her marketing and publishing decisions demonstrate she was indeed an integral figure in the 'longer and more distinguished history' of her branch of the Newbery family.[41]

The Evolution of Elizabeth Newbery's Legacy

Having established a fuller sense of Elizabeth Newbery's publishing output and its scope in both length and depth, the question remains: why have Elizabeth Newbery's professional accomplishments not been better recognized? Scholarship related to her role in the production of adult literature has been ignored, or glossed as 'merely financial' involvement; and her skilled marketing and branding of children's literature within the competitive market of her contemporaries has not been acknowledged.

In scholarship related to Elizabeth Newbery as a publisher, and in women's contributions to the book trades in general, there also seems to be a larger structural issue of what constitutes publishing activity – the assumption that funding a work, or selling books, does not carry the same weight as other activities such as liaising with authors and producing interesting titles. Therefore, the activities that Elizabeth Newbery engaged in were devalued within historical and cultural studies of the publishing business. There also seems to be a wilful ignorance of eighteenth-century women as publishers, despite primary evidence of their business activities. On one hand, Elizabeth Newbery's activities *have* been characterized as an unusual example of a female publisher. On the other hand, Elizabeth Newbery's narrative has historically been constructed through the perspective of 'she

---

41   Weedon, 'Richard Johnson and the Successors to John Newbery', 31.

published it, but' ... her manager [a man] was [really] in charge.[42] This final section walks through the history of Elizabeth Newbery's agency as publisher being questioned, first by Charles Welsh in 1885, and then by S. Roscoe in 1973.

In 1885, Charles Welsh, the biographer of John Newbery, briskly covers Elizabeth Newbery's career in his *Bookseller in the Last Century* in a mere two sentences. Meanwhile, he makes several references to her late husband Francis Newbery, whose production was relatively smaller than hers (about 131 editions), and to her successor John Harris. Welsh reports that Francis's widow, Elizabeth Newbery:

> ... carried on the business ... after his death. After some years she retired there from, drawing out of it, until her death in 1821, ... a yearly allowance of £500, and John Harris, who had long managed the business for her, succeeded to it.[43]

This brief account bookends Elizabeth's publishing industry activity between her husband and her successor; it focuses on Elizabeth's action of leaving the firm rather than her work within it. Welsh's account created the impression amongst scholars that 'Elizabeth had a merely caretaking role in the history of the prestigious Newbery firm'.[44] Jill Shefrin makes the case that Welsh is responsible for this misrepresentation of Elizabeth Newbery, which began with his 1885 account where he also asserts that Abraham Badcock actually ran the firm, at least initially before Harris 'took over' in 1797. Welsh explains that '[f]or some time before Harris, Mr Abraham Badcock, who died April 18, 1797, appears to have managed the business for Mrs Newbery'.[45] Shefrin refutes this understanding, explaining that:

> Evidence to support [Newbery as only a caretaker] is tenuous, derived largely from the surviving account books of Richard Johnson, a hack writer and compiler who provided the Newberys with a substantial number of manuscripts between 1770

---

42   The phrase 'she published it, but' is an adaptation of 'she wrote it, but' from Joanna Russ, *How to Suppress Women's Writing* (Austin: University of Texas Press, 1983).
43   Welsh, *Bookseller of the Last Century*, 85.
44   Shefrin, 'Elizabeth Newbery'.
45   Welsh, *Bookseller of the Last Century*, 85.

and 1792. These records show payments and records of orders from Elizabeth in 1780 and 1785; after that date they refer only to Abraham Badcock, her manager. Contemporary accounts of Badcock make clear his talents, but this is as much an argument for Elizabeth's business acumen as for her secondary role.[46]

Welsh's assertion that Badcock ran the firm operates on an understanding of a manager as someone with more authority than the publisher or owner, Elizabeth having both latter roles in this case. On the other hand, Shefrin points out, hiring a manager after roughly five years of successful business would be simply good business practice. The only primary evidence that exists shows that Badcock collected payments and processed orders, not that he was making upper-level decisions in regards to selection, rejection and author relations beyond paying them for their content. Welsh's bibliography, meanwhile, contains 178 references to the 'E. Newbery' imprint, enough of a presence, surely, to merit some attention to her publications within his introduction to the bibliography.[47]

Almost 100 years later, in 1973, Roscoe published his bibliography *John Newbery and his Successors*. While he discusses Elizabeth's work more than Welsh does, he relies directly upon Welsh's description of her as a passive figure in the Newbery legacy. Roscoe begins the section of his 'Introduction' dedicated to 'the fourth and last period in the family history' by acknowledging that Elizabeth 'dominated the period'.[48] Though he does acknowledge her output, he characterizes her firm as being run by her managers, and he questions her moral preferences. As we have seen, he was critical of her publishing choice of didactic titles for children. After describing her career, Roscoe writes:

> I have spoken of Elizabeth doing this and that. But was she really the master and active director of her publishing book-selling business? Or did she only lend her name (a valuable one in the trade, we may be sure, after all of those years), leaving the practical conduct of affairs in the active hands of her manager Abraham Badcock, and after him John Harris?[49]

---

46 Shefrin, 'Elizabeth Newbery'.
47 Charles Welsh, 'Catalogue of the Books Published by the Newberys', in *Bookseller of the Last Century* (Cambridge: Cambridge University Press, 2010), 168–335.
48 Roscoe, *John Newbery and His Successors*, 27.
49 Roscoe, *John Newbery and His Successors*, 32.

Roscoe suspects that Badcock, in particular, was running the firm. He explains, discussing Richard Johnson's correspondence with Badcock after 1785, and Johnson's ledger records:

> *The Grecian States* [by Johnson] was ledgered as compiled 'for Mrs Newbery' but later marked as paid for by Badcock. Of these ledger entries, all between 1785 and 1792, there are about thirty-seven. Clearly a substantial measure of the work of Elizabeth's firm was in Badcock's hands, if not under his ultimate control.[50]

Returning to Shefrin's point about Elizabeth's business acumen, the evidence these ledgers provide is that Badcock was the person who paid Johnson for his work. That Johnson recorded his work as 'compiled for Mrs Newbery' is evidence that he had at least some dealings with her; perhaps he compiled the work at her request, or after corresponding with her about the project. While certain details are unknowable, why would Johnson record her personal name, not just her professional imprint, in the process of doing business with the firm if she had no part of the transaction? Levy describes how Newbery 'established long-standing relationships with authors to produce content', which Johnson's experience appears to confirm. That Roscoe questions Elizabeth's role, going so far as to say 'the real motive power [in the firm] may have come from her managers Badcock and Harris',[51] ignores evidence of Elizabeth's activity, primary evidence that is recorded in the bibliography he produced. Levy argues that 'Roscoe's suggestion that she contributed to the decline in amusing work for children (such as that published by John Newbery) does not withstand scrutiny'.[52] Furthermore, Roscoe's depiction of Elizabeth's work largely relies on what Shefrin calls 'tenuous evidence',[53] and Levy concludes that Roscoe's opinions 'must rest on the unstated belief that only a man could operate a successful firm'.[54]

---

50   Roscoe, *John Newbery and His Successors*, 32.
51   Roscoe, *John Newbery and His Successors*, 2.
52   Levy, 'Towards a History of Women's Print'.
53   Shefrin, 'Elizabeth Newbery'.
54   Levy, 'Towards a History of Women's Print'.

Welsh and Roscoe included women in their bibliographies and the histories they published. However, I have made the case that they did not give Elizabeth Newbery adequate space or descriptive coverage for her labour and accomplishments, and I think this is true for other women. Both Welsh and Roscoe created narratives in the paratext of their bibliographies which impart the impression that while Elizabeth's name may have been the firm's imprint, she was not an active force or significant contributor to the Newbery legacy. They present an incomplete portrait of Newbery's involvement, at odds with the volume of production spearheaded by her imprint. This highlights a major issue in bibliographical scholarship: just because a woman is mentioned in a history or in a bibliography that does not mean that her agency as a historical person will be adequately covered.

Yet Elizabeth's firm was successful, and when she sold it to her successor John Harris, she successfully negotiated a £500 annuity as part of the sale. Roscoe describes this transaction as Harris buying her out,[55] but from another angle, this transaction can be read as a successful businessperson setting herself up for retirement and profiting from twenty-two years of work establishing the firm as, essentially, a brand. Newbery's professional achievements notwithstanding, Roscoe 'has no evidence as to the role of Harris in the conduct of the firm's affairs in the years leading up to Elizabeth's retirement'.[56] Therefore, his opinion of the transition from Newbery to Harris is not founded on knowledge of their professional relationship and the extent of Harris's work with the firm prior to the sale, but rather on gendered assumptions about women in business.

While there has been no evidence of Harris's involvement in the firm, and little evidence of Badcock's role – which appears limited, a position of bookkeeping rather than control – there is consistent evidence for Elizabeth's authority within the firm beyond publishing statistics – which is her imprint. It was common during this time to incorporate partners into the firm's imprint as they were brought on, a practice that spawned such long firm names as 'Longman, Rees, Orme, Brown, Green and Longman'. In contrast, Elizabeth never incorporated the names of Badcock or Harris

---

55   Roscoe, *John Newbery and His Successors*, 2.
56   Roscoe, *John Newbery and His Successors*, 32.

into her imprint; nor did she elaborate her imprint in homage to her connection to John Newbery.

For her entire career, Elizabeth's imprint read 'E. Newbery, at the Corner of St. Paul's Church-Yard', with minor grammatical variations in the address. Once Newbery sold the firm to Harris, he took on the imprint 'J. Harris, successor to E. Newbery, Corner of St. Paul's Church-Yard', again with minor address variants, for at least seventeen years, using it ninety-six known times in that span.[57] While it is plausible that Harris chose to keep Newbery's name in the imprint to recommend his works as part of the Newbery lineage, it is also possible that he was counting on Elizabeth's name, specifically, to be recognizable to customers: Harris was reprinting Elizabeth's titles, not John Newbery's, and by 1802 the market had evolved beyond what J. Newbery had 'fathered' thirty-five years prior. Elizabeth's consistent, singular imprint may indicate that Badcock and Harris held smaller positions in the firm's business than Welsh and Roscoe assert. For instance, the two were never described as partners. In contrast, consider the role William Davies (d. 1820) played in a contemporary firm: he became Thomas Cadell Jr's (1773–1836) partner *and* manager in that firm, and the imprint changed to 'T. Cadell and W. Davies, Strand' to reflect his position. Davies managed the business until he fell ill in 1813, though the firm retained the imprint with both men's names until 1820, when Davies died.[58] The addition and inclusion of Davies in the imprint indicates an elevated role above manager of accounts, whereas Badcock and Harris appear never to have risen above that type of managerial role.

Evidence for Elizabeth's active role in the firm comes most strongly from records of her finances, especially in reference to the sale of her business to Harris. The continued annuity paid to Elizabeth by Harris until her death suggests that at the time of her retirement, the firm was doing well enough financially to afford this expense. Harris was, in other words,

---

57 This information comes from searches executed within the Women's Print History Project.
58 H. R. Tedder, rev. Catherine Dille, 'William Davies', Oxford Dictionary of National Biography (2004), <https://doi-org.ezproxy.library.ubc.ca/10.1093/ref:odnb/7273>, accessed 30 January 2020.

buying a profitable business if such a deal were included in the sale. When Elizabeth died in 1821, her estate was worth 'some £20,000 in specific bequests', which equates to about £2.2 million today.[59] Her amassed fortune is telling of the work and success she had during her time as a publisher. Just as John Newbery had died a rich man after his efforts, Elizabeth set the same groundwork during her twenty-two-year career.

Elizabeth Newbery's will also speaks volumes as to how she conceived of women and their independence. Shefrin explains that 'her will is interesting for the careful provision of money for female relatives and dependents', with '[t]he money designated for her surviving sister, Susanna, who received the bulk of the estate, and that for Susanna's daughter, ... to be held in trust in such a fashion that it could not be used by their husbands'.[60] By specifying that only these two women could use the money given to them, Elizabeth demonstrates not only an awareness of patriarchal control over women, but a knowledge of how to leverage the system for the benefit of her female relatives. This 'careful provision' demonstrates that Elizabeth understood the value of women having financial independence, something she herself had earned through her career.

Additionally, there is the matter of her name showing up in publications both before and after her time as publisher. Roscoe explains that he first found her name 'in the imprint of the *Middlesex Journal,* numbers 587–91, in 1772–3', eight years before she took over Francis's firm, not seeing her name in that publication again until after the year of her husband's death'.[61] Both Ozment and Cait Coker have explained that women were probably involved in publishing within family units, even when their names did not appear in imprints. It seems possible in this case that Elizabeth assisted her husband in his business before she inherited it, and her name in the imprint of the *Middlesex Journal* stands as proof of this activity that probably continued, though with the absence of her name. In any case, the

---

59 Bank of England, 'Inflation Calculator', Bank of England (2020), <https://www.bankofengland.co.uk/monetary-policy/inflation/inflation-calculator>, accessed 30 January 2020.
60 Shefrin, 'Elizabeth Newbery'.
61 Roscoe, *John Newbery and His Successors,* 26.

subsequent success of her firm after Francis's death is also probably due in part to her proximity, if not her involvement, in the publishing process while he was alive. Male publishing lineage often went from father to son, or from publisher to apprentice (as was the case with John Newbery); in both instances the younger person learned from the older person before taking over the business, only ready to continue it on after years of practice and education. It seems probable, as has been shown to be the case for many women in the period, that Elizabeth was well-prepared to take over her husband's firm upon his death from her own education in the business, learning from Francis in a role akin to apprenticeship, borne out of a necessity to assist in the family business.[62] While her involvement or observance of Francis's firm was the training ground for her knowledge and expertise in publishing, in her retirement she felt the absence of the trade: Shefrin describes how Elizabeth 'retained an interest in publishing' after retirement, with her name appearing on the *Ladies Most Elegant and Convenient Pocket Book* in 1804, and again, as a joint publication, on the fifteenth edition of the *New Oxford Guide* in 1810, both titles she had published prior to the sale to Harris. Her participation in these two works probably came, as Shefrin suggests, out of a continued interest in works to which she still owned the rights.[63] Elizabeth's activities both before and after the span of her twenty-two-year career indicate that she had an interest in publishing; however, the nature of this interest cannot be defined after the fact. Regardless, this portrait of her activity shows her to be capable, intelligent, successful and involved, an important figure in the publishing landscape of the latter half of the eighteenth century.

62 Hunt, Tamara L., 'Women's Participation in the Eighteenth-Century English Publishing Trades', *Leipziger Jahrbuch zur Buchgeschichte* 6 (1996), 47; Bell, Maureen, *A Dictionary of Women in the London Book Trade 1540–1730* (Loughborough University of Technology, 1983).
63 Shefrin, 'Elizabeth Newbery'.

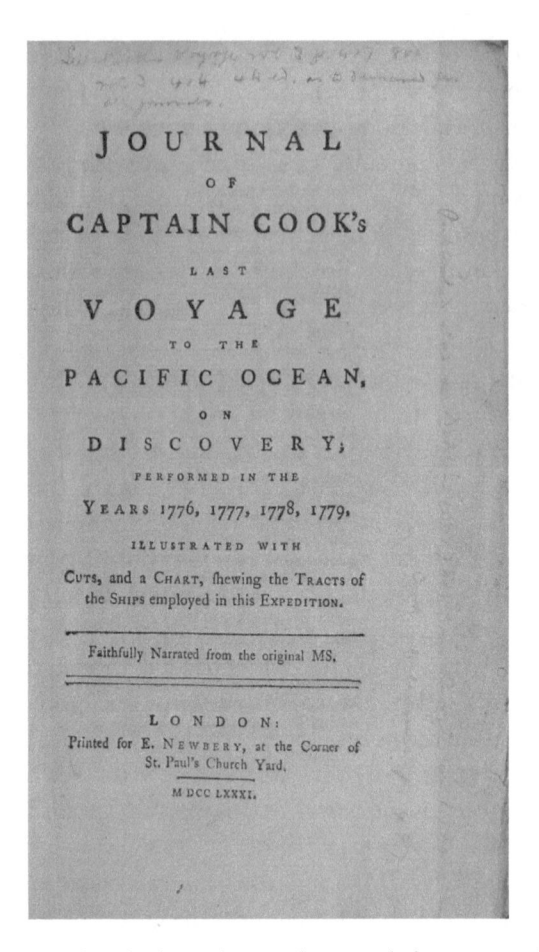

Figure 2.2. James Cook and John Rickman, eds, *Journal of Captain Cook's Last Voyage to the Pacific Ocean, on Discovery* (London: E. Newbury, 1781). Image courtesy of the University of British Columbia Library Digitization Centre.

Conclusion

Having considered the historical description of Elizabeth's work, what is the impact of these descriptions on how she is considered today? Coker notes that we are still grappling with the ramifications of women being described as atypical within the book trades; normalizing women's participation in this industry has not yet fully been achieved.[64] This chapter offers three recent examples that highlight the process whereby the narrative for Elizabeth Newbery as a publisher is still obscured. The first comes from Levy, who discovered a reference that attributed the publication of the 1781 edition of the *Journal of Captain Cook's Last Voyage to the Pacific Ocean, on Discovery* to a man named 'Edward Newbery' (Figure 2.2). The imprint on the book is 'E. Newbery', as it was published by Elizabeth; however, with only the initial 'E.' present, 'Edward' was supplied by this reference as publisher of this title. Levy and others have attempted to locate a real person named Edward Newbery, but with no success. Conversely, Roscoe, the British Library and *ECCO* list Elizabeth Newbery as the publisher for this title. Levy has concluded that, 'the invention by at least one scholar of one "Edward Newbery" as publisher of this book must have been motivated by a narrow and false conception of the kinds of works that Elizabeth Newbery published', perhaps operating under assumption that Elizabeth only published children's books.[65]

In an extension of this oversight, there are at least two more recent rare book title catalogues misidentifying Elizabeth in regard to *Cook's Last Voyage*. Both catalogue entries, one for a 1781 copy and one for the 'new' edition, fail to identify Elizabeth Newbery as the publisher, despite each catalogue including images of the title pages, which clearly bear her imprint. The 1781 catalogue entry states that the publisher was 'F. Newbery', attributing the work to her late husband, despite the initial in the imprint clearly reading 'E'.[66] The 'new' edition catalogue entry identifies the publisher as 'E. Newbery', but also misidentifies her as Francis in the book's description: 'Newbery recognised the potential of Rickman's anonymous journal, correctly assuming that it would be as successful as Marra's account

---

64 Coker, 'Finding Women in the Historical Record'.
65 Levy, 'Towards a History of Women's Print'.
66 Hordern House, 'Journal of Captain Cook's Last Voyage to the Pacific Ocean', Hordern House Rare Books, Manuscripts, Paintings (2020), <https://www.hordern.com/pages/books/4503917/cook-third-voyage-john-rickman/journal-of-captain-cooks-last-voyage-to-the-pacific-ocean-on-discovery-performed-in-the-years-1776/?soldItem=true>, accessed 20 January 2020.

of the Second Voyage, which *he* had also published.'[67] Although Francis Newbery did publish John Marra's *Journal of the Resolution's Voyage* (1775), this catalogue entry conflates both 'E.' and 'F.' Newbery into one person, overlooking the role publishers play in book production by paying them little attention.

This chapter has sought to unravel the faulty narratives from previous historical accounts of Elizabeth Newbery that were problematic because they (un)intentionally diminish her rich career and numerous accomplishments. While Newbery is one woman out of a known 459 women involved in the book trades of her period, it is important to reconsider how she has been described historically, and place these descriptions in conversation with Newbery's contributions to the publishing industry. Her personal life story and knowledge of her career enriches the narrative of women working in the book trades, and provides an example of the type of deep research needed to understand the complex network of contributions women made to the industry, contributions which have been historically ignored or described as unusual. To reiterate what Levy et al. have stated in the 'Aims and Objectives' of the WPHP, 'the hundreds of women we have found active in the trades, and the thousands of books they had a hand in printing, publishing and selling, offer a fertile beginning for reconstructing [women's] contributions to the history of print and their involvement in commercial networks'.[68] Uncovering, and then normalizing, women's contributions to the eighteenth-century book trades provide a better understanding of the complexities of the industry at the time, and resists anachronistic understandings of women and labour being applied to this history.

---

67 Maggs Bros. Ltd, 'Journal of Captain Cook's Last Voyage to the Pacific Ocean, on Discovery; Performed in the Years 1776, 1777, 1778, 1779, and 1780. Illustrated with Cuts, and a Chart, Shewing the Tracks of the Ships Employed in this Expedition', [italics added].
68 Levy et al., 'Aims and Objectives'.

HANNAH LYONS

3 Letitia Byrne (1779–1849) and the 'Prejudice Against Employing Women as Engravers'

On Friday 26 February, 1819, the 40-year-old printmaker, Letitia Byrne, left her home at 54 Upper John Street, Soho, London, carrying a small copperplate etching. The single sheet image depicted the picturesque town of Plympton nestled in the rolling, bucolic hills of the Devonshire countryside (Figure 3.1). Byrne's destination was the home of the landscape painter, Joseph Farington (1747–1821), who lived a fifteen-minute walk away at 35 Charlotte Street, Fitzroy Square.[1]

Farington, who by 1819 was 72-years-old and had enjoyed tremendous influence in the metropolitan art world, had known Letitia all her life.[2] He had been a longstanding collaborator and friend of her late father, the distinguished engraver and print publisher, William Byrne (1743–1805). However, Letitia's visit to Farington was not merely to catch up with an old family acquaintance; her print of the view of Plympton was etched after one of Farington's drawings and she was seeking his judgement on her proof. Farington had commissioned Letitia to make the frontispiece for his *Memoirs of the Life of Sir Joshua Reynolds*, and her proof illustrated

---

[1] This research is based on a chapter of my PhD thesis, '"Exercising the ART as a TRADE": Professional Women Printmakers in England, 1750–1850' (Birkbeck: University of London, 2021)', which examines the role, status and output of professional women printmakers working in late eighteenth and early nineteenth-century Britain. I would like to thank my supervisors, Professor Kate Retford and Dr Sarah Grant, as well as Anna Jamieson and Christine Slobogin.

[2] As so many Byrne family members will be discussed in this chapter, they will be referred to by their first names.

Figure 3.1. *Plympton*, Letitia Byrne (etcher) and Joseph Farington (painter), *Memoirs of the Life of Sir Joshua Reynolds: With Some Observations on His Talents and Character*, Joseph Farington, 1819, London: T. Cadell and W. Davies, frontispiece. Image courtesy of the Victoria and Albert Museum, London.

the eminent artist's birthplace. *Memoirs* was to be published by Cadell & Davies, booksellers to the Royal Academy of Arts, in March of that year.[3]

'Cadell called …', Farington had written in his diary on 19 January, 1819, 'he agreed to my proposal to have a Print of Plympton, the place where Sir Joshua was born, engraved by Miss L. Byrne to accompany the Narrative.'[4] Farington may have asked Letitia to make the print out of

3   Joseph Farington, *Memoirs of The Life of Sir Joshua Reynolds; With Some Observations on his Talents and Character* (London: Printed by Strahan and Spottiswoode, Printers-Street; For T. Cadell And W. Davies, In The Strand, Booksellers To The Royal Academy, 1819).
4   Joseph Farington, *Diary*, Tuesday 19 January, 1819. All Farington references are taken from: Kathleen Cave, ed., *The Diary of Joseph Farington*, 16 vols (New Haven and London: Yale University Press, 1978–84).

a sense of duty to her father; but, more likely, it was because of her respected reputation as a 'reproductive' engraver of topographical scenes – a reputation developed over a continuous career of almost twenty-five years. Although Letitia Byrne's *ouevre* is largely unknown today, by 1819 her prints had been praised by her contemporaries as showing evidence of 'great and progressive attainments in the art'.[5] Furthermore, since 1799 she had exhibited twenty-one watercolour landscape views at the Royal Academy of Arts – the principal institution in Britain for the exhibition of contemporary art. Given Farington's 'unparalleled ability and assiduity as a networker ... he seems to have known every painter, patron and dealer in London', which art historian Mark Hallett has recently noted, his decision to commission Letitia to etch the frontispiece to his latest project demonstrates that this most well connected of artists was clearly very confident of her abilities with the etching needle.[6] However, when recording the activities of 26 February in his diary that evening, Farington wrote: 'Miss L. Byrne called with an impression of the view of Plympton – notwithstanding Her ingenuity, she said there is a prejudice against employing women as Engravers.'[7]

Though concise, this diary entry alerts us to the gendered prejudices that Letitia Byrne felt that she faced in early nineteenth-century London. Crucially, it indicates that her extensive experience as a professional printmaker, working for large, male-run, commercial publishers, led her to believe that the status of male printmakers was superior to that of their female counterparts. Letitia implied that, by privilege of their gender, men were able to find work more easily in the overcrowded, metropolitan print market. This chapter will use the case study of Letitia Byrne as a lens to view the challenges that women printmakers faced when attempting to

---

5   *The Analectic Magazine, containing selections from Foreign Reviews and Magazines, together with Original Miscellaneous Compositions, and a Naval Chronicle* (Philadelphia: Moses Thomas, 1817), vol. 9, 47.

6   Mark Hallett, '1804: Pleading with Joseph Farington', in Mark Hallett, Sarah Victoria Turner and Jessica Feather, eds, *The Royal Academy of Arts Summer Exhibition: A Chronicle, 1769–2018* (London: Paul Mellon Centre for Studies in British Art, 2018), <https://chronicle250.com/1804>, accessed 12 January 2020.

7   Farington, *Diary*, Tuesday 26 February, 1819.

pursue a professional career in late eighteenth- and early nineteenth-century London. Firstly, it will highlight the centrality of the family workshop in framing and encouraging Letitia Byrne's printed productions, exploring the opportunities that being born into her trading family afforded. Secondly, it will demonstrate the strategies that Letitia employed to make a living – and a reputation – in London's rapidly expanding, male-dominated trade.

The Byrne Family

Letitia Byrne's extensive career, which spanned over fifty years, has been poorly documented; the information that I have garnered about her role and status within the artistic establishment has primarily been obtained through historical accounts that focus on her male relatives.[8] Despite the vast literature that exists on print culture, there are very few publications dedicated to those women who worked in this historically male preserve, usually via familial and workshop networks, particularly those practising in Britain in the long eighteenth century.[9] In recent years, print

8   For brief information of Letitia and her siblings, see: J. M. Wheeler, 'The Byrne Family and the Old Watercolour Society', *The Old Watercolour Society's Annual Volume* 48 (1973), 21–39; Timothy Clayton and Anita McConnell, *Byrne Family (per. 1765–1849), Engravers and Painters* (Oxford: Oxford University Press, 2007). <http://www.oxforddnb.com/view/10.1093/ref:odnb/9780198614128.001.0001/odnb-9780198614128-e-65026>, accessed 17 May 2018 and David Alexander, *Caroline Watson & Female Printmaking in Late Georgian England* (Cambridge: Fitzwilliam Museum, 2014), 27.
9   A select list includes: Frank Weitenkampf, *Catalogue of a Collection of Engravings, Etchings and Lithographs by Women, Exhibited April 12 to 27, 1901* (New York: The Grolier Club, 1901); Judith K. Brodsky, 'Some Notes on Women Printmakers', *Art Journal*, 35:4 (1976): 374–77; Elizabeth. Harvey-Lee, *Eve: Women as Models; Women as Printmakers* (North Aston, Oxon: Elizabeth Harvey-Lee, 1992); Elizabeth Harvey-Lee, *Mistresses of the Graphic Arts: Famous and Forgotten Women Printmakers* c.1550–c.1950 (North Aston, Oxon: Elizabeth-Harvey Lee, 1995); Elizabeth Harvey-Lee, *Unsung Heroes: A Selection of Neglected, Forgotten, Anonymous or Underrated Printmakers* (North Aston, Oxon: Elizabeth

specialists have acknowledged that men *and* women played significant roles. Antony Griffiths explains when discussing his methodology for *The Print Before Photography:* 'I have also abbreviated by referring to engravers, artists and collectors as "he" rather than "he or she", which would be more accurate.'[10] Aligned with, but separate from this, is the treatment of women printmakers in feminist art historical scholarship. Although feminist scholars have made important and significant progress in reconstructing the careers and output of women artists, this attention has largely focused on women working in media held in higher regard than print, such as painting and sculpture. The output of women artists such as Letitia Byrne, who made their living creating 'reproductive' prints, has been overlooked in favour of recovering and reconstructing the lives of women who created 'original' works of art.[11] Therefore, Joseph Farington's diary, which is scattered with snapshots of Letitia's everyday life, from her early years, through to her 'long days' working as a professional printmaker, is revelatory.[12] Though it must be treated with some caution – it is, to some extent, a self-aggrandizing presentation of Farington's important role at the heart of the British art scene – it is also a unique window onto the eighteenth-century London art world in which Letitia grew up and

---

Harvey-Lee, 1999); Lia Markey, 'The Female Printmaker and the Culture of the Reproductive Print Workshop', in Rebecca Zorach and Elizabeth Rodini eds., *Paper Museums: The Reproductive Print in Europe 1500–1800* (Chicago: The David and Alfred Smart Museum of Art, The University of Chicago, 2005), 51–75; David Alexander, *Caroline Watson & Female Printmaking in Late Georgian England* (Cambridge: Fitzwilliam Museum, 2014); Madeleine Viljoen, 'Printing women: Three centuries of female printmakers, 1570–1900', <https://www.nypl.org/printing-women-selections>, accessed 1 October 2017.

10 Antony Griffiths, *The Print Before Photography: An Introduction to European Printmaking 1550–1820* (London: British Museum Publications, 2016), 12.

11 The narrative that reproductive prints are wholly imitative has been rightly dismissed by print scholars such as Antony Griffiths, who has long argued that reproductive images 'have an independent life' from the works they are made after. See: Antony Griffiths, 'The Print as Translation', in Antony Griffiths, ed., *The Print Before Photography: An Introduction to European Printmaking 1550–1820* (London: British Museum Publications, 2016), 464.

12 Farington, *Diary*, Tuesday 20 February, 1821.

in which she came to work – a world witnessing the search for and establishment of the 'British' school of art.

Letitia's father, William Byrne, was one of those British printmakers who had witnessed and participated in London's transition from a market of continental imports and 'artistic obscurity' in the early half of the eighteenth century to its dominance of the international print market, becoming 'the most important centre for the production of new prints'.[13] Having trained as an arms engraver in Birmingham, and then in London and Paris in the mid-eighteenth century, William first achieved recognition for his exceptional engraving of *Villa Madama*, after a painting by Richard Wilson (1713–82), the highly influential Welsh landscape painter.[14] The engraving won him a premium of twenty-five guineas at the Incorporated Society of Artists of Great Britain in 1765, and John Boydell published it that same year.[15] This period of professional advancement paralleled the growth of William's family: in 1774, he married his first wife, Ann Taunton (dates unknown) and the couple had their first child, Anne Frances, in 1775.[16] Their second daughter, Mary, followed a year later and on 24 November 1779 they welcomed their third child, Letitia. Another daughter, Elizabeth, was born in 1784 and John, the only son, came in 1786 (Table 3.1).

13 Timothy Clayton, *The English Print: 1688–1802* (New Haven and London: Yale University Press, 1997), xii.
14 Timothy Clayton and Anita McConnell, *Byrne Family (per. 1765–1849), Engravers and Painters* (Oxford: Oxford University Press, 2007), <http://www.oxforddnb.com/view/10.1093/ref:odnb/9780198614128.001.0001/odnb-9780198614128-e-65026>, accessed 17 May 2018.
15 It appears to be this engraving that first linked William to Joseph Farington. Farington was Wilson's pupil and was in his Covent Garden studio when William made the engraving in 1765. On William's death, Farington also claims that he knew William for 'more than 42 years'.
16 J. M. Wheeler, 'The Byrne Family and the Old Watercolour Society', *The Old Watercolour Society's Annual Volume* 48 (1973), 23. Furthermore, Ann is recorded as William's 'dear wife' in the will that he made in 1776. He later married Marianne Francotte, 'Governess to Lord Donegal', as his second wife in 1792, so it is probable that Ann died sometime between 1786 and 1792 – perhaps after giving birth to John. London Metropolitan Archives; London, England: 89/mry1/175.

Table 3.1. A diagram of the Byrne family tree, 2020 © Hannah Lyons.

Byrne Family Tree

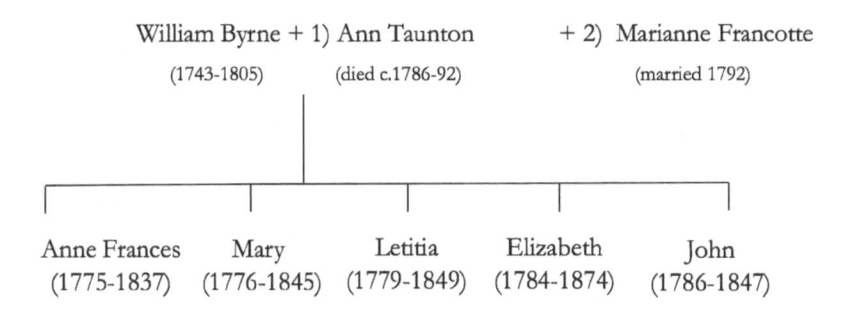

William Byrne + 1) Ann Taunton   + 2) Marianne Francotte
(1743-1805)   (died c.1786-92)   (married 1792)

Anne Frances	Mary	Letitia	Elizabeth	John
(1775-1837)	(1776-1845)	(1779-1849)	(1784-1874)	(1786-1847)

It was in the traditional setting of his own home that William began to teach *all* of his five children the techniques of etching and engraving. Apprenticeship was the standard route into the profession, with the apprentice indentured to their master typically for seven years, usually begun between the ages of 13 and 16 years.[17] But the print scholar David Alexander, whose pioneering research on women printmakers has been central to my research, previously noted only two cases where girls were formally apprenticed to an engraver in this period.[18] Thus being born into a printmaking family, and thereby receiving informal training, was almost the only way for a woman to enter the profession.[19] Surviving apprenticeship registers record that William took on at least six male apprentices, so why did he (along with many other male engravers) also teach his son and, especially, his daughters?[20] It may well be that they showed a particular aptitude for

17 Griffiths, *The Print before*, 235.
18 Alexander, *Caroline Watson*, 55.
19 Another way of entering the trade could be marrying into it. Husbands sometimes trained wives as engravers (e.g. Catherine Blake was trained by husband William Blake), or to run their businesses. See Reese Irwin's chapter in this volume.
20 William's apprentices, in order of the date they roughly entered into their apprenticeships, include: Samuel Middiman, 1766; John Boyne, c.1770; John Landseer c.1770–80; Frederick Vanderkiste, 1774; Thomas Underwood, 1788 and J. Dauthemare, 1796.

drawing, and William and his wife felt that such talent deserved further instruction. However, more importantly (and likely) it is because their assistance was crucial in the workshop that supported the household's economy. Regardless of their gender, their labour enabled the smooth running of the family business. In exchange for this labour, all William's children received training in a specialist trade, which gave them core skills – and vital networks – through which they could earn a living in the future. William probably shared the same sentiments as the painter Thomas Gainsborough (1727–88), who wrote in a letter to a friend in 1764 that he would teach his daughters: 'to paint Landscape; and that somewhat above the common Fan-Mount stile … that they may do something for Bread'.[21]

In 1795, aged only fourteen or fifteen years old, Letitia made a set of thirteen etchings after prints by a variety of seventeenth-century Dutch artists, revealing that her father had given her access to significant, imported continental prints by some of Europe's most accomplished and celebrated landscape and animal painters.[22] The frontispiece of this series is a confident interpretation of a print designed by the pioneering animal painter Paulus Potter (1625–54), etched after his death by his fellow countryman Marcus de Bye in 1664 (c.1639–c.1670). Like de Bye, Byrne has purposely and clearly asserted her authorship – and her link to her father – on the plate. Her careful translation reveals how, at a young age, she had managed successfully to acquaint herself with the tonality and marks of de Bye's etching. She made some subtle changes to the composition, for example, the addition of horizontal shading on the stone and lack of it in the sky, but the etching corresponds very closely, even in size, to the Dutch print.

With work published by Darling & Thompson on 1 January 1795, Letitia was the only one of the Byrne children who created impressions for the London market at such a young age, indicating that her skill with the etching needle was notable within her large, artistic family. Detailed

---

21 John Hayes, ed., *The Letters of Thomas Gainsborough* (New Haven and London: Yale University Press, 2001), 26.
22 A set of these prints in The Bancroft Library Collection, University of California, Berkeley, carry the publication line: 'London Pubd Jan 1 1795 by Darling & Thompson Gt Newport Street'.

in their execution, these prints indicate Letitia's solid technical grounding and the quality of the material available to her. William's use of prints by the Dutch masters in his training process was not uncommon. In the studio of the reproductive engraver, copying the prints of previous masters was an important training exercise, and had been since the sixteenth century. However, aside from learning to etch by copying the prints of older, famed Masters, William also took his children's training beyond the studio, so that they could practise their draughtsmanship. Farington wrote: 'Byrne goes to Windsor tomorrow for a few days with his family to afford them an opportunity of drawing from trees in the Park.'[23]

The Royal Academy of Arts and the European Print Market

Farington, who dined with the Byrne family regularly and often gave his own landscape drawings to the children to copy, noted Letitia's particular talents: '[William] Byrne called. His 3 daugtrs. [sic.] Possess extraordinary talent for drawing & etching – The eldest flowers, the second is now employed in painting miniature, the youngest in etching.'[24] As he notes, Letitia's two elder sisters, Anne Frances and Mary, were beginning to specialize in flower and miniature painting; both women exhibited several examples at the Royal Academy in the final decade of the eighteenth century.[25] But why did these women practise in these artistic preserves?

It is necessary to understand the works that all of the Byrne sisters made in the context of the 'hierarchy of genres' that pervaded early modern

---

23   Farington, *Diary*, Sunday 5 July 1801.
24   Farington, *Diary*, 16 November 1794. I believe that Farington is referring to Letitia 'etching', as Elizabeth would have only been 10 years old; his references to 'the eldest' 'the youngest' etc are often inconsistent and incorrect.
25   For more on Anne Frances Byrne, see: Paris Amanda Spies-Gans, 'Exceptional, but not exceptions: Public exhibitions and the rise of the woman artist in London and Paris, 1760–1830', *Eighteenth-Century Studies*, 51:4 (2018), 401.

European art theory, criticism and institutions.[26] In this hierarchy, absorbed from the French art theory that dominated the Académie Royale in Paris, 'history painting' enjoyed the highest status, for it was concerned with the historical, the political, the religious and the classical, as well as with stimulating the imagination. Portraiture followed, then genre painting, then landscape. Still-life painting was at the bottom of this academic scale as it focused on direct observation and apparently required little from the imagination. In London, the Royal Academy of Arts emulated the Académie Royale and their foreign counterparts, affirming that history painting should be at the peak of this academic hierarchy.

Another hierarchy implemented by the Academies focused on media: prints were not permitted to be exhibited at the annual exhibitions of the Royal Academy in London, unless submitted by an engraver who had been elected as an 'Associate Engraver'.[27] Furthermore, drawings copied after other paintings were prohibited. Yet Letitia navigated the Academy's rigid submission restrictions: she revealed her professional ambition and ensured that her work would be visible to the public by submitting watercolour landscapes.[28] Although her exhibited works have

26   A good survey and bibliography of this can be found in: 'Genres and contested hierarchies', in Linda Walsh, eds, *A Guide to Eighteenth-Century Art* (Chichester: Wiley Blackwell, 2017), 57–121.
27   The Royal Academy of Art refused to grant full academic status to engravers. For a detailed account of the 'engravers' battle' with the Royal Academy, see: Sarah Hyde, 'Printmakers and the Royal Academy Exhibitions, 1780–1836', in David Solkin, ed., *Art on the Line: The Royal Academy Exhibitions at Somerset House, 1760–1836* (New Haven and London: Yale University Press, 2001), 217–28.
28   The works that Letitia exhibited at the Royal Academy of Arts, preceded by the year of exhibition, are: (1799) *View of Wilsden Church;* (1800) *View of the old church at Macclesfield;* (1801) *View in Derbyshire; View of the West Tower, Derbyshire, View of Matlock, Derbyshire; View of Winfield Manor;* (1802) *A Park Scene; A Landscape; View from Shooter's Hill;* (1803) *The Remains of Eastwood, Hall; A Scene from Nature;* (1804) *A View upon the Thames;* (1819) *Flowers;* (1822) *Eton College from the Playing Fields;* (1838) *Chateau du Versailles;* (1839) *Landscape;* (1840) *Mill near Capel Cerig;* (1842) *Scene near Conway, North Wales;* (1846) *Linton, North Devon;* (1847) *View of Easby Abbey, Yorkshire;* (1848) *Another view of Easby Abbey, Yorkshire.*

proved difficult to trace, as are any reviews of them in the press, the fact that she did exhibit her art on the walls of such a prestigious institution signalled not only to the public, but also to the network of publishers and artists whose work she could engrave, that she was a highly trained and proficient, professional artist.

The watercolours that Letitia exhibited at the Royal Academy were topographical in content, depicting views of London as well as of the English countryside, from neighbouring Middlesex to Derbyshire. Stimulated by the influence of theories on the picturesque, the beautiful and the sublime, and supported by improvements in country roads, throughout the eighteenth-century antiquaries and domestic tourists travelled across the country in pursuit of inspirational landscapes and architectural ruins. Images after specific places were desired, not just by high profile collectors – most notably, King George III – but also by the middling sort. William Byrne had tapped into this phenomenon with his numerous and ambitious topographical publications, including *Antiquities of Great Britain*[29] and *Britannia Depicta*.[30] He spearheaded these projects, working as engraver and often publisher too, uniting the most skilful contemporary engravers and draughtsmen in London to profit from the contemporary demand for views of British sites.

Though all of William Byrne's daughters had been instructed in drawing and etching, it was only Letitia who, as a young woman, pursued printmaking further, and some of her first forays into etching plates for the European print market were for these large, topographical publications, collaborating on impressions with her father. *Donnington Castle taken from a Field Adjoining the Road to East Astley from Newbury,* made for *Britannia Depicta,* and also published in January 1805 as a single sheet print, is co-signed by Letitia and her father: 'Engraved by W. and L. Byrne' (Figure 3.2). Made after a drawing by J. M. W. Turner (1775–1851), who provided William with numerous watercolours to translate into engravings,

29   David B. Morris, *Thomas Hearne and his Landscape* (London: Reaktion Books, 1989). Chapter Three 'The Antiquities of Great Britain' describes the complicated breakdown of the numerous volumes and individually published prints, 24–51.
30   Morris, *Thomas Hearne,* 120.

the image depicts the gatehouse to the ruined fourteenth-century castle, overlooking the Lambourne Valley. The castle was no doubt chosen to feature in the publication because of its historic status: it had been defended by King Charles I during the English Civil War before it was lost to the Parliamentarians. However, Turner has ensured that it is the valley where the focus of this image is placed, on the figures and cattle idling around in the foreground and middle ground.

The print was made by the more complex and laborious processes of etching and engraving; where most of the plate was etched, but engraving was added to strengthen parts of the composition. It is difficult to ascertain which parts of the print Letitia put her hand to, and which parts William created. Yet, given William's established experience with the burin, it is

Figure 3.2. *Donnington Castle Taken from a Field Adjoining the Road to East Ilsley from Newbury*, William and Letitia Byrne (etchers) and J.M.W. Turner (painter), 1805. Image courtesy of Yale Center for British Art.

possible that Letitia made the initial etching of the castle, the landscape and the human figures, with William finishing the plate by engraving the sky. Letitia had already demonstrated her skill in making prints of animals in their natural habitats, so it is possible that she etched these as well as some of the finer details in the foreground of image. The art historian Samuel Redgrave, writing in 1874, proposed such a mode of collaboration: 'His [William's] pupils – in his later years his own son and daughters – were employed in the etching, and he occupied himself more in the finishing of his plates.'[31] As we can see in the publication line, William published the jointly signed print from their home-cum-workshop at 79 Titchfield Street. In doing so, he brought Letitia's name to the market for topographical engravings, ensuring that her art was seen by a much wider audience that those who frequented the London exhibitions.

'Published by Letitia Byrne'

At the time of William Byrne's sudden death in September 1805, all four of the unmarried children (Mary, the second daughter, had married the painter, James Green, in February 1805) had come of age: Anne was 30 years old; Letitia was 26; Elizabeth was 21 and John was 19 years old. For William's unmarried 'spinster' daughters, life without their father would have presented a very different prospect to that faced by their brother.[32] However, as Naomi Tadmor writes, the concept of the family household in eighteenth-century Britain was flexible and it was not uncommon for unmarried siblings to set up a 'new' household together.[33]

[31] Samuel Redgrave, *A Dictionary of Artists of the English School: Painters, Sculptors, Architects, Engravers and Ornamentists* (London: Longmans, Green and Co, 1874), vol. 2, 51.
[32] Robert B. Shoemaker, *Gender in English Society, 1650–1850: The Emergence of Separate Spheres?* (London: Longman, 1998), 142.
[33] Naomi Tadmor, 'The Concept of the Household Family', in *Family and Friends in Eighteenth-Century England: Household, Kinship, and Patronage* (Cambridge and New York: Cambridge University Press, 2001), 18–43.

Indeed, Robert Shoemaker takes this further when he argues: 'it was primarily when single women or widows were able to remain within a family context ... that they enjoyed the best living conditions.'[34] The unmarried Byrne siblings did not disperse, but remained together, although William's second wife, Marianne Byrne, eventually moved to another property in London.[35] Although, in the late eighteenth century, it was common for widows to continue their husband's trade, it seems that William's son and daughters were better equipped to continue the family business he had started.

It was his son John who took over his business affairs.[36] Given John's lack of visibility in both contemporary accounts and on printed impressions before this time, this strongly indicates that gender was more important than age, experience and skill when it came to continuing this family workshop. Although William had taught all his children the skills required for printmaking, and had clearly wanted and encouraged them all to flourish in their respective professions, Letitia was undoubtedly the most prolific and experienced printmaker. Anne Frances, meanwhile, was the eldest child. However, it was neither of these women, but instead their brother, John, who inherited the most important professional role: head of William's posthumous business affairs. That John took over William's workshop does not mean that they (Anne Frances and Letitia) were any less loved by their father, 'but by modern standards girls received a worse deal than did their brothers ... it is also clear that girls were a lower priority when it came to distributing the family resources, whether of a material or symbolic kind' explains historian Margaret Hunt in *The Middling Sort*.[37] Hannah Barker's research on late Georgian family partnerships echoes

---

34 Shoemaker, *Gender in English Society*, 144.
35 'Mrs Byrnes lodges in Cleveland Street': Farington, *Diary*, Thursday 16 July 1807.
36 William wrote two wills during his adult life. See: *Records of the Prerogative Court of Canterbury, Series* PROB 11. The National Archives, Kew, England: PROB 11/1024/220 and PROB 11/1439/146.
37 Margaret R. Hunt, *The Middling Sort: Commerce, Gender, and the Family in England*, 1680–1780 (Los Angeles and London: University of California Press, 1996), 82.

Hunt's conclusions: 'Sons were still considered more worthy of public attention than daughters.'[38]

At the same time that John was taking over William's business affairs, Letitia produced eight prints depicting contemporary, idealized views of England, Wales, Italy and colonial India. Abandoning the seventeenth-century Dutch artists who had inspired her first series of prints, all of these works evoke some of the prime visual characteristics of British Romanticism: individuals dwarfed by the immensity of a mountain range or dramatic clouds swirling tempestuously over the ruins of a classical Roman folly. These prints were not made for an illustrated book, but rather were published as single sheet prints.

This indicates that, aged 26 years, Letitia was really honing her skills as a specialized, topographical engraver. Furthermore, she was ambitious enough to publish on her own account; each of the eight impressions carries the line: 'London, Published Dec. 1, 1805, by L. Byrne, No.79 Titchfield Street'. The prints were after the work of contemporary British landscape artists who were known to her: Sawrey Gilpin (1733–1807); Thomas Hearne (1744–1817); John 'Warwick' Smith (1749–1831); Thomas Daniell (1749–1840); Francis Nicholson (1753–1844); George Barrett the Younger (1767–1842) and George Samuel (d.1823). Letitia had clearly inherited her father's network of engravers, painters and publishers – an invaluable gift for an aspiring printmaker-publisher, and one on which she was quick to capitalize. She had everything that she needed to work as a professional engraver and publisher: ambition, precocious skills that had been honed through thorough training and a supportive family and a studio with materials and tools.

It is possible that Letitia published these prints in the hope that the profits she would earn, by retaining the plates herself and selling her impressions, would bolster the family's finances. Despite her father's early prosperity, William's financial situation had been precarious, worsened during the years of war with France, and he died much in debt.[39] However,

---

38 Hannah Barker, 'Family, Firms, Partnerships, and Independent Traders', in *The Business of Women* (Oxford: Oxford University Press, 2006), 115.
39 The Seven Years' War (1756–63) and The War of American Independence (1778–83) significantly affected the print trade between London and Paris. For more on this,

notwithstanding the commercial possibilities for these prints, she evidently had difficulty attracting purchasers. So far, only one surviving set of the eight topographical prints, at the British Museum, together with one surviving single sheet print of *A Cross at Clearwell*, in the collection of the National Trust's Kingston Lacy, has been identified.[40] Likewise, advertisements or reviews for these prints in the press seem absent. After this presumably expensive but seemingly unsuccessful undertaking, the plates were sold to Thomas Palser (1789–1843), an established male publisher based on the 'Surrey Side' of Westminster Bridge, who printed them again on 1 January 1809. That this later series can be found in numerous collections in Britain and North America suggests that Thomas Palser had much more success than Letitia in marketing and selling these works. She abandoned print publishing after this project, and for her future forty-five years working as an engraver in London, she never again attempted to self-publish her prints.

Working for the Illustrated Book Trade

Despite these professional setbacks, Letitia did not stop producing high-quality topographical and antiquarian impressions, and, throughout the early nineteenth century, Letitia and, later, her sister Elizabeth continued to work independently on commission for publishers who harnessed the contemporary demand for picturesque views. Elizabeth's absence during previous years in the Byrne story is explained by a note from Farington: 'Miss Byrne called & took back etchings of views in Devonshire to finish. She spoke of the long indisposition of her youngest sister supposed to be caused by an adhesion of the Liver.'[41] Such illness could be devastating, preventing a professional from earning a living for months or years. Once again, we return to the economic benefits of the

---

see: Tim Clayton, *The English Print, 1688–1802* (New Haven and London: Yale University Press, 1997), 281.
40   See British Museum: 1875,0710.4158 to 4165.
41   Farington, *Diary*, Thursday 18 January 1821.

Byrne siblings maintaining a household together. As Alannah Tomkins notes, single women 'without access to a male breadwinner ... a father or brother ... were usually dependent on their own work for their survival and as such disadvantaged ... unless they were disposed to group together'.[42] Here Elizabeth could rely on the household to keep her from falling into poverty, though this would have inevitably put more pressure on those who were fit enough to work.

Throughout the first two decades of the nineteenth century both Letitia and Elizabeth produced numerous impressions for five of the six volumes of *Magna Britannia; being a concise topographical account of the several counties of Great Britain*, published by Cadell & Davies from 1806–22. All of their work for this large publication involved translating artwork by their key supporter, Joseph Farington. He writes:

> John Byrne and his sister Letitia called & I delivered to her a drawing of Trematon Castle made with Black pencil for Messrs. Lysons's Magna Britannia, for her to make a finished etching for it, which she agreed to do for 8 guineas.[43]
>
> Lysons told me he had communicated to Caddell & Davies His intention to have etchings done by Miss L. Byrne from my sketches of several subjects in Cornwall, which they quite approved of.[44]

This passage is particularly revealing, indicating that in 1810 Letitia was charging eight guineas for a medium sized, single sheet, topographical etching on copper. This was not a vast sum, and Letitia was charging less in 1810 than she had done four years earlier, when her brother told Farington that 'his sister wd. Make finished etchings of a certain size for 12 & 15 guineas.'[45] Did Letitia charge less because she needed the work? Or was a smaller sum promised because of the sheer number of smaller prints that Letitia (and Elizabeth) would contribute to this publication?

---

42 Alannah Tomkins, 'Bodily causes of female poverty: Illness and the lifecycle', in Hannah Barker and Elaine Chalus, eds, *Women's History: Britain, 1700–1850: An Introduction* (London: Routledge, 2005), 157.
43 Farington, *Diary*, Saturday 31 March 1810.
44 Farington, *Diary*, Wednesday 11 April 1810.
45 Farington, *Diary*, Tuesday 8 April 1806.

I called on Miss L. Byrne. She expressed Her desire & that of her sister to devote themselves to the works published by Cadell & Davies, and that they would engage in no other work if drawings should be delivered to them to work from. In 6 weeks they shall have finished their present commissions.[46]

Letitia produced eleven etchings for *Magna Britannia Volume the third Containing Cornwall*, with Elizabeth producing seven. One of the etchings that Letitia made for *Magna Britannia* was *Roche Rocks*, an image of a rocky outcrop in central Cornwall celebrated for its religious and geological significance. Farington's drawing (Figure 3.3) copied in Letitia's print (Figure 3.4) are both now at the Yale Center for British Art, permitting a rare opportunity to study print and drawing together.

Figure 3.3. *Roche Rocks* (graphite on thin paper), Joseph Farington [n.d.]. Image courtesy of Yale Center for British Art.

46   Farington, *Diary*, Friday 10 August 1810.

Letitia Byrne (1779–1849)

Figure 3.4. *Roche Rocks* (etching), Letitia Byrne, 1818. Image courtesy of the Victoria and Albert Museum, London.

Farington has depicted the craggy rock rising from an open heath from the southeast view, where the entrance to the famous chapel, and the granite steps rising towards it, can be most easily seen. The ruined fifteenth-century structure, shaded by the immense rocks rising above it, particularly appealed to eighteenth-century tourists because of its association with the Arthurian legend of Tristan and Isolde, who famously hid in it to escape their pursuers. This dramatic formation, and its romantic associations, made it an ideal destination for these domestic tourists, who Farington also captures in the drawing.

Letitia's translation incorporates very subtle changes. The formation appears even more striking when etched, conspicuously jarring with the flat, surrounding countryside and the white of the sky, where Letitia has allowed the paper to make a contrast with the etched line. Letitia asked for Farington's advice throughout the process, and the two conversed on the merits of other artists too:

> Miss L. Byrne called to speak abt. the etchings she & Her sister are doing from my drawings of subjects in Cornwall.[47]
>
> Miss L. Byrne called with three etchings made by Her from my sketches in Cornwall. She spoke of a Young man, Mr Norris, who resides at Tenby in South Wales. He has devoted much time to making sketches from nature particularly the remains of Abbeys, Castles & C. She said His outlines are very neatly executed, but that He has no knowledge of light and shade.[48]

Outside of the encouraging interactions between Letitia and Farington, the relationship between printmakers and those who ran the larger commercial publishing businesses was not always an easy one. The financial situation of the engraver in this period was often precarious and the possibility of falling victim to external economic forces a constant worry – as demonstrated by the debt which William accrued during the 1790s and Letitia's apparent failure to establish herself as an independent print publisher. In 1817, Letitia complained: 'Six weeks ago Mutlow (Clerk to Cadell & Davies) had informed her that she was not to make any more etchings for the *Magna Britannia*.'[49] Letitia's frustration with the commercial publishers developed, as her complaint to Farington that there was 'a prejudice against employing women as Engravers' reveals.[50] Letitia's comment is the most overt, contemporary reference I have found to the patriarchal institutional and commercial structures in place in eighteenth-century London that made it more difficult for women printmakers to earn a living. She clearly had an astute awareness of the issues of the contemporary art world that she inhabited. However, she was also keenly alert to her status as a woman, and how, despite her talent, this could marginalize her within the male-dominated print trade.

47 Farington, *Diary*, Thursday 13 December 1810.
48 Farington, *Diary*, Saturday 22 December, 1810.
49 Farington, *Diary*, Monday 3 March, 1817.
50 Farington, *Diary*, Tuesday 19 January, 1819.

Letitia Byrne (1779–1849)

Why did Cadell & Davies stop employing Letitia to make prints for their work? It is unlikely to have been that she was charging too much for her labour. Indeed, as we have seen, it seems that her costs had slightly dropped for her work on *Magna Britannia*. It is possible that previous disagreements between her brother and Cadell & Davies were affecting the work of the whole family. Earlier in 1808, as Farington notes, John had been commissioned to etch a view of Chester, after John 'Warwick' Smith (with whom both Letitia and William had previously worked):

> Which Cadell & Davies did not approve. I found the drawings very negligently executed and altogether unworthy of such a work as they were made for, & I told J. Byrne that certainly a work carried on in such a way wd. do no credit to anybody concerned in it, at the same time adding that having such drawings to work from I could not judge what He might be able to do from better drawings.[51]

Farington's criticism of Smith's draughtsmanship should be read as a means of, once again, advising and assisting the Byrne family; he was sympathetic, not wanting their work to be perceived unfavourably, and he was keen to make sure that they did not endanger their reputation. When John had tried to remove the sky from the print:

> The plate had been injured & He had destroyed it; He had therefore now no claim upon Cadell & Davies but for His plate of Launceston. He complained of the rude manner in which Davies had treated him, who had also refused to pay Him any money till He had spoken to me. He said after such treatment He should not think of being again employed by them. I gave him my opinion that it would perhaps be better to look over it.[52]

Despite Farington's attempts to keep the peace, 'Davies spoke to me of Young Byrne, saying He had been made a man of too soon, that when remarks had been made upon His work He took them ungraciously.'[53] Taking over William's business affairs as well as being the new socio-economic power as head of a family cannot have been easy for this nineteen-year-old. John was judged, as William would have been, on

---

51 Farington, *Diary*, Tuesday 9 August, 1808.
52 Farington, *Diary*, Thursday 9 February, 1809.
53 Farington, *Diary*, Friday 10 June, 1808.

how he managed the family's economic affairs. Once again, it was Joseph Farington who was there to guide him, and advise him on how it was best to conduct his business and ensure the reputation of the 'worthy family'. Furthermore, these passages seem to imply that Letitia lost her work with Cadell & Davies because of John's previous confrontation. Not only does this indicate that within the printmaking family, the reputation of each individual was tightly interwoven with those with whom they shared a familial connection, but it also further demonstrates that the decision for John, the male, to take over the family business, had backfired.

'The Louvre of London'

Thus, throughout the first two decades of the nineteenth century, arguably the most difficult after the loss of the Byrnes' father, Joseph Farington remained an important friend, particularly to Letitia. His patronage contributed to the Byrne family's supply of work, and he gave crucial advice to all of the Byrne siblings as they navigated the challenging urban print market. His patronage mirrors, in many ways, the printmaker Caroline Watson's professional relationship with the writer William Hayley as recently evidenced by David Alexander.[54]

Despite the family's problems with Cadell & Davies, Letitia, Elizabeth and John continued to receive commissions for book illustrations throughout the early to mid-nineteenth century. In the second decade of the century, the siblings attracted a very high-quality commission: producing plates for William Young Ottley's large and lavish *Engravings of the Most Noble the Marquis of Stafford's Collection of Pictures in London, arranged according to Schools, and in Chronological Order, with Remarks on Each*.[55] Ottley (1771–1836), an artist turned printer, curator and dealer,

---

54 Hayley employed Watson to create plates regularly in the early nineteenth century. Alexander, *Caroline Watson*, 24–25.
55 William Young Ottley, *Engravings of the Most Noble the Marquis of Stafford's Collection of Pictures in London, arranged according to Schools, and in Chronological*

compiled the four-volume illustrated catalogue recording the internationally lauded collection of paintings belonging to George Leveson-Gower, 2nd Marquess of Stafford (1758–1833), displayed at his London home of Cleveland House.[56] In 1803 Stafford had inherited both the house and one of the greatest art collections in France, if not Europe, from his maternal uncle, Francis Egerton, 3rd Duke of Bridgewater (1736–1803).[57] Stafford styled the remodelled Cleveland House as 'The Louvre of London'.[58]

Ottley's was a prestigious publication, clearly aimed at a refined, cultivated and elite audience.[59] Indeed, the catalogue was sold at extortionate prices, ranging from £35 14s for a folio edition, to £171 14s for a 'de luxe elephant folio', and was dedicated to Royalty and 'The rest of the Noblemen and Gentlemen of the British Institution' (Stafford was one of the Founding Members of the British Institution). Elizabeth, Letitia and John were three of the twenty-nine engravers who contributed to the huge volume, all making their prints after the drawings of William Marshall Craig (c.1765–c.1834), who acted as intermediary draughtsman, and who copied 293 paintings.[60] To be involved in the catalogue that interpreted and illustrated 'the single most important private collection of Old Masters' in Britain must have been a real source of pride for the siblings, not to mention an important source of income – though there is no record of how much they were each paid for this job.[61]

     Order, with Remarks on Each Picture (London: Longman, Hurst, Rees, Orme and Brown, 1818).

56 His full name was George Leveson-Gower, Second Marquess of Stafford, Earl Gower from 1786–1803 and created 1st Duke of Sutherland in 1833.

57 Egerton had purchased many of the paintings from the collection of Philippe II, Duke of Orléans, sold in London in the 1790s by his great grandson, Louis Philippe II.

58 As quoted in: Peter Humfrey, *The Stafford Gallery: The Greatest Art Collection of Regency London* (Norwich: Unicorn Press, 2019).

59 For more on this publication, see: Humfrey, 'Displaying and Recording the Stafford Gallery', 137–95.

60 Humfrey, *The Stafford Gallery*, 179.

61 Holger Hoock, '"Struggling against a Vulgar Prejudice": Patriotism and the Collecting of British Art at the Turn of the Nineteenth Century', *Journal of British Studies*, 49:3 (2010): 587.

For this publication Letitia contributed eight landscape prints after seventeenth-century continental masters of the German, Dutch or Flemish schools. Four were after Aelbert Cuyp (1620–91); the remaining four were after Joos de Momper (1564–1635), Jan Baptist Weeninx (1621–c.1659), J. V. Capeller and J. M. Blankhop. Elizabeth, meanwhile, made impressions after still-lifes of flowers and fruit, engraved after four continental artists: the Dutch painters, Jan Davidsz de Heem (1606–83/4); Jan van Huysum (1682–1749); Jan Van Os (1744–1808); and the Italian painter Filippo Lauri (1623–94). Finally, John produced two prints after the French master, Claude Joseph Vernet (1714–89). All of the siblings therefore translated the work of Older Masters who, in the academic hierarchy of six 'Schools' into which the publication was organized, comprised 'the Third Class of our Catalogue'.[62]

Aside from their inclusion in the publication, the prints were also published individually throughout 1810–18, by a long list of established publishers: 'Longman, Hurst, Rees, Orme & Brown, J. White, Cadell & Davies, P. W. Tomkins, 54 New Bond Street'. Four of Letitia's prints by Aelbert Cuyp, all of which were part of 'Class the Third – Schools of Germany, Flanders and Holland &c', were united on the same page and are particularly small, measuring on average only 8 cm high by 10 cm wide. Here, in at least three of the engravings, Letitia is utilizing her skills, as we have seen elsewhere, in translating landscape scenes with animals and figures. But she also made an engraving after one of Cuyp's most magnificent sea-pieces: *Fleet at Nijmegen*.[63] This was one of the largest Netherlandish pictures in Stafford's collection, as evidenced by its central placement in the tripartite Old Gallery – the largest space in the Stafford Gallery.[64] That Letitia was chosen to translate such a work demonstrates her reputation; Ottley and the publishers would have been keen to place the engraving of this most fine painting into the hands of only a trusted and competent engraver.

---

62   Ottley, *Engravings of the Most*, 10. The six schools were: 'Lower Italian and Upper Italian; Dutch; Flemish and German; Spanish; French; and English'.
63   Now in a private collection. See: Figure, 106 in Humfrey, *The Stafford Gallery*, 166.
64   Humfrey, *The Stafford Gallery*, 164.

In May 1828, the publication was advertised in *The Standard*:

> The Stafford Gallery, at a very Reduced Price ... for a limited period, at the following very reduced prices: Prints, 4 Vols, folio, half-bound uncut, £12 12*s* – Published at £35 14*s*. India Proofs, 4 Vols, folio, half-bound, uncut £31 10*s* – Published at £71 8*s*. Coloured and Mounted in four Portfolios £52 10*s* – Published at £171 14*s*. The work contains 291 Engravings (besides 13 Plans of the rooms) executed in the line manner by Finder, Fittler, C. Heath, Schiavonetti, Tomkins, Neagle, Mitan, J. Wright, Milton, A. Smith, Elizabeth and Letitia Byrne, Dauthemare, Warren, Landseer, Romney, Wothington, Piccart and other eminent artists.[65]

At a time when the publication was losing money, Elizabeth and Letitia appear to be evoked 'as eminent artists' in an appeal to potential buyers, to generate more sales. By 1828, it does seem that the two sisters had emerged as the most notable engravers in the Byrne family. The status of Letitia and Elizabeth was equal, if only on paper, to John Landseer (their father's former apprentice), Luigi Schiavonetti 'and other eminent artists'.[66]

Conclusion

In the early months of 1822, Letitia and Elizabeth Byrne etched and engraved, together, the print, *The House from the Lawn, Oatlands Park*.[67] The impression depicts the north facing façade of the Gothic Oatlands mansion, where a trio of finely dressed figures – presumably a mother, father and young daughter – stroll out on to the lawn towards the foreground. Three animated dogs bound towards them. The print was published by

---

65 'Advertisements & Notices', British Library Newspapers (2018), <https://go.gale.com/ps/i.do?p=GDCS&u=29002&v=2.1&it=r&id=GALE%7CY3202660456&asid=1657339200000~1acb59bd>, accessed 17 October 2018.

66 English engraver John Landseer (1769–1852) was father of artist Edwin Landseer (1802–73); Italian-born engraver and etcher Luigi Schiavonetti (1765–1810).

67 See: Letitia and Elizabeth Byrne, after John Byrne, *The House from the Lawn, Oatlands Park,* etching with engraving. Royal Collection Trust / © Her Majesty Queen Elizabeth II 2020, RCIN 702988.

John Byrne from 54 Upper John Street, Soho, which, in 1822, he shared with his sisters. John had sketched the scene himself, while William Daniell (1769–1837), a friend and collaborator of their father's, had produced the final drawing from which Letitia and Elizabeth worked. This impression is one of many prints that the family worked on together in the early to mid-nineteenth century, and it aptly demonstrates the continued significance of the family workshop in the lives of women printmakers like Letitia Byrne, allowing them not only to share domestic arrangements, but also to work together. Although her brother took control of the workshop after their father's death and, by 1822, was clearly able to self-publish prints himself, Letitia, and her female siblings made crucial contributions to the household unit, their artistic skills helping to ensure that the family did not fall into poverty during a highly insecure financial period. With the aid of their network, most importantly Joseph Farington, they harnessed and took advantage of the market for book illustrations, primarily of topographical, picturesque domestic tourist sites. Not only was their output for these publications large – much larger than scholars have previously noted – it also rose in status, ensuring that by the second decade of the nineteenth century they could turn their hand to one of the most lavish art historical volumes on the London market.

Four months before *The House from the Lawn, Oatlands Park* was published, Farington had visited Letitia and Elizabeth to invite them to dinner:

> Miss Byrne and her sister Letitia I called on & invited them to dine with me on 26th inst. – They told me that they breakfast every morning of the year at seven o'clock and of course in the winter by candlelight. Such is their desire to make long days for their incessant industry. I left an invitation for their Brother.[68]

In the Royal Academy's annual exhibition catalogue for 1847, two years before her death, Letitia was listed as an 'Honorary Exhibitor'.[69] Though many engravers had boycotted the Royal Academy because of its refusal

---

68 Farington, *Diary*, Tuesday 20 February, 1821.
69 Algernon Graves, *The Royal Academy of Arts: A Complete Dictionary of Contributors and Their Work from Its Foundation in 1769–1904* (London: Graves and Bell, 1905), 63.

to grant engravers full membership, Letitia and her siblings needed to capitalize on the artistic presence and prestige that the annual exhibitions afforded them and their work. By celebrating her watercolours with this accolade, the Royal Academicians and the exhibition selection committee acknowledged the contribution that she had made to British art throughout the first half of the nineteenth century. Letitia Byrne's 'incessant industry' did, then, ensure that she achieved professional recognition in the London art world. Yet, notwithstanding her extensive training and the benefits she derived from her family's supportive workshop, as well as her connections with the upper echelons of the London art world and her demonstrable skill with the burin, her career reveals the issues that women printmakers faced. Despite the invisibility of women printmakers in nineteenth-century historical accounts, as well their silence in the largely male-focused British art histories of the nineteenth and twentieth centuries, the fact that Letitia Byrne's prints survive in so many institutions today is a testament to her artistic and commercial success and her undeterred ability to navigate 'the prejudices against employing women as Engravers'.

DIANNE ROMAN

4 The *Olive Branch* and Female Compositors, Writers and Editors, 1836–57

In the early nineteenth century, changes in the social fabric of America meant that craft professions, such as those in textiles and printing, shifted from the domestic to the industrial. As early as 1792 in Pawtucket, Rhode Island, for example, Samuel Slater had successfully moved the traditionally female industry of spinning from the home to the factory.[1] Just north of Boston in Lowell, Massachusetts, the Merrimack Manufacturing Company, which opened in 1823, similarly moved both the process of cloth-making and its female workers into a factory setting.[2] American women had participated in all aspects of the printing trade in family-based shops since its establishment in 1639.[3] In her reviews of occupations performed by Colonial and Early Republic women in America, Elizabeth Anthony Dexter discusses the variety of money-making endeavours of women, including tavern host, shopkeeper, dress and lace maker and various printing and publishing trades.[4] A more accurate view, especially of the publishing trade, can be

1 Blanche Higgins Schroer, 'Slater Mill Historic Site', National Register of Historic Places Inventory-Nomination: Old Slater Mill (1975), <https://npgallery.nps.gov/NRHP/GetAsset/NHLS/66000001_text>, accessed 20 April 2020.
2 Carl Bridenbaugh, *Cities in Revolt: Urban Life in America, 1743–1776* (London: Oxford University Press: 1971), 124–5.
3 For women in the early American printing trades see: Leona M. Hudak, *Early American Women Printers and Publishers 1639–1820* (Metuchen: Scarecrow Press, 1978); Isaiah Thomas, *The History of Printing in America: With a Biography of Printers and an Account of Newspapers* (Barre: Imprint Society, 1970).
4 Elisabeth Anthony Dexter, *Colonial Women of Affairs: A Study of Women in Business and the Professions in America Before 1776* (Cambridge: The Riverside Press, 1924).

found in an 1868 article in *Harper's New Monthly Magazine*. Looking back to 1830, the article comments on the "almost exclusively" home and household duties of the middle-class women of that day.[5] According to the *Harper's* article, such women in the first quarter of the nineteenth century were not prepared to work outside the home, except in areas of teaching, as a governess or as a seamstress, marriage being their intended future.[6] Domestic work performed outside their own home was considered degrading. If the need for self-support arose, they were woefully unprepared.

The transition from family business to industrialization was accompanied by growing resentment towards women's involvement in the printing trades. Authorship was one avenue of economic sustenance which remained open to women, especially Protestant women from the middle- and upper-middle classes with English ancestry, who wrote and published a variety of material ranging from personal journals and local stories to novels and religious tracts.[7] But female opportunities for employment as compositors, once an accepted function in a family printing shop, were eroded, the work being considered too hard for women whose employment would undercut wages and demasculinize the profession.[8] Despite these negative assessments of female employment, however, women were still involved in the trade. The *Olive Branch*, a weekly newspaper published in Boston from 1836–1857, is one example of a publication that employed women at this time. During a one-month fellowship at the American Antiquarian Society in Boston, I was able to review the first few years of the *Olive Branch*,

---

Elisabeth Anthony Dexter, *Career Women of America: 1776–1840* (Francestown, New Hampshire: Marshall Jones Company, 1950).

5   'Woman's Work and Wages', *Harper's New Monthly Magazine*, 37:220 (September 1868), 546–53.
6   'Woman's Work and Wages', 547.
7   Nina Baym, *Women's Fiction: A Guide to Novels by and about Women in America 1820–70* (Urbana: University of Illinois Press, 1993), xi.
8   Ava Baron, 'Questions of Gender: Deskilling and Demasculinization in the U.S. Printing Industry, 1830–1915', *Gender & History*, 1:2 (Summer 1989), 182–7; Walker Rumble, *The Swifts: Printers in the Age of Typesetting Races* (Charlottesville: University of Virginia Press, 2003), 71.

collecting evidence on the variety of women employed there. This chapter highlights my findings and discusses a few of the women who began or supplemented their professional careers at the *Olive Branch*.

Early Nineteenth-Century Female Employment in Printing Outside the Home

In the printing trade the job of typesetting, for example, was considered both pleasant and respectable for a female, but it required training through an apprenticeship.[9] With its roots in the English and European craft guilds as a means of controlling the supply of labour, such training required apprentices to live at the home of the master printer for the term agreed, initially seven years in Europe.[10] Helen Sumner, in her 1910 Senate Report, states that apprenticeships were never intended for females, except in the case of domestic duties such as sewing and spinning.[11] If a girl was offered an apprenticeship, in most cases it was as cheap labour, and no trade or skill was taught. Belva M. Herron notes the differences in training within the print shop: men served a four-year apprenticeship becoming versed in all aspects of the trade while women were provided a six-week course in typesetting of straight matter only, which resulted in the role of typesetter being the sole printing employment option for women.[12] Abbott and Herron, and probably the *Harper's* article, relied on

9 'Woman's Work and Wages', 550; Edith Abbott, *Women in Industry: A Study in American Economic History* (New York: D. Appleton and Company, 1918), 249–56.
10 Patrick Duffy, *The Skilled Compositor, 1850–1914: An Aristocrat among Working Men* (Burlington, Vermont: Ashgate Publishing Company, 2000), 49; Rollo G. Silver, *The American Printer 1787–1825* (Charlottesville: Bibliographical Society of the University of Virginia, 1967), 1.
11 Helen L. Sumner, *Report on Conditions of Woman and Child Wage-Earners in the United States,* Senate Report to 61st Congress 2nd Session (Washington, DC: Government Printing Office, 1910), 30.
12 Belva Mary Herron, *The Progress of Labor Organization Among Women, Together with Some Considerations Concerning Their Place in Industry* (Urbana: University

a variety of statistical material, such as the *United States Industrial Census of 1822*, *Documents Relative to the Manufactures of the United States*, 1832, and C. D. Wright's *First Report of the Massachusetts Bureau of Labor*, 1870.[13] These statistics show that women were employed in industries like printing, in smaller numbers than their male counterparts. Although no specific employers are mentioned, each author discusses the difficulties women encountered in both obtaining training and maintaining steady employment.[14] Women were employed in weekly newspapers and two possible New York employers of women in printing were *Scientific America* and *The World*.[15] Beyond these statistics, no documentation has been found for the hiring of women in specific print shops or newspapers in the early 1800s.

No complete bibliography exists today documenting all of the early newspapers in America. The most thorough research on early American newspapers was conducted by Clarence S. Brigham in 1947, resulting in a two-volume *History and Bibliography of American Newspapers 1690–1820*.[16] Websites such as *Chronicling America* (hosted by the Library of Congress) and *Nineteenth Century U.S. Newspapers* (hosted by GALE) also provide information and links to numerous historic newspapers.[17] Although searchable, these digital repositories provide only a cross-section of early American newspapers, not complete listings. No employment information is provided beyond occasional names of individuals associated with the specific publication, usually as printer or editor. In the earliest days of printing in America, the printer often performed all the jobs in the shop. Ann Franklin's

---

of Illinois, 1905), 15–16. Straight matter is plain, straightforward lines of composition. Thomas MacKellar, *The American Printer: A Manual of Typography* (Philadelphia: MacKeller, Smiths & Jordan, 1885), 218.

13   Abbott, *Women in Industry*, 66–7; Herron, *Progress of Labor*, 445.
14   Abbott, *Women in Industry*, 246–61; Herron, *Progress of Labor*, 457–66.
15   'Woman's Work and Wages', 549.
16   Clarence S. Brigham, *History and Bibliography of American Newspapers 1690–1820*, 2 vols (Worcester: American Antiquarian Society, 1947).
17   *Chronicling America*, <https://chroniclingamerica.loc.gov/>, accessed 26 April 2020; *Nineteenth-Century U.S. Newspapers*, <https://www.gale.com/c/nineteenth-century-us-newspapers>, accessed 26 April 2020.

printing career, for example, included the three roles of printer, publisher and editor; and two of her daughters were possibly typesetters.[18] The job of typesetter ('compositor', 'type setter' or 'typo') appears in publications usually as part of a eulogy on printing, such as the poem 'Jonathan's Visit to a Printing Office', or as a complaint about poorly trained boys or women as in the notice 'Distressing Occurrence Expected'.[19]

Surprisingly, the article 'Female Printer' in the *Monongalia Mirror* states that 'in Boston, probably there are some 200 girls employed in printing-offices'.[20] As was customary in the early nineteenth century this article was reprinted from another newspaper, a standard practice of early American newspapers being participation in an 'exchange' with other papers.[21] No specific printing office or newspaper is cited in the 'Female Printer' article as an employer of female typesetters, but credit is given to the *Olive Branch* as the paper the information had been taken from. A second article in *The Southern, Tarboro'* entitled 'Female Typesetters' attests to the *Olive Branch* employing women as compositors.[22]

The *Olive Branch*: Early Beginnings on a Rocky Road

Chronicling America lists the *Olive Branch* as published weekly from 1836 to 1857 with the tag line 'Not a religious paper, neither an organ of the

---

18   Hudak, *Early American Women Printers*, 33–48.
19   'Jonathan's Visit to a Printing Office', *The Northern Star, and Farmers' and Mechanics' Advocate* (29 June 1833); 'Distressing Occurrence Expected', *Richmond Enquirer* (22 November 1833).
20   'Female Printer', *Monongalia Mirror* (24 December 1853).
21   Ryan Cordell, 'Reprinting, Circulation, and the Network Author in Antebellum Newspapers', *American Literary History*, 27:3 (2015), 435–6; Terence A. Tanner, 'Newspapers and Printing Presses in Early Illinois', *American Periodicals*, 3 (1993), <http://www.jstor.org/stable/20771045>, accessed 9 June 2021. This multiplicity of reprinting today is referred to as Viral Text and is being researched at Northeastern University, Boston, <https://viraltexts.org/>, accessed 20 April 2020.
22   'Female Typesetters', *The Southern, Tarboro'* (21 May 1853).

Methodist Protestant Church'. Printer and editor information are provided but there are no links to actual examples of the paper. The three individuals listed as editors and printers are E. R. Boyle (1837); T. F. Norris (1837–1853); and E. A. Norris (1854–1857).[23] Reverend Thomas Folsom Norris is credited with involvement in the creation of the *Olive Branch* and its editorial and financial support throughout his lifetime.[24] The newspaper was initially conceived to support the cause of a breakaway group of members within the Methodist Church in America. In his article of 15 February 1851, Norris reminisces about the inception of the newspaper.[25] He cites a 'specimen paper' called *Olive Branch* produced by a church member, L. H. M. Cochran, which answered a request for a local publication for the Protestant reformers.[26] The first known issue is dated 12 November 1836 (Vol. 1, No. 18). Assuming a consistent weekly printing, the first issue would have been published on 16 July 1836.[27]

Beginning with Number Eighteen, the *Olive Branch* is a four-page, cotton-rag newspaper with each page measuring approximately 15.6 × 22.25 in, or 39.7 × 56.5 cm.[28] Each page is divided into five columns with vertical rules between each column. On the outside/front page, the masthead includes a graphic of the name with an illustration of an ark surrounded by water and a dove carrying an olive sprig centred between the words 'Olive' and 'Branch' that extends across the width of the page. This graphic is set off by full-page width double thick-and-thin black lines. Centred below one set of double-lines, in printed hand-set type, is the publisher information and cost. S. Rowland Hart was the publisher and the price was two dollars per year, in advance. Below this is the volume, issue, date and numbering followed by a third thick-thin horizontal line. No information

---

23   'About the Boston Olive Branch', *Chronicling America* <https://chroniclingamerica.loc.gov/lccn/sn84023639/>, accessed 25 April 2020.
24   T. H. Colhouer, *Sketches of the Founders of the Methodist Protestant Church* (Pittsburgh: Methodist Protestant Book Concern, 1880), 393–4.
25   Thomas F. Norris, 'Boston Olive Branch: Its Editors', *Olive Branch* (15 February 1851).
26   No copies of this specimen paper have been located, making it difficult to know the full intention of the paper, its structure and its content.
27   No initial prospectus has been found.
28   The full printed sheet would have been 31.25 × 22.25 in or 79.375 × 56.5 cm.

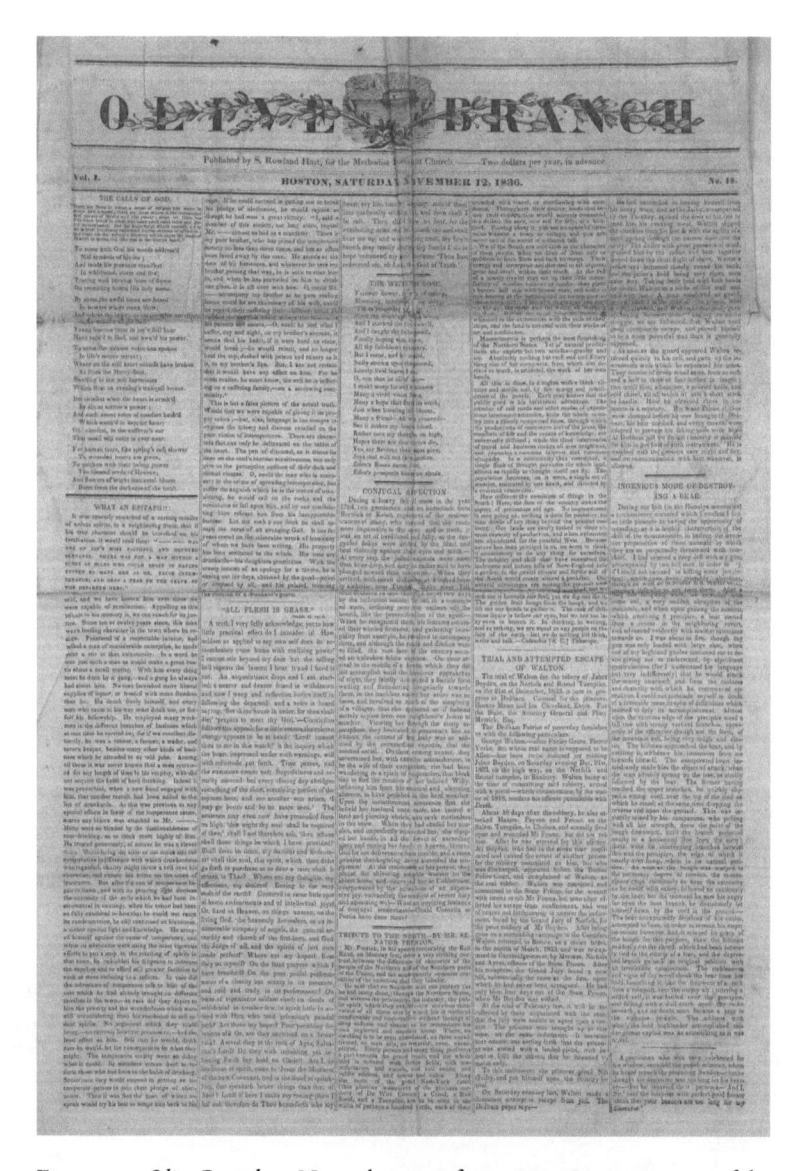

Figure 4.1. *Olive Branch*, 12 November 1836, frontmatter. Image courtesy of the American Antiquarian Society Collection.

is provided for either the artist or the editor. Aside from the tag-line 'for the Methodist Protestant Church' little information is offered regarding the organization, nor does the paper reflect any specific doctrine. The majority of the outside page is consumed with short articles of a moralistic tenor with titles such as 'The Calls of God', 'What an Epitaph!!!' and 'All Flesh is Grass'. No authors are identified.[29]

Pages two and three contain the text of a letter by 'Caroline', general news items from other papers, shipping news, listings of marriages and deaths, Sunday School news and the prices of country produce. Page four concludes with several short anonymous pieces and the printer's address is given as 37 Exchange St. The front pages of the next issues contain a variety of short stories, usually moralistic in nature, under the subtitles 'Miscellaneous' and 'Temperance Department' along with one or two poems. The centre two pages regularly provide information on the church, the positive growth of the Methodist Protestant reform and critiques on the Methodist Episcopal. Noteworthy items from other newspapers, federal and local news finish off the centre spread, and the back page offers poetry and short items. This format was well established by the end of the first volume.

The first year of the *Olive Branch* seems to have been rather turbulent and the paper had had several initial owners. Due to the paper's failure to break even, three of them voted to suspend publication and Norris purchased the paper between issues forty-three and forty-six.[30] On the front page of the 5 June 1837 issue, Reverend T. F. Norris and E. R. Boyle are listed as the proprietors and publishers.[31] By 1 July 1837 E. R. Boyle was sole editor, Hart's name was removed as printer and a new address (62 Cornhill, Boston, second story over Burnham's Book-store) is given.[32] An editorial by Boyle indicates that this issue was published earlier than usual, although it is dated as published on a Saturday, like all other issues.[33] He

---

29   Front page, *Olive Branch* (12 November 1836).
30   Norris, 'Boston Olive Branch: Its Editors'.
31   Front page, *Olive Branch* (5 June 1837).
32   Front page, *Olive Branch* (1 July 1837).
33   Edward R. Boyle, 'Our paper goes', *Olive Branch* (1 July 1837), 2.

reports a change in management and reminds ministers of their obligation to increase readership while assuring the readers that the paper will remain one they welcome. By the fifth issue of Volume Two more changes appear. The type is blacker, creating a darker, denser page, perhaps due to the new printer using a different typeface, newer type or applying more ink than the previous printer. The same initial graphic is used for the masthead but with fewer horizontal rules. A new slogan, again centred below the graphic, states 'Devoted to the Interest of Christianity, Mutual Rights, Literature, and General Intelligence'.[34]

Early Parameters Defined for the *Olive Branch*

The first known prospectus for the *Olive Branch*, published in the 2 June 1838 issue, introduced the upcoming third volume which would 'sustain the same character as in the current volume'.[35] Basically, it would remain a four-page folio paper with general reading material on the outside page and the inside pages continuing to contain church information with a 'fearless exposure' of the Episcopal Methodists, designated as 'old Methodists'. Local, state and federal news alongside items clipped from various newspapers would complete the centre, with material aimed at women and youth on the back page. This is the format established since Volume One, Number Eighteen. Topics of 'polemical divinity, politics, the slave question and all kindred objects' would be avoided and no pains would be spared to make the *Olive Branch* an acceptable and useful family paper while continuing to provide readers with choice material from other papers.[36] As with news items, this literary exchange would provide Norris with story material to copy and republish.[37] The paper would continue to engage a variety of excellent writers for literary contributions,

34 *Olive Branch* (19 August 1837).
35 'Prospectus of the Third Volume of the Olive Branch', *Olive Branch* (2 June 1838).
36 'Prospectus of the Third Volume of the Olive Branch'.
37 See footnote 21 for information on this practice.

although whether paid, and in addition to those copied from other publications, is not clear. I found no actual listing of the publications in this exchange, but the 11 June 1842 issue published a 'Notice to Exchanges', stating that the 300 publications in the exchange with the *Olive Branch* were 150 too many and some would be discontinued.[38] Over the ensuing years the *Olive Branch* saw many changes. The type used and the masthead graphic changed every few years and the paper grew from five columns to seven with an increased page size, but its structure and content remained the same.

Women Setting Type at the *Olive Branch*

Little else is known about the owners of the *Olive Branch* as employers. No company name or business records appear to have survived. What is known about the paper and its employees has been obtained from various articles across the issues of the *Olive Branch* and in other newspapers of its day. The 'Female Typesetters' article mentioned earlier, found in various newspapers, provided this information:

> Female Typesetters
>
> The Boston Olive Branch, on which females are employed as compositors, says: 'Our rooms are well carpeted, and the girls do not come in till 9 or 10 o'clock in the morning, retiring in good season, seldom making over seven or eight hours a day. – Smart compositors can in that time earn from $6 to $8 a week. We have also a female clerk out of the three we employ.'[39]

Another article titled 'Female Printers' printed in the *Jackson Standard* again identified the *Olive Branch* as a newspaper in Boston that hired

---

38 'Notice to Exchanges', *Olive Branch* (11 June 1842).
39 'Female Typesetters', *Spirit of Jefferson* (10 May 1853); 'Female Typesetters', *The Southern, Tarboro'* (21 May 1853); 'Female Type-Setters', *Meigs County Telegraph* (31 May 1853).

women: 'We have for sixteen years employed at least half females ... because they were more to be depended upon than many journeymen.'[40] None had ever failed to perform their work, none had willingly left the paper's service except for marriage, and five had found matrimonial matches amongst the printing staff. Those who had left for marriage returned occasionally when the paper needed additional help. If women were not hired for the first issue of the newspaper, they would have been soon afterward, by the time Norris became the owner. This article describes their working conditions, with a carpeted work room and a separate lunchroom that included a piano for entertainment. A few men were also employed in the shop: a foreman who excelled in proofreading and at least one individual to do the heavy lifting.

The *Mirror's* 'Female Printers' article, also reprinted in the *Cooper's Clarksburg Register,* states that the majority of female typesetters in Boston worked in weekly newspaper or magazine offices.[41] A common school education and three months of practice were the only qualifications needed for these women to be employed, earning between eighteen to twenty cents per thousand ems set.[42] This rate was equivalent to two-thirds the rate men were paid at the same time.[43]

These articles do not specify if the women employed at the *Olive Branch* had initially participated in any training program or if they learned on the job. As Herron states, their job would be setting straight matter only.[44] The majority of the four pages of five columns each are a continual grey, indicating a text-only document, no advertisements, no graphics. The type used is primarily the same size throughout, with few interruptions except for an occasional heading or sub-heading. The centre pages with information on country produce prices and the rare list are the exceptions. An occasional

40 'Female Printers', *Jackson Standard* (26 May 1853).
41 'Female Printers', *Monongalia Mirror.*
42 Payment by the em was piece work.
43 'Female Printers', *Monongalia Mirror;* 'Female Printers', *Cooper's Clarksburg Register* (4 January 1854). For the varying wages paid to male compositors in the early 1800s see Ethelbert Stewart, *A Documentary History of the Early Organizations of Printers* (Washington, DC: Government Printing Office, 1905).
44 Herron, *Progress of Labor,* 15–16.

poem, usually centred within the column, disturbs the monotony. As the paper grew in physical size and number of columns, the denseness of the text remained constant. This was a labour-intensive job for a typesetter. The foreman of the printing shop would proofread the text and any errors found were the responsibility of the typesetter to correct. Speed and accuracy were the primary skills, as undoing even a single misspelled word could result in resetting a major section of the type. The rate of pay, eighteen to twenty cents per thousand ems set, was for accurate type set; one was not paid for mistakes that had to be redone.[45]

Opportunities to Publish but Not Necessarily for Pay

The 'Prospectus of the Third Volume' claimed the *Olive Branch* was a family paper and towards the end of the seventh volume Norris described it as principally secular and highly ranked among other American literary papers.[46] With the conclusion of its seventh year its layout increased to seven columns per page, or a full twenty-eight columns of reading matter without advertisements. The family or literary paper of the early nineteenth century today is known as a story paper, 'a weekly periodical that imitated the format of conventional newspapers but was filled with popular fiction'.[47] The traditional format was the folio: a single large sheet, printed on both sides and folded once, resulting in four pages, exactly like the *Olive Branch*. According to the third-year prospectus, content came

---

45 MacKellar, *The American Printer*, 233–4. For an extensive overview of the workings of a print shop, see the chapter 'The Foreman or Overseer', 218–34.
46 'Prospectus of the Third Volume of the Olive Branch'; 'Boston Olive Branch'; Thomas F. Norris, *Olive Branch* (13 May 1843).
47 Daniel A. Cohen, 'Making Hero Strong: Teenage Ambition, Story-Paper Fiction, and the Generational Recasting of American Women's Authorship', *Journal of the Early Republic*, 30:1 (Spring 2010), 86. Due to the low cost of newspaper printing in America, the family paper/story paper was similar to the chapbook of Europe, a cheaply printed form of popular literature. Mary Noel, *Villains Galore: The Heyday of the Popular Story Weekly* (New York: Macmillan Company, 1954), 2–3.

from the exchange, whereas information on the eighth volume claimed the 'best writers would be employed'.[48] These weeklies provided opportunities for young, amateur writers to write for pay, however little; and the more sentimental and sensational the better. According to John Townsend Trowbridge's memoir *My Own Story: With Recollection of Noted Persons* (1903), the standard cry from Boston weekly editors was 'Stories, give us stories!'[49] Trowbridge considered the *Olive Branch* as one of the best of the weekly papers. When he began publishing in the *Olive Branch* Trowbridge was paid, if poorly:

> The pay was small, but I had no longer any difficulty in getting my articles published. The most flourishing of these papers paid its writers only two dollars a column [...]. Some paid only half those rates, while others kept to 'the good old rule, the simple plan', of paying very little, or nothing at all.[50]

Once a story or poem was published it became free material for reprinting in other papers belonging to the exchange. Like the reprinting of the 'Female Typesetters' article, authorship and copyrights were irrelevant: not only might a work be copied, but the author's name might not be included with the reprint.[51] Noel suggests that these early authors were honoured to be copied and published in a variety of papers, even without compensation.[52] Only when the author's name was dropped was it problematic. In her biography of Fanny Fern, Warren calls this practice 'literary piracy', yet Fern took the reprinting of her work as an indication she was sought after.[53]

---

48 'Boston Olive Branch' (13 May 1843); I understand 'the best writers would be employed' to indicate that at least some writers were paid by 1843. There is no mention of discontinuing the use of the exchange.
49 John T. Trowbridge, *My Own Story: With Recollection of Noted Persons* (New York: Houghton, Mifflin and Company, 1903), 135–6.
50 Trowbridge, *My Own Story*, 136.
51 Noel, *Villains Galore*, 9–10.
52 Noel, *Villains Galore*, 9–10.
53 Joyce Warren, *Fanny Fern: An Independent Woman* (New Brunswick: Rutgers University Press, 1992), 92.

In the early development of the weekly story paper, around the 1830s, amateur authors were less likely to use their own name. Across the pages of the *Olive Branch*, numerous stories are left unsigned or published under a pseudonym. The first female author identified in the *Olive Branch* is Louisa H. Medina, with her story *Ellen: or the Beauty of Holiness* on the front page of the 19 August 1837 issue.[54] This was a two-column short story, considered 'a sketch' and designated as a reprint from the *Ladies' Companion*. No issue or date was given for the *Companion*. Virtually unknown today, Medina was a sensational New York playwright in her day, known for works of startling and terrible catastrophe. The first woman in the American theatre to earn her living exclusively as a playwright, she authored the first 'long-run' play on an American stage, the melodrama *The Last Days of Pompeii*.[55] 1837 was the pinnacle of her career, as she died mysteriously in 1838, at the age of about 25.[56] Because *Ellen* was a reprinted item in the *Olive Branch*, Medina would not have received any financial compensation, though fortunately her name was included.

Early Women Authors and the *Olive Branch*

In 1839 the name Caroline Orne (sometimes 'C. Orne', 'C. F. Orne' and 'Mrs C. Orne') began appearing with prose and poems. Eventually I identified two different individuals, one with a middle initial of 'F', and the other designated as 'C. Orne' or 'Mrs'. According to John S. Hart's *Female Prose Writers of America* (1842), Mrs Caroline Orne was originally a Chaplin.[57] Born in Georgetown, Massachusetts, as a married woman

---

54 Louisa H. Medina, 'Ellen: or the Beauty of Holiness', *Olive Branch* (19 August 1837).
55 Miriam López Rodríguez, 'Louisa Medina, Uncrowned Queen of Melodrama', in Miriam López Rodriguez and Maria Dolores Narbona Carrión, eds, *Women's Contribution to Nineteenth-century American Theatre* (Valencia: Universitat de València, 2004), 29.
56 Rodríguez, 'Louisa Medina', 33.
57 John S. Hart, *Female Prose Writers of America* (Philadelphia: E. H. Butler and Company, 1852), 396.

she published only prose. Her first piece was published in the *Ladies' Magazine*, an early editorial work of Sarah Josepha Hale. Early on Mrs Orne did not sign her work or used the ubiquitous 'anonymous', making it difficult to identify all of her writings.[58] Caroline F. Orne, sometimes designated as 'C. F. Orne', was a poet. She published two books of poems, *Songs of American Freedom* and *Sweet Auburn*. Her work focused on the wild beauty of Cambridge, Massachusetts. She spent her entire life in Cambridge and died in 1905.[59]

Among the prolific female authors who published early on in the *Olive Branch* was Lydia Howard Huntley Sigourney whose sentimentality is well displayed in the poem 'The Boy's Last Request' published in the *Olive Branch* in 1838.[60] As the child lies dying, his last request to his mother begins: 'Half-raised upon his dying couch, his head Drooped o'er his mother's bosom –like a bud'.[61] Between 1840 to 1850 her name in the *Olive Branch* was regularly connected with verse and hymns.[62] She signed her work with variations of her name, including 'L. H. Sigourney' and 'Mrs Sigourney' and, in an article reprinted in the *Olive Branch* supporting her editorial position on the annual publication *Religious Souvenir*, she is described as an 'esteemed and distinguished lady' to whom the literary and religious public is much indebted.[63]

Ann Sophia Stephens, another *Olive Branch* contributor, was a Connecticut native who set her mind to a writing career as a young girl.[64] In 1831, at the age of 21, she married the publisher of the monthly literary

58 Hart, *Female Prose Writers*, 396–7.
59 Mary Isabell Gozzaldi, 'Gerry's Landing and its Neighborhood', *The Proceedings of the Cambridge Historical Society* 13 (1918), 81–8; Thomas William Herringshaw, *Herringshaw's Encyclopedia of American Biography of the Nineteenth-Century* (Chicago: American Publishers Association, 1904).
60 'The Boy's Last Request', *Olive Branch* (25 August, 1838).
61 'The Boy's Last Request'.
62 Hart, *Female Prose Writers,* 76; Anne E. Boyd, ed., *Wielding the Pen: Writings by American Women of the Nineteenth Century* (Baltimore: John Hopkins University Press, 2009), 54–63.
63 'Mrs. Sigourney', *Olive Branch* (25 August, 1838).
64 Baym, *Woman's Fiction*, 176.

Portland Magazine and began writing for it.[65] After the family moved to New York in the mid-1830s she turned to various popular magazines and weeklies for publication. Stephens's work was melodramatic and her romances were set in a fantasy world with strong independent women as her main characters.[66] Her earliest work, 'Love in a Cottage', appeared in 1840 and her serialized stories in the *Olive Branch* were reprints from other publications. 'Love in a Cottage' and 'The Queen's Vow' were from the *Ladies' Companion* and 'My Friend's Marriage' was from the *Maine Monthly Magazine*.[67] Stephens was the editor of the *Ladies' Companion* during the time her stories were published in that magazine and reprinted in the *Olive Branch*.[68] Today she is best known as the author of *Malaeska* (1860), the first dime novel which was a reprint of her 1839 serialized publication.[69] Stephens was known to travel for her career, leaving her husband at home with the children.[70]

A contributor new to the *Olive Branch* in 1841 was Lydia Jane Pierson, whose poem 'The Wildwood Home' indicates her style:

> There are fitting homes for the haughty minds,
> Yet a wildwood home for me,
> Where the pure, bright waters, the mountain winds,
> And the bounding hearts are free.[71]

Little is known of her: she is thought to have been born in 1802 in Middletown, Connecticut, and after an apparently idyllic childhood

---

65   Baym, *Woman's Fiction*, 176; Boyd, *Wielding the Pen*, 46–50; Sarah Josepha Buell Hale, *Woman's Record, Or, Sketches of All Distinguished Women* (New York: Harper and Brothers, 1855), 796–7.
66   Baym, *Woman's Fiction*, 180–8.
67   Ann S. Stephens, 'Love in a Cottage' (Chapter 1), *Olive Branch* (4 July 1840); 'The Queen's Vow, a Tale of Elizabeth' (concluded), *Olive Branch* (8 August 1840); 'My Friend's Marriage', *Olive Branch* (24 September 1842).
68   'Stephens, Ann S.', House of Beadle & Adams Online (August 2018), <https://www.ulib.niu.edu/badndp/stephens_ann.html>, accessed 11 June 2021.
69   'Stephens, Ann S.', House of Beadle & Adams Online.
70   Baym, *Woman's Fiction*, 176; Boyd, *Wielding the Pen*, 46–50.
71   Lydia Jane Pierson, 'The Wildwood Home', *Olive Branch* (6 November 1841), 2.

she moved, aged fifteen, to Canandaigua, New York.[72] Within two years she married a Mr Pierson and two years later was living in rural Pennsylvania.[73] No publication before 1841 is known, but in 1846 a collection of her poems was published as *The Forest Minstrel*.[74] She became the primary writer for the Philadelphian magazine the *Ladies' Garland* and in the 1850s moved to Adrian, Michigan.[75]

A widow with five children to support, Sarah Josepha Hale launched her literary career with the novel *Northwood: A Tale of New England* in 1827.[76] She has been immortalized by her poem 'Mary Had a Little Lamb' and the American holiday of Thanksgiving Day that she championed. By the time her works appeared in the *Olive Branch* in the 1850s, she was already the editor of *Godey's Ladies Book*, a position she held for over fifty years.[77]

From Seamstress to Author

In the early 1850s, a struggling widow brought a story she had written to the office of the *Olive Branch* hoping for publication.[78] She was paid fifty cents and only after it was published.[79] The woman was Sarah Payson Willis, the daughter of the newspaperman Nathaniel Willis and the sister

---

72 Boyd, *Wielding the Pen*, 68–73; Hale, *Woman's Record*, 769; Caroline May, *The American Female Poets: with Biographical and Critical Notices* (Philadelphia: Lindsay and Blakiston, 1848), 303.
73 Boyd, *Wielding the Pen*, 68–73; Hale, *Woman's Record*, 769.
74 Lydia Jane Pierson, *The Forest Minstrel* (Philadelphia: J. W. Moore, 1846).
75 Boyd, *Wielding the Pen*, 68–73; Hale, *Woman's Record*, 769–70; Frank Luther Mott, *A History of American Magazine: 1741–1850* (Cambridge, MA: Harvard University Press, 1930), 672: James Grant Wilson and John Fiske, eds, *Appleton's Cyclopædia of American Biography* (New York: D. Appleton and Company, 1888), 703.
76 Baym, *Woman's Fiction*, 64.
77 Baym, *Woman's Fiction*, 75–7; Boyd, *Wielding the Pen*, 127–31; Hart, *Female Prose Writers*, 93–9.
78 Warren, *Fanny Fern*, 92–3.
79 Warren, *Fanny Fern*, 92.

of the poet and editor N. P. Willis. At the age of 26 Sarah had in 1837 married Charles Harrington Eldredge.[80] The couple had three daughters but sadly, at the age of seven, their oldest daughter Mary died and the following year Charles also passed, a victim of typhoid, leaving Sarah in dire financial circumstances. At her father's insistence she married Samuel P. Farrington, whom she later divorced due to cruelty.[81] Divorce being considered scandalous by her father, a deacon, neither he nor her in-laws would help her.[82]

Having grown up in a newspaper family and excelling in writing as a student, Sara turned to writing to supplement her meagre income as a seamstress.[83] Her first published article 'The Model Husband' appeared in the 28 June 1851 *Olive Branch* under the pseudonym of 'Clara'.[84] Initially Willis used a variety of pseudonyms, including 'Jack Fern', 'Olivia', 'Olivia Branch' and 'Tabitha' in the *Olive Branch*. She used 'Mrs S. P. Eldridge' for an article she published in *The Mother's Assistant, Young Lady's Friend* and may also have been 'Aunt Emma'.[85]

'The Model Husband' was quickly picked up and reprinted in other newspapers without any additional remuneration for Willis.[86] Three weeks after its initial publication another piece by 'Tabitha' was published in the *Olive Branch* titled 'Thoughts on Dress'. Several contributions by 'Tabitha' followed; then on 6 September 1851 Willis used the name 'Fanny Fern' for the first time, again in the *Olive Branch*.[87] The article was 'The Little Sunbeam', a child's tale published on the fourth page under the 'Youth's Department' sub-heading. Within two years, Fanny Fern had become a

---

80   Warren, *Fanny Fern*, 54–74.
81   Warren, *Fanny Fern*, 83.
82   Warren, *Fanny Fern*, 76–89.
83   As an adult Sara dropped the 'h' from her name. Warren, *Fanny Fern*, 5.
84   Warren, *Fanny Fern*, 92.
85   Warren, *Fanny Fern*, 99; William Cushing, *Initials and Pseudonyms: A Dictionary of Literary Disguises* (New York: Thomas Y. Crowell and Company, 1885), 101; Cushing, *Initials and Pseudonyms: A Dictionary of Literary Disguises, Second Series* (New York: Crowell and Company, 1888), 57, 265.
86   Warren, *Fanny Fern*, 92.
87   Warren, *Fanny Fern*, 98.

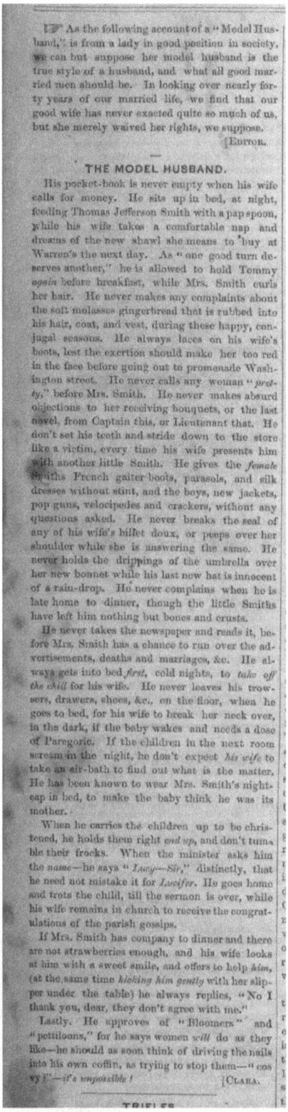

☞ As the following account of a "Model Husband," is from a lady in good position in society, we can but suppose her model husband is the true style of a husband, and what all good married men should be. In looking over nearly forty years of our married life, we find that our good wife has never exacted quite so much of us, but she merely waived her rights, we suppose.
[EDITOR.

THE MODEL HUSBAND.

His pocket-book is never empty when his wife calls for money. He sits up in bed, at night, feeding Thomas Jefferson Smith with a pap spoon, while his wife takes a comfortable nap and dreams of the new shawl she means to 'buy at Warren's the next day. As "one good turn deserves another," he is allowed to hold Tommy *again* before breakfast, while Mrs. Smith curls her hair. He never makes any complaints about the soft molasses gingerbread that is rubbed into his hair, coat, and vest, during these happy, conjugal seasons. He always laces on his wife's boots, lest the exertion should make her too red in the face before going out to promenade Washington street. He never calls any woman "*pretty*," before Mrs. Smith. He never makes absurd objections to her receiving bouquets, or the last novel, from Captain this, or Lieutenant that. He don't set his teeth and stride down to the store like a victim, every time his wife presents him with another little Smith. He gives the *female* Smiths French gaiter boots, parasols, and silk dresses without stint, and the boys, new jackets, pop guns, velocipedes and crackers, without any questions asked. He never breaks the seal of any of his wife's billet doux, or peeps over her shoulder while she is answering the same. He never holds the drippings of the umbrella over her new bonnet while his last new hat is innocent of a rain-drop. He never complains when he is late home to dinner, though the little Smiths have left him nothing but bones and crusts.

He never takes the newspaper and reads it, before Mrs. Smith has a chance to run over the advertisements, deaths and marriages, &c. He always gets into bed *first*, cold nights, to *take off the chill* for his wife. He never leaves his trowsers, drawers, shoes, &c., on the floor, when he goes to bed, for his wife to break her neck over, in the dark, if the baby wakes and needs a dose of Paregoric. If the children in the next room scream in the night, he don't expect *his wife* to take an air-bath to find out what is the matter. He has been known to wear Mrs. Smith's nightcap in bed, to make the baby think he was its mother.

When he carries the children up to be christened, he holds them right *end up*, and don't tumble their frocks. When the minister asks him the name—he says "*Lucy—Sir*," distinctly, that he need not mistake it for *Lucifer*. He goes home and trots the child, till the sermon is over, while his wife remains in church to receive the congratulations of the parish gossips.

If Mrs. Smith has company to dinner and there are not strawberries enough, and his wife looks at him with a sweet smile, and offers to help *him*, (at the same time *kicking him gently* with her slipper under the table) he always replies, "No I thank you, dear, they don't agree with me."

Lastly. He approves of "Bloomers" and "petticoats," for he says women *will* do as they like—he should as soon think of driving the nails into his own coffin, as trying to stop them—"cos vy !—*it's impossible !*
[CLARA.

Figure 4.2. Clara, 'The Model Husband', *Olive Branch*, 28 June 1851. Image Courtesy of the American Antiquarian Society Collection.

national sensation, although few individuals knew her true identity. It was not unusual to find a full page in the *Olive Branch* dedicated to her, such as page three of the 7 August 1852 issue which included four articles written by Fern: 'The Model Grandmamma', 'The Model Grandpapa', 'The Model Step-Mother' and one untitled reflection on human behaviour, alongside a letter to the editor asking 'Who is Fanny Fern?' by Almira.[88] Almira thought for sure Fanny Fern was Mrs Mary A. Denison, but others suggested that possibly Reverend Norris might be Fanny Fern.[89] By the time 'No, Almira, no!' was published, Willis was being paid two dollars a column, writing two columns for the *Olive Branch* and one column for the *True Flag* every week.[90] She eventually moved to New York, where she wrote exclusively for Robert Bonner's *New York Ledger* as the highest-paid journalist of her time.[91] Her fiction drew on her personal experiences and in her autobiography, fictionalized under the title *Ruth Hall,* she was scathing towards her family's treatment of her when she was destitute.[92]

Louisa M. Alcott

Another well-known American writer who debuted in the *Olive Branch* was Louisa May Alcott, initially anonymously, then under pen names. Alcott chose 'Flora Fairfield' as her alter ego for her family-orientated writings, reserving 'A. M. Barnard' for more gothic thriller and unladylike prose that never appeared in the *Olive Branch*.[93] Although writing since childhood, Alcott did not attempt to publish until she was about

---

[88] Almira, 'No, Almira, no!', *Olive Branch* (7 August 1852).
[89] Almira, 'No, Almira, no!', Warren, *Fanny Fern*, 102.
[90] Warren, *Fanny Fern*, 101; The *True Flag* was one of many story papers produced in Boston in the mid-nineteenth-century, Noel, *Villains Galore*, 46–55.
[91] Warren, *Fanny Fern*. 143–7; Noel, *Villains Galore*, 63–66.
[92] Warren, *Fanny Fern*, 120–42; Baym, *Woman's Fiction*, 250–1.
[93] Harriet Reisen, *Louisa May Alcott: The Woman Behind Little Women* (New York: Holt and Company, 2009) 124, 208–9.

eighteen. Her first published article 'The Rival Painters' debuted in the *Olive Branch* in 1852.[94] Like Fern, Alcott would write her autobiography as fiction in the book *Little Women,* portraying herself in the character of Jo March.[95] In chapter fourteen of *Little Women,* Jo informs her neighbour Laurie that she has dropped off two stories at a local newspaper office hoping to be published. Two weeks later Jo reads to the family a newly published story, 'The Rival Painters', using the actual title Alcott had used for her first published story.[96] The *Olive Branch*, a weekly family paper, was read by many families including the Alcotts. In fact, by the age of sixteen Alcott had created a family newspaper called the *Olive Leaf* modelled after the 'popular weekly the family liked'.[97] In *Little Women,* Jo March similarly creates a family newspaper called the 'Pickwick Portfolio', filled with original tales, local news and funny advertisements.[98]

From Author to Editor

In the 21 October 1854 issue of the *Evening Star* from Washington D.C. an article appeared titled '*Rather Spicy*', written in answer to a request the *Olive Branch* had received inquiring about the female compositors at the newspaper and the possibility of a few relocating to Nashville, Tennessee for employment.[99] The writer of this pithy response, who claimed the job title of 'editress', compared the potential future of a female compositor in the developing community of Nashville with that of one living in Boston. The working conditions and extracurricular activities were juxtaposed, and the writer informed her readers that the *Olive Branch* offered a third

---

94 Reisen, *Louisa May Alcott*, 118.
95 Reisen, *Louisa May Alcott*, 2.
96 Louisa M. Alcott, *Little Women: or, Meg, Jo, Beth and Amy, Volume 1* (Boston: Robert Brothers, 1880), 216–29.
97 Reisen, *Louisa May Alcott*, 111–12.
98 Reisen, *Louisa May Alcott*, 118; Alcott, *Little Women*, 148–52.
99 'Rather Spicy', *Evening Star* (21 October 1854).

avenue of employment (in addition to typesetting and writing): that of editorship. As in the case of the 'Female Printer' article, the article appeared with no name; but two women are known to have transitioned from writing for the *Olive Branch* to editing it: Mary A. Dennison and Eliza Ann Woodruff Hopkins.[100]

Mary A. Denison (M.A.D.)

Of the many individuals who signed their works with initials, 'M.A.D.' appeared in November of 1841. Over time additional signatures, including 'Mrs C. W. Denison', 'Mrs Denison' and 'Mary A. Denison' were used by this person. The C. W. Denison stood for Charles Wheeler Denison, the Reverend C. W. Denison, also a writer for the *Olive Branch*.[101] Mary Denison initially published poetry with a religious undertone under her own initials and her name first appeared in the *Olive Branch* with her serialized story 'The Haunted House and the Idiot Boy: A Tale Founded on Facts' in the 13 May 1848 issue.[102] After this, she interchanged her signatures, and by 3 May 1851 her name with the title 'Assistant Editor' appeared under Norris's on page two.[103] Denison's editorial role began when her husband, until then himself assistant editor of the *Olive Branch*, accepted a position in California and moved there while she remained in Boston due to poor health.[104] Mary, already writing for the *Olive Branch's* 'Youth' and 'Ladies' sections, took over some of the editorial duties vacated by her husband.[105] She remained in this position until the paper's

---

100   Norris, 'Boston Olive Branch: Its Editors'; 'A Word to Our Readers', *Olive Branch* (7 July 1855); E. A. Norris, 'Volume 22d of the Boston Olive Branch', *Olive Branch* (22 November 1856).
101   Cushing, *Initials* (1885), 408.
102   Mrs M. A. Denison, 'The Haunted House and The Idiot Boy: A Tale Founded on Facts', *Olive Branch* (13 May 1848).
103   'Boston Olive Branch', *Olive Branch* (3 May 1851).
104   Norris, 'Boston Olive Branch: Its Editors'.
105   Norris, 'Boston Olive Branch: Its Editors'.

demise in 1857, and was therefore possibly the 'editress' who wrote the 'Rather Spicy' article. After the *Olive Branch*, Denison continued to write for other periodicals such as *Gleason's Pictorial Dollar Weekly* and the *Literary Companion*.[106]

Eliza Ann Woodruff Hopkins (EAWH)

The second woman who transitioned from writer to editor at the *Olive Branch* was Eliza Ann Woodruff Hopkins who often signed as EAWH. She appears first as a writer in the 7 July 1855 issue, introduced by Norris as a 'new contributor, and one of much merit'.[107] Like numerous women authors of her day such as Fern and Hale, Woodruff Hopkins needed to support her family. She was not a widow, but the wife of a man who made poor choices and chased after dreams.[108] The family moved several times around Wisconsin and in Chicago, Illinois. Eventually the husband left for California leaving Eliza behind to pay all the bills and support the children. She turned to writing and editing and forged a successful career. Her descendants believe she may have been an editor in Ohio in the early 1850s.[109] Eventually Woodruff Hopkins moved to Boston, securing employment at the *Olive Branch*, and told her life story in *Ella Lincoln*.[110]

106   Lynne Thomas, 'Denison, Mary A.', House of Beadle & Adams Online (August 2018), <https://www.ulib.niu.edu/badndp/denison_mary.html>, accessed 2 May 2020.
107   'A Word to Our Readers'.
108   Joann Rivers, 'Eliza Ann Woodruff Hopkins Selected Writings', <http://josfamilyhistory.com/htm/hopkins/hopkins-eliza/eawh-articles/eawh-artsintro.htm>, accessed 2 June 2020.
109   Joann Rivers, *Official Rivers-Hopkins and Related Families Website* (March 2012), <http://joConclusionsfamilyhistory.com/htm/hopkins/woodruff/woodruff-eaw-early.htm>, accessed 2 May 2020.
110   Joann Rivers, 'Eliza Ann Woodruff Hopkins: As an Adult', <http://josfamilyhistory.com/htm/hopkins/hopkins-eliza/eawh-adult.htm> accessed 4 May 2020; Eliza Ann Woodruff Hopkins, *Ella Lincoln; or, Western Prairie Life an Autobiography* (Boston: James French and Company, 1857).

Conclusion

My initial research was in identifying where American women in the early nineteenth century had been employed in the capacity of typesetter, using digital repositories such as *Chronicling America* and *Nineteenth Century U.S. Newspapers*. The discovery of the 'Female Printer' article in the *Monongalia Mirror* was not just important for this but also introduced me to the *Olive Branch* and opened the door to exploring other employment opportunities for women within the larger publishing sphere. The lack of an initial *Olive Branch* prospectus, as well as a specimen paper and the first seventeen issues, left me wondering if any specific target audience had been originally envisaged. If so, I would think it was the Methodist Protestant Church members. The first available issues have a moralistic tone, but no specific audience is apparent, and within a year, Medina's sensational story covers the front page. The third-year prospectus mentions church members but focuses on the *Olive Branch* as a 'family paper' and by the end of the seventh year it was a secular one. Reverend Norris must have been keenly aware of what readers wanted and adjusted the tone of the paper accordingly. From 'Female Printer' to 'Rather Spicy', the working environment at the *Olive Branch* is characterized as a positive one. Regardless of the pay, the female typesetters are presented as content with their employment. An overview of standard print-shop practices of the day along with the various depictions offered in the three autobiographies would be good to compare with the image presented in the articles. If other printing opportunities for women are discovered, how might they compare to the *Olive Branch*? Having personally worked in a print shop, I have a hard time imagining one with a carpeted floor.

One month is a very short time to investigate a newspaper published over twenty-one years. I maintained a chart with each female name I encountered as I reviewed the various issues along with individuals only identified by single word names or initials and have attempted to accurately identify as many as possible. The initials and pseudonyms dictionaries of William Cushing (1885, 1888) have been exceeding helpful in identifying some of the cryptic author information I encountered. Currently I am about

50 per cent successful, as some initial sets have been used by numerous individuals and not all names have been collected into cross-references. I am also confident there are individuals I have missed. This use of pen names is still a common practice in the literary world, as seen in Nora Roberts is J. D. Robb and Jill March, Stephen King is Richard Bachman and Joanne Rowling is J. K. Rowling and Robert Galbraith.[111] Although not as well known today, the frequent appearance of names such as Orne, Stephens and Pierson justifies their inclusion here. What a delight it is to identify the *Olive Branch* as the publication that first published both Sara Willis and Louise M. Alcott and to discover the works of Denison and Hopkins. For Hale, an already established author and editor, the reprinting of her work in the *Olive Branch* was beneficial for the paper, though not necessarily for her. The free exchange of material in nineteenth-century publications is akin to today's online viral information exchange. Success can be measured in how popular one's tweets become. Warren's calling this practice 'literary piracy' is a modern-day sensibility. In 1850, Willis understood this as her opportunity for greater exposure and success.

More time is needed to fully review all the volumes and issues, not just the early years. This would allow me to chart the longevity of each woman's represented works and discover additional female contributors. If such a thing as a complete list of publications in the literary exchange Norris was involved with is not possible to obtain, compiling a list of each one identified across the pages would nevertheless be beneficial. This would allow for cross-checking of the articles with the designated publication for completion and accuracy of information. The *Olive Branch* is not a well-remembered periodical today, but I have found it to be full of valuable examples of the multiple employment opportunities it offered women during its duration.

---

[111] Nora Roberts, Wikipedia, <https://en.wikipedia.org/wiki/Nora_Roberts>, accessed 12 June 2021; Stephen King, Wikipedia, <https://en.wikipedia.org/wiki/Stephen_King>, accessed 12 June 2021; J. K. Rowling, Wikipedia, <https://en.wikipedia.org/wiki/J._K._Rowling>, accessed 12 June 2021.

PATRICIA THOMAS

5 'Choice Type' and 'Elegant Founts': Advertising in Elizabeth Heard's Truro Printing Office

On 13 June 1823 *The West Briton and Cornwall Advertiser* printed the following notice from its publisher's widow:

> Elizabeth Heard … deeply sensible of the very liberal patronage conferred on her lamented husband, returns her most grateful acknowledgements to his Friends and to the Public at large, for the numerous favours already bestowed; and begs to state, that it is her intention to continue the Business, as it was carried on by her late Husband. [She] most respectfully assures those who may honour her with their commands, that the most unwearied assiduity, and the most unremitted attention shall be employed to give that satisfaction which gratitude and the interest of her infant family equally require it should be her aim to afford.[1]

Recent studies of historical business demonstrate that nineteenth-century middle-class women like Elizabeth were not inevitably the gendered domestic stereotypes they were once thought to have been, nor was the work they engaged in restricted to the so-called feminine trades.[2] Widowhood was the entry point into business for many women. Numerous widows in the eighteenth century 'stepped [seamlessly]' into their husband's shoes and Elizabeth seems to have followed that practice in the nineteenth century.[3] Her husband John Heard had died on 18 May 1823, just three

1   Elizabeth Heard, 'Elizabeth Heard, Widow and Executrix of the Late John Heard', *The West Briton and Cornwall Advertiser* (hereafter *West Briton*) (13 June 1823), 1.
2   Jennifer Aston, *Female Entrepreneurship in Nineteenth-Century England: Engagement in the Urban Economy* (London: Palgrave Macmillan, 2016); Katrina Honeyman, 'Doing Business with Gender: Service Industries and British Business History', *Business History Review*, 31/3 (2007), 471–93.
3   Hannah Barker, 'Women, Work and the Industrial Revolution: Female Involvement in the English Printing Trades, c.1700–1840', in Hannah Barker and

weeks prior to the notice above. He left 'the amiable widow' with four children under the age of ten and a business, all of which resided in and operated out of the premises at 30 Boscawen Street, Truro.[4] She spent the following forty-five years living up to her statement of intent towards her clients, her family and the public of Cornwall. That she chose to continue in the business she inherited and conducted it 'with eminent success' is testament to her talents as a shrewd and capable businesswoman.[5] That she was said to have done so for 'close upon sixty years' suggests that her involvement in the business prior to her husband's death was substantial.[6]

I first encountered Elizabeth's work in pursuit of a small handbill in the Courtney Library at the Royal Cornwall Museum in Truro. Since then I have done considerable sleuthing in the Library archives and, while Elizabeth remains in many ways a spectral figure to me, additional investigative legwork will serve to bring her work more fully into the light. Meanwhile, this chapter offers glimpses of her contribution to the business of printing in the nineteenth century.

Contexts, Archival Source and Outline

This study of Elizabeth's printing office sits within the contexts of research on provincial printing and the analysis of typographical form. Scholars have recently paid a 'great deal of attention' to provincial printing

---

Elaine Chalus, eds, *Gender in Eighteenth-Century England: Roles, Representations and Responsibilities* (London: Routledge, 1997), 81–100, 91.

4   *Royal Cornwall Gazette* (24 May 1823). Due to borough rearrangements, 30 Boscawen Street became 32 in the 1830s.

5   'From Stage Coach to the Jet Age: The Story of the West Briton in Nine Reigns: The West Briton through 150 Years: The West Briton 1810–1960 and Royal Cornwall Gazette Established 1801: 150th Anniversary Supplement' (Truro: The West Briton, 1960), 10.

6   'Obituary', *The Bookseller*, 117 (30 September 1867), 668.

'Choice Type' and 'Elegant Founts' 113

businesses in the late 1700s and into the 1800s.[7] This chapter adds to the more recent research on non-metropolitan printers by historians who take the study of printing practices away from the urban centres, into the provinces and beyond them into the empire. David Osbaldestin and Diana Mackarill's individual research on the Gitton family at Bridgnorth and Rob Banham's study of the printers Guy & Balne situate this research on Elizabeth's printing house within the context of family businesses.[8] However, none of these examine Cornish printers and, as John Hinks notes, few studies investigate women's printing practices.[9] To reinstate women in the narratives of printing history, this chapter more specifically builds on the work of print culture and family businesses undertaken by historian Hannah Barker. Barker's research on women in printing provides a model for the study of working women 'towards the upper end of the scale', in other words, women of property such as Elizabeth Heard.[10]

7   Diana R. Mackarill, 'George and George Robert Gitton, Printers, Bridgnorth', *Journal of the Printing Historical Society*, ns 4 (2002), 31–62, 31; see also John Hinks, 'Local and Regional Studies of Printing History', *Journal of the Printing Historical Society*, ns 5 (2003), 3–14. Hinks notes that the fields of printing history and book history have of late taken on an interdisciplinary, and subsequently more vibrant, approach to the subject of print. John Hinks, 'The History of Printing and Print Culture: Contexts and Controversies', *Midland History*, 45/2 (2020), 134–44.
8   David Joseph Osbaldestin, 'The Art of Ephemera: Typographic Innovations of Nineteenth-Century Midland Jobbing Printers', *Midland History*, 45/2 (2020), 208–21; James J. Connolly, Patrick Collier, Frank Felsenstein, Kenneth R. Hall and Robert G. Hall, eds, *Print Culture Histories Beyond the Metropolis* (Toronto: Toronto University Press, 2016); Mackarill, 'Gitton'; Robert Banham, 'Guy & Balne: Printing Families', *Journal of the Printing Historical Society*, ns 5 (2003), 17–42; see also Michael Twyman, *John Soulby, Printer, Ulverston* (Reading: University of Reading, 1966).
9   Hinks, 'Printing and Print Culture'.
10   Barker, 'Women, Work', 84. Studies of business women outside the printing trades which also worked to promote an understanding of historical women as independent and entrepreneurial include Gabrielle Durepos, Alan McKinlay and Scott Taylor, 'Narrating Histories of Women at Work: Archives, Stories and the Promise of Feminism', *Business History*, 59/8 (2017), 1261–79; Helen Doe, 'Gender and Business: Women in Business or Businesswomen? An Assessment of the History of Entrepreneurial Women', in John F. Wilson, Steven Toms, Abe de Jong and Emily Buchnea, eds, *The Routledge Companion to Business History* (London: Routledge, 2016), 347–57. Studies of Women printers include Paula McDowell, 'On Behalf

Many of the women that Barker names in her list of widows or daughters, however, operated as printing house proprietors either in London or other larger centres, rather than in the counties, like Cornwall.[11] Moreover, with the notable exception of Osbaldestin, few studies of historical printing offices address the specifics tools – the type designs and typography – of the advertising material produced in them.

While this chapter examines the advertisements printed at the Heard printing office, it does not focus specifically on advertising practice *per se*. Rather, typefaces and typography form the basis of and provide a lens through which to analyse examples of advertising. This analysis draws on mid-twentieth century studies by printing historians. Among these are Nicolete Gray, P. M. Handover and Ruari McLean who explore the ideas and events that gave rise 'suddenly and without warning' to the aesthetic innovations in early nineteenth-century type designs.[12] As foundational studies they remain invaluable to research the typefaces themselves and their practical application in individual printing offices. Particularly relevant to some of the typefaces described in this chapter was the typographic historian James Mosley's identification in 1966 of a series of highly decorated wooden letters from the foundry of Louis John Pouchée. Mosley was able to confirm their provenance when, in 1988, he discovered a type specimen book of the idiosyncratic founder.[13]

Like many provincial printing proprietors of the time, Elizabeth was a book and music publisher and seller, stationery supplier, commodity merchant and insurance agent, and she operated a circulating library and book club. At this point in the research, it appears that the business records attached to any of those activities either no longer exist or are yet to be

---

of the Printers: A Late Stuart Printer-Author and Her Causes', in Sabrina Alcorn Baron, Eric N. Undquist and Eleanor F. Shevlin, eds, *Agent of Change: Print Culture Studies after Eliabeth Eisenstein* (Amherst: University of Massachusetts Press, 2007), 125–39.

[11] Barker, 'Women, Work', 85.
[12] Nicolete Gray, *Nineteenth Century Ornamented Typefaces with a Chapter on Ornamented Typfaces in America by Ray Nash* (London: Faber & Faber, 1976), 8.
[13] James Mosley, *Ornamented Types Prospectus* (London: I. M. Imprimit in Association with the St Bride Printing Library, 1992).

discovered.[14] This suggests that, like many of the records of women's business activities from that time – as distinct from their work practices – 'the relatively formal "traces" of an organization ... [are] dominated by male voices and male concerns.'[15] As fortune would have it, a collection of primary material in the form of job files and copies of the *West Briton* exist in the Courtney Library and they provide evidence of Elizabeth's printing production. The newspaper editions begin in 1810 and run up to and beyond Elizabeth's death. The job files are limited to the years 1838–47. Thus, like many ephemera collections, they are incomplete, but sufficiently substantial for analysis as examples of both advertising and typographic practices.

To give some focus to Elizabeth and her printing practice, this chapter begins by tracing her early life through to her marriage. It then turns to discuss the businesswoman: Elizabeth Heard, printer at Truro. An initial discussion of her practice focuses on the job files through analysis of a small selection of advertisements. The discussion then turns to an examination of advertisements in the *West Briton* to explore how the type designs available in the printing house began to change the look of the newspaper page at this time. This includes an advertisement announcing to her clients the acquisition of the Pouchée types, which is an example of how Elizabeth used the newspaper to advance her own business interests. Finally, the chapter explores more deeply the additional tools – typographical and architectural – that she used to advertise the business.[16] This examination of Elizabeth's work provides some evidence for a growth in the provincial printing trade that was, in the eighteenth century, 'less active than [in]

14 Hopefully, more records of Elizabeth's life and her business will emerge. Nevertheless, each trip to Truro and every internet search brings her a little more into the light.
15 Durepos et al., 'Narrating Histories of Women at Work'. See also Doe, 'Gender and Business: Women in Business or Businesswomen?'.
16 At times this chapter may state 'Elizabeth printed', and the phrase serves as shorthand for the responsibility she had for all branches of her businesses.

London'.[17] It tells the story of one woman, among a growing number, who operated her own business under her own name. It also adds regional specificity to the understanding of economic life in the nineteenth century, and the significant contributions that women have made both prior to and after the death of their husbands.

Elizabeth Goodridge Heard: Background

Elizabeth Goodridge was born in London, probably in the parish of St Andrew's, Holborn in 1787. She was the only child of Nathaniel Goodridge, a carpenter, and Margaret Macfarlane. Baptized at St Luke's, Finsbury in 1788, she appears to have lived in London until her marriage in 1811.[18] Her maternal uncle Andrew Macfarlane was a bookbinder in Poppin's Court, off Fleet Street; it may have been he who was the connection between his niece and John Heard. John, originally from Devon, had worked in a number of printing houses in London, and in 1808 ran a printing house in Falmouth in partnership with William Penaluna of Helston. Immediately prior to his and Elizabeth's marriage, John was the printer and publisher of Truro's newly minted Reformist newspaper *The West Briton and Cornwall Advertiser*.[19] When he died after only thirteen years of marriage, it was Elizabeth who oversaw the flourishing of all branches of the business, including the jobbing work conducted in the printing house.[20] So far, my research finds no evidence that associates

---

17 Barker, 'Women, Work', 85.
18 Finsbury parish christening records for 20 January 1788 recorded her birth date a month earlier, but not its location. St Bride's marriage register of 7 November 1811 recorded the marriage of John Heard, widower and Elizabeth Goodridge, spinster. Their marriage also was recorded in the *Monthly Magazine, or, British Register*, 32 (1811), 516, and by Heard himself in the *West Briton* on 15 November 1811.
19 Jeremy Black, *The English Press 1621–1861* (Stroud: Sutton, 2001).
20 'Elizabeth Heard', in *Cornish Women of Note from the Merry Maidens to 1980: A Collection of Brief Biographical Sketches*, loose leaves in folder, n.d. 942.370099, Kresen Kernow, Redruth. For a comprehensive discussion of the incidence and

Elizabeth with any newspaper or printing house other than her own, and I can only speculate about what she was doing prior to her marriage aged 23. Her father was a successful tradesman, so she may not have needed to be in paid work. She was also unlikely to have had a hand in the practical side of her business, being proprietor rather than artisan.

Remarriage was not common at this time among women who took over the running of their late husbands' businesses. Barker speculates that independence and age gave widows a welcome status and power that they would not otherwise have had as single or married women.[21] Certainly, Elizabeth appears to have kept control of the various branches of her business, even to the point of exercising power over her sons, at least within the business context. John MacFarlane and Edward Goodridge – the latter 'trained and influenced by his mother' – successively entered into the management of the *West Briton* as they reached adulthood.[22] John MacFarlane became the manager of the *West Briton* in 1850, but died in 1858. His younger brother Edward Goodridge succeeded him in the role. However, like many printers' widows, Elizabeth remained the printer and publisher of the newspaper and the driving force behind the wider business and its activities until her death on 10 September 1867.[23] The fact that her sons eventually managed the newspaper branch of the business rather than engaged in composing or presswork, as their father presumably did, positions the family as middle-class employers.[24]

---

longevity of printers' widows as proprietors in the nineteenth century, see Emma L. Greenwood, 'Work, Identity and Letterpress Printers in Britain, 1750–1850', PhD thesis, University of Manchester, 2015, and Barker, 'Women, Work'.

21 Barker, 'Women, Work'.
22 'Elizabeth Heard', in *Cornish Women*; Brian Elvins, 'Cornwall's Newspaper War: The Political Rivalry Between the *Royal Cornwall Gazette* and the *West Briton* 1810–1831', *Cornish Studies* 2nd ser. 11 (2001), 143–72, fn 35.
23 Rebecca Warren Davidson, *Unseen Hands: Women Printers, Binders and Book Designers* (Princeton: Princeton University Press, 2005).
24 The 1861 census records that Elizabeth employed '18 men and 16 boys'. Cornwall Online Census Project, 1861, 'Civil Parish of Borough Of Truro, Eccl. District of Truro St. Mary', Folio 7 Page 7. <http://sites.rootsweb.com/~kayhin/61594b.html>, accessed 17 April 2018.

Elizabeth Heard, Printer at Truro

The advertising material printed at Heard's printing house conformed to a 'new fashion' in display advertising designed to promote goods and services.[25] For printers, the nineteenth century was a time of experimentation and exuberance. Early nineteenth-century British type founders designed a visual vocabulary to serve the needs of an emerging advertising industry that responded to expanding markets for industrially produced goods, the often-separated loci of production and consumption and the growing habit of 'reading the street'.[26] These types were designed to attract a market that was habituated to visual novelty, one that increasingly saw the world as a visual text.[27] Large, ornamented types, through size, graphic weight and spatial arrangement, subverted the typography that emulated the book page which readers had been accustomed to for centuries.[28] Appreciation of the types has been mixed. At the end of the nineteenth century, the typographic critic John Southward characterized them as 'execrable' and demonstrating a 'want of taste' in both their designers and users.[29] Like Southward, early twentieth-century critics such as Daniel Berkeley Updike and Stanley Morison considered

---

25   Talbot Baines Reed, *A History of the Old English Letter Founders, with Notes Historical and Bibliographical, on the Rise and Progress of English Typography* (London: Eliot Stock, 1887), 340.

26   Kevin J. Hayes, 'Visual Culture and the Word in Edgar Allen Poe's "The Man of the Crowd"', *Nineteenth Century Literature*, 56/4 (2002), 445–65, 448, <https://www.jstor.org/stable/10.1525/ncl.2002.56.4.445>, accessed 9 January 2019.

27   P. D. Glennie and N. J. Thrift, 'Modernity, Urbanism and Modern Consumption', *Environment and Planning D: Society and Space*, 10 (1992), 423–43, 430.

28   Nomenclature: I use the word 'ornamented' and 'types' to describe the metal designs identified by Gray, Handover and McLean. For the Pouchée designs that began life as wooden letters, I use 'decorated' and 'letters'. I use 'types' when I discuss the material objects rather than the designs and 'typeface' for specific designs. 'Fount' is any of the many versions of a typeface, for example, bold or italic.

29   John Southward, *Progress in Printing and the Graphic Arts during the Victorian Era* (London: Simpkin, Marshall, Hamilton, Kent and Co. Ltd, 1897), 9 & 10.

these advertising display types rebarbative, part of 'a tide of bad taste.'[30] However, Gray argues that they were 'an efficient means to an essentially utilitarian and only accidentally aesthetic end.'[31] Their primary value was their function. These types often appeared on large placards or posters pasted on any vertical surface accessible to the public eye in both rural and urban settings. The types, and the innovative ways that printers deployed them on the page, are evident in Heard's jobbing work.

Jobbing Advertising

In 1897 Southward argued that 'jobbing work ... might be regarded as the least important of the ... printing business.'[32] It has taken many decades for historians to acknowledge the value of jobbing ephemera for the evidence it offers of the workings of a printing house, no less than the glimpses it provides of the quotidian events and circumstances in the social, economic, political and cultural life of the time. Attitudes have changed since the 1960s, due in large part to the work of the many printing historians who have investigated printing beyond its mechanics and outside of or beyond the book.[33] Librarians' and archivists' appreciation of the value of collecting, archiving and, most importantly, providing retrieval

---

30   Daniel Berkeley Updike, *Printing Types: Their History, Forms and Use*, II, 4th edn (New Castle: Oak Knoll Press & London: The British Library, 2001), 196; Stanley Morison, *Type Designs of the Past and Present* (London: The Fleuron Ltd, 1926).
31   Gray, *Ornamented Typefaces*, 15. Many of these typefaces were rehabilitated for the 1951 Festival of Britain and remain popular. See: Stephen Coles, 'Festival of Britain', Fonts in Use (2021), <https://fontsinuse.com/uses/3802/festival-of-britain>, accessed 8 December 2021.
32   Southward, *Progress in Printing*, 5 & 6.
33   Hinks, 'Printing and Print Culture'; James Raven, 'Print Culture and the Perils of Practice', in Jason McElligott and Eve Patten, eds, *The Perils of Print Culture: Book, Print and Publishing History in Theory and Practice* (London: Palgrave Macmillan, 2014), 218–37; Michael Twyman, 'The Long-Term Significance of Printed Ephemera', *RBM A Journal of Rare Books, Manuscripts and Cultural Heritage*, 9/1 (2008), 19–57.

systems for this material has alleviated some of the historical difficulties of access encountered in studying ephemera.[34] The material in the Courtney Library, though limited and not digitized, is a good example of this trend. It comprises an orderly, discrete collection of official announcements (Elizabeth printed considerable political literature); private communications (persons warning trespassers or offering rewards for lost or stolen animals); commercial advertising (much related to mining, real estate, agriculture and emigration); and advertisements for her own business.

Collections of the jobbing work of contemporaneous printers in other provincial towns indicate similar acquisitions of up-to-date typographic materials. Good examples are the John Soulbys (father and son), the firm of Guy & Balne and any number of lottery printers who adopted, and possibly even made individual letters (often wooden) for display advertisements in the early nineteenth century.[35] Advertisements printed by Hawkshead of Lancaster in 1823 and Soulby of Ulverston in 1826 display examples of Pouchée's ornamented types, although the decorated letters examined by Mosley and reproduced in Heard advertisements are not evident.[36]

Compositionally, the work produced by the Heard printing house conforms to the contemporaneous trend in advertising material of 'picking out individual words or lines of copy in large, bold type, according to their assumed significance' to the overall message.[37] Beyond its visually arresting value, this had two advantages: first, the message could be grasped quickly by passers-by without requiring them to read the whole; second, it could also be surmized by a semi-literate reader through the shorthand of the picked-out words. Additionally, Elizabeth used types that indicate a feeling for the appropriate matching of form to content. This is evident in two ephemeral pieces produced for the auctioneer Mr Tippet's sale of the contents of Chevelah House in 1847 (Figures 5.1a and b).

34   Elizabeth Holcombe, 'Difficult to Find and Keep: Providing Access to Ephemera Collections', *Australian Law Lirbrary*, 10/2 (2002), 113–24.
35   Rob Banham, 'Lottery Advertising 1800–1826', *Journal of the Printing Historical Society*, ns 13 (2009), 17–60.
36   'Maurice Rickards Collection of Ephemera', Centre for Ephemera Studies, University of Reading, Reading.
37   Twyman, 'Long-Term Significance', 36.

CHEVELAH HOUSE, NEAR TRURO.

ELEGANT MODERN
HOUSEHOLD FURNITURE,
Grand and Cottage Piano Fortes, Oil Paintings, Milch Cow, Pony Carriage, Pony, Harness, and Miscellaneous Effects.

MR. TIPPET
HAS BEEN INSTRUCTED TO OFFER FOR SALE BY

PUBLIC COMPETITION
PEREMPTORILY,

On MONDAY, the 3rd of MAY next, and following day,
AT TEN O'CLOCK IN THE FORENOON OF EACH DAY.

AT CHEVELAH HOUSE, KENWYN,
Within about a mile and a half of the Borough of Truro, the residence of H. H. Browne, Esq.,

THE WHOLE OF HIS ELEGANT MODERN

HOUSEHOLD
FURNITURE,
COMPRISING,

Mahogany Four-post and other Bedsteads, with Moreen and other Drapery, several fine seasoned Feather Beds, Mattrasses, Palliasses, Mahogany and other Chests of Drawers, Mahogany and other Washstands, Wardrobes, Toilet and other Glasses, Toilet Sets, Mahogany Cane-seat and other Chairs, Mahogany Dining and other Tables, Rosewood Loo and other Tables, Easy Chairs, Carpets, Hearth Rugs, Fenders, Fire Irons, Sofas, Couches, Cellaret, Moreen and other Curtains, What Not, Barometer, Passage and other Lamps, Knives and Forks, Tea Urns, Napkin Press, Plated and other Candlesticks, Set of Castors, a great variety of Glass, Dinner and Tea Services, Kitchen and Culinary requisites in every variety, Iron Furnace, Brewing Utensils, and miscellaneous effects.

ALSO,

A GRAND PIANO FORTE by STODART,
A ROSEWOOD COTTAGE ditto by BROADWOOD,
The tone of both of which are brilliant and delectable.

Several good Oil Paintings and Prints.

And, a Milch Cow in Calf, Pony Carriage and Harness, useful Pony, Saddles, Bridles, a Cucumber Frame, &c., &c.

The whole may be inspected on Saturday prior to the first day of Sale, when Catalogues will be ready for delivery price 6d. each, returnable to purchasers.

For further particulars, application may be made at Mr. TIPPET'S OFFICE, in Pydar Street.

Dated Truro, April 28, 1847.

HEARD AND SONS, PRINTERS, BOOKBINDERS, STATIONERS AND MUSIC SELLERS, BOSCAWEN STREET, TRURO.

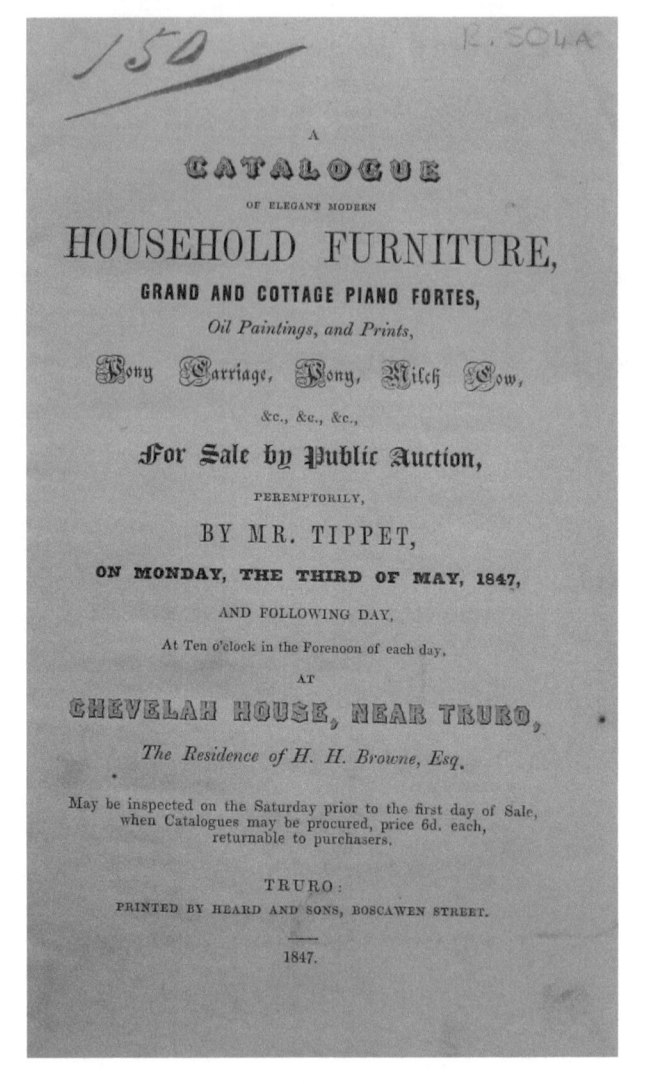

Figure 5.1. a. Advertising poster for Tippet of Pydar Street, Heard and Sons, 1847; b. Catalogue front cover for Mr Tippet of Pydar Street, Heard and Sons, 1847. Images used with the permission of the Royal Institution of Cornwall, Courtney Library (Heard Collection).

'Choice Type' and 'Elegant Founts'

Using a variety of large founts of Egyptian and Fat Face, 'MR TIPPET' advertises a 'PUBLIC COMPETITION' for the sale of 'HOUSEHOLD FURNITURE' the location being 'AT CHEVELAH HOUSE, KENWYN', with a special mention of the sale of 'A GRAND PIANO FORTE by STODART' and a lesser (by dint of its quieter typographic demeanour) 'ROSEWOOD COTTAGE ditto by BROADWOOD'. Fat Face was the first typeface specifically designed for advertising. A 'genial ... open-hearted' typeface, it epitomized the profligacy and extravagance of the Regency.[38] The Egyptian typeface – originally called Antique after a fashion for antique forms – reflected a simultaneous interest in things Egyptian, fostered by the collection of Egyptian artefacts gathered after the Napoleonic War and deposited in the British Museum. It is now known as a slab serif, a name that describes its slab-like horizontal and verticals strokes. Mr Tippet and the furniture for sale are portrayed as solid and reliable through their sturdy Egyptian garb. The auctioneer, the goods and their location are each picked out for attention and maximum impact. Disparate and less emphatic typographic treatments supply ancillary information on the particularity of goods, dates of the sale, location of the property, arrangements for inspection and the location of Mr Tippet's office. Almost the entire message comprises one long sentence, punctuated by the loud graphic presence of the display types.

Conversely, the cover of the catalogue for the sale of the household furniture, while it too is one long sentence, is smaller in size and shows some typographic restraint. However, it employs a greater variety of ornamented types to pick out many of the same words to impart the 'elegant' modernity that the message claims for the goods. It begins with a Tuscan Ornamented ('CATALOGUE'), followed by 'HOUSEHOLD FURNITURE' set in a compressed Fat Face, its slender strokes implying a gracefulness in the furniture of which it speaks. The nineteenth-century Tuscan typeface – based on a letterform from the fourth century – was a product of the same Regency impetus towards playfulness and generosity as was the Fat Face.[39] 'Pony Carriage, Pony, Milch Cow' appear in a small text

38   Gray, *Ornamented Typefaces*, 34.
39   Gray, *Ornamented Typefaces*, 34. These typefaces variously display bifurcated or trifurcated, but always curled, terminals.

type from the foundry of Henry Caslon – each initial letter a playfully decorated blackletter typeface. A Figgins Black ('For Sale by Public Auction') lends a quasi-legal tone to the proceedings. England was the birthplace of common law and blackletter became 'the dominant letter shape'[40] in the visual language of English common law. The letter thus had considerable significance to an English reading public. Like many other printers, Heard predominantly employed blackletter for words related to legal transactions. Finally, like its counterpart above, an Ornamented Tuscan – one of the many to emerge from the foundries of Henry Caslon and Vincent Figgins – forms 'CHEVELAH HOUSE, NEAR TRURO'. These lines are interspersed with a series of roman and italic text founts. Unlike the poster that advertises the event, this page is lively, but moderately so.

Even more lively and the most visibly poetic are Pouchée's decorated letters. In a flyer that advertised their 'previous stock of *well-selected and choice type*' Heard and Sons noted that they had 'made very extensive purchases of *the most elegant founts*' calculated to produce '[p]rinting in a style of typographical beauty rarely attained' (Figure 5.2).[41] It is tempting to imagine that these 'founts' are those advertised as 'ornamented letters' in Figure 5.3a.[42] The limitations of the job files make it impossible to know for certain, but these letters were available and there is no reason to suggest that Elizabeth would not have added them to the Pouchée types she purchased and advertised in 1824. It is unlikely that they were the Wood & Sharwood copies that Gray thought them to be because there is no evidence in any of the Heard examples of the lower case that Mosley attributes to this foundry.[43] Additional evidence comes in Pouchée's characterization of the letters on the advertisement as 'entirely new devices from well-executed designs', which suggests that these were the metal types cast from stereotypes of his original, elaborately carved wooden letters. Mosley notes that

40   Kasia Solon Cristobal, 'From Law in Blackletter to "Blackletter Law"', *Law Library Journal*, 108/2 (2016–9), 181–216, 183.
41   'Heard and Sons', R751, Royal Institution of Cornwall, Courtney Library (Heard Collection), Truro (italics in original). Sometime after 1842, when her sons would have been adults, 'E. Heard' became 'Heard and Sons'.
42   Louis John Pouchée, *Specimens of Stereotype Casting from the Foundry of L.I.Pouchée*.
43   Gray, *Ornamented Typefaces*; Mosley, *Prospectus*.

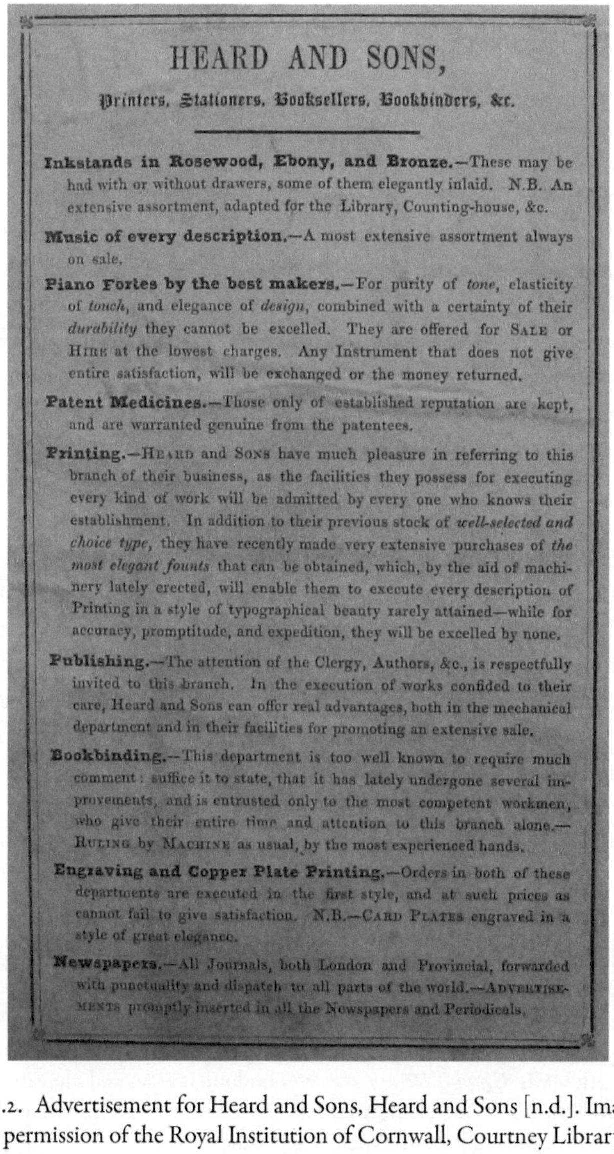

Figure 5.2. Advertisement for Heard and Sons, Heard and Sons [n.d.]. Image used with the permission of the Royal Institution of Cornwall, Courtney Library (Heard Collection).

this is 'very welcome evidence' of the genesis of the types, which reinforces the need for much more work to be done on provincial printing to provide a full picture of early nineteenth-century practices of type-founding and the distribution of type designs.[44]

Pouchée's letters burst onto the visual landscape with an exuberant energy uninhibited by any sense of restraint. In a publication on decorative printing, to which Pouchée subscribed, the printer William Savage admired the harmony and proportion of the letters, declaring that the 'Ornamented Letters' were 'a new feature' in 1818 and were 'superior to those now in use'. He went on to postulate that they would 'be looked on as peculiarly applicable where the subject is conviviality, masonry, or music'.[45] The generous rotundity of the Fat Face style of the letter was invigorated by Pouchée's decorations, its plumpness allowing for all manner of flora, fauna and masonic symbols to take up residence within its portly form. Like their less decorative fellows, these letters were very much of their time and came into their own when, as Savage comments, they were 'calculated for posting Bills, &c.'.[46] In these letters, form – 'the physical qualities ... that give it individuality' – signifies content in a *symbolic* sense.[47] Readers' psychological ability – a process that does not change over time – to extract semantic meaning from visual cues and to decode their symbolic signs through cultural habituation allows advertisers to mediate their messages through tools such as type design.[48] In tune with their time, these letters were truly 'all dressed up with something to say' in the flamboyant commercial and consumer culture of that time.[49] The form of these particular

44 James Mosley, Personal Communication, 24 October 2018.
45 William Savage, *Practical Hints in Decorative Printing with Illustrations Engraved on Wood and Printed in Colours at the Type Press* (London: Longman, Hurst, Rees, Orme and Brown, 1822), 73.
46 Savage, *Practical Hints*, 73.
47 Meredith Davis, *Graphic Design Theory* (London: Thames and Hudson, 2012), 86.
48 John R. Doyle and Paul A. Bottomley, 'The Massage in the Medium: Transfer of Connotative Meaning from Typeface to Names and Products', *Applied Cognitive Psychology*, 23 (2008), 396–409.
49 Jeffrey Jass and Terry Childers, 'All Dressed Up with Something to Say: Effects of Typeface Semantic Associations on Brand Perceptions and Consumer Memory', *Journal of Consumer Psychology*, 12/2 (2002), 93–106.

NEW LETTER FOUNDRY.

L. I. POUCHÉE,
TYPE FOUNDER,
LITTLE QUEEN-STREET, LONDON.

TYPES
OF THE MOST DURABLE QUALITY, AND OF EVERY CHARACTER.

PRESSES, INK,
AND ALL OTHER REQUISITES FOR PRINTING, FURNISHED WITH PROMPTITUDE, ON TERMS OF ADVANTAGE.

FAC-SIMILES, CHARACTERISTIC DESIGNS,
AND
GENERAL SUBJECTS,
CUT WITH ACCURACY AND TASTE, IN BRASS OR WOOD.

CAST METAL ORNAMENTS
IN GREAT VARIETY, OF IMPROVED EFFECT, FROM DRAWINGS, BY HIGHLY QUALIFIED ARTISTS.

AN EXTENSIVE AND SUPERIOR ASSORTMENT OF

Ornamented Letters
OF ENTIRELY NEW DEVICES,

From well-executed Designs.

BRASS ORNAMENTS FOR PRINTERS AND BOOK-BINDERS.

Book-Binders' Tools of every Description.

HEAD LINES FOR NEWSPAPERS.
Rules, Letters, Card-Borders, &c.
IN STOCK, AND CUT OR CAST TO PATTERN.

☞ THE FANCY LETTER USED IN THIS PAPER, IS FROM THE FOUNDRY.

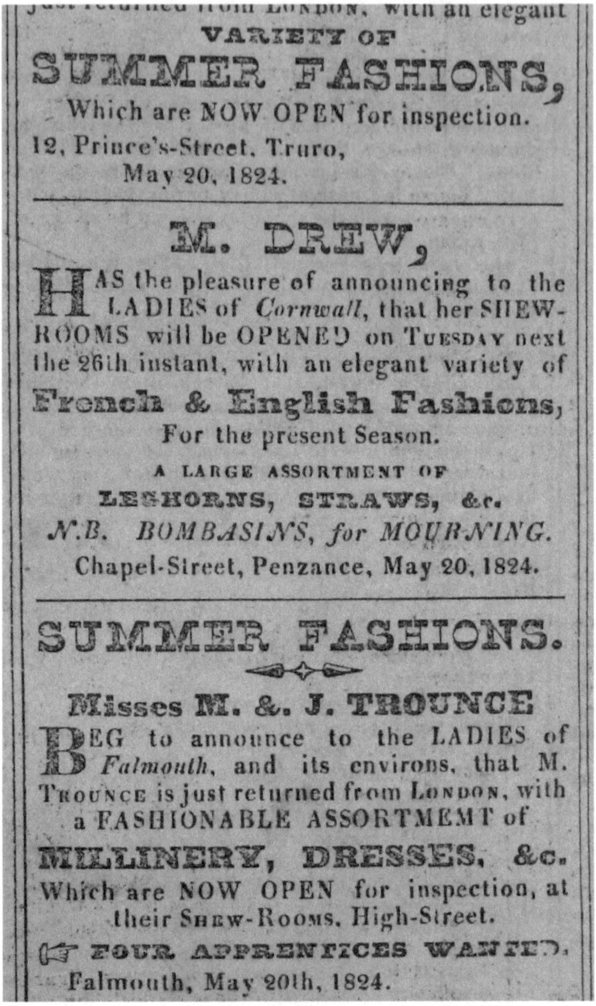

just returned from LONDON, with an elegant
VARIETY OF
SUMMER FASHIONS,
Which are NOW OPEN for inspection.
12, Prince's-Street, Truro,
May 20, 1824.

M. DREW,

HAS the pleasure of announcing to the LADIES of *Cornwall*, that her SHEW-ROOMS will be OPENED on TUESDAY next the 26th instant, with an elegant variety of

French & English Fashions,
For the present Season.
A LARGE ASSORTMENT OF
LEGHORNS, STRAWS, &c.
N.B. BOMBASINS, for MOURNING.
Chapel-Street, Penzance, May 20, 1824.

SUMMER FASHIONS.
→•←
Misses M. & J. TROUNCE

BEG to announce to the LADIES of *Falmouth*, and its environs, that M. TROUNCE is just returned from LONDON, with a FASHIONABLE ASSORTMENT of

MILLINERY, DRESSES, &c.
Which are NOW OPEN for inspection, at their SHEW-ROOMS, High-Street.
☞ FOUR APPRENTICES WANTED.
Falmouth, May 20th, 1824.

Figure 5.3.a. Advertisement for L. I. Pouchée; b. Advertisement using Pouchée types, *The West Briton and Cornwall Advertiser*, 13 February 1824 (details). Images used with the permission of the Royal Institution of Cornwall, Courtney Library.

'Choice Type' and 'Elegant Founts' 129

letters went further to mediate the message and convey its content *literally* in an advertisement produced by the Heard printing house in 1847.[50]

The 'STOCK' advertised is actually livestock (Figure 5.4a) and the word contains within its letters all of the hogs, ewes, steers and cows advertised in the sale. Pouchée's decorated letters are joined on the piece by a compressed Fat Face advertising 'SHORT HORN BULLS', in which the sharp and spiky terminals of the typeface render them a little menacing in spite of the shortness of their horns. The bluntness of Pouchée's plain, trifurcated Tuscan presents the less threatening female 'HEIFERS'. Preceding the decorated 'STOCK', a relatively small, squat Egyptian imbues the words 'BREEDING & FAT' with connotations of fecundity. Annotations on the top left of this advertisement indicate that there were to be '100 plain' and '100 coloured' printed, but 'plain' is the only one to have survived. The Heard printing office also used the Pouchée letters decorated with flowers to announce a 'meeting', the auction of a 'sloop' and the sale of a variety of nursery 'trees' (Figure 5.4b). The job files offer no evidence of any others Heard may have held. Nor did it limit its use of ornamented types to discrete advertising pieces, which are evident, though less vibrantly, in the columns of the *West Briton*.

Advertising in the *West Briton*

TO OUR READERS

We have this day the gratification of presenting the WEST BRITON to its numerous friends in an enlarged format ... for the pleasure of presenting our friends with a sheet which, in point of typographical arrangement is commensurate with the increased importance of our local interests.[51]

---

50   I have used this example from 1847 because it affords opportunities for additional analysis. There are others decorated with farm stock and with flowers that date from 1838.
51   *West Briton* (24 July 1846), 1 (italics in original).

THE

Annual Sale

AT

TRETHURFFE,

(IN THE PARISH OF LADOCK,)

WILL BE HELD

On TUESDAY, the 28th of September next,

WHEN, AS USUAL, A VARIETY OF

BREEDING & FAT STOCK,

CONSISTING OF

HOG RAMS,	FAT OXEN,
STORE EWES,	STEERS,
FAT WETHERS,	COWS & HEIFERS,

ALSO, PURE BRED

SHORT HORN BULLS

AND HEIFERS,

WILL BE OFFERED FOR

Sale by Public Auction.

Refreshments will be provided at One, and the Sale to commence at Two o'clock P.M.

N.B. Three months' credit will be given to purchasers of the Breeding Stock on approved security.

T. GERRANS,

AUCTIONEER &c.

Grampound August 28, 1847.

HEARD AND SONS, PRINTERS, BOOKBINDERS, AND STATIONERS, TRURO.

'Choice Type' and 'Elegant Founts' 131

Figure 5.4.a. Advertising poster for T. Gerrans, Auctioneer &c, Heard and Sons, 1847; b. Advertising poster for W. Salter, Heard and Sons, 1839. Images used with the permission of the Royal Institution of Cornwall, Courtney Library (Heard Collection).

Developments in newspaper advertising that had begun in the early 1800s gained momentum in the years Elizabeth managed the *West Briton*. By tradition, advertisements appeared on the first page of newspapers, but such was the demand that a few years later they had spilt over onto the following pages, and this demand continued to increase. Elizabeth purchased new types in March 1828, which allowed her to increase the advertising and editorial content within the existing six columns.[52] She also replaced the existing masthead typeface with a Fat Face. A further increase in size to eight columns in 1846 heralded a masthead change to

---

52 *West Briton* (21 March 1828), 4. John had begun with five and increased it to six in 1820 and Elizabeth had increased it to seven by 1842.

a blackletter with elaborately decorated initial letters for each word. This points to a considered response to changing conditions, including the acquisition of new types. Elizabeth advised her readers that the *West Briton* not only had the highest circulation, but was 'the largest sheet, at its price, in the west of England', each a boon to readers and advertisers alike.[53] It was enlarged again in 1851, this time increasing its four pages to eight, with the change alluded to in an editorial she addressed 'to our advertising friends, [to whom] then, we have to intimate that this department of the paper shall receive additional care, and our new type and increased space will enable us to give greater prominence to their favours'.[54]

Taking the opportunity to reinforce this message, Elizabeth advertised 'to printers' the sale of a cistern for wetting paper, which was being sold due to the 'enlargement of the West Briton'.[55] In 1860 the newspaper was again enlarged and 'new and improved type' was purchased to celebrate its fiftieth anniversary.[56] The jubilee number was printed for the first time on a flatbed, steam-operated press, a far cry from John's first edition in 1810, which was small in size and printed on a hand-operated press. As usual, the typographic arrangements kept pace with these changes. Earlier text-based and column-constrained advertisements utilized simple generic woodcuts and employed larger versions of the standard eighteenth-century blackletter and script typefaces, and italic founts. Gradually the advertisements became larger and more enticing through an increasing use of more imaginative imagery. This followed a trend in advertising, prompted by a shift in the understanding of goods and services as culturally symbolic, rather than solely utilitarian and 'the persuasive, emotional [and symbolic] dimensions of advertising' were well established by the early nineteenth century.[57] For the most part, these advertisements (for products such as Warren's Blacking and the London Genuine Tea Company) were sent intact – bar the name

53   *West Briton* (24 July 1846), 1.
54   *West Briton* (3 January 1851), 4.
55   'To printers', *West Briton* (8 January 1851), 3.
56   *The West Briton through 150 Years*, 15.
57   Liz McFall and Paul du Gay, 'Consuming Advertising: Consuming Cultural History', in Alison Anderson, Kevin Meethan, R. Steven Miles, and Steven Miles, eds, *The Changing Consumer: Markets and Meanings* (London: Routledge, 2002), 74–89.

of the local distributor – to newspapers across Britain. This produced a culturally progressive effect of erasing both space and time and connecting socially aspirational shoe polishers and tea drinkers across the kingdom. Type designs also entered into this new world.

With the exception of a Figgins Tuscan in 1820 on the newspaper's masthead, John had not used display faces for headings. Only in 1821 did he deploy the soon-to-become ubiquitous Egyptian. Elizabeth was more typographically adventurous and made good use of the 'terse and compact' Egyptian.[58] In addition to its popular appeal, it was an ideal face for a newspaper as it worked compatibly with the body type. By 1824 Elizabeth was using a number of these small but highly visible faces for the headings and sub-headings in the newspaper's advertisements. The advertisement for Pouchée types in the editions of 30 January, and 6 and 13 February 1824 were an example of what type design scholar Alexander Lawson notes was a 'hardsell' by founders, a departure from the restrained Latin quotation previously seen in specimen books. In turn Elizabeth promoted the types to her advertisers (Figure 5.3a).[59] A rival newspaper, *The Royal Cornwall Gazette,* perhaps not wanting the *West Briton* to gain an advantage, printed the same advertisement.[60] However, it had to advise its clients that 'their own [fancy types] having not yet arrived' would be supplied by another printer, who was not Elizabeth Heard. Elizabeth added her own comment to the advertisement, noting that 'the fancy letter used in this paper is from the foundry'.[61] We see one of these types at work in Figure 5.3b; the Italian typeface from a number of advertisements in May is among the numerous occasions that she used it in newspaper advertising, sometimes even before she published the Pouchée advertisement. Using the Italian and other similar typefaces changed the look of the newspaper page, which took on something of the visual display of jobbing advertisements, albeit with less exuberance. In addition to the Pouchée advertisement, Elizabeth

58 Gray, *Ornamented Typefaces,* 29.
59 Alexander Lawson, *Anatomy of a Typeface* (Boston: David R. Godine, 1990), 312.
60 *The Royal Cornwall Gazette, Falmouth Packet and Plymouth Journal* (7 February 1824), 1.
61 *West Briton* (30 January 1824), 1.

used other ornamented types to promote her business both in the newspaper and in flyers.

Advertising the Heard Business and Premises

> Mrs Heard and Sons have great pleasure in announcing to their Friends, that the extensive improvements which have for some time past been making in their Premises, BOSCAWEN STREET, *Truro*, being nearly completed, they ... very respectfully solicit the attention of their Friends thereto.[62]

Elizabeth's self-promotion indicates that she was aware of the value of both public relations and the advertising of her own business. Promotion of the various branches of the Heard business took up considerable space in all of the editions of the newspaper held in the Library. In the same announcement that she 'solicit[ed] a continuance' of the favour accorded to her husband in June 1823, Elizabeth advertised that she would satisfy all requirements for printing, bookbinding and 'the very best quality' stationery.[63] By August, she was expressing gratitude for the 'liberal support', at the same time as she advertised the arrival of new books (at '25 per cent under the London prices'), 'PRINTING AND BINDING' ('Executed with Neatness, Accuracy and Dispatch') and '*WRITING PAPERS*' ('on the most reasonable terms').[64] She continued to position her business favourably throughout her life.

As early as 1830 Elizabeth was in competition with nine bookbinders, six booksellers and stationers, eleven insurance agents and six letterpress printers, some in Boscawen Street.[65] Ensuring that prospective advertisers knew what her business offered was an important part of her approach.

62   *West Briton* (16 April 1847), 1 (italics in original).
63   *West Briton* (13 June 1823), 1.
64   *West Briton* (15 August 1823), 3 (italics in original).
65   Extract from Pigot's Directory of Cornwall, 1830, 169–72. Like most printers of the time, the Heard business included most of these somewhat related activities.

'Choice Type' and 'Elegant Founts' 135

One flyer in particular demonstrates the printing office's incidental use of its available typefaces to advertise the goods and services of all the branches of the business. In Figure 5.5a, 'E. HEARD' sets the tone in a large fount of expanded Egyptian. It is followed by 'ALMANACKS' in a tall – dimensionally book-like – fount of compressed Fat Face. Pouchée's Italian announces 'POCKET BOOKS' and a shaded Egyptian introduces 'ANNUALS'. Founts of Egyptian (italic and roman) advertise a 'LIST OF FAIRS' and 'WRITING PAPER' respectively. Sandwiched between these, in one long sentence, are additional offerings set in various founts of text types: upper case, upper and lower case, condensed and otherwise, italic and roman, large and small. A further flyer of the same time is typographically more restrained in terms of its size but shows advertisers a few more of the typefaces available to them. Various items for sale are set in small founts of Figgins Script, upper case condensed sans serif (probably Figgins, again) and Figgins' English Ronde, a script typeface that Figgins hoped would be 'found useful, as a variety for circulars'.[66]

A further tool Elizabeth used to bring her business to the minds of the public was her premises. Most notable on these advertisements is the deployment of the Heard premises, a Georgian building of four storeys, the large ground floor a generously fenestrated frontage. Bookending the image are repetitions of what the Heard business had to offer. The lettering on the building itself declares it to be the premises of the 'West Briton Office', a bookseller, a printer and a stationer. 'Heard' is displayed above each of the two doors. The building was an advertisement in architecture. Displayed in print, it became an advertisement for everything that went on inside the architectural space. The space itself underwent considerable expansion at the end of the 1840s.

The year 1846 had been a particularly good one for the Heards: the larger newspaper sported new types and its increasing circulation rates contributed to the success of all branches of the business. Although there are no figures to indicate a thriving jobbing office, the number and variety of ephemera in the job files suggest that it too enjoyed considerable success. However, by 1847 these were not the only innovations and events; Elizabeth

66 Vincent Figgins, *Specimen of Printing Types* (London: 1834).

had some rather more exciting news to impart to the public. During the year, the Boscawen Street shop was renovated substantially. It already had a significant presence in a street that was known for its genteel shopping establishments: mercers, drapers, chemists and grocers among them. The area around Boscawen Street had been Truro's commercial centre since the eighteenth century, but it had been an important crossroads (with St Nicholas Street) since the twelfth century.[67] Boscawen Street was a newly named thoroughfare, having once been two streets with a row of buildings in between. When this Middle Row was demolished in 1794, the streets which had been Market and Fore Streets became Boscawen Street, called so after Admiral Edward Boscawen.[68] It backed onto the Kenwyn River and so afforded ease of both trade and industry.[69] Hinks points to a renaissance in English provincial towns in the eighteenth century that saw an elevation of culture that was independent of London.[70] By the nineteenth century, Boscawen Street, with its fashionable Georgian buildings, reflected this cultural shift. The buildings accommodated the families, servants and premises of numerous middle-class family businesses; among them were printers who benefited from the growth in consumption and advertising. The 1851 census shows Elizabeth, for example, with three live-in servants, Jane Hodge, Ann Perkin (or Kerkin) and Stephen Tregenza, who also appear on the 1861 census, ten years later.

The newly renovated shop in this fashionable street now took on a more stylish demeanour with an enlarged area to accommodate 'an extensive and valuable collection of books' – advertised in the newspaper on 6 April 1847 and through a flyer on 13 April. On 14 May, under the

---

67 Graeme Kirkham, Cornwall and Scilly Urban Survey: Historical Characterization for Regeneration: Truro, HES Report2003R077, Cornwall City Council, December 2003, <https://books.google.co.nz/books/about/Truro.html?id=UklygEACAAJ&redir_esc=y>, accessed 9 December 2019.
68 'Boscawen Street', Hare family history, <https://sites.google.com/site/harefamilyhistory/truro-cornwall>, accessed 17 November 2017.
69 HES Report, 2003.
70 John Hinks, 'Baskerville's Birmingham: Printing and the English Urban Renaissance', in Caroline Archer-Parré and Malcolm Dick, eds, *John Baskerville: Art and Industry of the Enlightenment* (Liverpool: Liverpool University Press, 2017), 25–41.

ALMANACKS,		ALMANACKS,
POCKET BOOKS,		POCKET BOOKS,
ANNUALS,		ANNUALS,
&c. &c.,		&c. &c.,
FOR 1842.		FOR 1842.

E. HEARD,

PRINTER, BOOKBINDER, BOOKSELLER, STATIONER, &c., &c.,

Boscawen-street, Truro,

HAS JUST RECEIVED A VERY EXTENSIVE ASSORTMENT OF

ALMANACKS,

POCKET BOOKS, &c. FOR 1842,

Of all sizes and prices. Also a great variety of

ANNUALS,

For CHRISTMAS PRESENTS and NEW YEAR'S GIFTS, including the Gallery of Beauty, the Parterre, the Drawing-room Scrap Book, the Keepsake, the Book of Beauty, Heath's Picturesque, the Musical Bijou, the Piano-Forte Album, the Forget Me Not, the Friendship's Offering, &c.

With all ALMANACKS, sold by E. HEARD, will be given a

LIST OF FAIRS,

To be held in Cornwall, in 1842, about which great pains have been taken to make it accurate, and especially to add those places whose fairs have been established within the present year. The list is so arranged, that the whole may be seen at one view, with the month and day on which each is held.

A few New and Second-hand
GOOD TONED PIANO-FORTES FOR SALE OR ON HIRE.

E. H. has always an excellent list of

WRITING PAPERS,

TO BE SOLD REMARKABLY CHEAP.

Figure 5.5. a. Advertising flyer for E. Heard, printer, bookbinder, bookseller, stationer, &c, Heard and Sons 1842; b. *A Sketch of the Interior of the Shop of Mrs Heard and Sons Truro*, c.1847. Images used with the permission of the Royal Institution of Cornwall, Courtney Library (Heard Collection).

heading of 'New Piano Forte Saloon', Elizabeth again promoted the value of her newly renovated shop for its 'Collection of Piano Fortes', such as had never been seen before 'in this part of the Kingdom' and one unlikely to be available outside of London. She repeated these advertisements on 9, 23 and 30 April, and 7 and 21 May, and issued flyers with the same information. Along with these advertisements, she commissioned an engraving of the interior of the shop, a high-studded room lined floor to ceiling, first with wide drawers, then shelves of books. (Figure 5.5b). The room is flooded with light that streams in from the large windows and lunettes in the centre of the image. The image reassures the Victorian viewer that many desirable goods are available at the Heard shop. Paintings and sketches of fashionable people punctuate the wall space, echoing the real people browsing, buying or selling below. Well-stocked glass display cases on the left-hand counter space show off the myriad items for sale. A circular table display presents a series of containers – urns, vases, candle-holders of all shapes and sizes – some plain, some fancy, some exotic. An oval mirror set high on the back wall reflects the shop floor, rendering it visually larger. Beyond the laden table lies a large glass cabinet stuffed with all manner of objects that are too indistinct to identify. Evidence of how Elizabeth used this image remains unknown; unlike the advertising material, it does not indicate print run numbers, so the production run and distribution are also a mystery. There is a lightly coloured version of this view, which brings a certain vivacity to it.[71]

The Research Road Ahead

In spite of what Elizabeth's printed output has to say about her life and work, there is so much I do not know about this mid-nineteenth-century woman of business. At present the apparent lack of business records prevents identification of her printing staff, just as records, possibly yet to emerge, may tell us of her London life. Something that gets a little closer to who she was lies in contemporary reports. A woman of many accolades and obituaries, she was described as a 'gifted young woman' at her marriage, who become Cornwall's 'most able and amiable businesswoman', a woman of 'great business capacity'.[72] An obituary of 'this estimable lady' stated that there was 'no woman connected with the book and newspaper trade who was better known and more respected than Mrs Heard'.[73] So

---

71 Mrs Heards [sic] and Sons Shop Truro (Interior), *Known by Nunn: A Catalogue of Cornish Printers 1750–1850*, <http://www.knownbynunn.org.uk/list-images/entry/6141/>, accessed 7 December 2021.
72 *The West Briton through 150 Years*, 10; 'Obituary', *Royal Cornwall Gazette* (12 September 1867), 3.
73 'Obituary', *The Bookseller*, 668.

widely known was she that the *New York Tribune* published her obituary a few weeks after death.[74] On the Friday after her funeral, the *West Briton* reported that many of the shops were closed and a good number of 'her' townsfolk followed her funeral procession to St Mary's. The mayor, speaking at a town council meeting, reminded the councillors that they 'had recently lost an old inhabitant of the town ... whose memory they must ever revere, as one who was remarkable and pre-eminent among the wise and good inhabitants of the town of Truro'. There followed a number of accolades to her 'great private and social worth', her 'integrity of character', 'the talent she brought to bear on every pursuit' and her 'good deeds' towards the poor. Her son Edward Goodridge, who was present at the meeting, attested that 'if ever there was an excellent and public-spirited woman in the county, she was one'.[75] It is as frustrating as it is intriguing that he goes on to mention the copious correspondence she had with Cornishmen throughout the county and all around the world; correspondence that may exist and simply waits to be found.

While Elizabeth may have learned much from her late husband in his business dealings, his printing sensibilities and his political leanings, I would like to know what she brought to him. The newspapers and job files indicate that she operated within prevailing printing conventions; locating business records may reveal a singular flair for interpreting those protocols and bring to light her relationships with the many men and boys she employed. Further research will seek also to know more of who she was: a woman who was daughter, wife, mother and grandmother, and an inspiration to her fellow Cornishmen and women. She outlived her husband, two of her sons (one, Campbell Charles, seems to have died as an infant) and a daughter. Knowing who she was and how she dealt with the joys and vicissitudes of her life is as intriguing as knowing what she did. While this chapter has brought Elizabeth Heard – woman and businesswoman – a little more into the light, I am confident that ongoing research promises to bring her life and work into even sharper focus.

74 'Mrs Elizabeth Heard', *New York Tribune* (1 November, 1867).
75 'The Late Mrs Heard, of Truro', *West Briton* (19 September 1867), 8.

ERIKA LEDERMAN

6 *Examples of Art Workmanship*: The Victoria and Albert Museum's Educational Publishing Initiative and Its Female Institutional Photographer

Between 1868 and 1871 the South Kensington Museum – now the Victoria and Albert Museum (V&A) – published a series of photographically illustrated volumes under the series title *Examples of Art Workmanship of Various Ages and Countries.* Launched in partnership with the Arundel Society for the Promotion of Art, the series was originally produced for distribution to schools of art as part of an officially sanctioned 'Deposit Loan' programme, with a mandate to extend the visual resources of the South Kensington Museum (SKM) to students. This publishing partnership coincided with the 1868 appointment of Isabel Agnes Cowper (1826–1911), the SKM's first female Official Museum Photographer, whose role in the museum's photographic studio is now slowly being uncovered. This chapter will identify the volumes from the *Art Workmanship* series illustrated with Cowper's photographs, describing the circumstances of production, the series' reception and circulation, and exposing the breadth and agency of Cowper's influential role in the SKM's educational publishing programme. This analysis of Cowper's work and career will also reveal the fictions and biases inherent in prevailing nineteenth-century print culture histories that obscured her professional narrative, exposing the role of gender in the image-making ecology of the museum and the marginalization of women photographers.

Mrs Cowper

On the evening of 8 February 1868, Henry Cole (1808–82), the visionary founding director of the SKM, recorded in his diary a visit to his home by Charlotte Thompson, the widow of Charles Thurston Thompson (1816–68), the SKM's first Official Museum Photographer. Two weeks earlier, Thurston Thompson had died unexpectedly while on official museum business in Paris. His death left the museum without an Official Photographer and his widow had an important message to convey. Cole wrote:

> In the E[venin]g Charlotte [Thompson] came and resolved to have nothing to do with Photography in future: proposed ... that Mrs Cowper sh[oul]d take up the Artistic work but not the Trade.[1]

Considered at face value, Charlotte's message relates to staffing issues of the museum's photographic service, but viewed within the context of the museum's educational publishing activities, it is packed with meaning. Cole's diary entry is thus an excellent starting point for locating the photographs of Isabel Agnes Cowper and uncovering the web of networks she negotiated in order to develop and progress her professional life.

To unpack these meanings it is necessary to consider Charlotte's message within the context of the timeline of the museum's photographic activities. The roots of the SKM photographic service lay in the 1851 Great Exhibition. Cole was intimately involved in the Exhibition's organization, placing Thurston Thompson, his brother-in-law, in charge of photographic arrangements. It was from the profits of the Exhibition that the SKM was established in 1852.[2] With a mandate to encourage wider public engagement with the arts, Cole aimed to 'place objects of the highest art within

---

1   Henry Cole, 'Diary' [Typed transcript] (1868), General Collection, National Art Library.
2   For a history of the V&A see Julius Bryant, *Art and Design for All* (London: V&A Publications, 2012).

the reach of the poorest person'.[3] From the very beginning photography was employed and collected by the SKM towards this purpose. In 1856, when Cole formalized the terms for making 'negatives & positives officially', installing Thurston Thompson as Official Museum Photographer in a dedicated photographic studio, the first museum photographic service came into being.[4] A series of photographs of mirrors on loan at the museum from Thurston Thompson's tenure shows the photographer reflected in the glass. His conscious recording of himself at work in the newly minted profession suggests pride in his work and an increasing public recognition of the new vocation.[5]

'... a Discovery Which Is to Art What the Printing Press Was to Literature'[6]

From the beginning, Cole conceived of the museum's photographic activities as an educational tool to dramatically extend the range of visual resources available to artists and students. This conviction fits with the SKM's status as a division within the Privy Council Committee for Education – essentially a school with a public collection with a mission to progress an arts and design curriculum in Britain. Towards this end, photographs were sourced in tandem with the activities of the Circulation Collection, established to distribute specimens beyond the walls of the

3 Anthony Burton, *Vision & Accident: The Story of The Victoria and Albert Museum* (London: V&A Publications, 1999), 80.
4 Cole, 'Diary' (20 July 1856). For a history of the South Kensington Museum photographic service see Anthony Hamber, *A Higher Branch of Art: Photographing the Fine Arts in England, 1839–1880* (Amsterdam: Gordon and Breach, 1996), 393–470 and John Physick, *Photography and the South Kensington Museum* (London: Victoria and Albert Museum, 1975).
5 See V&A museum nos. 32638, 32639, 33579, 39793, 39833.
6 Alfred H. Wall, 'On Photographic Reproductions', *British Journal of Photography*, 9 (15 April 1862), 145.

institution to regional schools of art. In January 1868 these activities were extended with the Deposit Loan programme, which sanctioned the long-term loan of art examples, (including photographs), to schools of art for use as models and assessment tools, reinforcing the South Kensington collections-based curriculum.[7]

'Post Will Not Be Filled Up at Present'

Thurston Thompson's death on 19 January 1868 was unexpected and disruptive to the flow of museum operations.[8] At the time of his death the number of negatives registered since the service's inception was approximately 7,500.[9] While Thurston Thompson was not the source for all these negatives, his death left a hole in the operation of the photographic service and disrupted the continued production of negatives. Negotiations for the photographically illustrated *Art Workmanship* series would have been in the works at the time of Thurston Thompson's death. The Arundel Society was not in the business of photography, so while the museum had a store of negatives, the partnership would have assumed the continued production of negatives by the museum's Official Photographer.

Three days after Thurston Thompson's funeral the first application for the position vacated by his death was received from a Mr H. Sharpe. By 8 February, when Thurston Thompson's widow made a case for Mrs Cowper, four further applications had been recorded, including one from Stephen

---

7   See Science and Art Department, *Report on the System of Circulation of Art Objects on Loan from the South Kensington Museum for Exhibition: As Carried on by the Department from its First Establishment to the Present Time* (London: George E. Eyre & Spottiswoode, 1881).
8   'Obituary: Charles Thurston Thompson', *The Art-Journal* 30 (1 April 1868), 73.
9   See *Register of Negatives and Lantern Slides* (V&A Museum: 1866–91), Museum Archive, MA/94/4–6.

Examples of Art Workmanship

Thompson (no relation), a well-regarded photographer of antiquities and the fine arts who had worked at the British Museum.[10]

Despite the keen interest from qualified candidates as well as an existing trained assistant, the decision was made to discontinue the position (at least officially).[11] In reply to Stephen Thompson's application the department wrote: 'My Lords consider it undesirable to renew the office of official photographer and accordingly abolish it.'[12] This resolution was reinforced in the published minutes of the department: 'My Lords regret Mr. Thurston Thompson's death, and recognize his services and great ability. Post will not be filled up at present. Division of work among qualified artists to be tried.'[13] Considering that the official minutes confirmed the elimination of the position and the museum was already regularly contracting with outside firms and photographers, it is not surprising that all histories record that the position was abolished. But as anthropologist Anne Laura Stoler has demonstrated, it is often outside the written official prescriptions, among the 'ragged edges' of the archive, where disruptions to the clarity of official mandates are located.[14]

10   See *Abstracts of Correspondence* (V&A Museum: 1868), Museum Archive, MA/4/5, 2–5.
11   During the brief period of Thurston Thompson's illness leading to his death, Assistant Director Richard Thompson also proposed Thurston Thompson's 'man Wright'. See Cole, 'Diary' (18 December 1867).
12   'Applies for Post Vacant Thro the Death of Mr. Thompson' (1868), The National Archives, the Science and Art Department, ED84/145 4959.
13   'Photographer, Official: 12 February 1868', *Précis of the Board Minutes of the Science and Art Department, From 8th July to 23rd December 1869*, Science and Art Department (London: George E. Eyre and William Spottiswoode, H.M.S.O., 1872).
14   Ann Laura Stoler, *Along the Archival Grain* (Princeton: Princeton University Press, 2009), 2.

'Cowper, I. A. Applies for Post'

On 10 February 1868, two days after Cole recorded the visit of Thurston Thompson's widow, an entry in the *Abstracts of Correspondence* records: 'Cowper, I. A. applies for post vacant by Mr. Thompson's death.'[15] The original application has not been located and no official decision on the application is recorded. There is no record of Cowper being paid a salary or an annual 'retainer' as Thurston Thompson received for his services.[16] Yet two weeks later, on 24 February, correspondence from Cowper (now with a gender specific title) is recorded: 'Mrs. Cowper describes order for six negatives.'[17]

From this point on we stumble upon her name repeatedly, written into fragments of the institutional archive, recording photographs and negatives received from 'Mrs Cowper', as well as correspondence relating to her photographic activities at the museum. By 8 July 1868 her address is listed at 3, The Residences, dedicated housing for museum senior staff including Cole and his family.[18] Gathered, these fragments reveal that while Cowper was never formally acknowledged as the Official Museum Photographer, she consistently engaged in photographic activities on behalf of the department for over twenty-three years until her retirement in December 1891, indicating that she was the *de facto* Official Museum Photographer.[19]

Cowper's name is not found among the membership lists of any of the photographic clubs or societies that proliferated from the birth of

15   *Abstracts of Correspondence* (1868), MA/4/5, 6.
16   For details of Thurston Thompson's terms of employment, see *Report from the Select Committee on the South Kensington Museum: Together with the Proceedings of the Committee, Minutes of Evidence, and Appendix* (London: House of Commons, 1860), 77.
17   *Abstracts of Correspondence* (1868), MA/4/5, 12.
18   Library Receiving Room Diary (V&A Museum: 1868), Museum Archive, MA/4/5, 129.
19   See *Photographs Registers* (V&A Museum: 1868–91), Museum Archive, MA/63/5/8–17; *Register of Negatives* (1868–91); MA/95/4–6 *Library Receiving Room Diary* (1868–91), MA/34/7–23; and *Abstracts of Correspondence* (1868–91), MA/4/5–41.

the medium and there is no evidence of her connection to these types of professional networks.[20] However, London census records provide a clue to a different but important network for Cowper – her family: 3, The Residences, South Kensington lists Richard Thompson, the SKM 'Assistant Director', as 'head' of the household, with Cowper, whose profession is listed as 'photographer', recorded as 'sister'. The eight other residents included two 'sisters', two 'nephews', two 'nieces' and two 'servants'. Comparing this data to previous census years reveals that Richard, Isabel and her sisters were siblings to the recently deceased Charles Thurston Thompson, and establishes that Cowper lived at the museum with her surviving siblings and four surviving children.[21]

The Thompson siblings were born to John Thompson, one of the most eminent wood engravers of his time, and his wife Harriot. Like their father, the Thompson children worked as wood engravers, publishing their work in popular books from the late 1830s through the 1840s. Thurston Thompson and Cowper even engraved illustrations for the critic John Ruskin's only work of fiction, *The King of the Golden River*, a children's fairy tale written for thirteen-year-old 'Effie' Gray (of the famous Victorian love triangle that included Ruskin whom Gray left to marry the Pre-Raphaelite painter John Everett Millais).[22] Cole was a frequent visitor to the Thompson household; when he wrote his treatise declaring wood-engraving to be a 'honourable, elegant and lucrative employment … every way becoming [ladies'] sex and habits', he had Cowper and her sisters in mind and he subsequently commissioned them to produce wood-engravings for his series of guides to important British galleries published in the 1840s.[23]

20   For a discussion of women and photographic clubs see Nicole Hudgins, *The Gender of Photography: How Masculine and Feminine Values Shaped the History of Nineteenth-Century Photography* (London: Bloomsbury Visual Arts, 2020), 137–206.
21   'Census London 1871', <ukcensusonline.com>.
22   Cowper's known biographical details to date have been published in Erika Lederman, 'Isabel Agnes Cowper: Official Museum Photographer at the V&A Museum', in *Feminism and Museums: Intervention, Disruption and Change Volume Two* (Edinburgh: Museums etc., 2018), 560–600.
23   Anon [Henry Cole], 'Modern Wood Engraving', *London and Westminster Review* (July 1838), 145–52.

Cowper's familial links to the network of photographic and print-making communities extended beyond her brother and father. Her late husband, Charles Cowper, whom she married in 1852, was just as deeply enmeshed in the communities. Charles, a chemist, had patented various inventions in photography and previously worked for Chance Brothers, the leading producers of photographic glass.[24] He also had deep roots in the world of printing, his father being one half of the team that invented a steam-powered press featured at the Great Exhibition.[25]

When Charles died in 1860, Isabel, with four young children and pregnant, had a family to support. There are many well-documented studies on the ways that gender constrained nineteenth-century women's abilities to create livelihoods for themselves. More recently, there have been studies highlighting the creative ways women went about procuring paid work within these constraints.[26] Cowper's career at the SKM is representative of one such 'creative way', illustrating how family connections were put to work as a resource for employment opportunities. Cowper's subsequent appearance contributing to the production of photographically illustrated books at the SKM is representative not only of what Elizabeth Edwards and Christopher Morton have referred to as the 'easy flow' that existed during the late nineteenth century between photography, engraving and printing, but is also evidence of the important role that family connections played in the professional lives of female photographers.[27]

24 'Charles Cowper', *Grace's Guide* (1862).
25 '1851 Great Exhibition: Official Catalogue: Class VI: Edward Cowper', *Grace's Guide* (1851).
26 For an analysis of the economic and social conditions of nineteenth-century working-class women see Sonya O. Rose, *Limited Livelihoods* (Hoboken: Taylor and Francis, 2012). For an analysis specific to women and the arts see Kyriaki Hadjiafxendi and Patricia Zakreski, eds, *Crafting the Woman Professional in the Long Nineteenth-Century: Artistry and Industry in Britain* (Abingdon: Routledge, 2016).
27 Elizabeth Edwards and Christopher Morton, eds, *Photographs, Museums, Collections* (London: Bloomsbury Academic, 2015), 9. Regarding the role of family in the nineteenth-century photographic community and museums see Thomas Galifot, 'La Parentèle au Risque de la Photographie? Amateures et Professionnelles au XIXe Siècle et au Début du XXe Siècle (France, Grande-Bretagne, États-Unis)', in *Parent-Elles* …. (Poitiers: Musée Sainte-Croix, l'Université de Poitiers [Criham]

Cowper probably acquired her skills in photography from both her brother and her husband. While no records beyond census data have been found concerning Cowper's activities between the time of her husband's death and her subsequent employment at the SKM, Cole's diary entry of 6 November 1867 provides a clue. He writes: 'Paris: Thurston Thompson arrived with Mrs Cowper.'[28] We know that Thurston Thompson was in Paris on official museum business through the negatives he made and Cole's diary entries. Cowper's appearance with him was probably in the role of assistant. This is not unusual; recent gender-focused research into the history of photography has shown that nineteenth-century women produced, exhibited and wrote about photography; they experimented with photographic technologies and performed a range of what are considered the ancillary roles (such as colourists, studio managers and retouchers). Thanks to this scholarship we know that Julia Margaret Cameron, for example, was one of *many* nineteenth-century female photographers, and that female photographic practices were not limited strictly to 'lady amateurs'.[29]

Cowper's skill as an accomplished wood-engraver, as well as her experience assisting her brother would have prepared her well for a role in the production of negatives for the photographically illustrated books published by the SKM. She would have developed the highly specialized visual skills to see images in reverse as well as to swap dark for light, skills that would enable her to quickly and accurately 'read' the quality of a negative

---

et l'association Archives of Women Artists, Research and Exhibitions, 2017) and Lynne Teather, 'Museum Keepers: The Museums Association and the Growth of Museum Professionalism', *Museum Management and Curatorship* 9 (1990), 25–41.

28   Cole, 'Diary' (1967).

29   Recent publications on the early history of women in photography include, Luce LeBart and Marie Robert, *Une histoire mondiale des femmes photographes* (Paris: Les Éditions Textuel, 2020); Naomi Rosenblum, *A History of Women Photographers* (New York: Abbeville Press Publishers, 2010); Marie Robert, Ulrich Pohlmann and Thomas Galifot, *Qui a peur des femmes photographes?* (Paris: Musée d'Orsay and the Musée de l'Orangerie, Éditions Hazan, 2016); Hudgins, *The Gender of Photography*; Lena Johannesson, Gunilla Knape and Eva Dahlman, *Women Photographers: European Experience* (Gothenburg: Acta Universitatis Gothoburgiensis, 2004).

and its suitability for printing. Cowper's (non)employment was a perfect pairing of existing skills with professional responsibilities.

'Under the Sanction of the Science and Art Department, for the Use of Schools of Art and Amateurs'

Until the mid-1860s sales of photographs at the SKM consisted mostly of loose prints or portfolios, with only a handful presenting as illustrations in commercially published books or catalogues.[30] This limited circulation coincided with the development and wide dissemination of the wet collodion on glass process. Even in large sizes these new rigid negatives were easier to manage than the previous calotype paper negatives developed by William Henry Fox Talbot. Used in conjunction with albumized paper, the glass negatives produced practically grainless prints, rendering unsurpassed detail and making them particularly well-suited for the commercial reproduction of works of art. The technology was rapidly adopted by the photographic community, including the SKM studio, and became the dominant process by the end of the 1850s.[31]

Despite these technological developments, few photographically illustrated publications were published by the SKM. This was due to a variety of factors, not least of which was the inability to integrate text and

---

30   Two early examples of photographically illustrated SKM publications include John Charles Robinson, *Catalogue of the Soulages Collection; Being a Descriptive Inventory of a Collection of Works of Decorative Art, Formerly in the Possession of M. Jules Soulages of Toulouse, Now ... Exhibited ... at the Museum of Ornamental Art, Marlborough House* (London: Chapman and Hall, 1856) and John Charles Robinson, *Photographic Illustrations of Works in Various Sections of the Collection* (London: Science and Art Department of the Committee of Council on Education, 1859). See also the bibliography of V&A publications, Elizabeth James, *The Victoria and Albert Museum: A Bibliography and Exhibition Chronology, 1852–1996* (London: Fitzroy Dearborn in association with the Victoria and Albert Museum, 1998).

31   Hamber, *A Higher Branch of Art*, 79–81.

photographs, a practice that would only emerge with the development of photomechanical processes in the 1880s.[32] Previously, while photography might be employed in the execution of other book illustration processes, such as wood-engraving, photographically illustrated books involving the labour-intensive mounting of individual prints onto the page, were not yet pre-eminent.[33]

From the very beginning the museum struggled to meet the public appetite for reproductions. The publishing partnership behind the seventeen volumes of *Examples of Art Workmanship* that were eventually published addressed this issue. Conceptually, it was an extension of an existing trade agreement between the Arundel Society and the SKM that transferred the sale and distribution of museum reproductions to the authority of the Society with the aim to distribute art reproductions made by the Science and Art Department (the governing body of the museum) to schools of art and the public in a more efficient and cost-effective way.[34] As part of the agreement the Society maintained a dedicated public sales room on museum premises, decorated with framed specimens and stocked with thematically arranged 'stall' books of mounted sample prints made from museum negatives.[35] This set-up encouraged the SKM to venture more boldly into photographically illustrated books, starting with volumes documenting the museum's highly popular series of loan portrait exhibitions in the mid-1860s.[36] In January 1868 the formal publishing partnership

32 See Hamber, *A Higher Branch of Art*, 38–51.
33 For a history of the use of photography in the production of photomechanical images see Geoffrey Belknap, *From a Photograph: Authenticity, Science and the Periodical Press, 1870–1890* (London: Bloomsbury Academic, 2016). See also Anthony Hamber, 'Facsimile, Scholarship, and Commerce: Aspects of the Photographically Illustrated Art Book (1839–80)', in Stephen Bann, ed., *Art and the Early Photographic Album* (Washington: National Gallery of Art, 2011), 123–50.
34 See extract from minutes in *Catalogues of Reproductions of Objects of Art: Electrotypes, Plaster Casts, Fictile Ivories, Chromolithography; Etchings, Photographs* (London: George E. Eyre and William Spottiswoode, H.M.S.O., 1869), n.p.
35 Hamber, *A Higher Branch of the Art*, 309.
36 For a chronological list of the SKM's nineteenth-century photographically illustrated publications see *Appendix B* in Hamber, *A Higher Branch of the Art*, 465.

with the Arundel Society was sanctioned by the Government through a minute of the House of Lords. As part of the agreement production was outsourced, with Cundall & Fleming engaged to print the albumen prints from museum negatives and the manufacture and binding handled by the firm of Bell & Daldy. The first volumes in the series of *Examples of Art Workmanship of Various Ages and Countries,* subtitled 'Under the Sanction of the Science and Art Department, for the Use of Schools of Art and Amateurs' launched in July 1868.[37]

Each title in the series covered a specific area of study of the decorative arts and architecture. In all instances but one they were issued in large folio format, consisting mostly of twenty labelled albumen prints mounted one to the page, accompanied by a letterpress title page and a list of photographs, with some volumes supplemented with an introduction or historical essay. The volumes destined for circulation to national schools of art and design were bound in Morocco leather, others were bound in printed card to be used in the National Art Library and South Kensington Museum Board Room as promotional material.

Examples of Art Workmanship of Various Ages and Countries

Of the seventeen volumes that were eventually published, four are illustrated exclusively with photographs made from Cowper's negatives. We know this from entries identifying them as such in the *Photographs Register, Register of Negatives* and, if the negatives have survived, through Cowper's signature on the negatives themselves, as seen in Figure 6.1.[38] One of the earliest volumes to be published, *The Treasure of Petrossa*, documents the SKM's first. international loan exhibition borrowed from the Romanian Government (Figure 6.2). It is illustrated exclusively with photographs made from Cowper's first negatives produced for the SKM.[39]

---

37 Hamber, *A Higher Branch of the Art*, 309.
38 The surviving glass negatives from the SKM's nineteenth-century photographic service, part of the V&A Museum Archive are currently being surveyed.
39 Register of Negatives (1868), MA/95/4, entry nos. 7543 to 7556.

Examples of Art Workmanship 153

Figure 6.1. *Negative No. 9088* (collodion on glass plate), Isabel Agnes Cowper
© Victoria and Albert Museum, London.

Cowper's next book was *Musical Instruments in the South Kensington Museum*, completed in 1869.[40] In 1871, Cowper produced twenty-four negatives for *Designs for Silversmiths*, photographing a selection of metalwork designs from the National Art Library.[41] The negatives for the

---

40 See *Register of Negatives* (1869), MA/95/4, entry nos. 8947 to 8966.
41 See *Register of Negatives* (1870), MA/95/4, entry nos. 9086 to 9097.

photographs used in the final volume in the series, *Fans of All Countries*, documented the May 1870 South Kensington Museum loan exhibition of fans.[42] None of these volumes were attributed to Cowper, though the surviving negatives used to make the photographs included in these volumes are marked with Cowper's signature, scratched into the collodion emulsion as seen in Figure 6.1.

The remaining thirteen volumes were produced from the stores of existing negatives, the majority made by Thurston Thompson, with one volume employing the negatives of Joseph Cundall and two illustrated with photographs by Pietro Dovizielli, commissioned by Cole in 1859 to document buildings in Rome.[43]

On at least two occasions Cowper contributed work to fill in the gaps of illustrations when existing negatives did not suffice. The first title to be released was a survey of the architectural ornament of the Cathedral of Santiago de Compostela in Spain with a special emphasis on the Portico de la Gloria, illustrated with Thurston Thompson's negatives made while on a dedicated overseas photographic campaign.[44] In this instance the photographer's name, Thurston Thompson, is printed on the title page, suggesting the level of renown that he had achieved as an institutional photographer. But, for the purposes of this history, a more telling detail is found in the index of the photographs. A symbol at the bottom of the page directs the reader: 'From their position in the Portico, the Archivolt and Tympanum of the Central Doorway could not be satisfactorily photographed; Nos 12, 13 and 14 were therefore taken from the Casts in the South Kensington Museum.'[45] We know that the cast of the Portico de la

42 See *Photographs Register* (1870), MA/63/5/8, museum nos. 70192 to 70199 and 70204 to 70215.
43 *See* Martin Barnes and Christopher Whitehead, 'The "Suggestiveness" of Roman Architecture: Henry Cole and Pietro Dovizielli's Photographic Survey of 1859', *Architectural History*, 41 (1998), 192–207.
44 For a detailed account of Thurston Thompson's work in Spain and Portugal see Lee Fontanella, *Charles Thurston Thompson E O Proxecto Fotográfico Ibérico* (Coruña, Spain: Xunta de Galicia, Consellería de Cultura e Comunicacion Social, Dirección Xeral de Medios de Comunicacion Social e Audiovisual, 1996).
45 Charles Thurston Thompson, *Examples of Art Workmanship of Various Ages and Countries: The Cathedral of Santiago de Compostella in Spain, Showing Especially the*

Examples of Art Workmanship 155

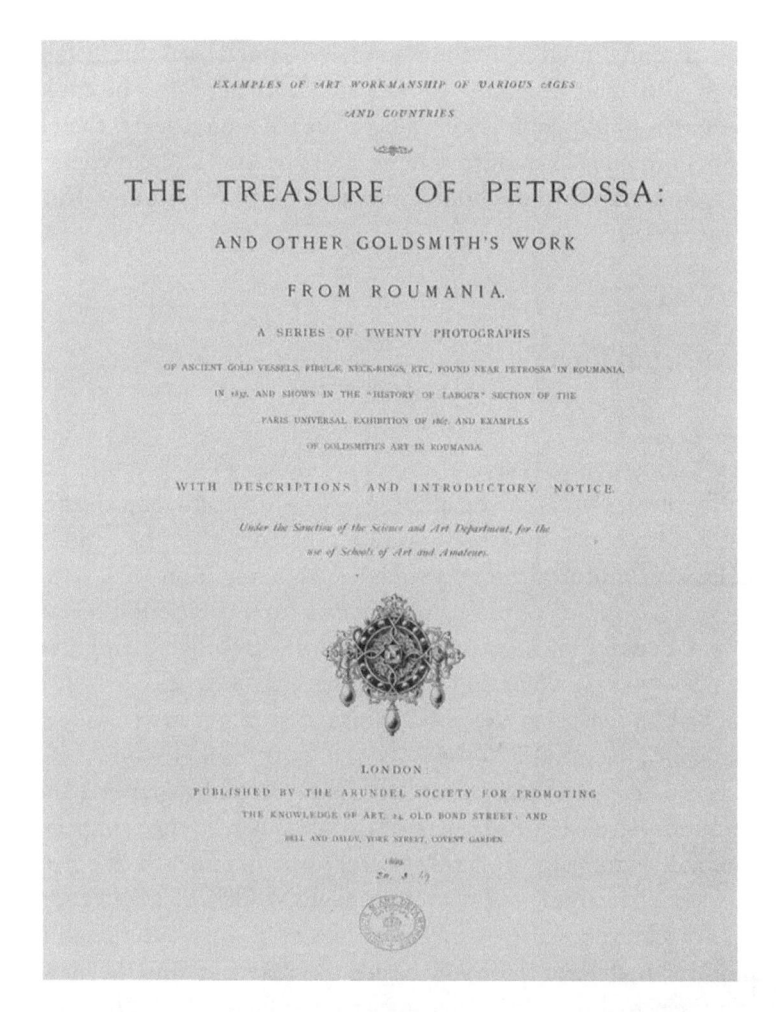

Figure 6.2. *The Treasure of Petrossa and Other Goldsmith's Work from Roumania: A Series of Twenty Photographs*, London: The Arundel Society for Promoting the Knowledge of Art and Bell & Daldy, 1869, title page © Victoria and Albert Museum, London.

Sculpture of the Pórtico de la Gloria by Mestre Mateo. A Series of Twenty Photographs Recently Taken by the Late Thurston Thompson. Under the Sanction of the Science and Art Department (London: Arundel Society for Promoting the Knowledge of Art, 1868).

Gloria (currently installed in the V&A Cast Courts) was not installed at the SKM until after Thurston Thompson's death, and thus he could not have taken the photographs. According to the museum registers these views were 'photographed from the cast in the SKM by Mrs. I. A. Cowper', yet all twenty photographs in the book are attributed to her brother Thurston Thompson.[46]

The 'Museum Effect'

There is a consistency of style throughout Cowper's contribution to the series. In most instances she photographed museum objects floating against a plain contrasting background, centred within the frame, with small margins, uniformly lit and removed from any contextual setting or background. A survey of museum negatives from this period reveals the consistent masking of negatives, a process of carefully coating the area of the plate glass surrounding the photograph (with either iron oxide or lampblack), removing any visual 'noise' that might exist as a result of cracked collodion emulsion, shadows or a 'busy' background. This practice accentuates the contrast between the object photographed and the background. Because the absence of extraneous references impacts the viewer's ability to gauge dimensions and sometimes depth, the masking process was oftentimes used to create a slight shadow to imply a sense of depth. To achieve a sense of scale, Cowper often inserted a small block reading 'one inch' into the frame beside the object, aiding the viewer to fathom the actual size of the object, as seen in Figure 6.3.[47] The presentation of objects in this manner is representative of what Svetlana Alpers has described as 'the museum effect': the isolation of an object from its context and subsequent transformation into art through the practice of

---

46 See *Photographs Register* (1868), MA/63/5/8, museum nos. 60135–60137 and 60798.
47 This is a method that was also employed by Thurston Thompson who, in addition to the scale, often included a small block with his name and title in the frame.

Examples of Art Workmanship 157

Figure 6.3. *Plate No. 6, Twelve-sided Vessel* (albumen print), Isabel Agnes Cowper, in *The Treasure of Petrossa and Other Goldsmith's Work from Roumania: A Series of Twenty Photographs*, London: The Arundel Society for Promoting the Knowledge of Art and Bell & Daldy, 1869 © Victoria and Albert Museum, London.

'attentive viewing'.[48] Presented in this way, accompanied by connoisseurial text, these volumes and the accompanying mounted photographs were put to work performing the didactic function of knowledge production. While this serves to control interpretation of the object, as Elizabeth Edwards repeatedly demonstrates, the 'subjective noise around photographic objects is deafening'.[49] In this instance, one could argue that the 'subjective noise' following from this presentation is the deafening silence of Isabel Agnes Cowper.

48 Svetlana Alpers, 'The Museum as a Way of Seeing', in *Exhibiting Cultures: The Poetics and Politics of Museum Display* (Washington: Smithsonian Institution Press, 1991), 27.
49 Elizabeth Edwards, *Raw Histories* (Oxford: Berg, 2010), 58.

Circulation

In the surviving National Art Library volumes from the series one still finds copies of department labels documenting the journey these volumes made among the schools of art as part of the Deposit Loan programme. A volume of *Italian Jewellery as Worn by the Peasants of Italy* travelled from Dudley, to Leamington, to Barrow-in-Furness, to Tunbridge Wells, to Southend, and back to Dudley and Barrow-in-Furness. Appendices attached to departmental *Annual Reports* provide data concerning the number of loans per year for each title. As an example, in 1872 the four volumes illustrated with photographs from negatives made exclusively by Cowper travelled to over 230 schools. During the years they were circulated, copies of each title were lent to approximately thirty different schools of art, though the more popular titles might be lent to over 100 different schools.[50]

The volumes were announced and reviewed in both the popular and art press. This contributed to their circulation internationally among the nascent museums and schools of art and design of North America and throughout the Empire.[51] The 'South Kensington System', with its deployment of material collections, was frequently emulated. 'This is the vision of South Kensington that was so attractive in the United States and throughout the Empire. What was copied by museums like the Metropolitan in New York was not South Kensington's type of collecting, but its usefulness, its educational vision.'[52] Ongoing research locates these volumes

50 *Nineteenth Report of the Science and Art Department of the Committee of Council on Education with Appendices* (London: George E. Eyre and William Spottiswoode, H.M.S.O, 1872), 438–9.
51 See, for example, 'The Arundel Society Will Shortly Publish ...', *The Express (London)* (*27 June 1868*), *3*; 'Photographs Taken for the Department of Science And Art', *The British Journal of Photography 14/361 (5 April 1867), 161;* 'Photography and the Fine Arts', *British Journal of Photography 15/426 (3 July 1868), 321;* 'The South Kensington Museum: The Photographs', *The Art-Journal 31 (1 January 1869), 18–19;* 'Fine-Art Gossip', *The Athenaeum 2122* (27 June 1868), 899.
52 Bruce Robinson, 'The South Kensington Museum in Context: An Alternative History', *Museum and Society*, 2:1 (2004), 9.

in the libraries of many of the North American museums and schools of art and design founded in the second half of the nineteenth century (including Philadelphia, Boston, Washington DC, Cincinnati, New York and Ontario), acquired as resources to support a collections-based curriculum modelled on South Kensington. Copies are also being uncovered in the databases of art libraries in Europe, including the Kunstbibliothek of the Staatliche Museen zu Berlin.[53] By 1871 no further *Art Workmanship* volumes were produced. Why the series was discontinued is unclear, though records suggest the enterprise was not profitable for either party.[54]

'Artistic Work but Not the Trade'

When Charlotte, Thurston Thompson's widow, stated that Cowper should take up the 'artistic work and not the trade' she was responding to a very specific set of circumstances concerning the operations of the photographic studio at the SKM at that time: circumstances that, as I will show, made Cowper a perfect candidate for the job. At the most literal level, the distinction between 'artistic' and 'trade' refers to the production of negatives, as opposed to the printing of positives from the negatives and the subsequent sale and distribution of those positives to the public. Charlotte's statement suggests that Cowper was hired to produce negatives, with the 'trade' to be handled by other firms. This is relevant in the context of the early reception of the museum's photographic service. In 1859 Cole had a plan to expand photography operations at the SKM. To this end the SKM was authorized to issue photographs of works of art to the public at cost, making the availability of cheap public photographs of works of art official government policy. This allowed for funding and a scaling up of the service, centralizing all government institutional photographic

---

53   For memo regarding distribution of volumes to Europe, see *Abstracts of Correspondence* (1869), MA/4/8, 66.

54   See *Abstracts of Correspondence* (1871), MA/4/10, 100 & 104. For details of Arundel Society's diminishing returns see also Hamber (1996), 309.

activities, including those of the British Museum, at South Kensington. On 1 October 1859 an item in the *British Journal of Photography* announced that the Office for Official Photography was open for business.[55]

Trade professionals, arguing that the Government unfairly undercut their prices and interfered with their ability to conduct business, fervently opposed this policy. The evidentiary statement taken at the 1860 Special Select Committee hearing from John Scott of the firm Colnaghi & Co. put it succinctly: 'It puts the entire monopoly of photography in the hands of a Government Department armed with the power to do that with the public money, which we have to perform with our own.' Scott, speaking on behalf of the photographic profession, deeply resented the special access to a national collection afforded to Thurston Thompson. He stated: 'My object is to show the operation of the Department of Science and Art upon our business, and thus upon the interests of photography in general; ... showing the extreme jealousy with which the interests of Mr Thurston Thompson were guarded by the department, and how they endeavoured to shut out every other photographer from everything touching that department.'[56] To sharpen the point, Scott noted that Thurston Thompson also happened to be Cole's brother-in-law, implicitly adding nepotism to the list of complaints. He declared: 'Mr. Thurston Thompson is not only photographer to the South Kensington Museum, but he is also bound to Mr. Cole by ties of relationship ... [A]nd Mr. Cole would naturally feel interested in what his own relative does, apart from his being photographer to the department.'[57]

As it turns out, it is possible that members of the trade opposing the establishment of the SKM Office for Official Photography experienced a period of *schadenfreude*. Despite Government support, the SKM photographic studio became a victim of its own success. The low costs increased

---

55 'Photographs taken for Government Institutions', *The British Journal of Photography* 6 (1859), 245.
56 *Report from the Select Committee* (1860), 48.
57 *Report from the Select Committee* (1860), 57. For an analysis of this controversial period of photographic activities at the SKM see Ronan Deazley, 'Photography, Copyright and the South Kensington Experiment', in Estelle Derclaye, ed., *Copyright And Cultural Heritage: Preservation and Access to Works on a Digital World* (Cheltenham: Edward Elgar Publishing, 2010), 77–110.

public demand to breaking point. The service, even with the support of extra staff for printing and expanded facilities, was unable to meet the increased orders and by 1863 most printing from negatives at the SKM ceased. Arrangements with various firms were put in place to meet the demand, but these proved equally unsatisfactory.[58]

In 1866 the first partnership with the Arundel Society was announced in a pair of Board minutes:

> In reference to the distribution of Art examples; after taking into consideration the several systems which had been adopted, either of direct sale by the Department to art Schools, &c., or by sale through Agents in the ordinary channels of trade, their Lordships were led to believe that a system might be adopted by which a public Society, not looking to large profits, might be found willing to undertake the responsibility of all commercial transactions connected with the purchase and sale of examples …. In reference to a communication on the same subject subsequently received from the ARUNDEL SOCIETY FOR PROMOTING THE KNOWLEDGE OF ART, their Lordships considered that Society a peculiarly eligible channel for assisting the action of the Department, and directed that arrangements for the publication and sale of Photographs, and other Art examples produced by the Science and Art Department, should forthwith be entered into with the Arundel Society.[59]

The partnership with the Arundel Society addressed the concerns of both the trade and the Department. As noted in the press: 'It will be remembered that some years ago objections were raised in the trade against the sale of photographs at low prices by the Government Department. To make things pleasant all round, the Arundel Society kindly consented to be the cat's paw on certain valid considerations.'[60] The arrangement meant that the trade was unable to levy accusations of monopolistic activities

---

58 Physick, *Photography and the South Kensington Museum*, 14.
59 As excerpted in *Examples of Art Workmanship of Various Ages and Countries: Italian Jewellery as Worn by the Peasants of Italy. Collected by Signor Castellani and Purchased from the Paris Universal Exhibition for the South Kensington Museum. Under the Sanction of the Science and Art Department, for the Use of the Schools of Art and Amateurs* (London: Arundel Society for Promoting the Knowledge of Art, 1868), n.p.
60 'Five Years of The Arundel Society', *The Art-Journal*, 36 (1874), 40.

and Thurston Thompson (Cole's brother-in-law), with a low tolerance for rivals, remained as Official Museum Photographer.[61]

With Thurston Thompson's death, installing a woman (who also happened to be related to Cole) as Official Museum Photographer would probably be overlooked by a trade agitated by what they believed to be unfair practices on the part of the Department. Cowper's (non)hire, effected as an informal arrangement, with compensation calculated per job, dodged the contempt already heaped upon the department (and Cole) concerning the previous arrangements of Thurston Thompson's employ, while allowing the SKM to maintain control of the production of negatives (and keeping the production of negatives 'in the family'). Research has yet to uncover any trade complaints concerning the SKM's apportioning of photographic work to Cowper.

Hiding in Plain Sight

While Cowper's employ seems to have been overlooked by contemporary rivals, she would have been hard to miss by historians of photography and publishing. Cowper, a woman, would not have been eligible for appointment into the Civil Service (as some of the earlier male photographers hired to assist Thurston Thompson had been in 1860) and thus would slip between the cracks of official records; even so, evidence of her work and role in the photographic service is easily identified.[62] Over a period of twenty-three years, between 1868 and 1891, Cowper's name is consistently listed in the *Photographs Registers* as the source for most of the photographs of museum objects. The surviving glass negatives, hundreds made by Cowper, all have either her initials or signature scratched into the collodion emulsion. This functioned as a way for Cowper to track monies owed to her: paid 3 pence per

---

61 *Report from the Select Committee* (1860), 48.
62 Physick, *Photography and the South Kensington Museum*, 14.

square inch of glass (the same paid to Thurston Thompson, though he was also on an annual retainer), marked negatives facilitated the tally of amounts due.[63] Similarly, Cowper is frequently referenced as a source in the *Library Receiving Room Diary*, where photographs were collected before the establishment of the Photographs Section, and a search of the *Abstracts of Correspondence* from the years of Cowper's residence documents her regularly submitted invoices.

Even after the *Art Workmanship* series ceased publication, Cowper continued to be responsible for most of the museum photography until her retirement in 1891. During her tenure she documented the construction of museum buildings, performed a survey of all the department's glass negatives, calculated costs for the photographing of the Bayeux tapestries and even took pictures of Cole's children. And she continued to take photographs of museum objects, many of which were used for books, lantern slides, journals and newspapers, including the popular press, eventually being used in conjunction with the photomechanical processes that would soon be regularly employed.[64]

Cowper was not without some sense of self-regard in terms of her skills as a photographer. Between 1871 and 1874 she exhibited examples of her work in the annual London International Exhibitions – in 1871 they were displayed directly adjacent to the work of renowned photographer Julia Margaret Cameron (1815–79).[65] These exhibitions were reviewed in the photographic press, with one mention of Cowper placed under the heading 'Pictures Most Worthy of Notice'.[66] And if there was any doubt

---

63 The *Register of Negatives* frequently notes the negative size in square inches and the amount paid, allowing for the determination of this statistic.
64 For an example of the use of Cowper's photographs by the popular press, see 'The Loan Art Collection In South Kensington Museum', *The Illustrated London News* 52 (18 April 1868), 393.
65 *Official Catalogues of the London International Exhibition* (London: J. M. Johnson & Sons, 1871, 1872, 1873, 1874).
66 'International Exhibition', *British Journal of Photography*, 18:590 (25 August 1871), 401. See also *BJOP* 18/576 (19 May 1871), 228; 20:679 (9 May 1873), 216; 21:727 (10 April 1874), 169. Cowper was also cited for her skill in the *Art-Journal* by critic F. Roubiliac Conder, who noted Cowper's 'silver photographs of lace for the South

of the extent of her responsibilities, Cowper in her letter of resignation cleared things up:

> In consequence of the retirement of my brother Mr. R. A. Thompson and removal from London I find it necessary to resign the post of Official Photographer which I have held for twenty-three years. I shall be obliged by your accepting my resignation from the 31st of December next.[67]

This is indexed in the archive as 'Official Photographer Resigns'.[68] This points to a recognition within the institution that Cowper was considered a member of staff, yet she has been excluded from the histories.

Cowper's choice of the word 'necessary' implies that her retirement was not entirely voluntary and that her professional position was contingent upon her male relative and her family ties to Cole and that her staff accommodation was dependent upon her brother Richard's position. With his departure, (and Cole's earlier retirement), Cowper was no longer eligible to remain in residence. Whatever the case, with Richard's retirement Cowper's twenty-three-year career running the SKM photographic studio was over.[69]

With all these signs pointing to a sustained and professional career as an institutional photographer, it is perplexing how contemporary institutional historians could have missed her. In the first history of the SKM's photographic service, published in 1975 by John Physick, there is no mention of Cowper. The first reference to her appears in a 1991 journal article written by photography historian Anthony Hamber where he writes: 'Isobel [sic] Cowper's career, like those of so many

---

Kensington Museum, which are considered to be the greatest success yet attained by the art' (Conder, 'Heliography' *The Art-Journal*, 9 (1 December 1870), 358).

67   Isabel Agnes Cowper, 'Mrs Cowper resigns her post as Photographer …' (V&A Museum: 5 November 1891), Museum Achive, ED 84/146 RP/1891/7403.
68   *Abstract of Correspondence* (1891), MA/4/41, 330.
69   Cole retired in 1873

nineteenth-century women photographers, may unfortunately never be fully reconstructed.'[70] Six years later, in 1997, the V&A's first Curator of Photographs, Mark Haworth-Booth, published a comprehensive survey of the history of photographic collection of the V&A, with no mention of Cowper.[71] Lee Fontanella, a historian of the life and work of Thurston Thompson, performed rhetorical gymnastics in order to marginalize Cowper's role in making of the photographs of the casts of the Portico de la Gloria. Taking into consideration the entry in the *Photographs Register* clearly identifying 'Mrs I. A. Cowper' as the photographer of the casts, Fontanella references the glimpses of Victorian architecture captured in the views. He acknowledges it is 'plausible' they are not the photography of Thompson, [but] rather of a woman photographer, J. A. Cowper [sic].'[72] He goes on to proclaim that they 'steal the day for their museological contextuality ...' and anoints them 'key images in the story of Thurston Thompson, whether or not they are images made by him.'[73] Histories of the Arundel Society pay scant attention to the short-lived programme with the SKM with no mention of Cowper.[74]

Cowper's role in the early days of the photographically illustrated book publishing industry places her squarely among the earliest women photo-bookmakers. The rank of 'first' goes to Anna Atkins (1799–1871), credited as the maker of the very first book illustrated with photographic images, regardless of gender (though in terms of commercially published photographically illustrated books, Henry Fox Talbot's *The Pencil of*

---

70 See Anthony Hamber, 'Henry Cole and the institutionalization of photography', *Photoresearcher* (2 June 1991), 30.
71 Mark Haworth-Booth, *Photography, An Independent Art* (London: V & A Publications, 1997).
72 The inability to accurately report Cowper's name speaks to Tanya Sheehan's critique of art historical structures invested in 'proper names'. See Tanya Sheehan, *Photography, History, Difference* (Lebanon: Dartmouth University Press, 2015), 1.
73 Fontanella, *Charles Thurston Thompson E O Proxecto Fotográfico Ibérico*, n.p.
74 See Tanya Ledger, 'A Study of the Arundel Society: 1848–1897' (unpublished PhD, University of Oxford: St. Hilda's College, 1978) and Lucina Ward, 'A Translation of a Translation: Dissemination of the Arundel Society's Chromolithographs' (unpublished PhD, The Australian National University, 2016).

Nature, published between June 1844 and April 1846 is regarded as the first).[75] Among the women, Cowper, with her contributions to the *Art Workmanship* series made in 1869, ranks fourth behind the London-based sisters Caroline (1840–1889) and Marie Bertolacci (1843–1929), whose series of reproductions of engravings of J. M. W. Turner's works were published in 1864, and Parisian Louise Laffon (active circa 1860s), who published her photographically illustrated examples of uniforms of French soldiers in 1866.[76]

Looking at Cowper's material contribution and circulation as part of this short-lived but influential publishing initiative locates her not only as an overlooked highly skilled photographer, but also as one of the nineteenth century's most widely circulated photographers. It places Cowper within a complex matrix of nineteenth-century networks, including those around publishing, arts education and photographic technologies. More broadly, Cowper's work, newly excavated, reveals larger stories concerning the role of gender in publishing, institutional practices and the historiography of photography, making it, as photography historian Kelley Wilder has stated, 'the stuff from which we write history'.[77]

75 See Larry J. Schaaf, *The Pencil of Nature: Anniversary Facisimile; Introductory Volume, Historical Sketch, Notes on The Plates* (New York: Hans P. Krauss, 1989) and Larry J. Schaaf, 'Third Census of Henry Fox Talbot's The Pencil of Nature', *History of Photography*, 36:1 (2012), 99–120.
76 See C. C. and M. E. Bertolacci, *J.M.W. Turner's Liber Studiorum after Engravings* (London: F. Pickton's & Messrs. Colnaghi, 1863–69). According to Anthony Hamber, who is constructing a chronology of photographically illustrated publications, these volumes straddle the categories of 'albums' and 'books' (see Anthony Hamber personal communication, 7 April 2020). Louise Laffon, *Album photographique des uniformes de l'armée Francaise* (Paris: Alexis Godillot, 1866).
77 Kelley Wilder, 'Not one but many: Photographic trajectories and the making of history', *History of Photography*, 41:4 (28 November 2017), 376. For a discussion of the ways in which museum objects write biographies of women, see Ann Whitelaw, 'Women, Museums and the Problem of Biography', in Kate Hill, ed., *Museums and Biographies: Stories, Objects, Identities* (Newcastle: Boydell Press, 2012), 75–86.

ARTEMIS ALEXIOU

7 Late Nineteenth-Century Periodical Texts and Paratexts: The *Women's Penny Paper/Woman's Herald* (1888–92)

Gérard Genette first introduced the concept of paratextuality in his 1987 treatise *Seuils*, which gained greater recognition in 1997 through *Paratexts: Thresholds of Interpretation*.[1] He argued that 'the literary work consists, exhaustively or essentially, of a text', yet, this text almost never appears 'without the reinforcement and accompaniment of a certain number of productions' such as an author's name, a title, a preface, illustrations.[2] Genette termed these productions 'paratexts', explaining that 'more than a boundary or a sealed border, the paratext is, rather, a *threshold*': paratexts represent 'a fringe of the printed text which in reality controls one's whole reading of the text'.[3] This chapter focuses on late nineteenth-century periodical paratexts, as they were presented in the pages of the *Women's Penny Paper/Woman's Herald* (27 October 1888–23 April 1892) – a general feminist periodical printed and published weekly by the Women's Printing Society, with Henrietta Müller as its sole proprietor and editor.[4] The chapter begins with a brief

---

1   Gérard Genette, *Seuils* (Paris: Editions du Seuil, 1987); Gérard Genette, *Paratexts: Thresholds of Interpretation* (Cambridge: Cambridge University Press, 1997).
2   Gérard Genette and Marie McLean (trans.), 'Introduction to the Paratext', *New Literary History*, 22 (1991), 261–72 (261).
3   Philippe Lejeune, *Le Pacte Autobiographique* (Paris: Seuil, 1975), 45 quoted in Genette, *Paratexts*, 2.
4   On 3 January 1891 the *Women's Penny Paper* was renamed as the *Woman's Herald*. The editor identified the two titles as one, so this article refers to the periodical as the *Women's Penny Paper/Woman's Herald*, or *Paper/Herald*.

overview of the paper's history, and then presents an analysis of iconic and material paratexts (e.g. mastheads, subtitles and page architecture), anchor texts and iconic paratexts (e.g. interviews and portraits), ending with an analysis of more complex paratexts featured in the advertising sections of the aforementioned papers.

Existing research reveals that late nineteenth-century women activists utilized various communication media for the purposes of their various campaigns, yet feminist periodicals are understood to be the medium that allowed them to extent their ideas to a much wider audience. Feminist periodicals allowed women activists to construct organized groups, while simultaneously acting as platforms from which they could influence public opinion at a time when print media were the most effective means for the dissemination of ideas.[5] Feminist periodicals, unlike other women's periodicals, reveal women communicating with other women in a variety of ways and for a diversity of political purposes.[6] With that in mind, this chapter argues that the *Women's Penny Paper/Woman's Herald (Paper/Herald)* presented, through its featured text and paratexts, a complex feminist message, whilst projecting a diversity of womanhoods.

The following discussion aims to analyse the textual and paratextual messages communicated through the *Paper/Herald*, by focusing on some of the emerging womanhoods that existed during the last two decades of the nineteenth century, revealing the significant and effective combination of messages communicated through design, text and image. It will also analyse the manner in which these multi-layered messages were used to drive the women's movement agenda. All primary material has been sourced through the *Gale 19th century UK Periodicals* database, provided by the British Library.[7] Mastheads, typesetting, titles and subtitles, texts, portraits and advertisements are examined within the socio-cultural and political context

[5] Maria DiCenzo, Lucy Delap and Leila Ryan, *Feminist Media History: Suffrage Periodicals and the Public Sphere* (Basingstoke: Palgrave Macmillan, 2010), 2.
[6] David Doughan and Denise Sanchez, *Feminist Periodicals, 1855–1984: An Annotated Critical Bibliography of British, Irish, Commonwealth and International Titles* (Brighton: The Harvester Press Ltd, 1987), xii.
[7] 'Nineteenth Century UK Periodicals', Gale (2022), <https://www.gale.com/intl/primary-sources/19th-century-uk-periodicals>, accessed 6 July 2022.

of the period, adopting Genette's concept of paratextuality, whilst occasionally involving ideas from twentieth- or twenty-first-century women's history, gender studies, printing history, fashion history and sociology.

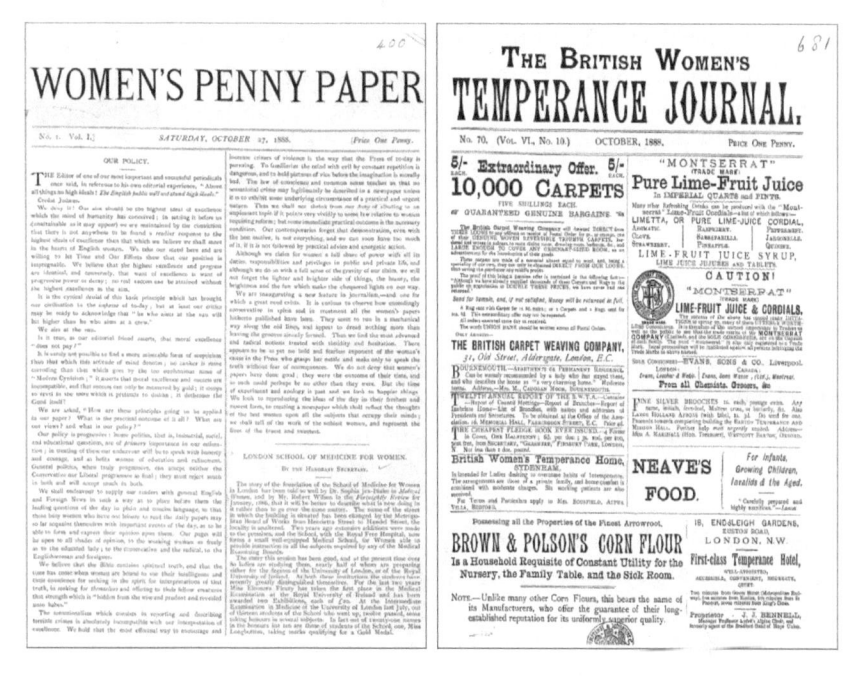

Figure 7.1. (Left to right) a. *Women's Penny Paper*, 27 October 1888, frontmatter; b. *The British Women's Temperance Journal*, October 1888, frontmatter © British Library Board, Gale, Nineteenth-Century UK Periodicals.

The *Women's Penny Paper/Woman's Herald*

The general feminist periodical *Women's Penny Paper* was first distributed on 27 October 1888, and, as mentioned above, was printed and published weekly by the Women's Printing Society, with Henrietta Müller as proprietor and editor. Reproduced on crown folio newsprint (15 × 10 inches), it initially consisted of twelve pages, later increasing to sixteen. It had a progressive editorial policy, and a focused interest in home politics, especially in regard to industrial, social and educational questions.

The original masthead of the *Women's Penny Paper* (Figure 7.1a), and all its subsequent versions up to Number 74, resembled the symmetrical mastheads of the reformist newspaper press (Figure 7.1b). From a practical perspective, the symmetrical design of this masthead, and the fact that it was text-based rather than illustration-based, allowed for an effortlessly executed, time-efficient, low-cost production. The main title occupied the text width and was positioned in the centre of the page. This created symmetry between form and space, because the masthead appeared to have a 'stable figure/ground' relationship, neutralizing negative space, which created a 'unified design'.[8] In turn, this unity provided the masthead with a sense of order, whilst assisting readability, both of which reflected sentiments of confidence and reliability.

As time passed, the titling in the masthead evolved (Figures 7.2a–d). Titles and subtitles generally carried a great significance in the printing trade where 'women had been the object of historical exclusion', and 'traditional enmity continued' until the 1900s.[9] In this case, the subtitle 'The Only Paper Conducted, Written, Printed and Published by Women' was a bold statement and a clear signifier of the paper's support for women's training and employment.[10] So the title and subtitle as verbal messages

---

8   Alex White, *The Elements of Graphic Design: Space, Unity, Page Architecture, and Type* (New York: Allworth Press, 2002), 19.
9   Felicity Hunt, 'The London trade in the Printing and Binding of Books: An Experience in Exclusion, Dilution and De-skilling for Women Workers', *Women's Studies International Forum*, 6 (1983), 517–24 (522).
10   The epigraph changed accordingly over the years, but the main premise remained.

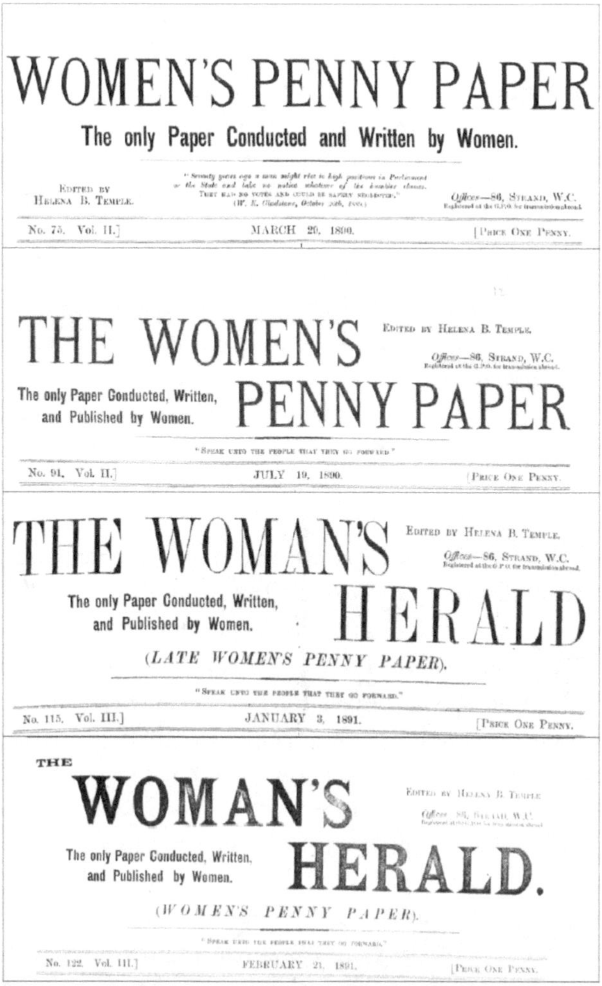

WOMEN'S PENNY PAPER

The only Paper Conducted and Written by Women.

EDITED BY HELENA B. TEMPLE.

"Seventy years ago a man might rise to high positions in Parliament or the State and take no notice whatever of the humbler classes. THEY HAD NO VOTES AND COULD BE SAFELY NEGLECTED." (W. E. Gladstone, October [illegible])

Offices—86, STRAND, W.C. Registered at the G.P.O. for transmission abroad.

No. 75. Vol. II.] MARCH 20, 1890. [PRICE ONE PENNY.

THE WOMEN'S PENNY PAPER

EDITED BY HELENA B. TEMPLE.

Offices—86, STRAND, W.C. Registered at the G.P.O. for transmission abroad.

The only Paper Conducted, Written, and Published by Women.

"SPEAK UNTO THE PEOPLE THAT THEY GO FORWARD."

No. 91. Vol. II.] JULY 19, 1890. [PRICE ONE PENNY.

THE WOMAN'S HERALD

EDITED BY HELENA B. TEMPLE.

Offices—86, STRAND, W.C. Registered at the G.P.O. for transmission abroad.

The only Paper Conducted, Written, and Published by Women.

(*LATE WOMEN'S PENNY PAPER*).

"SPEAK UNTO THE PEOPLE THAT THEY GO FORWARD."

No. 115. Vol. III.] JANUARY 3, 1891. [PRICE ONE PENNY.

THE WOMAN'S HERALD.

EDITED BY HELENA B. TEMPLE

Offices—86, STRAND, W.C. [illegible]

The only Paper Conducted, Written, and Published by Women.

(*WOMEN'S PENNY PAPER*).

"SPEAK UNTO THE PEOPLE THAT THEY GO FORWARD."

No. 122. Vol. III.] FEBRUARY 21, 1891. [PRICE ONE PENNY.

Figure 7.2. Figure 7.2. (Top to bottom) a. *Women's Penny Paper*, 20 March 1890, frontmatter; b. *Women's Penny Paper*, 19 July 1890, frontmatter; c. *Women's Penny Paper*, 3 January 1891, frontmatter; d. *Women's Penny Paper*, 21 February 1891, frontmatter © British Library Board, Gale, Nineteenth-Century UK Periodicals.

were important paratexts in themselves that were actively utilized by the editor in order to enforce the paper's editorial policy. Simultaneously, the inverted pyramidic typesetting of the subtitle seems equally purposeful and certainly fit for purpose, given that to the present day this practice is considered especially appropriate for subtitles that use centred type. Alex White argues that this arrangement offers a clean hierarchical structure that allows the reader to begin reading the longest part of the sentence, and then gradually move down to the shortest part.[11] Thus, the case could be made that the arrangement of the paper's epigraph was an intentional design choice, a choice that used the principles of 'good design' in order to put an emphasis on the verbal message of the subtitle.

On 29 March 1890, the National Press Agency took over as printers and with them came a number of changes: the subtitle changed because the *Women's Penny Paper* was no longer printed by women, and the subtitle's fount, size and length were altered too (Figure 7.2a). The subtitle changed to 'The only Paper Conducted and Written by Women' and was set in Lining Condensed Sans Serif No. 4.[12] The shorter subtitle allowed more space for the rest of the text in the masthead; however, it was the change in typeface that really enhanced the new subtitle's functionality. Lining Condensed Sans Serif No. 4 made long-distance reading easier, because each letter was much more symmetrical, rather than balanced, while the lack of serifs allowed a more or less equal white section in between all letters, which is not possible with most serif founts. The newly formed areas of white space allowed not only for a more experimental composition, but also for a rather successful grouping that communicated a more compact and concise message. In other words, the compositors 'put interesting information where it could be found', whereas in previous mastheads they typically put the editor's name on the bottom left-hand corner of the masthead, while the address and G.P.O. registration featured on the opposite corner which was a rather confusing arrangement.[13] One other notable

11   White, *The Elements of Graphic Design*, 34.
12   See Stephenson, Blake & Co. and Sir Charles Reed & Sons, *Specimens of Point Line Type* (Sheffield: Stephenson, Blake & Co., 1908).
13   White, *The Elements of Graphic Design*, 107.

change on this masthead was the change in the fount for the editor's name. The typeface remained the same, but the size was reduced, which made the overall phrase narrower, and more compact. This aided readability and gestalt by delivering the same message in a more concise manner than the original wider typesetting.[14]

The next change in the masthead came with issue Number 91 (Figure 7.2b). The typesetting of the titling was now changed from a traditional inverted pyramid to a progressive asymmetrical design. From a design perspective asymmetry suggests motion and activity. White explains that:

> [Asymmetry] is the creation of order and balance between unlike or unequal elements. Having no predictable pattern, asymmetry is dynamic. White space in an asymmetrical design is necessarily active, because it is integral to our perception of the positive elements.[15]

In other words, asymmetry is active, and it can 'evoke feelings of modernism, forcefulness, and vitality', which dynamic style complemented the new epigraph. One might argue that the new arrangement also projected the sense that women working for the *Penny Paper* were progressive, resilient and determined not only to succeed within a male-dominated sector, but also to introduce change. Figure 7.2c shows Number 115, which was the first issue of the paper as the *Woman's Herald*. It had its title typeset in Condensed Roman Modern, which bears a close similarity to the Lining Latin used by the paper for almost three years.[16] The whole title was capitalized, and it followed the same dynamic arrangement first introduced on 19 July 1890. However, this typeface was only used for the issues published during January of that year. By February, Condensed Roman Modern was replaced by Antique No. 8, a much heavier typeface (Figure 7.2d). This bold change in typeface literally and metaphorically

---

14 For more information on the concept of 'gestalt' see: Johan Wagemans et al., 'A Century of Gestalt Psychology in Visual Perception: Perceptual Grouping and Figure-Ground Organization', *Psychol Bull*, 138 (2012), 1172–217 (1174–5).
15 White, *The Elements of Graphic Design*, 35.
16 See: Miller and Richard, *Printing Type Specimens: Comprising a Large Variety of Book and Jobbing Faces, Borders and Ornaments* (Edinburgh and London: Miller and Richard, 1918).

served two purposes: first, it made the title noticeable from far away; and second, it created a clear sense of hierarchy to the masthead, making it very obvious that these two words formed the main title of the paper, and all else around it was secondary information. In this masthead, the new typeface allowed the title to be loud and powerful, demonstrating a sense of strength and self-determination, declaring to readers that the *Woman's Herald* was here to stay and stronger than ever. Most importantly, this choice of typeface demonstrated progressiveness, not because Antique No. 8 was aesthetically modern (if anything it appeared aesthetically old fashioned), but because a bold typeface was typically used in advertisements, and considered an *avant-garde* practice at the time. Antique No. 8 was later changed to Trajan, a typeface family listed under the jobbing and fancy types category in Miller & Richard's type specimen book. Both Antique No. 8 and Trajan were listed under the same price band, which excludes pricing as the reason for this change. Graham Hudson describes a decline of 'highly elaborate design' that took place in the 1880s, which was eventually replaced by a 'trend towards simplicity' that proliferated during the 1890s.[17] Therefore, Trajan conveyed simplicity and elegance, while implying a subtle connection with the past; connotations that created a paratextual message that combined the old with the new, implying unity of all women under the banner of universal sisterhood. These diverse messages, communicated through the use of certain typefaces, emphasized that the *Woman's Herald* was a modern confident paper with a clear objective and ambition, whilst the successful grouping of all the diverse elements in the masthead represented the universal sisterhood which Müller advocated. During the 1880–90s, two generational groups of feminists existed: those born before the 1850s, and those born after. Within that two-fold group, there were conservative, progressive, Liberal, Conservative, non-partisan, middle-class, working-class and many other groups of women. The *Woman's Herald* attempted to bridge these different groups of women through its content as well as its design choices, and by doing so it was breaking new ground.

17 Graham Hudson, *The Victorian Printer* (Oxford: Shire Publications Ltd, 1996), 21.

In addition to the paratexts discussed above, the size, paper quality and column arrangement of the periodical were also used to communicate specific messages familiar to the British female reader, which potentially would have influenced the overall meaning of the anchor text. There is evidence suggesting that by the late nineteenth-century female readers increasingly read men's broadsheet newspapers. However, this was mainly common practice amongst a small minority of middle-class or upper-class women, who were gradually beginning to be interested in politics and general public affairs. The reality was that the majority of female readers were mostly catered for by the typical three- or two-column periodicals.[18] Therefore, the vast majority of female readers across the social spectrum would have perceived this paper's crown folio size of eight to sixteen pages as a familiar format, because it was very close to, if not identical with, the size and pages used by the specialist women's periodicals to which they were accustomed.

Additionally, the thin newsprint paper in combination with the two-column arrangement would have intertextually associated the *Woman's Herald* with the British reformist newspaper press, which in itself was a familiar format to the more progressive readers, and to some of the working-class readers, given that the Chartist press had, in the past, used a similar format. Also, adopting a two-column arrangement was perceived as forward thinking, modern and tidy – so much so that American suffrage papers printed in the 1880s, which had originally opted for a spreadsheet format with seven columns (typically used by newspapers targeting male readers) changed to four columns or fewer by the 1890s. Undoubtedly, the two-column arrangement allowed an layout that was efficient and created a 'structured white space', which in turn assisted 'headings to stand out' whilst 'helping readers quickly find what they need[ed]'.[19] In other words, this clean design allowed potential readers to better understand the design personality of the paper, which in turn accentuated its editorial identity.[20]

18 Periodicals aimed at working-class men were also using the smaller periodical size with three or two columns, rather than the full broadsheet newspaper size.
19 White, *The Elements of Graphic Design*, 7.
20 White, *The Elements of Graphic Design*, 55.

Indeed, Müller's strategy was rather successful as audiences perceived the neat and minimalist design of the *Woman's Herald* as a great advantage; one reviewer described it as 'a smartly conducted journal and very readable', and another referred to it as 'crisp and newsy'.[21]

The 'Interview' Column

From the start, the *Paper/Herald* contained an interview and portrait on its front page. The text was typically written in a personal tone that aimed to establish a direct connection with readers, at the same time almost always including positive comments about the interviewee's noteworthy achievements.[22] As a result, the interview column created an intimacy between author and reader, whilst also acting as a source of inspiration. Simultaneously, the use of portraits paratextually underscored the idea of combining conventional and reformist models of womanhood, through the use of clothing and coiffure that were conservative, progressive or a combination of the two.

The illustrated celebrity interview was a common feature in the general illustrated press, as well as the cheap domestic and religious press and the ladies' papers, typically incorporating a description of the interviewee's domestic setting and a reference to their public and professional accomplishments.[23] The illustrated celebrity interview was capable of engaging with the reader on a personal level, because it offered a relatable portrayal of the interviewee. Hence, by using personal pronouns, and offering detailed

---

21   *Wakefield Free Press*, 'What our Contemporaries say of Us', *Women's Penny Paper* (27 July 1889), 10; *Women's Tribune*, 'What our Contemporaries say of Us', *Women's Penny Paper* (19 January 1889), 6.
22   Artemis Alexiou, 'Women's Words, Women's Bodies: Late Nineteenth Century English Feminisms in the "Interview" Column of the *Women's Penny Paper/Woman's Herald* (Oct. 27, 1888–Apr. 23, 1892)', *Women's History Review* 29 (2019), 1149–81.
23   Margaret Beetham and Kay Boardman, eds, *Victorian Women's Magazines* (Manchester: Manchester University Press, 2001), 59 and 202.

descriptions of the interviewees' domestic environment and their regular day-to-day activities as women made them appear more familiar to the average reader. This model of writing was typical for mainstream celebrity interviews, and was routinely adopted by most established interviewers.[24]

The interviews in the *Paper/Herald* also followed this style of writing. The vast majority of them included details about the interviewee's surroundings and personal possessions, while they made sure to include the interviewee's opinion on the 'woman's question'. For example, in the first interview published in the paper, part of the text focuses on the interviewee's personal taste and interior decoration, while also mentioning numerous domestic tasks in which she was typically involved. The author also dedicates approximately three-quarters of the article to the interviewee's achievements as 'a pioneer worker in the cause of women's rights', who had 'agitated for the removal of the unjust laws under which "women" suffer'.[25]

During the nineteenth century, the manner in which women chose to present themselves to the world held a great significance. 'Dress is not a covering merely, it's a symbol', wrote an avid reader of the *Paper/Herald*, a symbol of 'the mind of society' that has been of 'absorbing interest to women in general'.[26] Indeed, during this period clothing acted as a symbol, providing information about a person's social status, role and character, and because upper- and middle-class women were deprived of any other forms of power, they especially used non-verbal symbols such as dress for the purposes of self-expression.[27] As such, the portraits published with the 'Interview' column communicated paratextual messages about each interviewee's opinion on women's appearance, often enforcing conventional womanhood by means of typically feminine hair and dress styles,

---

[24] Troy J. Bassett, '"A Characteristic Product of the Present Era": Gender and Celebrity in Helen C. Black's Notable Women Authors of the Day' (1893), in Ann R. Hawkins and Maura Ives, eds, *Women Writers and Celebrity Culture in the Long Nineteenth Century* (Farnham: Ashgate, 2013), 151–68.

[25] Anon., 'Interview' *Women's Penny Paper* (27 October 1888), 4–5.

[26] H. R. S. Dalton, 'Notes and Letters: Dress as a Basis for Union', *Woman's Herald* (8 August 1891), 145.

[27] Diane Crane, *Fashion and its Social Agendas: Class, Gender, and Identity in Clothing* (Chicago: University of Chicago Press, 2000), 100.

on other occasions depicting women in an 'alternative style' of clothing and hair which challenged conventional understandings of womanhood.

A case in point is the interview and portrait printed in the *Paper/Herald* on 23 February 1889, which featured 35-year-old Mrs Florence Fenwick Miller (Figure 7.3a), a leading English journalist, elected member of the London School Board, and a well-known public speaker. One fifth of the main text comments on the books in her library and various souvenirs on display, whilst approximately three-fifths of the interview focus on her success as a professional journalist, public speaker and author of science books.[28] The feature then closes with a lengthy explanation on Fenwick Miller's decision to keep her maiden name after marriage during the 1870s – a decision that instigated numerous news reports and forced the Chairman of the London School Board to seek legal advice before he was able to refer to her as 'Mrs Fenwick Miller'.

In contrast to the main text, which presented Fenwick Miller as a progressive woman, her portrait presented her in conventional clothing and hair. Indeed, most images of her available in the public domain (see Figures 7.3b–d) show Fenwick Miller wearing her long brown hair tied up in a conventional style, similar to the 'brown, neatly combed heads of the virtuous governess and industrious wives' often depicted in Victorian fiction.[29] Adopting a conventional appearance was probably intentional, because it underscored 'the doctrine of separate spheres', allowing Fenwick Miller to appear non-threatening to her male contemporaries.[30] For feminists like her, born in the 1850s, it was not unusual to opt for more progressive dress and hair styles, yet she made a conscious decision to retain a mainstream appearance to underscore her womanliness. Fenwick Miller, therefore, used her hair as a symbol to seek power through a style that 'de-emphasize[d] resistance and instead emphasize[d] accommodation to mainstream ideas about attractiveness'.[31]

28　Anon., 'Interview', *Women's Penny Paper* (23 February 1889), 1–2.
29　Elisabeth G. Gitter, 'The Power of Women's Hair in the Victorian Imagination', *PMLA* 99 (1984), 936–54 (941).
30　Crane, *Fashion and Its Social Agendas*, 100.
31　Rose Weitz, 'Women and their Hair: Seeking Power through Resistance and Accommodation', in Rose Weitz, ed., *The Politics of Women's Bodies: Sexuality, Appearance, and Behavior* (New York: Oxford University Press, 2003), 138.

Figure 7.3. (Top left) a. Florence Fenwick Miller, *Women's Penny Paper*, 23 February 1889, frontmatter; (top right) b. Florence Fenwick Miller (detail), *Woman's Signal*, 3 October 1895 © British Library Board, Gale, Nineteenth-Century UK Periodicals; (bottom left) c. Florence Fenwick Miller, 1893 © Herbert Rose Barraud; (bottom right) d. Florence Fenwick Miller, c.1910–2 © George Deney.

This phenomenon when women seem to 'both struggle in a conscious and active way against their inequality, yet who also seem to accept, and even support their own subordination' has been described as 'accommodating protest'.[32] This middle-of-the-road approach to being a progressive woman during the 1890s allowed Fenwick Miller, and others like her, to appear feminine enough to their contemporaries, and therefore unobjectionable to the gendered *status quo* of the period. The power obtained by appearing unthreatening also enabled women like Fenwick Miller to advance further in their professional and political work than those women who were considered too radical. It would be unjust to claim that Fenwick Miller's feminine appearance was the main reason for her longstanding success both professionally and politically; however, choosing to appear conventionally feminine would probably have had a positive impact on her public work.

Another interesting example was the interview and portrait printed on 12 April 1890, featuring 35-year-old Lady Florence Dixie (Figure 7.4a), a Scottish writer, war correspondent and traveller. The editorial begins by describing Dixie in her study including a thorough depiction of her clothing and hair.[33] Then the author offers Dixie's comments on the position of women, and the remaining sections follow a strict question and answer structure. In total, almost seven-eighths of the text discuss women's causes such as education and parliamentary participation, women's rational dress and equal property rights, and the interviewee's achievements in her private and public life. Dixie commented on her life as a mother and teacher to her two boys, writer and traveller, and a woman with a regular exercise routine. The interview also reported on Dixie's womanly qualities, which included being well-dressed, neat, honest, caring and a natural leader.

According to the evidence available, this interview was the only one written and conducted by a male interviewer, whereas all other interviews published by the *Paper/Herald* are thought to be written by women.[34]

32 Arlene E. MacLeod, *Accommodating Protest: Working Women, the New Veiling, and Change in Cairo* (New York: Columbia University Press, 1991), xiv.
33 Anon., 'Interview', *Women's Penny Paper* (12 April 1890), 1–2.
34 See: Helena B. Temple, 'The "St. James's Gazette" on the "Women's Penny Paper"', *Women's Penny Paper* (26 April 1890), 318.

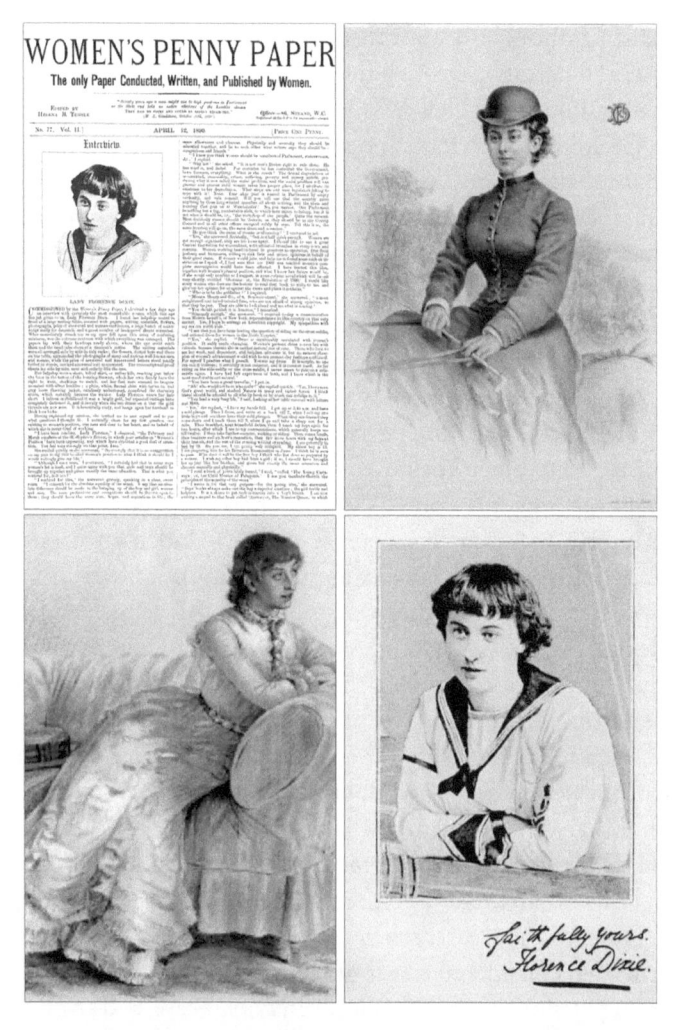

Figure 7.4. (Top left) a. Lady Florence Dixie, *Woman's Herald*, 12 April 1890, frontmatter © British Library Board, Gale, Nineteenth-Century UK Periodicals; (top right) b. Lady Florence Dixie, 1880; (bottom left) c. Lady Florence Dixie, 1883; (bottom right) d. Lady Florence Dixie, *Gloriana; or, The Revolution of 1900*, London: Henry and Company, 1890, frontispiece. Public domain.

With that in mind, it is important to note that this interview offers a more gendered narrative than all the others, even though the interviewer appears to be supporting New Women such as Lady Dixie and their work. For instance, in this interview the description on the interviewee's appearance and immediate surroundings are positioned at the very beginning, underlying the belief that the manner in which women present themselves or decorate their immediate environment holds more significance than what they practise or have to say. Furthermore, using a structured interview style often seen in newspaper interviews written by men and aimed at male readers, rather than a semi-structured interview style mostly seen in periodical interviews written by women and aimed at women readers, added its own masculine tone to this specific interview. Nonetheless, the celebrity interview blueprint noted above remains: conventional duties, progressive activities and women's suffrage have all been reported.

This interview, aside of the main text, also included a portrait of Lady Dixie in 'alternative style' dress, wearing a mid-length coiffure with a sailor's outfit. By the 1880s, boy's clothes were specific to this gender, and although they 'reflected the prevailing modes in both women's and men's costume', they mainly included 'fancy dress' styles influenced by military uniforms or antique dress.[35] In other words, sailor's outfits were considered conventionally masculine attire, even if they were meant to be worn by boys not adult men, but were later openly adopted by a section of progressive women as a symbol that allowed them to challenge established ideals of women's status in late Victorian society.[36] Simultaneously, mid-length hairstyles, although longer than the short haircuts for boys, often offered 'an autonomous pleasure' to the wearer when caressed by the wind, which, in itself, could have been considered an act of female emancipation.[37]

Wearing a sailor's outfit, specifically in Dixie's case, had an even greater significance, because she was in fact a traveller and travel writer. During

---

35   Jo B. Paoletti, 'Clothes Make the Boy, 1860–1910', *Dress* 9 (1983), 16–20 (16).
36   Diane Crane, 'Clothing Behaviour as Non-Verbal Resistance: Marginal Women and Alternative Dress in Nineteenth-Century', *Fashion Theory* 3 (1999), 249.
37   Frigga Haug, ed., *Female Sexualization: A Collective Work of Memory*, trans. by Erica Carter (London: Verso, 1999), 110.

the late nineteenth century, 'women travellers, seemingly free of domestic constraints, challenged the strict boundaries of the woman's sphere while appearing to operate within it'.[38] As a result, through their international travels women 'asserted their rights to self-determination and self-rule', and by doing so, they 'negotiate[d] the discursive boundaries of Victorian Britain's ideological sex-role socialization'.[39] Dixie, for instance, wrote in her monograph *Across Patagonia* (1880) that she travelled to 'an outlandish place, so many miles away [...], precisely because it was an outlandish place so far away'.[40] As such, as a woman interviewee appearing in alternative dress and haircut, whilst also being a woman traveller and travel writer in real life, Dixie was not only 'located outside of the dominant tradition', but was also 'doubly different' in terms of her 'more socially conformist female contemporaries and to male travellers of the period'.[41] Thus, although other portraits of Dixie depict her in rational outfits (Figure 7.4b) or aristocratic dresses (Figure 7.4c), the portrait selected to accompany her interview in the *Paper/Herald* was a reproduction of the image that accompanied her own book *Gloriana* (Figure 7.4d),[42] which suggests that editor and interviewee deliberately intended to intertextually associate the paper with Dixie's feminist utopia.

The Advertisements

In addition to the masthead and interview columns, advertisements had a paratextual role in the complex editorial message of universal sisterhood too. The first issue of the *Paper/Herald* consisted of 94 per cent editorial

---

38   Monica Anderson, *Women and the Politics of Travel, 1870–1914* (Madison: Fairleigh Dickinson University Press, 2006), 14.
39   Anderson, *Women and the Politics of Travel*, 14.
40   Dixie quoted in Anderson, *Women and the Politics of Travel*, 14.
41   Anderson, *Women and the Politics of Travel*, 17.
42   Lady Florence Dixie, *Gloriana; Or, The Revolution Of 1900* (London: Henry and Company, 1890).

content and 6 per cent advertising; yet, the last issue consisted of 64 per cent editorial content and 36 per cent advertising. Each weekly issue included numerous advertisements, which, although originally limited to the last page, eventually bled into the body of the paper, and in general they typically advertised beauty services and products, food/drink products, products and services to do with woman's dress, home, training/ education and health. Inevitably, with the increase in advertising the potential impact of advertisements may have increased too, and if there were a class of products that was advertised more than others, then this would naturally put its own paratextual impression on the already multi-layered identity of the *Paper/Herald*. Therefore, the remainder of this chapter focuses on the two most advertised categories of products and/or services: corsets and hair.

The French corset has chiefly been associated with the female figure, and although it was widely favoured by affluent seventeenth- and eighteenth-century upper-class women, during the nineteenth century's industrialization it was a consumerist product for the *bourgeoisie*, and was used by most women of this class.[43] For most women, wearing a corset was a signifier of social propriety, indicating a virtuous body belonging to a morally righteous woman. Simultaneously, a corseted body was seen as beautiful, erotic and feminine, emphasizing the breasts and hips, against a thinner waist, which in turn reflected a 'girlish innocence' and femininity.[44] Western society imposed the wearing of corsets on women from a young age through their adulthood. Valerie Steele argues that whatever it represented to different women, the corset in actuality was 'an instrument of physical oppression and sexual commodification'; a garment that applied 'disciplinary power' upon the woman's body, in order to make her 'docile' and feminine.[45]

---

43 Alisa Webb, 'Constructing the Gendered Body: Girls, Health, Beauty, Advice, and the *Girl's Best Friend*, 1898–99', *Women's History Review*, 15 (2006), 253–75 (260).
44 Webb, 'Constructing the Gendered Body', 261.
45 Valerie Steele, *Fetish: Fashion, Sex, and Power* (Oxford: Oxford University Press, 1996), 57; Michel Foucault, *Discipline and Punish: The Birth of the Prison*, trans. by Alan Sheridan (New York: Vintage Books, 1979) in Steele, *Fetish: Fashion, Sex, and Power*, 57.

Figure 7.5. (Top left) a. *Women's Penny Paper*, 16 March 1889, p. 8; (top right) b. *Women's Penny Paper*, 13 July 1889, p. 12; (bottom left) c. *Women's Penny Paper*, 13 December 1890, p. 127; (bottom right) d. *Woman's Herald*, 30 May 1891, p. 512 © British Library Board, Gale, Nineteenth-Century UK Periodicals.

Certainly, there were major differences between types of corsets. There were conventional corsets, healthy corsets and tight-laced corsets. Conventional, moulded corsets were mainstream and the type worn by most Victorian women, whereas tight lacing was 'a minority practice'.[46] With the advent of dress reform during the late nineteenth century, manufacturers opted to respond to the new market desire for healthy garments, and they began producing corsets for the health-conscious progressive New Woman (Figures 7.5a and b). Healthy corsets, unlike conventional corsets, were 'made of wool or cotton', and 'featured a straight-front busk, as opposed to a moulded waist', which supported the abdominal muscles without creating a distortion.[47] Healthy corsets allowed women to perform their daily activities, such as riding, cycling or nursing, without feeling restricted, and were openly favoured by contemporary qualified medical practitioners, for women compelled to wear one. Healthy corsets were a better alternative to the traditional corset, and as mentioned above, allowed women to assume power through accommodation.

Despite these differences, healthy corsets were still a product of the established patriarchal system. Even if the corset-wearing New Women only opted to wear the so-called healthy style, the metaphor represented by this fashion choice meant that the individual did not truly challenge the existing cultural expectations about women's roles, or affect 'the broader distribution of power by gender'.[48] While so-called healthy corsets may have allowed their wearers 'to resist subordination' figuratively and literally by increasing an individual's power of movement, the progressive New Woman was still part of a subordinate group, who assumed a conventional True Woman appearance, corset included. Susan R. Bordo argues that the corseted woman (even if she opted for a healthy corset) ultimately supported patriarchal ideologies and taste that defined 'a woman's body as her most important attribute', and changed a woman's identity through changing 'a woman's appearance'.[49]

46 Steele, *Fetish: Fashion, Sex, and Power*, 58.
47 Webb, 'Constructing the Gendered Body', 262.
48 Weitz, *The Politics of Women's Bodies*, 140.
49 Weitz, *The Politics of Women's Bodies*, 140–1.

Inevitably, the wearing of any corset still posed a gendered menace for women because this piece of clothing could also make them seem too feminine, and in patriarchal societies femininity indicates weakness and lack of competence.[50] In addition, therefore, to the strong paratextual messages of women's emancipation offered by the title, subtitle and the diverse textual and paratextual messages of progressive New Womanhood offered by the interview column, the advertisements of corsets in general would have added their own paratextual layer of communication to the paper's message – an awareness of the consumer market geared towards progressive New Woman's health, combined with conventional True Woman propriety. Yet, in terms of women's emancipation, the financial decision to accept these advertisements was rather inconsistent with the editorial aim of the *Paper/Herald*, because it did not truly challenge established patriarchal conventions.

However, the mixed paratextual messages presented through advertisements did not necessarily mean that the appeal of *the Paper/Herald* was affected in a negative way. For some readers, the advertising of corsets was probably not an issue because they, themselves, believed that continuing to wear conventional clothing did not necessarily negate their status as progressive women who aspired to be valuable members of society. For instance, a reader who considered herself 'a good example' of a woman explained she was 'the eldest of a family of five' who had lost both their parents at the same time, yet 'decided to keep on' supporting their household with herself 'at its head'; she then further elaborated:

> I am twenty-two and these are some of my daily duties: ordering the meals, teaching my two young sisters drawing, English, and music; a morning walk of two miles in and two miles out to our country town to do necessary shopping; looking after the clothes of myself and four children; arranging flowers and gardening, of which I am very fond; and paying visits in the afternoon. Now, the hindrance (?) to carrying out this constant labour of different kinds is, that since I was fifteen I have been brought up to wear close-fitting corsets and never lay them aside whatever my employment may be. I am not a tight-lacer but like always to wear well-made well-laced stays, and consequently have a slight well-proportioned figure and a neat waist.[51]

50 Weitz, *The Politics of Women's Bodies*, 142.
51 A Dainty Housekeeper, 'Correspondence: A Dainty Housekeeper', *Women's Penny Paper* (12 April 1890), 295.

The reader then ended her letter stating she thought it 'very hard that because one has a little womanly vanity about a nice appearance one should be considered incapable of being an active and useful member of society'.[52] On the other hand, however, there was a segment of the paper's readership that believed corsets, healthy or not, should be banned. A reader named Kora, who agreed with Mrs Ormiston Chant's advice that 'out-door work for women' should be sought 'on account naturally of the fresh air they meanwhile inhale', argued that it was also significant for women to know:

> The importance of allowing their waists to expand when they breathe, and not even confining them so little that if they were to leave off their corsets the dress body would not meet. This is I am sure, one of the reasons (if not the first) that retards woman's progress, and until women see this, their chance of the Suffrage is small. It may appear very insignificant to those who practise even the slightest pressure round their bodies, but to those who do not, it is of vital importance.[53]

Some might argue that advertising healthy corsets could have alienated the kind of readers who opposed the corset. Still, the impact of paratexts such as advertising and typography was probably not as significant as the impact of the main copy (interviews, letters to the editor). Consequently, as long as the *Paper/Herald* remained an inclusive platform, readers opposed to corsets were more likely to send in their opinions and initiate general conversations about topics with editors and other readers, as the evidence suggests, rather than completely withdrawing from the discussion or refraining from purchasing the paper.

Products related to the care of hair, especially long, healthy hair, was the theme of the second largest category of items marketed: dressing combs, hairdressers, hair additions, restorers, shampoos, hair treatments and hair curlers were only a few of the products and services that were regularly advertised in the pages of the *Paper/Herald*. Galia Ofek notes that 'the cultural expectation [was] that hair should [...] display the same order, neatness and cultivation which were required of them'.[54] Indeed, 'non-compliance

---

52   A Dainty Housekeeper, 'Correspondence', 295.
53   Kora, 'Notes and letters: Tight lacing', *Woman's Herald* (22 August 1891), 147.
54   Galia Ofek, *Representations of Hair in Victorian Literature and Culture* (Farnham: Ashgate, 2009), 34.

with such grooming injunctions could be interpreted as a declaration of dissidence'.[55] Hair was also connected with concepts of hygiene, commodity fetishism and sexuality. For instance, the advertisement of the Victoria Toilet Club (Figure 7.5c), which offered ladies' and gentlemen's hair-cutting rooms, also advertised Mrs Stidder's 'sanitary synthedine hair wash for promoting the growth, strengthening and beautifying the human hair'; Mrs Stidder's Victoria sanitary toilet cream 'for preserving and beautifying the skin'; and her 'infallible cure for chapped hands' that would 'make them beautifully soft and white'. The advertisement also shows that at the same premises, customers could find private baths for ladies and gentlemen, as well as 'every design of artificial hair for fashion and convenience', and 'wigs of all description' that could be used as 'invisible coverings for semi or complete baldness'. The advertisers used bold typefaces to draw readers' attention, and they also used images on either side: one full-body image of a woman in her dressing gown standing in front of the mirror combing her wavy, floor-length hair; a second head-only image of a woman, presumably after she has finished at the hairdresser's, wearing her artificial and natural hair up in a nice, neat hairdo, 'after it has been brushed by machinery'.

These types of advertisement communicated a plethora of consumerist paratextual messages that may have been at odds with the overall goals of the *Paper/Herald;* messages that were really about appearance but being framed as concern over one's health and hygiene. In these advertisements, hairdressers were cast into the role of 'the defenders of traditional social structures and divisions'.[56] 'For the ordinary woman, the so-called health revolution became a fundamental ingredient in women's modernization', while at the same time health products were used as a mechanism to condition women to focus on a commercial activity like personal grooming, by emphasizing 'the interconnectedness of the moral and physical life' more broadly.[57] Additionally, there was the emphasis 'on pleasure that

---

55   Ofek, *Representations of Hair in Victorian Literature and Culture*, 34–5.
56   Ofek, *Representations of Hair in Victorian Literature and Culture*, 35.
57   Regina Markell Morantz, 'Making Women Modern: Middle Class Women and Health Reform in 19th Century America', *Women's History*, 10 (1977), 490–507 (495, 491).

necessarily required leisure' implied through the 'recurrent motif of the woman looking into her mirror'; which suggested the ability of the products and services advertised to 'facilitate a satisfying reflection', that would, in turn, secure 'personal attractiveness and one's position in society'.[58] The same image could also have implied 'the inadequacy' of the woman's 'perceived image' when wearing her natural hair, or that 'the ideal woman was self-absorbed and pleasure-oriented enough to delight in her own reflection'.[59] 'Images of impossibly, unnaturally beautiful hair turn the consumer's own body – woman's hair – into a spectacle and a chimera', argues Ofek, while at the same time turning 'private rituals (like combing one's hair) into public ones'.[60]

Then, there was the problematic paratextual message of being in *vogue* and its relationship to commodity fetishism. Being in *vogue*, according to some advertisements, was achieved by promoting the purchase, hiring and/or usage of artificial hair. 'Fashion prescribed the ritual by which the fetish Commodity wished to be worshipped', writes Walter Benjamin, adding that fashion, in this case artificial hair, 'stands in opposition to the organic', and therefore, 'prostitutes the living body to the inorganic world'.[61] In other words, advertisements and consumer culture promoting order and artificiality paratextually suggested purchase of their products signified 'an advanced state of cultivation, sophistication and civilization and distanced hair from its organic, untidy origin'.[62]

In contrast to the Victoria Toilet Club's advertisement, which heavily exploited established True Womanhood desires, anxieties and constructions, Figure 7.5d shows an advertisement for Koko shampoo, which offered an alternative paratextual message that was heavily influenced by progressive

---

58 Lori Anne Loeb, *Consuming Angels: Advertising and Victorian Women* (Oxford: Oxford University Press, 1994), 42; Ofek, *Representations of Hair in Victorian Literature and Culture*, 40.
59 Anne Hollander, *Seeing Through Clothes* (New York: Viking Press, 1978), 397; Loeb, *Consuming Angels*, 42.
60 Ofek, *Representations of Hair in Victorian Literature and Culture*, 39.
61 Walter Benjamin and Harry Zohn, trans., *Charles Baudelaire: A Lyric Poet in the Era of High Capitalism* (London: Verso, 1973), 166.
62 Ofek, *Representations of Hair in Victorian Literature and Culture*, 35.

ideas of womanhood. The text incorporated in this advertisement may have not been much different from the typical fear-infusing and miracle-promising puffery that was typically used by advertisers of the period, while the photograph on the right emphasized this impossibility of floor-length hair that one could only find in mythological images. Nonetheless, the illustration positioned at the prominent top left corner told another story: the story of the progressive woman who is fearless enough to ride cross-saddle, implying that she was wearing trousers under her dress, and rebellious enough to go in public with her hair down and, like the militant Joan of Arc, or the controversial Lady Godiva, lead women's battle for equality. 'The longer, thicker, and more wanton the tresses, the more passionate the heart beneath them', writes journalist Celia Brayfield – an untamed sexuality that Koko's female heroine was proud to parade in public.[63] In contrast to the images produced by male artists, such as Dante Gabriel Rossetti, which typically depicted women with long thick hair in poses and settings that implied submissiveness and augmented sexuality, Koko's image was embracing the New Woman activist/warrior, who rebelled against socio-cultural conventions of sexuality and gender. Another interpretation of this same image, however, could also imply that women should focus on conventionally feminine matters, such as lustrous long hair, rather than other conventionally masculine matters, such as politics. It could be that this over-emphasis on sexuality and femininity aimed to 'conceal a certain appropriation of "masculine" traits and avert anxiety of retribution from her conservative society', because to many a woman riding cross-saddle, wearing trousers and being a warrior may have seemed as 'a phallic woman in possession of male potency'.[64]

[63] Celia Brayfield, 'A Lifetime Haircut', *The Times* (20 July 2004), 11.
[64] Ofek, *Representations of Hair in Victorian Literature and Culture*, 28.

Conclusion

While this chapter discusses only a fraction of the multitude of textual and paratextual material available in the pages of the *Paper/Herald*, it offers essential information on the ways that women of this period simultaneously used their agency through the feminist press, and as a means for political participation. By focusing on late nineteenth-century periodical paratexts, through a consideration of the mastheads, interview features and advertisements published in the general feminist periodical the *Paper/Herald*, this chapter reveals that these design, textual and visual choices allowed the paper to communicate messages that combined conventional and progressive elements of womanhood – in other words, a complex feminist message.

This inclusive approach to presenting women's experiences demonstrated to the readers of the *Paper/Herald* that women's contribution to politics and society was both nuanced and multi-layered, and could often be exceedingly effective without necessarily being restricted to a specific single model of progressive womanhood. It also demonstrated to its readers, who may have been anxious about disrupting the *status quo* in an abrupt manner that may have resulted in hostility towards them, that the progressive New Women honoured and respected their feminine qualities. In this way, if anything, any attempt for change could incorporate traditionally perceived attributes, rather than completely abandoning them.

Maggie Andrews and Sallie McNamara argue that 'there is a tendency when historians utilize media as a source for research for them to ignore the innate polysemia of popular texts, the multiple layers and contradictory meanings' often displayed in newspapers articles, or the cover pages of magazines.[65] Instead, this chapter has endeavoured to approach feminist periodicals from a more holistic perspective, simultaneously considering textual and paratextual messages present, in order to offer a more nuanced understanding of the messages communicated. In turn, it is anticipated

---

65 Maggie Andrews and Sallie McNamara, eds, *Women and the Media: Feminism and Femininity in Britain, 1900 to the Present* (New York: Routledge, 2014), 1–2.

that this contribution will allow an even better understanding of late nineteenth-century English progressive womanhood in particular, and Victorian feminisms in general, further expanding on women's history research by offering an interdisciplinary viewpoint. Moving forward with the goal of expanding the field of design history in a direction that allows design historians to create intersections with Victorian periodical studies, the aim of further research is to uncover more examples such as those presented, with the hope that this type of research method and analysis of primary sources inspires its wider use. Such inclusive research would allow not only appreciation of the history of design seen through the lens of gender and gendered communication, but also add to a better understanding of the roles of women in history in general, and their influence in the production of periodicals in particular.

ANGELA GRIFFITH

8 Elizabeth Corbet Yeats: Dun Emer and Cuala Presses and Irish 'Art Printing', 1903–40

In 1938 Elizabeth Corbet Yeats (1868–1940) brought the Japanese academic and Yeatsian scholar Shotaro Oshima on a tour of the Cuala Press's premises on Dublin's Baggot Street. In his account of his visit to the private press, Oshima noted that E. C. Yeats described what they did at Cuala as 'art printing'.[1] This chapter considers this term and contextualizes the production of printed images firstly at the Dun Emer Press (founded 1902), and later at the Cuala Press (founded 1908), under the directorship of E. C. Yeats. The two Presses are rightly celebrated for their seminal role in publishing contemporary Anglo-Irish writing in the first half of the twentieth century during William Butler Yeats's (1865–1939) tenure as editor, yet the artistry and agency of the visual material produced remains largely overlooked.[2] While siblings, the relationship between the director and the editor was fraught as each vied to assert their authority and their vision.[3] However, in the printing of images E. C. Yeats had full autonomy. Informed in part by the theories and practices of the British private press movement and an Irish revivalist aesthetic, her attitude to fine printing and the reproduction of imagery, and the extent to which she viewed the press as an

---

1   Liam Miller, *The Dun Emer later the Cuala Press* (Dublin: Dolmen Press, 1973), 88.
2   Writers included Padraic Colum, Lady Augusta Gregory, Ezra Pound, Oliver St John Gogarty, John Millington Synge, William Butler Yeats. For a catalogue of volumes printed at the Cuala Press see exhibition catalogue produced by the National Book League, *The Cuala Press 1903–1973* (Dublin: Dolmen Press, 1973).
3   Simone Murray, 'The Cuala Press: Women, publishing, and the conflicted genealogies of "feminist publishing"', *Women's Studies International Forum*, 27 (2004), 489–506, 496.

artistic enterprise will be considered. The discussion will also address her seemingly paradoxical ambivalence in using mechanically produced matrices when hand-printing images, an attitude at odds with many leading figures within the British private press movement. During the period of E. C. Yeats's stewardship, the Presses became a hive not only for writers but also for artists, many of whom were women, and their work almost exclusively visualized Irish themes. As she championed the artistic value of the prints and illustrations produced at Dun Emer and Cuala, their formal qualities and the extent to which the dictates of craft and tradition informed or determined their style and presentation will be assessed.

The work of the Dun Emer Press and subsequently the Cuala Press until E. C. Yeats's death in 1940, was singular in Ireland; no other private press of similar reputation or productivity operated before, or during, that time. Therefore, it was inevitable that E. C. Yeats would have looked beyond Ireland for direction and inspiration. Given the family's close association with London (the Yeats siblings and their parents were domiciled there from 1887; Elizabeth and her sister Susan moved to Dublin in 1902), in addition to Ireland's longstanding cultural, social and political relationships with the United Kingdom, it was inevitable that she would be guided by the theories and practices associated with the private press movement in England.[4] The Yeats family was closely acquainted with leading figures in London's artistic milieu, most significantly William Morris (1834–96). While she was initially motivated by Morris's Kelmscott Press, the stylistic approach eventually taken by E. C. Yeats for her own presses would differ greatly from that of Kelmscott. Her printed literary volumes – which were unillustrated – would be noted for their clarity and straightforwardness of design, echoing the restrained practices of T. J. Cobden-Sanderson (1840–1922) and Emery Walker (1851–1933) at the Doves Press.[5] With Walker as

---

4   For a cultural discussion of the Irish in London at the end of the nineteenth century see Fintan Cullen and R. F. Foster, *Conquering England: Ireland in Victorian London* (London: National Portrait Gallery, 2005).

5   William G. Blaikie Murdoch, art critic, writer and contemporary, described Elizabeth Yeats's work at Cuala as 'wholly simple, its beauty of a restful and

a mentor, E. C. Yeats would remain steadfastly faithful throughout her publishing career to the direct, uncluttered in-house style first devised in the early days of the Dun Emer Press.[6] However, in contrast to the refined austerity of her letterpress publishing E. C. Yeats would offset this by printing an extensive collection of illustrative prints and book plates designed by Irish artists. Under her guidance, the Dun Emer and Cuala Presses would produce artworks that reflected revivalist and nationalist definitions of Irish culture, and this material was disseminated nationally and internationally. As in the example of Irish revivalist literature, visual cultural production was directed by contemporary calls to create work that testified to a distinctive national identity.[7] Within nationalist ideologies, Irish identity was best represented by the rural landscape, its inhabitants and its local traditions, all of which were viewed as authentic and distinct from British-styled metropolitan centres.[8]

---

unobtrusive kind' quoted in Gifford Lewis, *The Yeats Sisters and the Cuala Press* (Dublin: Irish Academic Press, 1994), 119.

[6] Gifford Lewis, *Miss Elizabeth Corbet Yeats: A Centenary Tribute Celebrating her Life of Publishing Irish Books,* (Bethesda: Wild Apple Press, 2003), 1–9.

[7] Commentators included the writer, editor and artist George William Russell (Æ) (1867–1935) and art collector Hugh Lane (1875–1915) both of whom called for the creation of, and recognition of, a distinctive Irish school of art. See George Russell (Æ), Letter to editor, *The Daily Express* (10 December 1898) and Hugh Lane, *Catalogue of the Exhibition of Works by Irish Painters* (London: Guildhall Art Gallery, 1904).

[8] For a discussion of the importance of the visualization of rural life and landscape for Irish cultural identity in the first decades of the twentieth century see J. Crampton Walker, *Irish Life and Landscape* (Dublin: Talbot Press, 1926), 7–8, and Mike Cronin, 'The State on Display: The 1924 Tailteann Art Competition', *New Hibernian Review,* Autumn (2005), 50–71.

The Foundation of the Dun Emer and Cuala Presses

From their inception, the Dun Emer and Cuala Presses employed only women, each of whom was trained in all aspects of letterpress printing. E. C. Yeats's first press was part of a larger co-operative working under the name Dun Emer Industries. The initiative was first conceived by Evelyn Gleeson (1855–1944), a suffragette who encouraged women to seek out employment that was rewarding and that would enable them to live independent lives.[9] Gleeson, who trained in textile design and weaving, was known to the Yeats family through the Irish Literary Society in London. Gleeson approached the Yeats sisters and proposed that together they establish a craft enterprise in Dublin, specifically for the training and employment of young women. Their objective – according to their own promotional material – was to employ Irish hands, using the best of Irish materials, to make 'beautiful things'.[10] Gleeson's concept to train and engage women in the area of craft production echoed existing schemes in Ireland.[11] From the late 1800s, significant numbers of women who lived in impoverished rural areas were employed by philanthropically funded co-operatives, and later by government-sponsored relief agencies, to produce textiles and needlecraft which were marketed at home and abroad.[12] Following negotiations, in partnership with Susan and Elizabeth Corbet Yeats, Gleeson founded the Dun Emer Industries in 1902. The enterprise was located in Dundrum, a suburb of South County Dublin.

---

9   For further information on Gleeson see Karen E. Brown, 'Gender and the Decorative Arts: Evelyn Gleeson and the Irish Cultural Revival', in Éimear O'Connor, ed., *Irish Women Artists, 1800–2009: Familiar but Unknown* (Dublin: Four Courts Press, 2010), 61–78.
10 Anon., *The Dun Emer Industries Prospectus* (Dublin: Dun Emer Press, 1903).
11 For further information see Janice Helland, *British and Irish Home Arts and Industries 1880–1914: Marketing Craft, Making Fashion* (Dublin: Irish Academic Press, 2007).
12 Nicola Gordon Bowe, 'Two Early Twentieth-Century Irish Arts and Crafts Workshops in Context: An Túr Gloine and the Dun Emer Guild and Industries', *Journal of Design History*, 2:2/3 (1989), 193–206.

Gleeson provided the funding, while the Yeats sisters brought with them an extensive network of contacts in addition to their respective knowledge and skills. Susan Yeats was an embroiderer who trained at Kelmscott under May Morris, daughter of William. E. C. Yeats was also acquainted with the Morrises and she had the opportunity to see at first hand the workings of the Kelmscott Press. Previously E. C. Yeats had trained as a kindergarten teacher at the Froebel College in Bedford and was a visiting art mistress at the Froebel Society, Chiswick High School and at the Central Foundation School in London. Furthermore, she was a published author, providing text and illustrations for four painting manuals including *Brushwork studies of flowers, fruits and animals for teachers and advanced students* (1898).[13] Despite her professional accomplishments and reputation in art education, she decided, with the encouragement of Emery Walker, Morris's advisor, and the support of her family, in particular that of her brother the poet William Butler Yeats, to leave London and establish a private press in Dublin. Through both Yeats sisters, the Dun Emer Industries, and later the Cuala Industries, would serve as a conduit of Morrisian theories and practices in Ireland. W. B. Yeats described how the design principles of Kelmscott, and its practice, gratified 'his thirst for a truly national, aesthetically satisfactory, social-artistic movement with which he might identify himself'.[14] The private presses founded by his sister, the first of their kind in Ireland, would serve as a beacon for the cultural national revivalist movement.

A significant aspect of E. C. Yeats's association with Kelmscott was that she saw women working at the press, not only May Morris, but women who were hired as printing professionals.[15] She undertook a short course in

13 For a discussion of E. C. Yeats's training see Lewis, *The Yeats Sisters*, 32–42.
14 Robin Skelton, 'Twentieth-Century Irish Literature and the Private Press Tradition', *The Massachusetts Review*, 5:2 (1964), 368–77 (371).
15 Thomas Binning, a committed trade unionist and head printer at Kelmscott, negotiated union membership for the entire Kelmscott workforce resulting in the London Society of Compositors accepting its first female member: Elizabeth Carolyn Miller, *Slow Print: Literary Radicalism and Late Victorian Print Culture* (Stanford: Stanford University Press, 2013), 56; 'The Kelmscott Chaucer in Trinity College', in W. E. Vaughan, ed., *The Old Library Trinity College Dublin, 1712–2012* (Dublin: Four Courts Press, 2013), 265–71.

hand-printing with the Woman's Printing Society in London, an organization that was associated with the women's suffrage movement.[16] During her training, E. C. Yeats was instructed not only in composing and proofreading but also in business practices and workspace management to increase efficiency and productivity. In fact, the press would become one of the most productive and financially successful parts of the Dun Emer enterprise and this continued to be the case under the umbrella of the Cuala Industries, the new company formed by the Yeats sisters following a split with Gleeson in 1908. Both presses sustained their workforce by producing printed materials that appealed to a market fuelled by the Irish revivalist *zeitgeist* of the age. From the late 1800s to the first decades of the twentieth century an 'Irish consciousness' marked consumer culture.[17] Revivalist themes were not only explored in Dun Emer's and Cuala's literary volumes but would also dominate their popular and commercially successful series of individual hand-coloured prints, greetings cards and illustrated broadsheets.

The Printed Page and National Identity

A 1903 company prospectus outlined the ethos of the Dun Emer cooperative. One section stated, 'Everything as far as possible is Irish, the paper of the books, the linen of the embroidery, the wool of the tapestries and carpets. The designs are also of the spirit and the tradition of Ireland.' With reference to the printing of books the prospectus claimed, '(T)he first two books issued by the Dun Emer Press are now scattered over the world and have given pleasure to our country people in America and at home and to strangers interested in the art of hand printing.'[18] Like W. B.

---

16   Lewis, *The Yeats Sisters*, 37. An example of feminist tracts published by the Women's Printing Society included *'Veritas', What is Women's Suffrage and Why do Women Want it* (London, 1883).
17   John Strachan and Clare Nally, *Advertising, Literature and Print Culture in Ireland, 1891–1922* (London: Palgrave, 2012), 1.
18   Anon., *The Dun Emer Industries Prospectus* (Dublin: Dun Emer Press, 1903).

Yeats, others, such as the Irish writer, artist and social reformer George Russell (who wrote under the pseudonym Æ), recognized that the arts afforded pre-independence Ireland a platform where it could assert itself as a sovereign political and cultural entity.[19] Some decades later, following the establishment of the self-governed Irish Free State, an article from the Russell-edited *The Irish Statesman* stated, 'It is important that in our young state there should be a realisation of the importance of the arts to civilisation.'[20] W. B. Yeats also acknowledged the local importance of the arts, and observed that the work at Dun Emer, and subsequently Cuala, presented an opportunity to create finely crafted artefacts that 'moved a whole people and not a few'.[21] As expected of a former art student and an ardent supporter of William Morris, the quality of the printing and presentation of his work was of great import to W. B. Yeats. The considered design, the hand-printed page and the use of Irish materials in Dun Emer Press and Cuala Press publications were all read in nationalistic terms. The work of both presses was seen as an attempt to reintroduce the indigenous craft of hand printing in Ireland and to promote it in a revived form, characterized by the high production values, creativity and its distinctive 'Irishness'. The national value of the industries at Dun Emer and Cuala was also recognized by government agencies: Dun Emer received a grant of £120 from the Department of Agriculture and Technical Instruction, and later the Yeats sisters received support through an award of £100 from Arts and Crafts Society of Ireland.[22] The use of local materials and skills, together with references to earlier traditional forms, was

19   *Daily Express* (10 December 1898): in a letter to the editor, George Russell wrote of his regret that there was no distinctive sense of identity in Irish art and that few found visual inspiration from Irish life and traditions, as had been the case in Irish writing.
20   *The Irish Statesman*, 5 (1926), 647.
21   W. B. Yeats, 'Ireland and the Arts', *The United Irishman* (1901) quoted in Nicola Gordon Bowe, 'Wilhelmina Geddes, Harry Clarke, and Their Part in the Arts and Crafts Movement in Ireland', *The Journal of Decorative and Propaganda Arts*, 8, Spring (1988), 58–79 (58).
22   Vicky Cremin 'The Cuala Press and Its Origins', lecture script for Foxrock Local History Group, September 1989. TCD OLS Xerox 6 no.2.

seen to encourage regional vitality, as Irish art, crafts and literature attracted new audiences, both national and international.[23] The Dun Emer and Cuala Presses printed images of Irish subject matter in particular, which, as recalled by Susan Yeats after the death of her sister, 'became a very large part of the work of the Press, and have gone all over the world'.[24]

The Private Press, the Printed Image and the Irish Artist

The history of Irish artists and the printed image during the nineteenth century was varied and prolific as many became involved in producing designs for a diverse range of publications for the thriving British print industry.[25] Artists born in Ireland and who enjoyed international reputations, such as the nineteenth-century painters Daniel Maclise RA and William Mulready RA, followed the example of their British colleagues by working with leading publishers and engravers of the day.[26] From the mid-1800s publishers especially marketed their collaborations with artists, producing bespoke, limited-edition illustrated books, with images printed from hand-cut blocks or plates, and bound in hand-finished

23   Skelton, 'Twentieth-century Irish literature', 376.
24   Susan Yeats, *Elizabeth Corbet Yeats; born March 11th 1868 – died January 16th 1940*. (Dublin: Cuala Press, 1940). In a newspaper interview, Anne Yeats, daughter of W. B. Yeats, and director of the Cuala Press in its latter years described the prints as the Press's 'bread and butter' which helped to finance the printing of books. See Ida Grehan 'The Yeats family as printers and publishers', *Irish Times* (21 November 1975).
25   Angela Griffith and Philip McEvansoneya, 'Drawn to the Page; Irish Artists and Illustration, 1830–1930', *Irish Arts Review*, 29:3 (2012), 116–9.
26   Maclise's most celebrated contributions to British illustrations include Thomas Moore, *Moore's Irish Melodies* (London: Longmans, 1845); Alfred Tennyson, *Poems*, (London: Moxon, 1857); Charles Dickens, *The Chimes: A Goblin Story of Some Bells that Rang an Old Year Out and a New Year In* (London: Chapman & Hall, 1845); Mulready's illustrations include those for Oliver Goldsmith, *The Vicar of Wakefield* (London: John van Voorst, 1843).

covers. Artists were well recompensed for this activity and they also recognized the promotional and reputational benefits of having their work included in high-production-value volumes which were widely disseminated across the Empire and beyond.

In terms of process, the quality of illustrations depended on a sound working relationship between the artist and the professional engraver. Very few fine artists cut or engraved their own relief blocks or intaglio plates; until the emergence of photographic reproductive processes, prints after an artist's designs were produced by the hand of a trained craftsperson. Some artists were content to allow their designs to be translated from their original drawings with little correspondence with the engraver. Other artists worked closely with the professional cutter directing exactly how they wished their illustrations to be interpreted, engraved and printed.[27] Nonetheless, as the juggernaut of technical advancement loomed, new and evolving methods of photomechanical reproduction were developing, leading many to conclude that the hand-engraved, hand-printed illustrated book would be consigned to history.[28]

It was in this context that the private press movement emerged in the later nineteenth century and was in large part a reaction to the dominance of commercial mass publishing using industrial printing technologies. Led by William Morris's Kelmscott Press and followed by others such as Charles Ricketts (1866–1931) and Charles Haslewood Shannon's (1863–1937) Vale Press, private presses returned to earlier handcraft reproduction methods. The private press rebuilt working relationships with publishers, engravers and artists. Of key concern in private press illustrated volumes was the aesthetic relationship of text and image – where each was valued equally, each enhancing the other. In 1890, when he founded the Kelmscott Press, Morris believed that in order to produce what he considered to be an acceptable standard of publication, the making of books must be an inclusive handcrafted process, from the use of the hand press, the use of handmade paper,

---

27 *The Brothers Dalziel; A Record of Fifty Years of Work in Conjunction with Many of the Most Distinguished Artists of the period 1840–1890* (London: Methuen & Co. 1901), 42.
28 *The Brothers Dalziel*, vii.

the design of type and the design and execution of illustrative blocks. He argued that in order to recover the artistry of illustration, images should be printed from hand-cut woodblocks.[29] As private presses sought to ensure the quality of every aspect of their publications, many viewed them as works of art in their own right. Illustrated private press books would be distinguished by their use of artist-designed, hand-cut blocks or plates – or artist-drawn lithographs – for their imagery. Morris's theories and practices would garner the support of artists and craftspersons in his efforts to have fine design and traditional manual skills in printing recognized and celebrated; and among his most ardent supporters were the members of the Yeats household.[30]

A market for hand-printed illustrated books was cultivated by Morris and a number of private presses followed Kelmscott's example. The luxurious publications produced by the Vale Press used original hand-cut woodblocks as they argued it 'ensured greater sweetness of the printing'.[31] Among those artists who produced designs for Vale were its directors Ricketts and Shannon, Thomas Sturge Moore (1870–1944) and the Irish-born Elinor Monsell (1879–1954). As further evidence of the Yeats family's engagement with private press networks, Sturge Moore and Monsell would design pressmarks for the Dun Emer Press at the behest of W. B. Yeats. Later, the Golden Cockerel Press, owned and managed by Cork-born Robert Gibbings (1889–1958) from the 1920s, contended that artists should be involved in all aspects of illustrated printing in order to preserve the artistic integrity of their design.[32] In 1920, Gibbings, alongside artists including Eric Gill, Gwen Raverat and Northern-Irish artists Mabel Annesley and E. M. O'Rorke Dickey, was a founder member of the Society of Wood

29 S. C. Cockrell, *Essays from a Note by William Morris on his Aims in Founding the Kelmscott Press: Together with a Short Description of the Press … & an Annotated List of the Books Printed Thereat. Frontispiece by Edward Burne-Jones* (1898), 1–6. <https://archive.org/details/ANoteByWilliamMorrisOnHisAimsInFoundingTheKelmscottPressTogether>, accessed 26 November 2021.
30 Karen E. Brown, *The Yeats Circle: Verbal and Visual Relations in Ireland, 1880–1939*, (Farnham: Ashgate, 2011), 13
31 James Thorpe, *English Illustration: The Nineties* (London: Faber & Faber, 1935), 200.
32 For a personal account of practices at the Golden Cockerel Press see Robert Gibbings, 'The Golden Cockerel Press', *The Woodcut: An Annual*, 1/1 (1927), 13–26.

Engravers in London. One of its principles, in the face of the dominance of photomechanical printing processes, was to promote the use of hand-cut blocks for illustrated publishing.[33]

Yet, despite the insistence among key figures in the private press movement that the artistic value of illustration was highest when using a hand-cut matrix, a new generation of artists and printers emerged that was willing to exploit the expediencies of modern technologies. Industrial photomechanical methods were used by some publishers in reproducing artists' designs, including the collaboration between the publisher Elkin Mathews and the artist Aubrey Beardsley. Some private presses used industrial methods. James Pryde and William Nicholson at Beggarstaffs would reproduce Nicholson's woodcuts commercially through reproductive lithographic means.[34] Even the originator of the Arts and Crafts movement, William Morris, declared he did not wish to abolish all new technologies, but rather he maintained that producers should 'master our machines'.[35] Morris also recognized the necessity of accepting modern methods to guarantee greater public accessibility.[36] Therefore, following the past experiences and training of members of the Yeats family, the Dun Emer and Cuala Presses would combine letterpress printing with photomechanically produced images for their select illustrated publications. As noted by Schwarz, those that operated early twentieth-century private presses were directed by economic, social and technological conditions particular to their time and place.[37] The challenges facing E. C. Yeats were acknowledged by contemporary commentators:

> Miss Yeats had a harder task than many Englishmen who started presses: because she was working in a country which had no commercial standard of fine printing – while

33 Selborne, Joanna, *British Wood Engraving Book Illustration 1904–1940; A Break with Tradition* (London: Oak Knoll Press, 2001), 112.
34 Gordon N. Ray, *The Illustrator and the Book in England from 1790 to 1914* (New York: Pierpont Morgan Library, 1976), 178.
35 William Morris, *Art and its Producers; The Arts and Crafts Today* (London: Longman & Co., 1901), 15.
36 Elizabeth Cumming and Wendy Kaplan, *The Arts and Crafts Movement* (London: Thames and Hudson, 1991), 6–7.
37 Philip John Schwarz, 'The Contemporary Private Press', *Journal of Library History*, 5 (1970), 297–322.

we have had Baskerville and the University Presses, the Chiswick, the Aldine Series of Pickering, and the big firms of Ballantyne and Clay. With taste and wisdom, Miss Yeats attempted nothing fantastic. Her type, modelled on simple lines, is readable as well as beautiful, and her page has always seemed to us to be excelled by none of our more famous presses, except the Doves.'[38]

Additionally, if E. C. Yeats had wished to produce hand-cut illustrations and prints there was no tradition or extant community of wood engravers (or artist-printmakers) working in Dublin or on the island of Ireland in the first decades of the 1900s. In a letter to a customer's query dating from 1912, E. C. Yeats wrote: 'We cannot make woodblocks. I fear there are none done in Ireland now – but we could have a process block made in Dublin like we have for the Broadsides.'[39]

From the beginning, the Dun Emer and Cuala Presses used 'process blocks' for their printed imagery. A key reason for this was that while domiciled and working in London, E. C. Yeats and her brother, the artist and commercial illustrator (and leading artist at Dun Emer and Cuala) Jack Butler Yeats (1871–1957), were experienced in working with photo-mechanical methods as illustrators. At no time in their careers had E. C. Yeats or Jack B. Yeats produced hand-cut blocks or so-called fine art prints which may seem at odds given their close acquaintance with, and admiration for, Morris and his activities at Kelmscott. Instead, Dun Emer and Cuala would employ photoengraved blocks, a process developed by Walter Roberts in 1864. The method grew in popularity among commercial publishers initially, but it subsequently attracted artists working in illustration.[40] While some artists extolled the virtue of the hand-cut artist's block, photoengraving also had its supporters. During the photoengraving process, the artist's original drawing was transferred photographically to the metal plate before being mechanically processed. Through this process artists recognized that their line drawing was transferred in its truest form and

---

38 *The Observer*, undated; quoted in Cuala Press Brochure c.1925: Cuala Press Archive, 11535/49A/23.
39 Miller, *The Dun Emer later the Cuala Press*, 65.
40 F. J. Harvey Darton, *Modern Book Illustration in Great Britain and America* (London: The Studio Limited, 1931), 17.

was not subject to the vagaries of a human hand. Other advocates argued that, 'rather than destroying an artist's personality ... the line block certainly encourages freedom of pure draughtsmanship'.[41]

Among E. C. Yeats's personal collection of books was Charles Jacobi's *Some Notes on Books and Printing – A Guide for Authors Publishers and others*.[42] Jacobi had been managing partner of the Chiswick Press. Jacobi's chapter on 'Methods of Illustration' gives some further insight into E. C. Yeats's reasoning in terms of her choice of illustration process as used at Dun Emer and Cuala. E. C. Yeats's edition was published in 1902, the year that the Dun Emer Industries were founded. Jacobi notes that in past years, illustrations had become more frequent and that few publishers produce a book without illustrations or at least some form of typographical decoration. Jacobi presents the choices for the printer as being 'whether the designs are original or whether the pictures are mere reproductions of old subjects' and that the former allowed designs to be adaptable to the requirements of the printer; the vast majority of images printed at Dun Emer and Cuala Presses were from original designs. Jacobi goes on to state that 'today nearly all illustrations are mechanically' reproduced.[43] Practically, Jacobi underlines how photomechanical relief processes may be easily incorporated with letterpress type and highlights its cost-effectiveness as it eradicated the expenses associated with a professional engraver. He also makes the astute observation that while artists 'of repute' are producing illustrations, few of them trained as engravers nor were they willing to 'undertake the drudgery of such training'.[44] Furthermore, the original artwork was preserved and available for sale, which is exactly what Jack B. Yeats did, advertising the sale of his original drawings amongst Dun Emer and Cuala Presses circulars promoting the prints made from them.

E. C. and Jack B. Yeats's first experience of what would be described as 'art printing' was with the London publisher Elkin Mathews (1851–1921).

---

41 Darton, *Modern Book Illustration*, 28.
42 Cuala Press Archive: Elizabeth Corbet Yeats Collection: Press A Cuala Arch xBox 16 no.5.
43 Charles Jacobi, *Some Notes on Books and Printing: A Guide for Authors Publishers and Others* (London: C. Whittingham & Co., 1902), 33.
44 Jacobi, *Some Notes on Books and Printing*, 38.

Figure 8.1. *Specimen of 'A Broad Sheet'*, Elkin Mathews, London (Cuala Press Archive) © Estate of Jack B. Yeats, DACS London / IVARO Dublin, 2020. Image courtesy of the Board of Trinity College, Dublin.

Mathews, a neighbour of the Yeatses in London's Bedford Park, became a close family friend. He was a well-known figure in artistic circles in England and had been involved in publishing the graphic work of a number of artists, including the deluxe periodical *The Yellow Book*.[45] The association with Mathews in conjunction with key figures in the English private press movement demonstrated to E. C. and Jack B. Yeats the opportunities for artistic expression within printing. *The Yellow Book* presented a visual argument that images were more than illustrations, they were not secondary to text, but rather were on a par with the magazine's literary content – they were presented as independent artforms.[46] In 1902, Jack B. Yeats began a two-year partnership with Mathews, and with the assistance of E. C. Yeats, they produced a limited-edition series, issued monthly, entitled *A Broad Sheet*.[47] The publication – modelled on inexpensive popular ballad sheets which were sold by generations of street singers across British and Irish cities and fairs – was first published in January 1902. *A Broad Sheet*, produced as a limited edition of 300 per issue, comprised a single sheet of paper, printed on one side (Figure 8.1). The text, made up of lyrics and poetry, was provided by the Yeats family and their literary friends, some of whom were leading writers of the day, including W. B. Yeats, Lady Gregory, George Russell (Æ), John Masefield and Frederick York Powell. Images featured largely on *A Broad Sheet* page, asserting the importance of the visual content. They were distinctive in terms of their bold graphic style, their use of colour (applied by hand) and their dominant placement. The artist's role for *A Broad Sheet* was that of interpreter of the text rather than acting as a translator or transcriber of the writer's intent. The visual element was – at the very least – in partnership with the writing. As Lorraine Janzen Kooistra stated in her critical examination of *fin-de-siècle* illustrated

---

45 Artists included Aubrey Beardsley, Laurence Housman and Walter Sickert.
46 Linda Dowling, 'Letterpress and Picture in the Literary Periodicals of the 1890s', *The Yearbook of English Studies*, 16 (1986), 117–31. Dowling makes this argument citing how the content pages in *The Yellow Book* are listed as 'Literature' and 'Art' from the second issue – see *The Yellow Book: An Illustrated Quarterly*, Vol. II, July (1894), <https://archive.org/details/yellowjuly189402uoft>, accessed 26 November 2021.
47 During the first year, Jack B. Yeats also collaborated with the Jamaican-born artist and illustrator Pamela Coleman Smith.

Figure 8.2. *Design for an Irish-themed Greeting Card*, Elizabeth C. Yeats (Cuala Press Archive). Image courtesy of the Board of Trinity College, Dublin.

literature, artists had become increasingly independent of, or interpretative of, the texts their work accompanied.[48] Observing the practices of new publishing cultures in London, the redefinition of the artist's role from illustrator to contributor had a major impact on E. C. Yeats as she would go on to create an unprecedented environment for Irish artists to express themselves in print. *A Broad Sheet* would serve as a prototype for a similar illustrated publication first produced at Dun Emer Press, and later at the Cuala Press, entitled *A Broadside*.

48   Lorraine Janzen Kooistra, *The Artist as Critic: Bi-textuality in the Fin-de-Siècle Illustrated Book* (Aldershot: Scolar Press, 1997), 3.

The Art of Printing – *A Broadside*

By the time of E. C. Yeats's death in January 1940 sixty-seven books had been published under the Dun Emer and Cuala imprints.[49] Sold by subscription, these hand-printed volumes, as in the example of other private presses, were expensive and time-consuming to produce. However, by 1906, four years after the establishment of Dun Emer, the press diversified to include the production of hand-coloured prints. The director, based on her experience and knowledge of printing on mainland Britain, had determined that there was a market for such visual materials, and such materials would be economical and expedient to produce. E. C. Yeats was proven correct. Account books from 1925 show that artist-designed prints earned £422.10s, while literary volumes brought in a revenue of £260.5s. The earliest prints were designed by Jack B. Yeats and typically depicted Irish rural scenes and characters, such as an Irish cottage set in a rural landscape, point-to-point racing on a Western strand or a busy market town with a host of expressive characters. For the period up to 1940, ninety-seven individual prints have been catalogued.[50] The presses also produced Irish-themed greeting cards designed by Jack B. Yeats, his wife the artist Mary Cottenham Yeats, E. C. Yeats herself, Beatrice Elvery and Hilda Roberts among others (Figure 8.2).[51] Other printed ephemera included bookplates designed by E. C. and Jack B. Yeats, and other designers included George Atkinson and Thomas Sturge Moore – who designed a bookplate for W. B. Yeats. While some bookplate designs were in keeping with traditional armorial motifs, the majority of those by Jack B. and E. C. Yeats drew on Irish subjects.

---

49   For a list of titles see Lewis, *The Yeats Sisters*, 190–91.
50   National Book League, *The Cuala Press, 1903–1973: [Catalogue of] an Exhibition Arranged by the National Book League to Celebrate the Seventieth Anniversary of the Cuala Press, 11–30 June 1973* (1973), unpaginated
51   National Book League, *The Cuala Press*. The 1950 card catalogue advertised 129 designs by different artists.

This rich and varied visual content was in stark contrast to the restrained presentation of Dun Emer and Cuala Presses literary ventures. In a contemporary review, the critic William Garden Blaikie Murdoch described the Cuala book as having no 'distracting adornments, while the binding consists usually in a grey canvas back, sides of rough bluish paper, so the beauty of these Irish bibelots is ever a charming homeliness, as in a painting by Chardin'.[52] Other printers, while admiring of the composition and placement of type, were somewhat critical of the lack of decoration and illustration in Cuala Press books.[53] However, their austere aesthetic was formed initially as a result of E. C. Yeats's lack of training. The limits of her abilities were evident in the first Dun Emer book, W. B. Yeats's *In Seven Woods* (1903). She did not use a pressmark designed by Emery Walker because she did not know how to lock a block in the chase with type. However, by the second volume, George Russell's (Æ) *Nuts of Knowledge*, E. C. Yeats used a properly locked up block – with red ink – for the frontispiece, having learned to register two-colour printing. Yet, despite her new skills, other than the use of frontispiece motifs or pressmarks, Dun Emer and later Cuala Presses literary volumes were not illustrated. However, there was one related exception, a venture which saw text and image composed together on a page. The new publication recalled the previous successful collaboration of E. C. Yeats and Jack B. Yeats with Elkin Mathews – *A Broad Sheet* was reincarnated as *A Broadside* (Figure 8.3).

Unlike the single sheet *A Broad Sheet*, the new *A Broadside*, which was also published monthly in a limited edition of 300, was presented as a folded sheet, each page measuring 28 by 19 centimetres with pages 1, 2 and 3 printed. Cartridge paper produced in Saggart Mills south of Dublin city was used and the type was fourteen-point Caslon, the same type used for the presses' literary volumes, with the title heading printed in French Antique. Alongside traditional ballads and contemporary Irish and English writing, *A Broadside* was usually illustrated with two or three

---

52 W. G. Blaikie-Murdoch, 'The Cuala Press and its bookplates', *The Bookplate Booklet* 1:1 (1919), 9–20.
53 Claire Badaracco, 'Will Ransom, Elizabeth Yeats, and Press Publicity', *The Papers of the Bibliographical Society of America* 83:4 (1989), 524–32.

Figure 8.3. *Specimen of 'A Broadside*, Cuala Press, Dublin (Cuala Press Archive) © Estate of Jack B. Yeats, DACS London / IVARO Dublin, 2020. Image courtesy of the Board of Trinity College, Dublin.

photoengraved blocks, one for the front page, one occasionally for the second page and a single image, with no type, appeared on the third page.[54] All of the illustrations were designed by Jack B. Yeats, numbering just over 250 examples for the entire series which ran from 1908 to 1915. Colour was added to the images by hand – at no time did E. C. Yeats print illustrations, or individual prints, in colour, presumably due to a lack of knowledge on her part. She and each of her assistants applied the colours – as selected by Jack B. Yeats – by hand to each of the 300 issues published monthly. A time record exists for a second series of *A Broadside* which was produced in 1935. Pre-printing preparation time for each number was seventeen hours, type distribution was four hours and it took thirty-six hours to print the run of 300. The hand-colouring would take between sixty and ninety hours.[55] The commitment to the process of adding watercolour or gouache by hand to the printed image continued at the Cuala Press up to, and after, E. C. Yeats's death. At no time did she, or her assistants, seek training in colour printing. For E. C. Yeats hand-colouring brought an 'art' element to her printing, it became a unique and marketable feature of her work, and one that was clearly appreciated by the presses' patrons. This practice encapsulated her unconventional cross-disciplinary approach to image-making at Dun Emer and Cuala. The austerity of Dun Emer and Cuala Presses books contrasted significantly with the vibrancy of the presses' individual coloured prints. The disciplined design of the literary volumes became an established brand aesthetic for the presses. This was counterbalanced by E. C. Yeats's unconventional approach to print making and was reflected in her decision not to learn colour printing despite the fact that a number of private presses familiar to her, including Beggarstaffs and Lucien Pissarro's Eragny Press, printed in colour.[56]

E. C. Yeats's decisions were also informed by the inter-art relationships that marked the cultural climate of the period.[57] The Yeats siblings shared

[54] As for *A Broad Sheet*, writers for *A Broadside* included family friends such as Padraic Colum, John Masefield, James Stephens, Ernest Rhys and James Guthrie. Jack B. Yeats himself wrote under the pseudonym Wolfe T. McGowan.
[55] National Book League, *The Cuala Press*, unpaginated.
[56] Colin Franklin, *The Private presses,* 2nd edn (Aldershot: Scolar Press,1991), 171.
[57] Brown, *The Yeats Circle*, 1.

an appreciation for the Morrisian concept of the interconnectedness of the arts in an effort to create 'popular art'.[58] *A Broadside* exemplified a unification of the same – combining the visual and the textual – writing, design, fine art and craft. The popularity of the *Broadside* series and the presses' individual hand-coloured prints was also related to their dominant use of Irish rural themes, thus appealing to an Irish nationalist market at home and abroad.[59] Roy Foster has argued that 'their printing *oeuvre* enshrined a particular vision of the Irish Revival as well as the commodification of the Yeats family'.[60] Yet, as seen by their popularity, the transformation of revivalist ideas into relatively inexpensive artistic representations was an impactful, and appreciated, form of visual communication among diverse audiences.

'Art Printing' and Inference

While both the Dun Emer and Cuala Presses adhered to Arts and Crafts principles regarding the use of local materials and hand-printing, these very elements often led to a misunderstanding of the reproductive techniques used for its visual content. The in-house style for images, as primarily dictated by Jack B. Yeats, comprised bold expressively outlined forms that were seen by many to emulate the stylistic values of a hand-cut relief print. Historically, Dun Emer and Cuala images have been mistaken for woodcuts or wood engravings by commentators, auction houses and art institutions. The use of mechanically produced photoengraved zinc blocks at Dun Emer and Cuala was not readily known as evident in

---

58 Skelton, 'Twentieth-century Irish literature', 370.
59 While dominated by Irish subject matter, it is also important to note that Jack Yeats also explored other popular romantic themes in *A Broadside* including pirates and the American 'Wild West'.
60 R. F. Foster, *W. B. Yeats: A Life II: The Arch-Poet 1915–1939* (Oxford: Oxford University Press, 2003), 240, quoted in Brown, 'The Cuala Press Archive, 1902–86' (2013), 280.

a 1917 review for *To-day* magazine which described the prints as woodcuts.[61] Another example of this confusion was demonstrated in 1942 when Kenneth Clark curated a joint exhibition of works by Jack Butler Yeats and William Nicholson at the National Gallery in London. The display included printed designs by each artist, including Jack B. Yeats's artwork for Cuala. In his opening speech, which was published in the press, the Irish commissioner in London at the time, John Dulanty, claimed:

> ... what I know about [Jack B.] Yeats is that he is a major artist and a member of a distinguished family who are all against the mechanical. His sisters even made printing unmechanical with the Cuala Press, which they set up to provide a setting for their brother's woodcuts'.[62]

And yet when asked directly, as noted above, E. C. Yeats did not hide the fact that Cuala illustrations were not printed from hand-cut blocks. Furthermore, when her prints were exhibited in Irish Arts and Crafts Society and Guild of Irish art workers exhibitions they were described in catalogues as 'hand-printed and hand-coloured prints', or listed as 'black and white reproductions'.[63] However, as suggested in Dulanty's speech, the misconception may have been informed by the presentation of the enterprise in its literature as a handcraft venture, which, of course, in most respects it was – from the production of original designs to the use of a hand- press and handmade paper. In a promotional brochure dating from about 1931, it was claimed 'Each issue [*A Broadside*] contained three characteristic woodcuts by Jack Yeats ...'.[64] The brochure was a Cuala Press publication so one may ask why E. C. Yeats would have allowed this assertion to be published. Perhaps, as noted above, the public and critics

---

61   Eugene Mason, 'Mr. Jack B. Yeats and the Poets of a "Broadside", *To-day*, 2:8 (1917), 55–8.
62   Bruce Arnold, *Jack Yeats* (London: Yale University Press, 1998), 302.
63   The Cuala Press exhibited prints in displays including the Arts and Crafts Society of Ireland and the Guild of Irish Art Workers exhibition, Metropolitan School of Art, Dublin, 1917; Exhibition of Irish art, Royal Dublin Society, 1922, Aonach Tailteann, Dublin, 1924.
64   Aileen M. Goodwin, *The Cuala Press in Ireland: A Woman's Contribution to Fine Printing* (Dublin: Cuala Press, undated, c.1931).

persisted in describing the images as woodcuts and she believed it was futile to challenge this belief. Perceptions would also have been informed by the visual experience of the printed images themselves, the embossed nature of the print on the page, their vivid, graphic appearance emulating, to the unprofessional eye, the hand-cut relief prints of other private presses. Therefore, audiences had concluded, however wrongly, that the illustrations were woodcuts or wood engravings on formalist grounds. For collectors of fine publishing, and as espoused by other private presses, the artist-cut relief block was of greater artistic integrity and it seems that assumptions were made that E. C. Yeats shared this attitude and applied it at her press.

Conclusion

During her time as director, E. C. Yeats would steer her presses through the heady days of the Irish Revival movement, through war and rebellion and a global depression. Hers survived when the majority of private presses in Britain bowed to internal and external pressures.[65] And while unquestionably informed by the Morrisian private press model, she also had the independence of mind and vision to employ methods that would serve her, her staff and the needs of the artists employed by her, creatively and commercially. E. C. Yeats was a publisher of visual imagery that reflected the cultural agendas of the newly founded Irish Free State and her 'art printing' brought the work of Irish artists to an appreciative global market. Following the death of E. C. Yeats, George Yeats, the widow of W. B. Yeats, took over the running of the press. The writers Frank O'Connor and Seán O'Faolain became directors. And while the press would produce a number of new literary titles from the 1940s, the majority of prints issued under the new directorship were from the same

---

65 Kelmscott Press (1891–98); Vale Press (1894–1904); Eragny Press (1895–1914); Beggarstaffs (1894–99); Doves Press (1900–16).

process blocks ordered by E. C. Yeats in the 1910s and 20s. They were reproduced continuously either individually or as collections until the Cuala Press closed its doors in 1986. Serving a growing tourist market to Ireland in the 1960s and 70s, the popularity of Cuala Press 'art printing' remained unwavering and helped to ensure the viability of the press until the end. In the phrase 'art printing', art comes first and, as described by her niece, the artist Anne Yeats, for Elizabeth C. Yeats printing was an artform.[66] The printed image at Dun Emer and Cuala Presses represents an unconventional marriage of ideology, art, craft and technology.

---

66 Ida Grehan, 'The Yeats Family as Printers and Publishers', *The Irish Times* (21 November 1975).

ANIL AYKAN BARNBROOK

9 Suffragettes: Radical Design in Action, 1903–30

For the majority of citizens voting is the most notable type of political participation; other types of political involvement include campaigning, party work, contacting representatives and community organizing. Protest politics 'regarded as a distinct form of activism' and embodied in demonstrations, petitions and political strikes are also an alternative way of influencing politics.[1] From political activism comes protest design which has existed throughout the centuries, and become an increasingly popular and acknowledged force in society and the visual arts.[2] In the twenty-first century, different forms of protest and their resultant graphic languages have emerged worldwide as a response to global financial and political crises. The number of talks and discussions around the subject have expanded including two major exhibitions held in London: in 2014 *Disobedient Objects* at the Victoria & Albert Museum, and in 2018 *Hope to Nope: Graphics and Politics 2008–18* at the Design Museum.

In recent years the voice of activism has been amplified and more diverse populations have been engaged with the help of new technologies such as social media. Yet political activism is as old as political engagement itself, and as the contemporary activist design and research group Metahaven has stated:

---

1   Pippa Norris, 'Political Activism: New Challenges, New Opportunities', in Carles Boix and Susan C. Stokes, eds, *The Oxford Handbook for Comparative Politics* (Oxford: Oxford University Press, 2009), 628–49.
2   For early examples of visual protest, see the chapter *Early Developments: The Reformation and Social Comment, 1500–1900* in Liz McQuiston, *Protest!: A History of Social and Political Protest Graphics* (London: White Lion Publishing, 2019), 8–33.

> Every era, every generation, has to construct and reconstruct its political beliefs, and subsequent visuals, out of the stuff that surrounds it at any given moment. Protest signs will be made out of the cardboard, paper and textile available at that given time and place at a local hardware store; there is no hardware store selling 'political' cardboard, so even at that material level, a transformation always has to be made.[3]

Determined to gain the right to vote, a century ago the suffragettes did exactly this. They reconstructed the political landscape of their time, and to do so they created new tools and a new visual language. This chapter aims to show that the suffragettes were pioneers of modern political activism, and that modern protest design can often be traced back to their activities. In particular, it examines the impact of the diverse visual communication methods used on different stages of the Women's Social and Political Union's (WSPU) campaign to win votes for women in the first decades of the twentieth century in England. In his article 'Media and Militancy: Propaganda in the Women's Social and Political Union's Campaign' John Mercer argued that, despite the fact the WSPU brought an integrated, distinctive and sophisticated propaganda campaign to the suffrage movement it was neglected in suffrage histories.[4] By examining the WSPU's visual propaganda campaign, this chapter furthers this discussion.

Firstly, the chapter focuses on the WSPU branding – name, colour scheme, emblems, slogan – demonstrating how creatively the WSPU represented itself and through this creativity transformed the adversity it faced. Secondly, the chapter focuses on the WSPU publicity, and the creative artists who produced its visual work, giving a highly visible presence to the suffragist movement in London and around the UK. Thirdly, the chapter explores the more controversial design methods used by the suffragettes and how the visual language changed when the fight became more heated. Fourthly, the chapter focuses on the creative output and discusses the many innovative and unusual methods suffragettes used, which can be categorized

---

3 Metahaven, *Can Jokes Bring Down the Governments?* (Moscow: Strelka Press, 2013), 46–7.
4 John Mercer, 'Media and Militancy: Propaganda in the Women's Social and Political Union's Campaign', *Women's History Review*, 14:3&4 (2005), 472.

as 'guerrilla marketing' well before the term came into being.[5] Finally, the chapter concludes that winning the vote was achieved by building a methodical, persistent and highly visual graphic agitation and communication strategy. In this way the suffragettes not only reconstructed the political landscape of their time, they also created a strong visual language which was channelled using completely new tools.

Building the Brand

Name, slogan, colours and logo are essential elements of branding, and are typically used to define the identity of an organization and communicate with an intended audience.[6] 'Branding' is perceived as a commercial word, and even today some non-profit and left-wing organizations are sceptical of adopting a 'brand strategy'. However, even during the initial phases of the women's movement, the suffragettes understood the importance of branding to leverage their name and gain influence. When Emmeline Pankhurst (1858–1928) invited a number of women to her family home in Manchester to establish the organization for the fight for women's franchise in October 1903, their first task was to come up with a name: the *Women's Social and Political Union* (WSPU) was chosen.

Despite the fact they called their group the WSPU, they were known as 'suffragettes'. This title was first used in 1906 by the *Daily Mail* journalist Charles Hands as a term of derision in order to describe and differentiate them from the more 'law-abiding' suffragists.[7] The suffix '-ette' is used in a variety of diminutive formations: nouns denoting relatively small size or

---

5   'Guerrilla marketing' is an advertising concept that uses unconventional, imaginative and cost-effective tactics in order to promote a brand's products and services.
6   Catharine Slade-Brooking, *Creating a Brand Identity: A Guide for Designers* (London: Laurence King Publishing, 2016), 156.
7   *Daily Mail* (10 January 1906), 3, cited in Diane Atkinson, *Rise Up Women!* (London: Bloomsbury Publishing, 2018; Kindle edn, 2018) Loc 740.

imitation and substitute, especially for the distinctively feminine nouns such as 'kitchenette' or 'usherette'.[8]

Rather than shying away from this diminutive name, the WSPU embraced it; pronouncing it with a hardened 'g' sound (Suffra-GET-tes), implying they not only wanted the vote, but it would definitely be got.[9] They recognized this name as an opportunity to underline their core intention, which was to distinguish themselves from the constitutional suffragists and emphasize their action-oriented intentions. Furthermore, they endorsed the name by using it for their militant newspaper, *The Suffragette*, launched in 1912. By this action they transformed a popular diminutive word into a word of empowerment. From then on it became a trademark, so to this day 'suffragette' refers to any woman who fights or fought for women's suffrage all around the world.[10]

Following the choice of a brand name, another important branding decision is establishing a slogan. From the early stages of the movement, the WSPU founders agreed on the motto 'deeds, not words' which expressed their desire for political action instead of just discussions of women's suffrage.[11] However, they lacked a slogan that could stand on its own, which stated their mission openly, and which would attract attention in society and the media. A motto cannot be a substitute for a slogan, since the former acts as a guide for internal ideals, whereas the latter is used to attract attention and communicate the essence of what is represented.[12] The WSPU 'accidentally' found their slogan two years after their establishment, and arising out of an adverse situation.[13] The suffragettes' initial

[8] Macmillan Education Limited, '-ette', Macmillan Dictionary, <https://www.macmillandictionary.com/dictionary/british/ette>, accessed 25 April 2020.
[9] Atkinson, *Rise Up Women!*, Loc 740.
[10] Other languages have coined similar words in imitation.
[11] Emmeline Pankhurst, *My Own Story* (London: Eveleigh Nash, 1914), 38.
[12] Ambreen Shahnaz and Samina Amin Qadir, 'Branding the Higher Education: Identity Construction of Universities through Logos, Mottos and Slogans', *Journal of Research in Social Sciences (JRSS)*, 8:1 (2020), 57; Chiranjeev Kohli, Lance Leuthesser and Rajneesh Suri, 'Got Slogan? Guidelines for Creating Effective Slogans', *Business Horizons*, 50:5 (2007), 416.
[13] Pankhurst, *My Own Story*, 233.

intention was to influence political parties, but soon realized there was a press boycott against women's suffrage – their speeches at public events were not reported and articles about their cause were not published. On the eve of the 1905 general election, a protest was planned at a Liberal Party meeting at the Free Trade Hall in Manchester in order to break this boycott. During question time, the suffragettes intended to ask a question to the speaker while showing a banner saying: 'Will the Liberal Party Give Votes For Women?' and with this banner they expected the audience to understand the intention and nature of their presence there.[14] However at the last minute they realized it was impossible to get their large banner in the seating area, so cut the banner down to 'Votes for Women'.[15] The incident created a sensation in the media, and through this creative design solution the slogan of the entire suffrage movement came into being. 'Votes for Women' was a short and simple phrase that was memorable and directly defined their *raison d'être*.[16] From then on, the suffragettes ensured that the slogan appeared wherever a political speech took place, later becoming the title of the WSPU's official newspaper first published in October 1907.[17]

Alongside a name and slogan, the other prominent element of a brand's visual identity is the colour scheme. It affects the perception of the brand, and communicates a subliminal message regarding values and qualities.[18] Unlike the National Women's Suffrage Society who opted for the strong colour combination red, white and green, in 1908 the WSPU adopted a traditional Victorian colour combination: white for purity, green for hope and purple for dignity.[19] The colour scheme was announced just before the

14 Pankhurst, *My Own Story*, 233.
15 Pankhurst, *My Own Story*, 46.
16 A certificate from 1908 given to the WSPU members who had been imprisoned describes the cause as the ' "Votes for Women" Cause'. See Richard Pankhurst, *Sylvia Pankhurst, Artist and Crusader* (London: Paddington Press, 1979), 110.
17 Pankhurst, *My Own Story*, 50.
18 Meagan K. Cunningham, 'The Value of Color Research in Brand Strategy', *Open Journal of Social Sciences*, 5:12 (2017), 186.
19 Emmeline Pethick Lawrence, 'The Purple, White and Green', Programme of *The Women's Exhibition 1909* at the Prince's Skating Rink Knightsbridge, London, 13 to 26 May (1909) as cited in Lisa Tickner, *The Spectacle of Women: Imagery of the Suffrage Campaign, 1907–14* (London: Chatto & Windus, 1987), 265.

massive suffrage demonstration, *Women's Sunday*, at Hyde Park on 21 June where the official colours were introduced to the public. The unity of the colour scheme was displayed in the banners, in the dresses and accessories of the marchers and 'proved a very attractive means of stimulating the "esprit" of members and of propagating the movement'.[20] The colour scheme created a correlated visual language, it was simple and could potentially be understood by a wide audience. As the treasurer of the WSPU, Emmeline Pethick Lawrence (1867–1954), also pointed out: 'The colours have now become to those who belong to this Movement a new language of which the words are so simple that their meaning can be understood by the most uninstructed and most idle of passers-by.'[21]

Since the intention was to make the colours 'the reigning fashion' and 'nothing would so help to popularize the Women's Social and Political Union,' WSPU members were encouraged to wear these colours at all occasions.[22] With the advancement of printing, in particular the use of lithography in mass printing, it became possible to reproduce the colour scheme on every possible item from printed matter to their outfits.[23] It proved to be a strong marketing tool, and sales of a wide array of merchandise, such as tricoloured scarves, ribbons, sashes, handkerchiefs and jewellery, almost quadrupled in a year.[24]

The organization benefited greatly from Sylvia Pankhurst (1882–1960), a founding member of the WSPU and an artist who trained at the Manchester School of Art and Royal College of Art.[25] One of the first designs she handled for the movement was the membership card, printed

20 'The Colour Scheme', *Votes for Women*, 1:16 (25 June 1908), 258; The National Women's Social and Political Union, *Third Annual Report January 1–December 31 1908*, 6.
21 The National Women's Social and Political Union, Programme of *The Women's Exhibition 1909*, 13. Cited in Diane Atkinson, *The Suffragettes in Pictures* (Gloucestershire: Sutton Publishing, 1997), 86.
22 Emmeline Pethick Lawrence, 'Popularising the Colours', *Votes for Women*, 1:15 (18 June 1908), 249.
23 Lisa Tickner, *The Spectacle of Women: Imagery of the Suffrage Campaign, 1907–14*, 48.
24 The National Women's Social and Political Union, *Third Annual Report January 1–December 31 1908*, 6.
25 Pankhurst, *Sylvia Pankhurst, Artist and Crusader*, 27, 46.

around 1906/7 when the WSPU moved their headquarters from Manchester to London.[26] The design represented her political inclination towards the labour movement.[27] The card has the visual qualities found in many labour and left-wing images of the time which glorified the emancipation of the working class, depicted by strong women in work uniforms, as well as a suffrage banner with the message '*Votes*'.[28] In later years, however, her socialist, realist style evolved to be more symbolic. This change is best seen on the movement's emblems designed between 1908 and 1909: each emblem represented a different aspect of the organization together with the official colours, style and visual elements. The starting point for the emblem's style was the sentimental ideas of Pre-Raphaelite imagery, which were 'aesthetically and ideologically congruent with the image of womanliness' that the WSPU wished to convey.[29] The Pre-Raphaelites placed women in the centre of their paintings, depicting them in an idealized way that was typically melancholic and sensual and often passive and/or vulnerable. In contrast, however, Sylvia Pankhurst transformed them from submissive feminine stereotypes and depicted women in action, empowered and in control. For instance, the earliest emblem from 1908 illustrates a woman with wings, trumpeting for freedom which was originally designed for the cover of the first bound edition of the official newspaper *Votes for Women*.[30] Another emblem illustrates a woman opening barred doors, holding a 'votes for women' sash and breaking free, and which was used on the WSPU's 1908 Christmas card, and on the cover of the book *Prisons and Prisoners* (Lytton, 1914). One more emblem, from 1909, depicts a woman sowing seeds in the ground, which can be seen on numerous handbills that were used to promote the WSPU's public meetings. Subversive images such as these became characteristic of suffragette art and design and were used to transform the political landscape, attacking social norms and disrupting the status quo.

26   Pankhurst, *Sylvia Pankhurst, Artist and Crusader*, 62.
27   Pankhurst, *Sylvia Pankhurst, Artist and Crusader*, 25–6, 53–54, 75–99.
28   An image of the membership card can be found here: <https://www.bl.uk/collection-items/maud-arncliffe-sennetts-scrapbook-volume-1>, accessed 29 May 2020.
29   Tickner, *The Spectacle of Women: Imagery of the Suffrage Campaign, 1907–14*, 30.
30   Elizabeth Crawford, *Art and Suffrage: A Biographical Dictionary of Suffrage Artists* (London: Francis Boutle Publishers, 2018), 175.

Publicizing the Cause

The next step was to create public interest within London as well as other cities around the UK. To achieve this, the WSPU distributed printed material and merchandise, and took its campaign to the streets with spectacular demonstrations organized in collaboration with other suffrage groups. Artist ateliers played an important role in preparations of these spectacles. In particular, in order to help towards the preparations for the United Procession of Women (1907), the Artists' Suffrage League (ASL) was established, followed in 1909 by another artist studio called Suffrage Atelier (SA) which was founded 'to encourage artists to forward the women's movement, and particularly the enfranchisement of women, by means of pictorial publications'.[31] The ASL was mostly associated with fine art; they employed professional artists and encouraged non-professionals to submit work.[32] Even though significant members of the SA, such as Clemence Housman (1861–1955) and Laurence Housman (1865–1959), were also members of the WSPU,[33] the WSPU was not associated with any organized artists' leagues, instead relying on a small number of individual artists, such as Sylvia Pankhurst.[34]

In addition to their subversion of the Pre-Raphaelite style they also used the visual language of commercial fashion illustrations, transforming them into political propaganda. Examples of this are Hilda Dallas' (1878–1958) posters which were designed in 1909 for publicizing the newspaper *Votes for Women* (Figure 9.1). The figures are feminine, but not eroticized as was typically the case in commercial advertising. This became an effective way to communicate to the public that they were not a threat to the established ideal of womanhood, but were feminine as well as socially and politically capable: '"Womanly" women needed the vote' and 'the

---

31   Constitution of The Suffrage Atelier, see Tickner, *The Spectacle of Women*, 241.
32   Crawford, *Art and Suffrage*, 14.
33   Crawford, *Art and Suffrage*, 124–9.
34   Tickner, *The Spectacle of Women*, 241.

Figure 9.1. Advertisement for *Votes for Women*. Image courtesy of Schlesinger Library, Radcliffe Institute, Harvard University.

emancipation of feminine virtues into public life was a necessary condition of social reform'.[35]

An important part of the WSPU's visual identity was the official uniform introduced in 1908. The suffragettes disguised themselves in conventional female dress, just like Joan of Arc, 'the patron saint of the suffragettes' who made the journey through hostile French territory disguised as a soldier. The official dress was mainly white which, aside from symbolizing 'purity and innocence', was also 'a marker of class and gender'; gender signifiers softened their aggressive stance and was 'in contrast with the darker masculine colours of the period ... conforming to gender binaries': their official costume was 'reassuringly feminine'.[36] It was also a signifier of class, thereby enhancing the suffragettes' status and worth in the public eye.[37] Known for her militant spirit, the co-founder of the WSPU, Christabel Pankhurst (1880–1958), believed 'the House of Commons, and even its Labour members were more impressed by demonstrations of the feminine *bourgeoise* than of the feminine proletariat'.[38] All members were encouraged to wear their uniform at all times.[39] As well as presenting a lady-like presence and transforming the 'extremely unpleasant' suffragette image in the public eye, the uniform also played a vital role in creating a united movement, fostering professionalism and loyalty.[40] As important as was the suffragettes' uniform, many also used other outfits as a form of protest. For example, Christabel Pankhurst wore her academic gown to communicate that she was a university graduate, although she could not actually put her law studies into practice because as a woman she could not work as a lawyer.[41] Similarly,

35   Tickner, *The Spectacle of Women*, x.
36   Kimberly Wahl, 'Purity and Parity: The White Dress of the Suffrage Movement in Early Twentieth-Century Britain', in Jonathan Faiers and Mary Westerman Bulgarella, eds, *Colours in Fashion* (London: Bloomsbury Academic, 2016), 22.
37   Wahl, *Purity and Parity*, 24.
38   Christabel Pankhurst, *Unshackled: The Story of How We Won the Vote* (London: Hutchinson of London, 1919), 67.
39   'Concerning Dress', *Votes for Women*, 2:30 (1 October 1908), 5.
40   'The Suffragette and the Dress Problem', *Votes for Women*, 1:21 (30 July 1908), 348; 'Dress in the Colours', *Votes for Women*, 2:52 (5 March 1909), 413.
41   For the image of Christabel Pankhurst in her academic gown at the *Women's Sunday* in 1908 see Atkinson, *The Suffragettes in Pictures*, 108; Krista Cowman, *Women of*

another notable member of the WSPU, the 'working-class heroine' Annie Kenney (1879–1953), often proudly wore her cotton-mill worker's clothes.[42]

Although the WSPU is generally considered to be a group mainly consisting of middle-class women, the social background of the WSPU members was diverse. A few years after the movement was founded, most social classes were represented within the WSPU, including mill girls, teachers, merchant family members as well as 'ladies'.[43] The uniting link between these women was the frustration of their position in society. As Christabel Pankhurst explained: 'ours is not a class movement at all. We take in everybody – the highest and the lowest, the richest and the poorest. The bond is womanhood!'[44] The message of diversity was declared in the first issue of *Votes for Women*: 'come and join us, whatever your age, whatever your class, whatever your political inclination'.[45] The front cover of a much later issue in 1911 visually depicts the same message: women from different classes, ages and occupations marching united for the suffrage cause.[46]

Another example of the suffragettes' subversive fashion was the creation of jewellery. Sylvia Pankhurst designed a brooch called the 'Holloway Brooch' made to commemorate the suffragettes' incarceration at Holloway Prison.[47] The inspiration came from the symbol of the House of Commons and the broad arrow from prison uniforms.[48] The broad arrow is in the WSPU's colours, with silver chains on either side. Between them a portcullis is placed, which is also a part of the Houses of Parliament's crowned

---

the Right Spirit, Paid Organisers of the Women's Social and Political Union (WSPU) 1904–18 (Manchester: Manchester University Press, 2007), 24.

42 Diane Atkinson, 'Six Suffragette Photographs', in Maroula Joannou and June Purvis, eds, *The Women's Suffrage Movement: New Feminist Perspectives* (Manchester: Manchester University Press, 1998), 90.
43 Cowman, *Women of the Right Spirit*, 20.
44 June Purvis, *Christabel Pankhurst: A Biography* (Abingdon: Routledge, 2018), 329.
45 'The Battle Cry', *Votes for Women*, 1:1 (October 1907), 6.
46 Alfred Pearse, [front cover cartoon], *Votes for Women*, 4:169 (2 June 1911), 573.
47 'The Women Who Suffered', *Votes for Women*, 2:58 (16 April 1909), 553.
48 Neil R. Storey, *Prisons and Prisoners in Victorian Britain* (Cheltenham: The History Press, 2010), 54–5.

portcullis symbol. In manipulating one of the best-known authoritarian symbols, the design turned the symbol of the House of Commons into a mark of repression. The broad arrow motif became an iconic symbol in its own right, a badge of honour, worn by women who were imprisoned.[49] The suffragettes also carried banners with arrow symbols, referring to this design, in street demonstrations.[50]

Rallies and exhibitions provided the best opportunities at which to demonstrate the vast support for women's suffrage, as the suffragettes 'have been challenged by the Government to show numbers'.[51] They not only accepted the challenge and managed to gather thousands of people to the 'Women's Sunday' in 1908, but they also convinced the most critical newspapers that WSPU was worthy of appreciation:

> I am sure a great many people never realised until yesterday how young and dainty and elegant and charming most leaders of the movement are. And how well they spoke – with what free and graceful gesture; never at a loss for a word or an apt reply to an interruption; calm and collected; forcible, yet, so far as I heard, not violent; earnest, but happily humorous as well.[52]

In addition to uniforms, embroidered banners were also an important part of communicating the WSPU's aims at demonstrations. Embroidery is a skill which has been predominantly associated with women throughout history, yet the suffragettes subverted the feminine perception of this activity, by using it as a political tool.

The WSPU was aware of the impact of banners. It was, after all, 'a little white cotton banner, inscribed with the words, "Votes for Women", in black letters', which became important to the suffragettes on their first protest at the Free Trade Hall, Manchester.[53] For 'Women's Sunday' several banners were commissioned from professional artists, seven of which were

49 'Union Colours, Badges, &c.', *Votes for Women*, 2:73 (30 July 1909), 1015.
50 Atkinson, *The Suffragettes in Pictures*, 78.
51 The National Women's Social and Political Union, *Second Annual Report 1 January–31 December 1907* (London: Woman's Press, 1908), 10.
52 *Votes for Women*, 1:16 (25 June 1908), 261.
53 Sylvia Pankhurst, 'The History of the Suffrage Movement, Part II: The Beginning of the Militant Tactics', *Votes for Women*, 2:30 (1 October 1908), 3.

unfurled at a special ceremony two days before the main event.[54] Emmeline Pethick Lawrence promised to the donors of these banners that one day they would be 'treasured possessions to the women of the country'.[55] For the same rally 700 smaller banners were made by suffragettes from all around the country.[56] All banners, whether made by professionals or amateurs, were competent works of art and design that 'had an impact upon their audience and whose style also sent particular messages about feminism and femininity together'.[57] At the time, the *Daily News* reported:

> Gleaming in the sunlight the seven hundred banners told their own story ... the massed spectators read the mottoes aloud as they went by, 'Who would be free themselves must strike the blow', 'Not chivalry but justice', 'The only hope for the unemployed', '237 women were imprisoned for the vote' and '54 weeks of Holloway'.[58]

The other notable publicity initiative was opening the Woman's Press shop in order to sell WSPU's merchandise and publications. Opened in 1910, the shop was an extension of the literature department (1907) founded by the British Labour politician and suffrage campaigner Frederick Pethick Lawrence (1871–1961) for publishing and selling WSPU literature; soon after its opening, the sales increased and its premises rapidly expanded, leading to a shop at a central London location, which they hoped would

---

54 Tickner, *The Spectacle of Women: Imagery of the Suffrage Campaign, 1907–14*, 261; Emmeline Pethick Lawrence, 'Hyde Park Demonstration Fund', *Votes For Women*, 1:10 (14 May 1908), 164; 'Unfurling the Banners', *Votes for Women*, 1:16 (25 June 1908), 270.

55 Emmeline Pethick Lawrence, 'Hyde Park Demonstration Fund', *Votes For Women*, 1:10 (14 May 1908), 164.

56 Atkinson, *Rise Up Women!*, Loc 1788.

57 Paula Hays Harper, 'Votes for Women? A Graphic Episode in the Battle of the Sexes', in Henry A. Millon and Linda Nochlin, eds, *Art and Architecture in the Service of Politics*, (Cambridge: MIT Press, 1798), 150–61 as cited in Colleen Denney, *The Visual Culture of Women's Activism in London, Paris and Beyond: An Analytical Art History, 1860 to the Present* (Jefferson: McFarland & Company Inc., Publishers, 2018), 9.

58 *Votes for Women*, 1:16 (25 June 1908), 261.

attract passers-by.⁵⁹ In 1909, The Woman's Press became the headquarters of their newspaper *Votes for Women* and at the opening ceremony, literature representative Evelyn Jane Sharp (1869–1955) stated:

> it is not only the commercial side of our shop keeping that matters so much [...] [it is also the] enormous number of people who have heard about our movement for the first time through the work that has been done by the Woman's Press.⁶⁰

Through the Woman's Press, they also sold everyday 'middle-class' products in order to place their objectives at the heart of the household.⁶¹ This infiltration of their message into the most respectable of homes was achieved through the many items offered for sale, such as scarves, blouses, bags, belts, 'Pethick' tobacco pouches, 'Emmeline' and 'Christabel' bags, books, pamphlets, leaflets, stationery, games, blotters and playing cards.⁶² One of the most notable items was a tea-set, originally commissioned for the 'Women's Exhibition' at the Prince's Skating Rink at Knightsbridge, in May 1909.⁶³ Rather than typical Edwardian decorative patterns, Sylvia Pankhurst designed a modern and stylish range of tableware using the suffragette colours and angel-trumpet logo. They also produced and sold Votes for Women tea. Such products enabled those who did not participate at demonstrations or other public events to show support for the WSPU's cause.⁶⁴

In parallel with their increasing visibility, the suffragettes also attracted negative publicity. New printing technologies made picture postcards popular and affordable, and were often used by the suffragettes to defuse anti-suffragist propaganda. A popular theme for the postcards was the juxtaposition of good education and imprisonment for the suffrage cause.

---

59 Frederick Pethick Lawrence, 'The Romance of the Woman's Press', *Votes for Women*, 4:184 (15 September 1911), 793.
60 'Under the Clock', *Votes for Women*, 3:114 (13 May 1910), 533.
61 'Xmas Gifts at the W.S.P.U. Shops', *Votes for Women*, 3:92 (10 December 1909), 170. Also see the advertisement of the board game *Pank-a -Squith* in *Votes for Women*, 3:90 (26 November 1909), 141.
62 Under the Clock', *Votes for Women*, 3:121 (1 July 1910), 651.
63 Atkinson, *Rise Up Women!*, Loc 2649.
64 'Under the Clock', *Votes for Women*, 3:114 (13 May 1910), 533.

On one postcard Edith How-Martyn (1875–1954) was shown as a university lecturer as well as a prisoner in Holloway Prison.[65] Advances in printing also allowed the production of card and board games, which were popular amongst WSPU's supporters. The Woman's Press produced a simple deck of cards with the suffragette colours, Votes for Women slogan and prison arrows.[66] A popular card game was *Panko*, first advertised in *Votes for Women* just before Christmas 1909, which contained forty-eight cards of six different designs illustrated by Edward Tennyson Reed (1860–1933) of *Punch* magazine.[67] Several board games were also created such as 'the propaganda table game' *Pank-a-Squith*, representing Pankhurst versus Prime Minister Asquith.[68]

Satirical Cartoons and Controversial Advertising (or Shock Advertising)

The suffragettes' initial objective was building a favourable image to keep women's suffrage in the public eye, but when the fight became heated the visual language changed dramatically. They attempted both to tackle potentially difficult issues, and to influence public opinion on how the government treated women, with more direct information techniques and hard-line 'shock advertising'. The WSPU neither published nor commissioned as many posters as other suffrage organizations and ateliers; rather they concentrated on photographic postcards of their leaders and demonstrations.[69] Nevertheless they educated the public about women's suffrage

---

65 Elizabeth Crawford, *The Women's Suffrage Movement: A Reference Guide 1866–1928* (London: UCL Press. 1999), 388. An image of the postcard can be found here: (image 10), <https://visit.bodleian.ox.ac.uk/files/suffrageinaboxsources-postcardspdf>, accessed 15 June 2020.
66 Kenneth Florey, *Women's Suffrage Memorabilia: An Illustrated Historical Study* (Jefferson: : McFarland & Company, 2013), 113.
67 *Votes for Women*, 3:91 (3 December 1909), 157; Kenneth Florey, *Women's Suffrage Memorabilia*, 114.
68 *Votes for Women*, 3:90 (26 November 1909), 141.
69 Tickner, *The Spectacle of Women*, 27, 252–53.

and its broad benefits through *Votes for Women* and later *The Suffragette*. From issue 51 of *Votes for Women* they started using on the front page an editorial cartoon depicting the current political situation.[70] The cartoons were drawn and donated to the paper on a weekly basis by the accredited cartoonist Alfred Pearse (1855–1933) under the pseudonym 'A. Patriot'.[71] Pearse's cartoons were powerful, cleverly expressing each week's events, and 'always aroused considerable interest both inside and outside the movement'; thus many suffragists would cut and paste them into their scrapbooks.[72] Due to their popularity and success in communicating the WSPU's message, some of the cover cartoons were also produced as postcards and posters, leading to an exhibition at the Woman's Press in 1911.[73]

Satirical cartoons were deemed appropriate for the WSPU's sensationalist intentions, and were the main visual communication medium that *Votes for Women* used to criticize and ridicule the Prime Minister and his government. Certainly, humour helped to bring the messages to a wider audience, because humour has 'emphasis on the shared human background of oppressors and oppressed'.[74] The WSPU also used 'educational' cartoons whose aim was to describe the broad impact of women's suffrage.[75] Offering information based on real stories,[76] they informed the public about the economic and political inequality between the sexes and

70   Alfred Pearse, [front cover cartoon], *Votes for Women*, 2:51 (26 February 1909), 369.
71   'Features of this Issue', *Votes for Women*, 2:51 (26 February 1909), 370.
72   'WSPU Announcements', *Votes for Women*, 4:157 (10 March 1911), 366; Crawford, *Art and Suffrage*, 182.
73   'WSPU Announcements', *Votes for Women*, 4:157 (10 March 1911), 366.
74   Chloe Ward, 'Images of Empathy: Representations of Force Feeding in Votes for Women', in Miranda Garrett and Zoë Thomas, eds., *Suffrage and the Arts, Visual Culture, Politics and Enterprise* (London: Bloomsbury Publishing, 2018; Kindle edn, 2018), Loc 6386; Marjolein 't Hart, 'Humour and Social Protest: An Introduction', in Marjolein 't Hart and Dennis Bos, eds, *Humour and Social Protest* (Cambridge: Press Syndicate of the University of Cambridge, 2008), 18.
75   Alfred Pearse, [front cover cartoons], *Votes for Women*, 4:153 (10 February 1911), 301; 4:155 (1911), 333 and 4:168 (26 May 1911), 557.
76   For the examples of such stories see 'Old Grievances Unredressed', 4:155 (24 February 1911), 334; 'The World We Live In', 4:155 (24 February 1911), 339 and 'The Belfast Mother', 4:153 (10 February 1911), 303.

highlighted legal discrimination against women. These cartoons also emphasized that if women got the vote, they could contribute to the making of laws which could eventually improve their living conditions. As Emmeline Pethick Lawrence pointed out, the 'life and death struggle' was 'to get a great revolt of the women against their subjection of body and mind to men'.[77]

The year 1909 was marked by Emmeline Pankhurst as 'an important point' in their struggle, because they became determined 'never again to submit to be classed with criminals', and not to 'allow the Liberal government to treat them like ordinary law-breakers in future'.[78] In the same year the suffragettes became increasingly frustrated by the government's constant refusal to address their issues and the Prime Minister's refusal to meet them.[79] Consequently, they moved towards 'new and more aggressive forms of militancy' but the more determined they were, the more intolerant the police and authorities became.[80] To push their agenda to be recognized as political and not criminal prisoners, many of the suffragettes went on hunger strike while in prison.[81] Hunger strikes politicized their bodies and created a radical practice of non-violent protest that inspired others such as Mahatma Gandhi.[82] Force-feeding was introduced by the authorities as a deterrent as well as a punishment. The news of suffragettes being force-fed outraged the public, and it was then that the WSPU started using a new propaganda technique which today is referred to as 'shock advertising'.

Shock advertising 'deliberately rather than intentionally startles and offends its audience by violating norms for social values and personal ideals'.[83] This technique prospered in the 1980s: the Italian clothing brand Benetton's

77 Roger Fulford, *Votes for Women* (London: Faber and Faber, 1957), 143.
78 Pankhurst, *My Own Story*, 136.
79 Pankhurst, *My Own Story*, 138–48.
80 Pankhurst, *My Own Story*, 148.
81 'The Hunger Strike', *Votes for Women*, 2:71 (16 July 1909), 933.
82 Mahatma Gandhi, 'Suffragettes', *Indian Opinion* (28 August 1909), in *The Collected Works of Mahatma Gandhi vol. 09* (New Delhi: 1963), 324–26.
83 Darren W. Dahl, Kristina D. Frankenberger and Rajesh V. Manchanda, 'Does it Pay to Shock? Reactions to Shocking and Nonshocking Advertising Content among University Students', *Journal of Advertising Research*, 43:3 (2003), 268–80, 268.

usage of provocative subject matter is the best-known example.[84] The aim of this kind of advertising is to attract attention with controversial techniques that create strong reactions, in particular shock or distress. On the cover of *Votes for Women* issue 99 the WSPU controversially depicted the brutal force-feeding of suffragette prisoners. This image was also reproduced as a poster in four colours, in two sizes suitable for hoardings and windows.[85] These highly realistic images which 'affronted some of the deepest instincts within society concerning the sanctity and vulnerability of the female person' had great impact and increased the public's support for women's suffrage.[86] Forcible feeding became a propaganda weapon which was handed to suffragettes by the government. As Christabel Pankhurst pointed out, 'from the moment that women had consented to prison, hunger-strikes, and forcible feeding as the price of the vote, the vote was really theirs'.[87] The poster, designed by Alfred Pearse in 1910, was the reworked version of the cartoon published on the front cover of *Votes for Women*. It showcased the government's violence against women with the headline 'The Modern Inquisition Treatment of Political Prisoners under a Liberal Government', and asked voters to empathize with the suffragettes, urging them to 'Put a Stop to This Torture by Voting Against the Prime Minister'. In 1914 they printed an even more horrific cartoon cover for *The Suffragette* (No. 94). Signed by J. M., the cartoon depicts the face of a suffragette being forcibly fed behind bars; the tubes inserted into her nostrils and mouth by a man, while her body is held forcefully by disembodied hands. The cartoon had the controversial title 'Militant Women Tortured – Militant Men Received by the King' (Figure 9.2), referring to the WSPU's deputation which King George V refused to receive, whereas their male opponents were invited to Buckingham Palace to meet him.[88]

84 Pavel Skorupa, 'Shocking Contents in Social and Commercial Advertising', *Creative Studies*, 7/2. 68–81, 70.
85 'A Forcible Feeding Poster', *Votes for Women*, 3:99 (28 January 1910), 274.
86 Melanie Phillips, *The Ascent of Woman: A History of the Suffragette Movement and Ideas Behind it* (London: Abacus, 2007), 225.
87 Pankhurst, *Unshackled*, 146.
88 J. M., 'Forcible Feeding', [front cover cartoon], *The Suffragette*, 3:94 (31 July 1914), 273.

Figure 9.2. *The Suffragette*, 31 July 1914, frontmatter. Public domain. Image courtesy of LSE Library.

Shock advertising was also used for newspaper headlines, typographic posters and placards, with phrases that were direct, simple, clever and provocative. To increase impact, they were set in big, bold typography. For example, the placard designed to advertise *Votes for Women* issue 157 carried a controversial slogan: 'Man Prisoner Fed by Force' (Figure 9.3), referring to the women's suffrage supporter Alfred Abbey who was force fed during his prison sentence.[89] This placard showed that male supporters were ready to go to prison and go on hunger strike for the cause. It also demonstrated that regardless of the gender of a prisoner, the barbaric treatment of forcible feeding became the 'usual method' that the government used on supporters of women's suffrage. The placard became even more significant when it was displayed by the women's suffrage supporter, Hugh Franklin (1889–1962), at the end of his trial in Bow Street Magistrates' Court where he was accused of breaking Winston Churchill's window to protest against Alfred Abbey's treatment in prison. When he was given time to deliver his last words, he showed the placard and said that its message was his 'whole defence in a nutshell'.[90]

Moreover, the WSPU used the cover of their official newspaper as a shock advertising tool. On one occasion, a striking front page which carried just one word was created when all the workers in the WSPU's printing office were arrested on 2 May 1913 the day before the publication date.[91] Rather than the week's issue not being printed, they printed the single word 'Raided' in bold type. This issue 'had an enormous and unprecedented sale'.[92] Suffragette paper sellers displayed copies of the issue outside Bow Street Court where the preliminary hearing of the case took place.[93] Neither an article nor a front cover cartoon could have produced a more dramatic and poignant effect than this simple typographic front cover design.

---

89   'Forcible Feeding in Pentonville', *Votes for Women*, 4:157 (10 March 1911), 366; 'Man Prisoner Forcibly Fed. Mr. Churchill's Windows Broken in Protest', *Votes for Women*, 4:157 (10 March 1911), 368.
90   'A Month's Imprisonment for Mr. Franklin', *Votes For Women*, 4:158 (17 March 1911), 385.
91   Pankhurst, *My Own Story*, 310–1.
92   'Business as Usual', *The Suffragette*, 1:30 (9 May 1913), 499.
93   See Antonia Raeburn, *The Suffragette View* (London: David & Charles, 1976), 60.

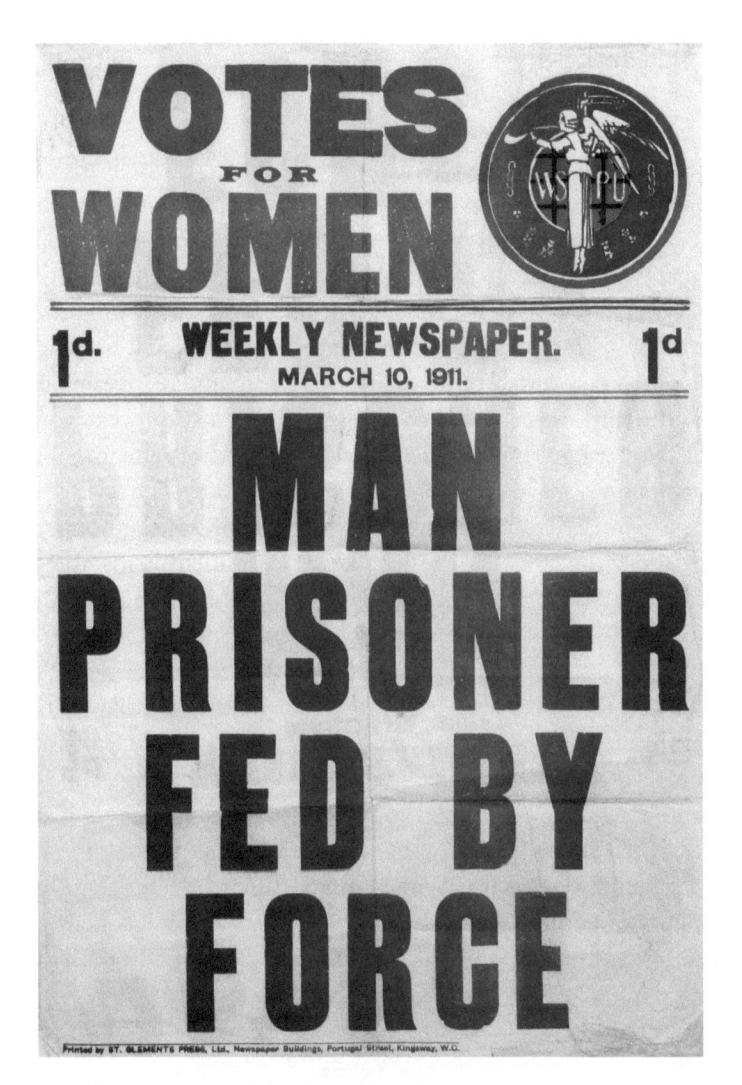

Figure 9.3. Front headline used as shock advertising, *Votes for Women*, 10 March 1911, frontmatter. Image courtesy of LSE Library.

Guerrilla Marketing

Suffragettes worked creatively with limited resources which they turned to their advantage. They became adept at finding alternative methods to traditional advertising, developing easily achievable, but effective tactics. Today, this type of strategy is called 'guerrilla marketing', which is the kind of low-cost advertising that promotes products or services in an unconventional way.[94] The concept was introduced in 1984, and it has since been used in political protests around the world. The many creative and unusual methods the suffragettes used can also be anachronistically categorized as 'guerrilla marketing'. The cheapest, yet, 'one of the most effective means of advertisement' was pavement chalking, and required a high level of artistic skill because it attracted interested crowds watching the announcements develop 'under the hand of [the] chalker'.[95] Prominent landscape painter and suffragette Marie Brackenbury (1866–1950), who studied at the Slade School of Fine Art, was well-known for her pavement chalking, even to the point where she signed her works with 'A Suffragette Pavement Artist'.[96] The WSPU's members also used other forms of 'guerrilla marketing', which resemble what we call 'graffiti' today. For example, Scottish artist and suffragette Marion Dunlop (1864–1942) created a large-scale rubber stamp and used purple ink used to imprint political messages inside the Houses of Parliament.[97] She also had her photograph printed in *Votes For Women* stencilling 'Votes for Women this Session' with 'her new machine', on the pavement outside the door of 10 Downing Street just before a cabinet meeting.[98] Another unusual guerrilla marketing method used by the

---

[94] Jay Conrad Levinson, *Guerrilla Marketing: Secrets for Making Big Profits from your Small Business* (Boston: Houghton Mifflin, 1984).
[95] 'Pavement Chalking', *Votes for Women*, 1:14 (11 June 1908), 234. Also see Pankhurst, *My Own Story*, 54 and Pankhurst, *The Suffragette*, 213.
[96] Crawford, *Art and Suffrage*, 46–7.
[97] Crawford, *Art and Suffrage*, 85.
[98] *Votes for Women*, 4:154 (17 February 1911), 321.

WSPU's members was driving four-in-hand coaches pulled with horses, carrying purple, white and green flags and placards advertising their official newspaper, *Votes For Women*.[99]

The suffragettes also used guerrilla marketing strategies to intervene in, and circumvent, the political system from which they were excluded. For example, to attract the attention of politicians, they decorated a boat and sailed down the Thames, then anchored it opposite the Houses of Parliament with a hired brass band and a big banner announcing the 'Women's Sunday' meeting in Hyde Park.[100] Their most unusual tactic was probably posting themselves as 'human letters' to the Prime Minister at Downing Street, in an attempt to deliver a message personally to him. All of the letters, however, were refused.[101] They even created maximum publicity by gaining access to, and being arrested at, places they could not normally reach: such as padlocking themselves to the railings of government buildings, which allowed them to protest first and then use the opportunity to make political speeches while they were being cut free and arrested. Sylvia Pankhurst explained they were using the chains 'both symbolically to express the political bondage of womanhood, and for the very practical reason that this device would prevent her being dragged speedily away'.[102] The suffragettes also used this tactic to divert the attention of the security guards while performing other acts of civil disobedience. For example, in 1908 two of the suffragettes padlocked themselves to the Downing Street railings to distract the police while two others attempted to enter number 10. The situation was repeated: this time they were all arrested, handcuffed and put behind bars. In this way they welcomed ridicule. 'Deliberately adopting "silly" behaviours as a counterpoint to over-formal and male dominated Edwardian politics', they created 'the women's alternative for doing something cruel' and 'the effect was the same'.[103]

99 For the other unusual methods of the suffragettes see ' "Votes for Women" Week. News from some the Workers', *Votes for Women*, 3:111 (22 April 1910), 473.
100 *Votes for Women*, 1:16 (25 June 1908), 270.
101 'Announcing the Deputation', *Votes for Women*, 2:51 (26 February 1909), 379.
102 Pankhurst, *The Suffragette*, 191.
103 See Atkinson, *Rise Up Women!*, Loc 1525; Pankhurst, *The Suffragette*, 192. Krista Cowman, ' "Doing Something Silly": The Uses of Humour by the Women's Social and Political Union, 1903–1914', in Marjolein t' Hart and Dennis Bos, eds,

A Very Modern Legacy

Graphic expression was central to the battle of the WSPU. 'Underpinning all their activities with visual propaganda and protest', they authentically reinvented political protest for the twentieth century onwards where visuality has become central to political dissent. In order to achieve the maximum outcome from a political act, they used their creativity and dark humour which are the two important parts of modern protest discourse.[104]

This highly professional and creative body of work shows that women's suffrage was not 'merely a fad of a few wealthy and leisured ladies'.[105] Instead their actions were thoroughly planned, articulated and sustained, and they 'accepted discipline, displayed capacity of organisation, courage and tenacity' and 'challenged traditional attitudes to women's abilities'.[106] At a time when the intellect and skills of women were not properly used, the WSPU cultivated a new type of professional and independent woman who used creativity and skills to achieve her goals. 'As a speaker, a pamphlet-seller, a chalker of pavements, a canvasser on doorsteps', she was needed.[107]

It was the 'sex disability' and 'the limitations set by men' and 'handicapping her ultimate career' which made the woman artist radicalize into the suffrage movement in the first place. Ending inequality and discrimination

---

Humour and Social Protest, 259. Emmeline Pethick Lawrence, 'The Tactics of the Suffragettes', *Votes for Women*, 1:6 (March 1908), 81.

104 See Marjolein t'Hart and Dennis Bos, eds, *Humour and Social Protest*; Altug Yalcintas, ed., *Creativity and Humour in Occupy Movements: Intellectual Disobedience in Turkey and Beyond* (London: Palgrave Macmillan, 2015) and Sabine Damir-Geilsdorf and Stephan Milich, eds, *Creative Resistance: Political Humor in the Arab Uprisings*, (Bielefeld: Transcript Verlag, 2020).

105 Fulford, *Votes for Women*, 121. Fulford stated that these claims were 'the old argument'.

106 Winifred Holtby, *Women and a Changing Civilization* (Chicago: Cassandra Editions, 1978), 53; Denney, *The Visual Culture of Women's Activism in London, Paris and Beyond: An Analytical Art History, 1860 to the Present*, 16.

107 Pankhurst, *The Suffragette Movement*, Loc 4247.

in education, scholarships and travel grants could only be possible with equal citizenship.[108] At the same time, the WSPU and suffrage ateliers provided women with the opportunity to work creatively, to educate each other, to collaborate and develop a career. Moreover, they acquired a sense of freedom and 'a life untrammelled by convention' which 'the artist needs for his development'.[109] The suffragettes' story reveals two histories, and two practices: 'that of the political campaign, and that of the artists who brought their particular skills and proclivities to its aid'.[110] The former highlights their contribution to the emancipation of women and the latter underlines the women's development as designers and artists through the suffrage movement. The suffragettes were an important milestone for the developing role of art and design in the struggle for women's liberation which still reverberates today.

---

108 Edith M. Mason-Hinchley, 'Why We Want the Vote: The Woman Artist', *The Vote*, 4:94 (12 August 1911), 199–200.
109 Mary Lowndes, 'Genius, and Women Painters', *The Common Cause*, VI:262 (17 April 1914), 31.
110 Tickner, *The Spectacle of Women, 1907–14*, x.

ABBEY REES-HALES

10 'The Woman Thoroughly Dominates': Lene Schneider-Kainer (1885–1971) and Weimar Lesbian Erotica

A sensitively drawn lithograph depicts two recumbent women, both *en déshabillé*, sprawled across a loosely sketched bed (Figure 10.1). Positioned at the front of the picture plane, a woman with flowing russet hair, dressed in a simple chemise, rests her head on the lap of her bare-breasted and fair-haired partner, as they clasp hands and gaze tenderly at one another. Rejecting the lesbophobic prurience that dogged many early twentieth-century renderings of lesbian women, the lithograph presents the couple neither as sexological specimens nor hypersexualized performers but as an ordinary, loving couple in a moment of quiet repose. This sensitive and sensual lithograph was just one of a series of thirty-two erotic and lesboerotic book illustrations created by the Austrian-Jewish artist Lene Schneider-Kainer (née Helene Schneider; Vienna, 1885 – Bolivia, 1971) in the early part of Germany's Weimar Republic (1919–33).[1] The series saw this now largely forgotten artist transgress oppressive notions of bourgeois female propriety in order to repeatedly depict nude and partially clad women, whether alone (Figure 10.2, left), in pairs (Figures 10.1 and 10.3) or threes (Figure 10.2, right), as they rest, recline and embrace.

Schneider-Kainer's ambitious suite of lithographs adorned a decidedly modern, unexpurgated German edition of Lucian of Samosata's ancient

---

1   I favour the specificity of *lesboerotic* over the ostensibly more generic but often decidedly androcentric *homoerotic*.

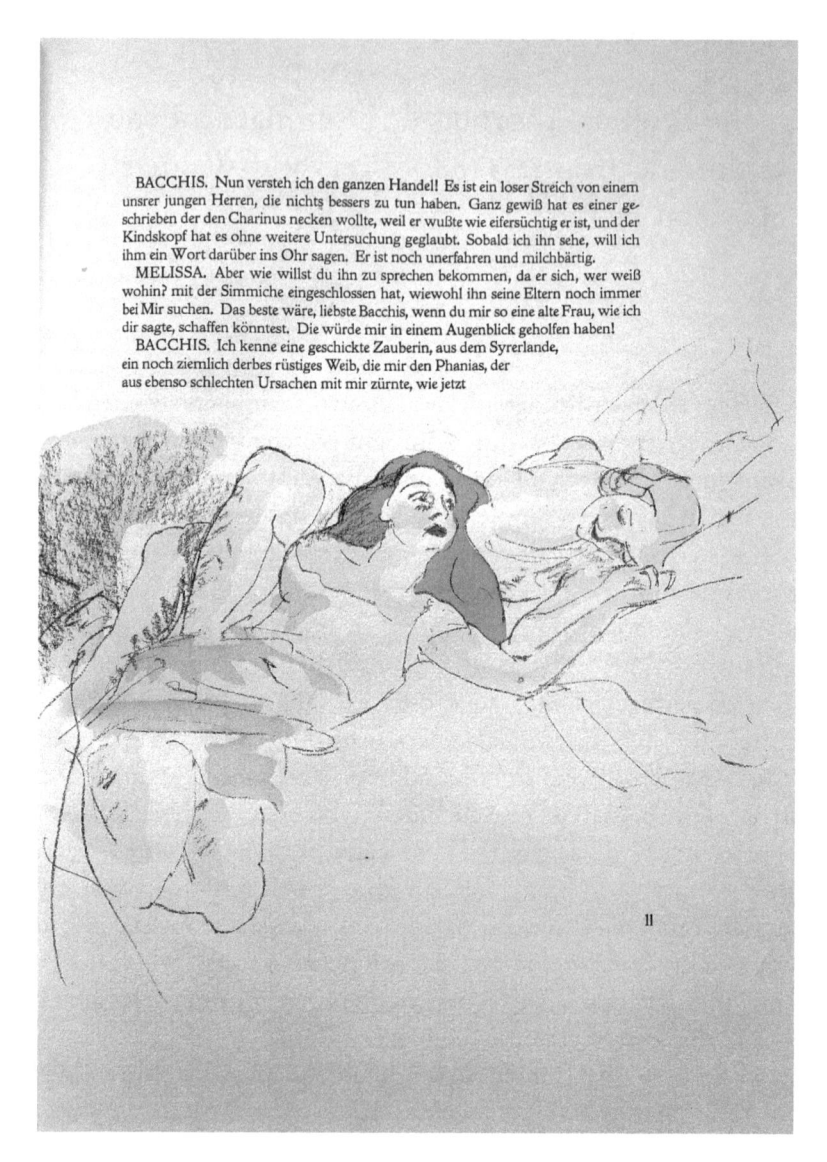

BACCHIS. Nun versteh ich den ganzen Handel! Es ist ein loser Streich von einem unsrer jungen Herren, die nichts bessers zu tun haben. Ganz gewiß hat es einer geschrieben der den Charinus necken wollte, weil er wußte wie eifersüchtig er ist, und der Kindskopf hat es ohne weitere Untersuchung geglaubt. Sobald ich ihn sehe, will ich ihm ein Wort darüber ins Ohr sagen. Er ist noch unerfahren und milchbärtig.

MELISSA. Aber wie willst du ihn zu sprechen bekommen, da er sich, wer weiß wohin? mit der Simmiche eingeschlossen hat, wiewohl ihn seine Eltern noch immer bei Mir suchen. Das beste wäre, liebste Bacchis, wenn du mir so eine alte Frau, wie ich dir sagte, schaffen könntest. Die würde mir in einem Augenblick geholfen haben!

BACCHIS. Ich kenne eine geschickte Zauberin, aus dem Syrerlande, ein noch ziemlich derbes rüstiges Weib, die mir den Phanias, der aus ebenso schlechten Ursachen mit mir zürnte, wie jetzt

Figure 10.1. *Untitled* (lithograph), Lene Schneider-Kainer, *Hetärengespräche* [The Dialogues of the Courtesans], Lucian of Samosata and Christoph Martin Wieland (trans), Berlin: Verlag Julius Bard, 1920. Image reproduced with the permission of Gesche Kainer.

text, the *Hetairikoi Dialogoi* [Dialogues of the Courtesans]. Advertised for subscription pre-publication, this deluxe edition of Lucian's text was published in around December 1920 by the Berlin-based Verlag Julius Bard as *Hetärengespräche des Lukian* [Lucian's Dialogues of the Courtesans].[2] Written in Attic Greek during the second century CE, but set in the then recent past, Lucian's series of fifteen fictitious conversations take place between the *hetairai* [courtesans] of Classical Athens and their mothers, colleagues, clients and attendants as they discuss topics encompassing witchcraft, same-sex desire, rivalry, infidelity, jealousy and sexual violence. Situated alongside Lucian's fourth dialogue, 'Melissa und Bacchis', the aforementioned lesbian lithograph is representative of the relationship between text and image in this luxury volume. Contrary to what Schneider-Kainer's tender depiction of a lesbian couple might suggest, the plot of Lucian's 'Melissa und Bacchis' dialogue is resolutely heterosexual. As this chapter demonstrates, this discrepancy between text and lesboerotic image would define Schneider-Kainer's Lucian lithographs. Concentrating upon female same-sex intimacy and jettisoning the trappings of antiquity, Schneider-Kainer's lithographs can hardly be said to illustrate Lucian's tale of conversing courtesans in a literal sense, a fact that was not lost on the influential German cultural historian and collector Eduard Fuchs (1870–1940).

Writing in 1926 in the concluding volume of his three-part *Geschichte der Erotischen Kunst* [History of Erotic Art], Fuchs drew upon Schneider-Kainer's lesboerotic reimagining of *Hetärengespräche* in order to prove his conviction that modern female artists were increasingly satisfying and satiating sexual longings, 'left unfulfilled by reality', through the creation of erotic art.[3] What was arguably more significant than Fuchs's reductive attempt at a psycho-sexological diagnoses of Schneider-Kainer and her female peers was his acknowledgement of the increased role played by female artists

2   Lucian of Samosata (c.125 CE–after 180 CE) was a Syrian-born and Athenian-domiciled satirist and rhetorician. Lucian of Samosata, Christoph Martin Wieland (trans.), *Hetärengespräche des Lukian*, illus. Lene Schneider-Kainer (Berlin: Verlag Julius Bard, 1920).

3   'seine von der Wirklichkeit unerledigt gelassenen Sehnsüchte'. Eduard Fuchs, *Geschichte der erotischen Kunst: Das Individuelle Problem, Zweiter Teil* (Munich: Albert Langen, 1926; repr. Berlin: Verlag Klaus Guhl, 1977), 382.

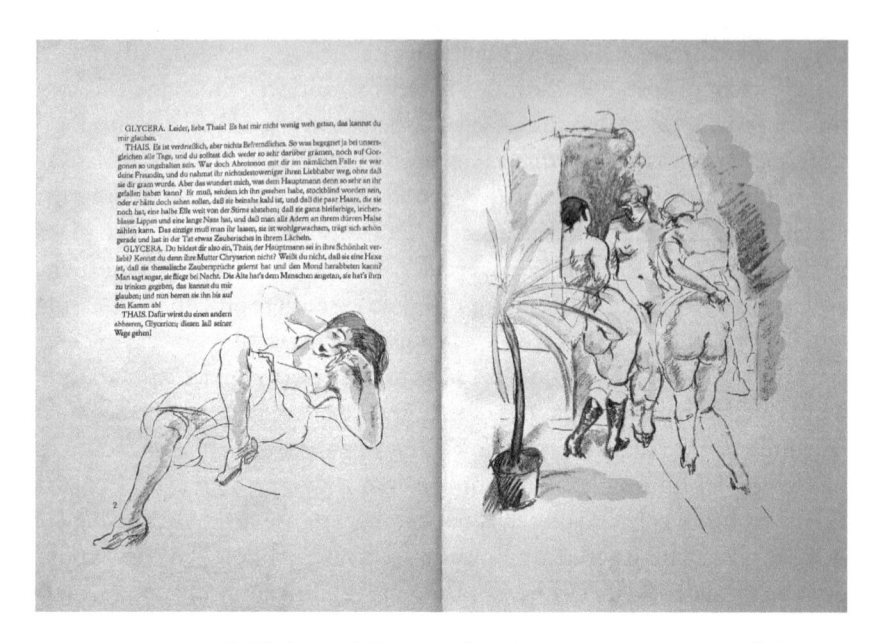

Figure 10.2. *Untitled* (lithographs), Lene Schneider-Kainer, *Hetärengespräche* [The Dialogues of the Courtesans], Lucian of Samosata and Christoph Martin Wieland (trans), Berlin: Verlag Julius Bard, 1920. Image reproduced with the permission of Gesche Kainer.

in the production of erotic art in the wake of the First World War. Alongside Suzanne Meunier (French; 1888–1979), Margit Gaal (Hungarian; active by 1920), Charlotte Berend (German; 1880–1967), Renée Sintenis (German; 1888–1965) and Gerda Wegener (Danish; 1886–1940), Schneider-Kainer ranks as one of the first female artists known to have produced overtly erotic graphic art expressly for publication. Others, including the Austrian-born Mariette Lydis (1887–1970), the Czech Surrealist Toyen (1902–1980), the German *Neue Sachlichkeit* [New Objectivity] artist Jeanne Mammen (1890–1976) and the American Clara Tice (1888–1973), soon followed in their wake. As the careers of these now largely forgotten female artists women hint at, academically trained women artists across Europe and the United States produced a sizeable and stylistically diverse body of erotic graphic art during the First World War and throughout the interwar period, ranging from mass-produced 'French postcards' and magazine illustrations, to fine art folios and bibliophilic books.

This particular facet of print culture is seldom acknowledged, let alone the subject of exhibitions and scholarly studies. Whilst in recent years the likes of Mammen and Toyen have benefited from feminist art historical reappraisal, on the whole this stylistically diverse coterie of female artists have been written out of histories of the period, resulting in a somewhat sanitized account of women's contributions to twentieth-century visual culture.[4] Focusing upon the erotic graphic art of Schneider-Kainer, this chapter seeks to play a small part in redressing this lacuna. This chapter will start by considering the role that the First World War and German November Revolution (1918–19) played in enabling Schneider-Kainer to contravene restrictive gender norms through her career choices during the latter half of the 1910s. Having situated Schneider-Kainer's venture into erotic art in relation to its wider social and cultural context, the second half examines Schneider-Kainer's decidedly lesboerotic reinterpretation of Lucian's *Hetärengespräche*, probing the startling disconnect between text and image. In placing its lens upon the semi-clandestine print erotica trade, this chapter seeks to challenge preconceptions about the types of illustrative work undertaken by early-twentieth-century female artists.

---

4   Karla Huebner, *Magnetic Woman: Toyen and the Surrealist Erotic* (Pittsburgh: University of Pittsburgh Press, 2020), and Camilla Smith, 'Sex Sells! Wolfgang Gurlitt, Erotic Print Culture and Women Artists in the Weimar Republic', *Art History*, 42:4 (2019), 780–807. Both of these were published after the paper upon which this present chapter is based was delivered. On Berend, see this author's essay, '"Mit einer ziemlich weitgehenden weiblichen Indiskretion": Charlotte Berends Anita Berber: Acht Originallithographieen (1919)', in Hemma Schmutz and Elisabeth Nowak-Thaller, eds, *Wolfgang Gurlitt Zauberprinz: Kunsthändler – Sammler*, exhibition catalogue, LENTOS Kunstmuseum Linz (Munich: Hirmer, 2019), 169–76.

Women's Dis/honourable Wartime Work: Contextualizing Schneider-Kainer's Advance into Erotica

As the German sexologist Magnus Hirschfeld remarked in 1931, and which largely holds true to this day, 'Everybody knows how the war affected the participation of women in industry'.[5] From propaganda posters to popular histories, the romanticized image of women flowing into the workplace for the first time, ensuring that the cogs of industry kept turning, continues to capture the public imagination. Even if the reality was considerably more nuanced than the popular image of the woman war worker suggests, with the mass mobilization demanded by the war, across the belligerent nations women of all ages assumed roles formerly the preserve of men, from the chemical industries to the transport sector, from metalworking to the printing trades.[6] Despite his sexological credentials and his conviction that the war had led to 'the creation of a new sexual morality', when Hirschfeld remarked that women 'entered practically every branch of productive activity' during the War, he was probably not thinking of more clandestine forms of employment.[7] However, if women stepped into male roles in state-sanctioned industries, they likewise stepped into them in state-censured sectors. A Berlin police report of April 1919 noted that women had become increasingly active in the pornography trade during the war, demonstrating that a numerical increase in women entering fields previously dominated by men does not necessarily

---

5   Magnus Hirschfeld, *Sittengeschichte des Ersten Weltkriegs* (Hanau: Schustek Verlag, 1929), translated as *The Sexual History of the World War* [anonymous translation] (New York: Cadillac Publishing, 1941), 14.

6   For instance, Ute Daniel, *The War from Within: German Working-Class Women in the First World War* (Oxford: Berg, 1997), 37–126. References to female printers can be found in: Renate Bridenthal, 'Beyond Kinder, Küche, Kirche: Weimar Women at Work', *Central European History*, 6:2 (1973), 155; Gail Braybon, *Women Workers in the First World War*, 3rd edn (London and New York: Routledge, 1981), 64.

7   Hirschfeld, *The Sexual History of the World War*, 13 and 14.

equate to a straightforward advancement of feminism.[8] It was not just from the disreputable world of pornography that increasing numbers of women were making a living during and following the war but also in the apparently more rarified world of elite erotic print culture, as the career of Schneider-Kainer testifies.

Born in Vienna in 1885 into middle-class Jewish family, Schneider-Kainer moved to Munich in 1907 and enrolled at the city's *Damen-Akademie* [Women's [Art] Academy], which had been founded two decades earlier as a reaction against the continued exclusion of women from the prestigious royal academies of the arts.[9] The *Damen-Akademie* enabled Schneider-Kainer to negotiate some of the many obstacles facing women artists in order to gain an education based on the model established by the royal academies, with modules offered in perspective, compositional theory, anatomy and, crucially, figure and life drawing.[10] Having left the *Damen-Akademie* in 1910, Schneider-Kainer moved to Paris and married fellow graphic artist Ludwig Kainer (1885–1967), with a son born the following year. The early part of the 1910s saw the young family move to Berlin, before relocating to the neutral Netherlands during the First World War. During this period Schneider-Kainer began to build a successful career as a painter of somewhat impressionistic oil on canvas portraits, still-lifes and cityscapes, yet that appears to have changed following the outbreak of the First World War.

In the summer of 1915, as wartime mobilization saw increasing numbers of women workers enter sectors formerly the preserve of men, Schneider-Kainer made her first furtive steps into a rather different former male enclave: erotic print culture. In August of that year, six of Schneider-Kainer's

---

8   Report of Berlin police, 5 April,1919, ZStA Merseburg, Rep. 77, Tit. 380, Nr. 7, Adh. 1, Bd. 2, cit. Gary D. Stark., 'Pornography, Society, and the Law in Imperial Germany', *Central European History*, 14:3 (1981), 221.

9   I am very grateful to Gesche Kainer for sharing information about her grandmother's life with me. Further biographical material is drawn from: Louise Fargo Brown, 'Elena Eleska', *The Horn Book Magazine*, XXI, September *1945*, 337–43, and Anon., 'Longing, Prayer, Surrender: Diary of an Incredible Journey Translated into English', *LBI News* 94 (2014), 12–13.

10 Yvette Deseyve, *Der Künstlerinnen-Verein München e.V. und seine Damen-Akademie: Eine Studie* […] (Munich: Herbert Utz Verlag, 2005), 68–89.

gestural female nude studies were published in the influential German Expressionist journal *Die Weißen Blätter* [The White Sheets].[11] Drawn in a lively and gestural manner in graphite and charcoal, the *Die Weißen Blätter* series built upon Schneider-Kainer's earlier training at the *Damen-Akademie*, where she would have been able to attend life drawing classes, albeit only as elective modules and not as part of the core curriculum.[12] Due to anxieties pertaining to female propriety, female students were restricted to working from partially draped child and adult female models; the adult male life model remained firmly off limits. Schneider-Kainer responded to and subverted such educational limitations and confounded gendered expectations by making the female nude a defining feature of the intimate graphic works that she produced from 1915 onwards. In style and pose, however, Schneider-Kainer's female nude studies, whether the *Die Weißen Blätter* series or the later *Hetärengespräche* lithographs, were, as will become apparent, anything but academic. Not content with merely gaining commissions for magazine work, the following year Schneider-Kainer exhibited a lithograph simply entitled *Akt* [nude] at an exhibition of graphic art organized by the *Freie Secession* [Free Secession], a stylistically diverse, independent association of Berlin artists.[13] The brevity of the print's title belies the boldness of such a move. In not simply portraying a study of the female nude – and moreover, the female nude freed of edifying mythological or religious trappings – but publicly exhibiting it at one of Berlin's major exhibiting societies, Schneider-Kainer announced herself to the Berlin art world as a thoroughly modern female artist.

With Schneider-Kainer having relocated to Berlin in around 1917, the cultural climate of the German capital enabled her to become increasingly bold in her choice of subjects, a fact that did not go unnoted by the German art critic and editor Karl Scheffler (1869–1951). Reviewing an exhibition of Schneider-Kainer's work, held at Wolfgang Gurlitt's Berlin gallery in February 1917, Scheffler praised Schneider-Kainer's 'ingenious

---

11   *Die Weißen Blätter*, 2: 8, *August 1915*, 956, 962, 990, 1017 and 1041–42.
12   Deseyve, *Der Künstlerinnen-Verein München e.V.*, 198–200; 205–06.
13   *Katalog der Schwarz-Weiss Ausstellung der Freien Secession Berlin 1916*, 47.

talent, shrewd insight and graceful audacity'.[14] It may come as something of a surprise that a critic who less than a decade earlier had asserted that woman was 'quite incapable' of 'creative power' should reserve such praise for a female artist.[15] What was similarly surprising was that Scheffler was responding to an exhibition which showcased the full range of Schneider-Kainer's work. Genres that were deemed appropriate to the abilities and sensibilities of the so-called fairer sex (landscapes, portraits and flower paintings) were displayed on the walls of the Galerie Gurlitt alongside Schneider-Kainer's altogether more audacious foray into a decidedly male enclave: erotic fine art prints.[16] Such unlikely praise from this unrepentant misogynist was not, however, proffered without reservations. 'It is fortunate', Scheffler cautioned, 'that this artist does not know how deep the water is, on whose thin ice she skates so boldly'.[17] Boldness, be it in terms of subject matter, style, mark making, self-presentation or sexuality, was actively encouraged if the artist happened to be born a man. It was not so encouraged if one happened to be born a woman. If such rhetoric was an attempt to keep the woman artist in check, then Schneider-Kainer appears to have paid little heed. The gentle eroticism of Schneider-Kainer's wartime works on paper was soon eclipsed by the temerity of the erotic

14 'einem geistreichen Talent, von kluger Einsicht und graziöser Verwegenheit'. Karl Scheffler, 'Kunstausstellung: Berlin', *Kunst und Künstler: illustrierte Monatsschrift für bildende Kunst und Kunstgewerbe*, 15 (1917), 344.
15 'Der schöpferischen Kraft, im Schaffen wie im Genuß der Kunst, ist die Frau durchaus unfähig, weil ihr die Triebfeder dazu fehlt: der fanatisch vorwärts drängende Wille'. Karl Scheffler, *Die Frau und die Kunst: eine Studie* (Berlin: Verlag Julius Bard, 1908), 29–30.
16 Anon., *Kollektiv-Ausstellung: Lene Schneider-Kainer; Miniaturen, Johanna Freund-Kampmann*, exhibition catalogue, Galerie Gurlitt, Berlin (Berlin: Fritz Gurlitt Verlag, 1917), unpaginated. The rabidly misogynistic psychiatrist Paul Julius Möbius claimed that flower paintings, still lives and portraits were the only genres which female artists could 'grapple' with. Paul Julius Möbius, *Über den physiologischen Schwachsinn des Weibes* (Halle: Verlag von Carl Marhold, 1900), 12–13.
17 'Es ist das Glück dieser Künstlerin, dass sie nicht weiss, wie tief dass Wasser ist, auf dessen dünner Eisdecke sie so kühn Schlittschuh läuft'. Scheffler, Kunstausstellung, 1917, 344.

lithographs which she would produce during the early postwar period for the Verlag Julius Bard.

A New Erotic Renaissance Threatens Germany: Revolution and the German Print Boom

On 28 October 1918, a mutiny of German sailors in the port city of Kiel initiated the German November Revolution which, whilst dismissed by many as a failure, brought about the abdication of Kaiser Wilhelm II and the proclamation of the German Republic on 9 November 1918. On 12 November, only a day after the Armistice was signed, Germany's interim revolutionary government unveiled a raft of progressive reforms. Censorship was ostensibly rescinded and suffrage was granted to all German citizens aged twenty years and over. Women may have been enfranchised on exactly the same terms as men but rather than this ushering in a new era of female emancipation, with the gradual return of approximately six million servicemen, the restoration of patriarchal order became a priority for the new Republic.[18] Schneider-Kainer defied wider postwar employment trends by making her mark in a male-dominated sector at precisely the moment when postwar demobilization decrees forced thousands of women workers out of other male sectors.

Writing in *Der Sammler* [The Collector], a journal for bibliophiles, exactly a year after the tumultuous events of November 1918, the reactionary critic Ludwig Sternaux cautioned of a new threat facing the defeated nation. Taking aim at the Revolution and Republic for fostering a climate of moral permissiveness, Sternaux bewailed: 'A new erotic Renaissance threatens

---

18   By March 1919 female employment had been cut to below pre-war levels. Ingrid Sharp, 'Gender Relations in Weimar Berlin', in Christiane Schönfeld and Carmel Finnan, eds, *Practicing Modernity: Female Creativity in the Weimar Republic* (Würzburg: Königshausen und Neumann, 2006), 2.

Germany. The Public Prosecutor? My God, that was once upon a time, the fear of him has disappeared with the old regime.'[19]

The old regime may have disappeared but with the retention of the obscenity clause from the Imperial Criminal Code, the threat of the public prosecutor remained. Artists and publishers still ran the risk of prosecution for disseminating *unzüchtig* [obscene] materials.[20] Yet the ostensible abolition of censorship in November 1918, however patchy its application was in reality, undoubtedly contributed to an increase in the production of text and image of a sexual nature during the early postwar period. Almost as soon as the Armistice had been signed and censorship abolished, the Republic's numerous critics lamented that the revoking of censorship had 'worked like the opening of a sluice gate', unleashing a 'flood of smut' onto an impressionable German public.[21] For the most part, these outraged commentators were concerned with the moral conduct of newly enfranchised women and with the 'moral filth' on stage, screen and print.[22] Sternaux, however, directed his ire against a very small and elite band who had by and large evaded condemnation: the producers and distributors of limited-edition erotic print folios and illustrated books, whom he likened to avaricious *Kriegsgewinner* [war profiteers], profiting out of the misery and uncertainty of the early postwar period.[23]

Despite his alarmist rhetoric, Sternaux's comments were not entirely unfounded. Against a backdrop of spiraling inflation, the years 1919 and 1920 witnessed the publication of an unprecedented number of

19 'Eine neue erotische Renaissance bedroht Deutschland. Der Staatsanwalt? Mein Got, das war einmal, die Furcht von ihm ist mit dem alten Regime verschwunden'. Ludwig Sternaux, 'Eros als Rattenfänger', *Der Sammler: Deutsche Kunst und Antiquitäten Börse*, 9:48 (29 November 1919), 5.
20 German courts defined *unzüchtig* material in suitably vaguely terms as 'anything that offends the public's sense of modesty and morality in a sexual sense', see: Stark, 1981, 213.
21 Badische Landtag, 42. öffentliche Sitzung, 31 July 1919, 1627–30, Stadtarchiv Freiburg, C4/XII/30/6, cit. and trans. Kara L. Ritzheimer, *'Trash', Censorship, and National Identity in Early Twentieth-Century Germany* (Cambridge: Cambridge University Press, 2016), 160.
22 See Ritzheimer, 'Trash', Censorship, and National Identity, 160–219.
23 Sternaux, 'Eros als Rattenfänger', 5.

limited-edition print folios and illustrated books.[24] The more liberal censorship legislation ushered in by the November Revolution, and enshrined in the Weimar Constitution of August 1919, encouraged publishers and artists to be increasingly bold with their output, as alluded to in comments made by the publisher Reinhard Piper (1879–1953). 'It was the era of "private printings"', Piper ruminated in 1947, 'And not, surprisingly, it was above all erotic works which were well-suited for such private printings.'[25] Indeed, it was during this period that Schneider-Kainer produced a number of erotic etchings, lithographs and graphic folios for the *Privatdrucke der Gurlitt-Presse* [Gurlitt's Private Printing Press], the imprint which Gurlitt had established for the production and distribution of costly, hand-printed erotica. Gurlitt's postwar promotion of Schneider-Kainer's graphic art was consistent with his growing reputation as a purveyor of elite erotic print culture, and his not unrelated record of exhibiting and commissioning limited-editions prints, both erotic and otherwise, from female artists including Berend and Sintenis.[26]

Publishers who during the *Kaiserreich* had focused upon respectable literary and artistic tomes, leaving erotica and pornography for clandestine societies and private presses, now increasingly diversified into a sector that they had previously shunned. Such was certainly true of the Verlag Julius Bard, a publishing house better known for fine art postcards, art historical tomes and classics of the German Enlightenment than for elite erotica. Seemingly emboldened by the ostensible abolition of censorship

24 Starr Figura, 'German Expressionism: The Graphic Impulse', in Starr Figura, ed., *German Expressionism: The Graphic Impulse*, exhibition catalogue (New York: Museum of Modern Art, 2011), 31.
25 Reinhard Piper, *Vormittag: Erinnerungen eines Verlegers* (Munich: 1947), 419, cit. and trans. Stefan Kutzenberger, '"The Pleasure of Being Beaten": Gustav Klimt and Lucian's Dialogues of the Hetaerae', in Tobias G. Natter, Franz Smola, Peter Weinhäupl, eds, *Klimt: Up Close and Personal: Paintings, Letters, Insights*, exhibition catalogue, Leopold Museum (Vienna: Verlag Christian Brandstätter, 2012), 146 + 150.
26 Print portfolios by Berend, Sintenis and Schneider-Kainer are advertised in: *Almanach auf das Jahr 1920* (Berlin: Fritz Gurlitt Verlag, 1920), vi; 'Mappenwerke', *Das Graphische Jahr: Fritz Gurlitt* (Berlin: Fritz Gurlitt Verlag, 1921), 37, 39, 50–51 and 60–61.

and buoyed by the thriving market for costly erotic bibliophilic books, the commissioning editors at Bard commissioned Schneider-Kainer to illustrate a deluxe edition of Lucian's *Hetärengespräche*. Lavishly illustrated with Schneider-Kainer's series of unapologetically lesboerotic lithographs, the Verlag Julius Bard's unexpurgated edition of *Hetärengespräche* was, as I will demonstrate, very much a product of the 'new erotic renaissance' of which Sternaux had warned.[27]

'Perversion' in Print: Promoting and Publishing the Verlag Julius Bard Edition of *Hetärengespräche des Lukian* (1920)

Evidently deemed sufficiently enticing, a monochrome copy of Schneider-Kainer's 'Melissa und Bacchis' lithograph, as described in the opening paragraph of this chapter, was selected to adorn the prospectus that the Verlag Julius Bard (henceforth referred to as Bard) issued to promote its deluxe edition of *Hetärengespräche*.[28] Printed on machine-made paper, bound in hardback and featuring card boards, the standard edition of *Hetärengespräche* could be pre-ordered for 250 marks. For 1,600 marks one could purchase one of the seventy-five deluxe copies printed on fine Bütten paper, and bound in calf parchment and textured Saffiano leather. If that failed to satisfy the appetites of the most ardent of bibliophiles, for the princely sum of 2,000 marks one could obtain one of the twenty-five ultra-deluxe copies, bound in pigskin and hand-coloured by Schneider-Kainer herself.[29] The purchaser of the deluxe edition was not simply paying for a few daubs of watercolour or gouache but for the privilege of owning an original art object, betraying the hand of the artist. With lithography traversing both elite and popular culture, the use of hand-colouring elevated the mass-reproducible print to the vaunted sphere

---

27   Sternaux, 'Eros als Rattenfänger', 5.
28   Anon., *Werbeprospekt des Julius Bard Verlags* (Berlin: Verlag Julius Bard, 1920), unpaginated.
29   *Werbeprospekt*, unpaginated.

of the original art object. The option to preorder, the tiered edition and the high price indicated that whilst Bard might have had little experience of marketing erotica, he knew that an illustrated edition of Lucian's text was an enticing prospect for collectors, even if it was not an enticing prospect for *völkisch* German classicists hellbent on traducing Lucian's reputation.[30]

Somewhat incongruously and seemingly as an afterthought, Bard's prospectus also promoted a rather different suite of prints by Schneider-Kainer. The publication in question was *Die Schönsten Fische aus dem Aquarium* [The Most Beautiful Fish in the Aquarium], a somewhat whimsical folio of fifteen hand-coloured lithographs of tropical fish. Given the highly disparate subject matter (ancient eroticism and aquatic animals) and the divergent audiences the two would have inevitably appealed to, it might seem surprising that a commissioning editor not only chose to promote these uneasy bedfellows side by side but had selected the same female artist to illustrate them.[31] In rather overblown language, the prospectus declared that 'it is nonetheless a totally new undertaking when a modern female artist [...] pictorially captures the most beautiful fish in the Berlin aquarium.'[32] Crucially, Bard shied from emphasizing the very thing that was indeed the groundbreaking undertaking: the instance where the female artist not only transgressed notions of bourgeois female propriety by depicting the female nude but depicted her in such an overtly sexualized manner.

The boldness of Schneider-Kainer's venture into erotica is underscored when we consider that in early twentieth century Germanic discourse, the female artist was repeatedly cast as a sexually-deviant 'degenerate'. Echoing the criticisms that would be levelled at the emancipated postwar *neue Frau*

---

30 On anti-Semitic readings of Lucian in early-twentieth-century German scholarship see Manuel Baumbach, 'Lucian in German Nineteenth-century Scholarship', *Lucian of Samosata Vivus et Redivivus, Warburg Institute Colloquia*, 10, 2007, 191, 197 and 201.
31 *Werbeprospekt des Julius Bard Verlags*, unpaginated.
32 'So ist es ein in der allgemeinen Entwicklung liegendes, aber doch in unserer Kunst ganz neuartiges Unternehmen, wenn eine moderne Künstlerin [...] die schönsten Fische aus dem Berliner Aquarium im Bilde festhält', *Werbeprospekt des Julius Bard Verlags*, unpaginated.

[New Woman], women artists, Scheffler warned in his highly influential and deeply misogynistic polemic, *Die Frau und Die Kunst* [Woman and Art; 1908], were prone to prostitution and lesbianism.[33] According to Scheffler, the dangers of being a woman artist did not end there. In her assumption of male privileges, the female artist, Scheffler asserted, was immediately transformed into 'an insufferable hermaphrodite [...] fluctuating between the gender ideals of nature and the ones belonging to the 'third sex'.[34] If often more subtle and insidious, prejudices pertaining to the abilities, sensibilities and sexual inclinations of the woman artist would continue to circulate and define artistic discourse in the wake of the War, Revolution and the founding of the Weimar Republic, as Bard's promotion of Schneider-Kainer's Lucian lithographs evinces.

In commissioning a deluxe edition of *Hetärengespräche*, illustrated by a modern Austrian artist, Bard immediately evoked and encouraged comparisons to Julius Zeitler's (1874–1943) earlier edition of Lucian's text (1907). Edited and translated by Franz Blei (1871–1942), the Zeitler edition was illustrated with a series of sparing erotic collotypes by Gustav Klimt (1862–1918). Printed on handmade paper and featuring elegant bindings by the Wiener Werkstätte co-founder, Josef Hoffmann (1870–1956), the Zeitler edition was the kind of bibliophilic offering that Bard appears to have been keen to rival.[35] Over a decade may have passed since Zeitler's publication but with the recent deaths of Klimt and other cultural figures of 'Vienna 1900', it had not been forgotten by publishers or collectors. Nor had it been forgotten by public prosecutors, with a copy of the Zeitler edition seized by a Berlin regional court earlier in 1920 on the grounds of suspected obscenity. Far from being deterred by such censure, Bard was keen to situate Schneider-Kainer's Lucian lithographs in relation to those

---

33 Scheffler, *Die Frau und die Kunst*, 41–2.
34 Scheffler, *Die Frau und die Kunst*, 41–2.
35 Lucian and Franz Blei (trans. and ed.), *Hetärengespräche des Lukian*, illus. by Gustav Klimt (Leipzig: Julius Zeitler, 1907). Tobias G. Nätter, 'Gustav Klimt and Lucian's dialogues of the courtesans: A masterpiece of erotica, the range of tis significance, and Greek antiquity', in Stella Rollig and Tobias G. Nätter, eds, *Klimt and Antiquity: Erotic Encounters* (Prestel Verlag, Munich, 2017), 8–25.

of her recently deceased Viennese compatriot, even if it was to announce her point of departure:

> After Klimt, it is now a modern female artist, Lene Schneider-Kainer, who sets out to reflect the spirit of this naïvely refined masterpiece of world literature through the rhythm of soft outlines. However, whereas the Viennese master introduced the sultry breath of desperate fervor into his Lucian images, it is Mrs Schneider-Kainer's fortunate lack of self-consciousness and her agility that enable her to give pure expression to the joyful frivolity of Greek grace in her coloured lithographs.[36]

Betraying the conflation of creativity with male heterosexual desire, the illustrations of the sexually profligate Klimt gave visual form to the 'sultry breath of desperate fervor', the unnamed author of the Bard prospectus proclaimed. Quick to assert the essential femininity of Schneider-Kainer's erotic lithographs and by default the femininity of the artist, Schneider-Kainer's visual interventions were contrastingly defined in reassuringly feminized terms. The apparent threat posed by women's entry into a male sphere had to be defused, and defused in distinctly gendered terms. Attempts to package Schneider-Kainer's work as soft, pure, naïve, frivolous, graceful and essentially feminine wilfully belie her originality – a quality which was rendered a male preserve – but also, the radical eroticism of Schneider-Kainer's Lucian lithographs. In 1920, such overt eroticism (lesboerotic or otherwise) had little precedent amongst the public works of female artists, even if it inevitably had a precedent in their private works.[37]

---

36 'Nach Klimt unternimmt es nun eine moderne Künstlerin, Lene Schneider-Kainer, den Geist dieses naiv-raffinierten Meisterwerks der Weltliteratur in der Rhythmik zarter Linien widerzuspiegeln. Während aber der Wiener Meister den schwülen Hauch einer krampfigen Inbrunst in seine Lukianbilder hineintrug, besitzt Frau Schneider-Kainer die glückliche Unbefangenheit und Leichtigkeit, um die frivol-frohe Grazie des Griechen in ihren farbigen Steinzeichnungen rein ausdrücken'. *Werbeprospekt*.

37 Käthe Kollwitz produced a number of erotic works on paper but they were not intended for public view. Rosemary Betterton, *An Intimate Distance: Women, Artists and the Body* (London: Routledge, 1996), 43.

'Scenes of Lesbian Love Predominate': Lene Schneider-Kainer's Lesboerotic Reimagining of *Hetärengespräche*

Across the forty-seven pages of Bard's folio-sized edition of *Hetärengespräche*, Schneider-Kainer assumed what had formerly been a masculine privilege in repeatedly depicting the nude or partially clad female form. Rejecting the conventions of the academic nude – naturalistically coloured, carefully modelled, highly idealized and invariably located in a biblical or mythological narrative – Schneider-Kainer portrayed the ancient *hetaira* in an altogether more modern manner. Contrary to the original ancient source, lesbianism rather than prostitution became the overwhelming focus of the Schneider-Kainer's lively lithographic sketches. Her style ranges from almost cartoonish small-scale sketches to more sensitive, analytical renderings, as exemplified by the aforementioned 'Melissa und Bacchis' lithograph. Colour is used sparingly but consistently throughout. Bands of pink and peach wash are used to suggest the roundness of the female form whilst accents of jewel-like colour, be it a shock of russet hair or a daub of carmine red for the eroticized zones of the mouth and nipple, focus the viewer's gaze. For all Schneider-Kainer's apparent audacity in depicting nude and scantily clad women as desirable and desiring modern subjects, the patchy and partial training in life drawing that she received at the *Damen-Akademie* during the early 1900s is borne out in this series of prints. The lithographs see Schneider-Kainer appearing to grapple with anatomy: bodies are peculiarly proportioned and lack three dimensionality, breasts appear to emerge out of armpits, thighs intersect with torsos at impossible angles and limbs dwindle away. 'To be an artist on par with men', the art historian Paula Birnbaum contends, 'women needed to claim mastery' of the genre of the female nude.[38] Schneider-Kainer's Lucian lithographs, works which are simultaneously confident and sensitive, carefully observed and anatomically flawed,

---

38   Paula Birnbaum, *Women Artists in Interwar France: Framing Femininities*, 2nd edn (London and New York: Ashgate, 2011), 161.

remind us just how hard it was for early twentieth-century women artists, denied equality of opportunity, to attain such 'mastery'.

Whilst it is possible that Schneider-Kainer may have worked directly onto the lithographic stone, it is more likely that she would have drawn upon a specially prepared sheet of transfer paper; the process being ideally suited to maintaining the spontaneity of her original drawings. The printer, in this case the esteemed Berlin-based fine art printer Hermann Birkholz, would have then transferred Schneider-Kainer's designs to the stone and printed them, overprinting layers of colour to mimic the fluidity and translucency of watercolour.[39] Rather than the text assuming the dominant role, it would seem that Schneider-Kainer's lithographs dictated the layout of the text, which was printed subsequently at the Spamersche Buchdruckerei [Spamersche Book Printing Works] in Leipzig, a city which boasted a well-established network of publishers and collectors of privately printed erotica.[40] This was precisely the audience who Bard would have hoped to appeal to with this lavishly illustrated edition of Lucian's dialogues, offered in a choice of three different editions of varying levels of luxuriousness.

Seven of Schneider-Kainer's compositions are formatted as full-page lithographs, including the third lithograph accompanying 'Glycera und Thais' (Figure 10.2). The remaining twenty-five are either inset into the body of the text as unframed vignettes, which wrap around the text or sit alongside it, with a clear divide between pictorial space and textual element (Figures 10.1 and 10.3). Word and image might at times cling to one another but as we will see, they do not necessarily correspond to one another. The majority of deluxe illustrated books coming out of Germany in the

---

[39] Information about the printing of the volume is taken from the prospectus and the *Hetärengespräche* colophon page; the former refers to the prints being *Steinzeichnungen* [stone drawings], thus it would seem that they were stone lithographs rather than offset lithographs. Birkholz is best remembered for his thirty-year working relationship with the artist Käthe Kollwitz. Jutta Bohnke-Kollwitz, ed., *Käthe Kollwitz, Die Tagebücher* (Berlin: Akademie-Verlag, 1989), 623.

[40] On Leipzig's role in the erotica trade, see: Camilla Smith, 'Challenging Baedeker Through the Art of Sexual Science: an Exploration of Gay and Lesbian Subcultures in Curt Moreck's Guide to 'Depraved' Berlin (1931)', *Oxford Art Journal*, 36:2 (2013), 253–54.

immediate postwar period, as exemplified by Gurlitt's nine-volume erotic series, *Der Venuswagen* [The Chariot of Venus; 1919–20], were, like Zeitler's earlier edition of *Hetärengespräche*, formatted with text printed on the verso and image printed on the opposite recto.[41] Regardless of how ambitious or innovative the publication, early twentieth-century German illustrated books largely obeyed this typographical formula; Bard's *Hetärengespräche* did not. Refusing to assume a subservient role as visual translations of Lucian's text, Schneider-Kainer's lithographs brazenly displayed little deference to the authority of the ancient printed word.

If a classicizing aesthetic had long been exploited by artists and publishers to justify the depiction of copious amounts of bare flesh whilst reassuring the viewer that so-called deviant sexual practices were the preserve of distant lands and epochs, Schneider-Kainer rejected such a convention.[42] Despite the antiquity of Lucian's text, Schneider-Kainer neither ensconced her female subjects in imagined classical settings nor attired them in pseudo-classical garb. In this respect, her Lucian series presents an important precedent to the series of sapphic lithographs that Wolfgang Gurlitt commissioned from Jeanne Mammen in around 1931 to illustrate an ill-fated German edition of Pierre Louÿs's pseudo-Sapphic prose poems, *Les Chansons de Bilitis* [The Songs of Bilitis; first published 1894].

Whilst Mammen transposed Louÿs's ancient Greek setting to the lesbian bars, brothels and bedrooms of Weimar Berlin, such overt references to urban modernity (sapphic or otherwise) are nowhere to be found in Schneider-Kainer's earlier illustrative undertaking. On occasion, undergarments and footwear codify Schneider-Kainer's sapphic subjects as modern women. However, the majority of her lithographs are devoid of any such sartorial clues as to the antiquity or modernity of the subjects depicted. It is left uncertain as to whether Schneider-Kainer's female subjects are to be interpreted as ancient Athenian *hetairai* or German *neue Frauen* [New Women]. The sharply suited, crop-haired, bar-hopping *Bubi* [butch] lesbian woman who has come to symbolize the fabled sexual freedoms of

---

41   *Der Venuswagen* was a nine-volume series of deluxe illustrated books published by the *Privatdrucke der Gurlitt-Presse*, see Smith, Sex Sells!, 788–94.
42   For instance, the homoerotic photographs of Wilhelm von Gloeden (1856–1931).

the Weimar Berlin had no place in Schneider-Kainer's *Hetärengespräche* lithographs, just as she had no place in early postwar erotic print publications produced for a heterosexual male audience. The lean figure of the tuxedo-clad *Bubi* was by no means a product of the Weimar Republic period but several years before the birth of Berlin's lesbian press, she was nowhere near as pervasive or popular a print presence as she would become in the latter years of the Weimar Republic. The lesbian women who populate Schneider-Kainer's lithographs are instead resolutely (and perhaps less 'threateningly') feminine in style and appearance. In 1920, the feminine lesbian, a stock figure in what Jack Halberstam has branded the 'heteropornographic imagination', was an altogether more marketable commodity than her masculine female partner, at least where the anticipated heterosexual male audience was concerned.[43] In 1920 – several years before the likes of the German lesbian magazine *Die Freundin* [The Girlfriend; 1924–33] demonstrated the demand for female-authored images of sapphic love – it seems doubtful that Bard would have been fully conscious of, or at all interested in, the commercial viability of a lesbian and bisexual audience.[44]

Only one of Lucian's fifteen dialogues, the fifth dialogue, 'Leäna und Clonarion', discusses female same-sex desire, yet as the German bibliophile Emil Tuchmann rightly noted in 1929, 'scenes of lesbian love predominate' in Schneider-Kainer's *Hetärengespräche* illustrations.[45] Evidencing Tuchmann's conviction that in Schneider-Kainer's hands, 'all women are construed as erotically excited, even where the scene illustrated perhaps does not make it seem absolutely necessary', dialogues which are completely devoid of the slightest trace of eroticism or lesboeroticism are infused with a sapphically sensual rather than a sororal air.[46] Far from detailing a lesbian

---

43   Jack Halberstam, *Female Masculinity* (Durham and London: Duke University Press, 1998), 61.
44   Lucienne Frappier-Mazur, 'Marginal Canons: Rewriting the Erotic', *Yale French Studies*, 75 (1988), 116.
45   'Szenen lesbischer Liebe herrschen vor'. Emil Tuchmann, 'Schneider-Kainer, Lene' in Leo Schidrowitz, ed., *Bilder-Lexikon: Literatur und Kunst* (Vienna and Leipzig: Verlag für Kulturforschung, 1929), 564.
46   'alle Frauen werden als erotisch erregt aufgefasst, auch da, wo die dargestellte Situation es vielleicht nicht als unbedingt erforderlich erscheinen liesse'. Tuchmann, Schneider-Kainer, Lene, 564.

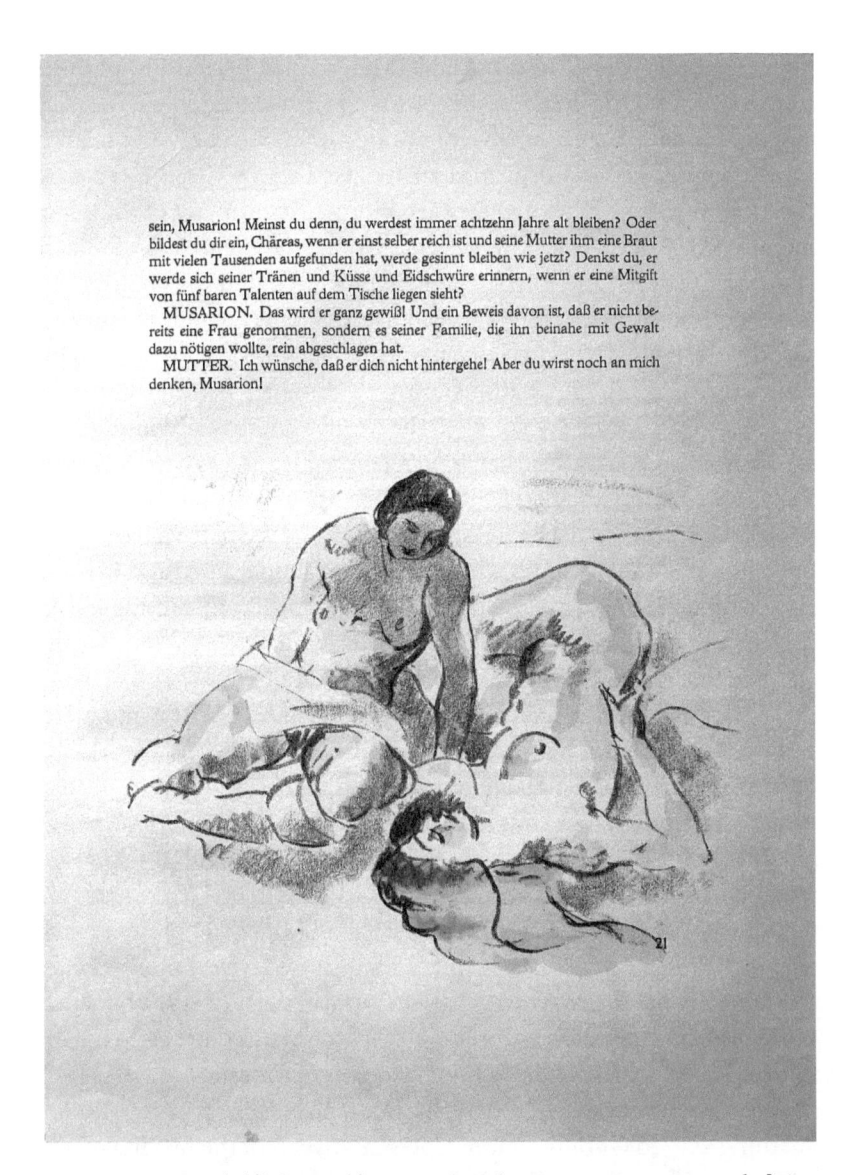

sein, Musarion! Meinst du denn, du werdest immer achtzehn Jahre alt bleiben? Oder bildest du dir ein, Chäreas, wenn er einst selber reich ist und seine Mutter ihm eine Braut mit vielen Tausenden aufgefunden hat, werde gesinnt bleiben wie jetzt? Denkst du, er werde sich seiner Tränen und Küsse und Eidschwüre erinnern, wenn er eine Mitgift von fünf baren Talenten auf dem Tische liegen sieht?

MUSARION. Das wird er ganz gewißl Und ein Beweis davon ist, daß er nicht bereits eine Frau genommen, sondern es seiner Familie, die ihn beinahe mit Gewalt dazu nötigen wollte, rein abgeschlagen hat.

MUTTER. Ich wünsche, daß er dich nicht hintergehe! Aber du wirst noch an mich denken, Musarion!

Figure 10.3. *Untitled* (lithograph), Lene Schneider-Kainer, *Hetärengespräche* [The Dialogues of the Courtesans], Lucian of Samosata and Christoph Martin Wieland (trans), Berlin: Verlag Julius Bard, 1920. Image reproduced with the permission of Gesche Kainer.

sexual encounter, the plot of Lucian's 'Melissa und Bacchis' is resolutely heterosexual, seeing a jilted *hetaira* conspire with a female friend to engage the services of a sorceress capable of reuniting her with her male beloved. Rather than depicting conspiring courtesans (a scene with limited erotic appeal), Schneider-Kainer depicted the more enticing image of the lesbian couple in bed, as described at the start of this chapter (Figure 10.1). Similarly, in both the third and seventh dialogues, 'Philinna und ihre Mutter', and 'Musarion und ihre Mutter' (Figure 10.3), dialogues which see mothers chide their daughters for their lack of business acumen, Schneider-Kainer does not portray intergenerational mother-daughter pairings but rather intragenerational, same-sex couples. The women's nudity and interlocking poses suggest a sexual rather than filial relationship. This is particularly apparent in 'Musarion und ihre Mutter', which opens with a sketchily drawn vignette depicting two bare-breasted women as they hold each other in a close embrace and concludes with yet another tender portrayal of naked young women in bed, gazing lovingly at each other. Depicting lesbian couples in bed, 'Musarion und ihre Mutter' and 'Melissa und Bacchis' suggest sexual intimacy without explicitly depicting it.

As the classicist Kate Gilhuly has argued, Lucian's *hetaira* is 'not merely an object to exchange, a mute representative of the material world' but rather, as instigator of the dialogues, she is 'an agent participating in an exchange'.[47] These exchanges might concern sexual transactions but they are first and foremost verbal exchanges, with Lucian's female subjects engaging in spirited conversations with their mothers, attendants, colleagues and predominately male clients. Entirely eschewing the male presence from Lucian's dialogues, Schneider-Kainer's focus is exclusively upon women, prompting Tuchmann to remark that 'the woman thoroughly dominates'.[48] Depicting intragenerational women, either alone or in mute embraces, we get little sense of these lively and occasionally acrimonious exchanges in Schneider-Kainer's ensuing lithographs. Her female subjects instead become something akin to Gilhuly's 'mute representative[s] of the material world'.

---

47   Kate Gilhuly, 'Excess Contained: Prostitution and the Polis in Classical Athens', PhD dissertation, University of California, Berkeley, 1999, 122.
48   Tuchmann, Schneider-Kainer, Lene, 564.

Despite this, Schneider-Kainer's portrayals of same-sex desire refrain from the performative pornographic prurience on display in the numerous depictions of lesbian couples produced by her male peers, for instance in the voyeuristic etchings of Schneider-Kainer's Gurlitt stablemate, Otto Schoff (1884–1938).[49] Schneider-Kainer's handling of female same-sex desire is marked by sensitivity and tenderness that sets it apart from the depictions of the hyper-sexualized lesbian that dominated Weimar erotic visual culture. To assume that the erotic works produced by women artists are somehow inherently more sensitive, as the Bard prospectus appeared to imply, and less voyeuristic than those produced by their male peers would be a reductively essentializing approach to take. If Schneider-Kainer's portrayals of lesbian women are marked by a greater empathy towards her subjects then that was surely owing to her greater personal respect for women and not by simple virtue of her gender.[50]

Teasingly ambiguous in their identities, Schneider-Kainer's sapphic subjects defy easy categorization. If Schneider-Kainer's subjects are to be read as prostitutes, whether ancient or modern, then they are certainly not defined by their profession; they are instead defined by their loving relationships with one another not by business transactions with their predominately male clients. With her focus entirely upon women as they listlessly wait around and as they share unguarded moments of tender intimacy with one another, Schneider-Kainer's lithographs recall the body of prints, paintings and sketches that Henri de Toulouse-Lautrec (1864–1901) produced during the first half of the 1890s, depicting the private lives and lesbian loves of Parisian state-regulated prostitutes.[51] Given the oft-repeated early twentieth-century belief that lesbianism was particularly frequent amongst prostitutes, might Schneider-Kainer have similarly decided to depict the

---

49 See for instance, *Sappho, oder die Lesbierinnen*, illus. Otto Schoff, trans. Balduin Möllhausen, Alfred Richard Meyer, ed., *Der Venuswagen* (Berlin: Privatdrucke der Gurlitt-Press, Fritz Gurlitt Verlag, 1920).
50 This is supported by the recollections of the artist's granddaughter, Gesche Kainer, who informed me of her grandmother's lifelong interest in women's rights.
51 Henri de Toulouse-Lautrec, *Les deux amies*, 1894–95 (Gouache on cardboard, 64.5 × 84 cm; Zurich: Emil Bührle Collection) and *L'abandon*, 1895 (Oil on board, 45.7 × 67.7 cm; private collection) are two representative examples.

private lives of lesbian prostitutes?[52] Whilst there may have been no textual justification for such a move, there was certainly a commercial motivation. Doubly deviant, the lesbian prostitute represented, as the literary scholar Gretchen Schultz notes, the 'deepest form of depravity imaginable'.[53] She was a figure who could excite sexological curiosity, moral condemnation and sexual arousal alike, making her the ideal subject for erotic prints.

Cliched tropes, be it garish face paint, fur stoles, fanciful headwear or black stockings, that would codify Schneider-Kainer's female subjects as sex workers are largely absent from her lithographs. Also missing from Schneider-Kainer's lithographs is the misogynistic violence routinely meted out against the prostitute in contemporaneous paintings and prints by *Neue Sachlichkeit* artists Otto Dix (1891–1969) and George Grosz (1893–1959). The fresh-faced, healthy-looking feminine young women who populate Schneider-Kainer's prints have nothing in common with the haggard, cadaverous harbingers of disease and death who so often haunt works produced by Schneider-Kainer's male peers. The widespread postwar fears of venereal disease – with an estimated 500,000 new cases in Germany in 1919 alone – do not loom large in Schneider-Kainer's lithographs; they make their presence more subtly felt.[54]

Only one of Schneider-Kainer's thirty-two lithographs can be interpreted at all confidently as relating to the working lives of prostitutes: the depiction of three women listlessly waiting in line that accompanies the opening dialogue, 'Glycera und Thais' (Figure 10.2). Positioned against a shadowy backdrop, a blonde-haired woman, dressed only in a pair of heeled boots, is flanked by two female companions, standing with their backs to the viewer and their chemises hoisted over their haunches to reveal their

---

52   The sexologist Albert Moll (1862–1939) claimed that a quarter of Berlin prostitutes were lesbians. Albert Moll cit. Havelock Ellis, *Studies in the Psychology of Sex*, Volume 2 (3rd edn) (Philadelphia: F.A. Davis Company, 1931), 210.

53   Gretchen Schultz, *Sapphic Fathers: Discourses of Same-Sex Desire from Nineteenth-Century France* (Toronto, Buffalo and London: University of Toronto Press, 2015), 174.

54   Julie R. Stubbs, 'Rescuing ' "Endangered Girls": Bourgeois Feminism, Social Welfare, and the Debate over Prostitution in the Weimar Republic', PhD dissertation, University of Michigan, 2001, 96.

bare buttocks. Far from alluring and seductive, they appear jaded and lethargic; a world away from the ingenues, coquettes and vamps who more typically inhabit erotic illustrated books, folios and popular postcards of the early postwar period.[55] This particular plate appears to allude to Germany's much-contested system of *Reglementierung* [state-regulated prostitution] and specifically, to the routine gynaecological examinations that the system forced women to endure.[56] With their skirts lifted in readiness, it is the wearisome waiting around for such an inspection that Schneider-Kainer seems to refer to in this image. In choosing this moment of lethargic anticipation and resignation, Schneider-Kainer evoked a series of oil sketches that Toulouse-Lautrec created in 1894, which not only depict this very subject but do so in a remarkably similar manner.[57]

The year that the Bard edition of *Hetärengespräche* was published, German prostitutes increasingly began to mobilize, forming their own unions and even founding a newspaper, the appositely named *Der Pranger* [The Pillory], which called on sex workers to 'break [the] chains' of their oppression.[58] Asserting demands for improved working conditions and sharply critiquing the 'lucrative' state-regulated 'sale of women's flesh', these newly enfranchised women shone a light on the hypocrisy of bourgeois morality.[59] Against a backdrop of vocal calls for the reform of *Reglementierung*

---

55   See for instance postcards, folios and illustrated books by illustrators and artists including Meunier, Gaal, Schoff, Édouard Chimot and Franz Christophe.

56   In Berlin, *Reglementierung* prescribed where a woman could live, the streets she could traverse, the buildings she could pass and the attractions she could visit. Abraham Flexner, *Prostitution in Europe*, 2nd edn (New York: The Century Co., 1914), 415–19.

57   Toulouse-Lautrec's depictions of women waiting for medical examinations include *Rue des Moulin*, 1894 (Washington: Chester Dale Collection, National Gallery of Art) and *La femme de maison blonde*, 1894 (Paris: Musée d'Orsay). Mary Hunter, 'The Waiting Time of Prostitution: Gynaecology and Temporality in Henri de Toulouse-Lautrec's Rue des Moulins, 1894', *Art History*, 42:1 (2019), 68–93.

58   *Der Pranger*, 1:18 (1920), 5, cit. and trans., Julia Roos, 'Weimar's Crisis Through the Lens of Gender: The Case of Prostitution', PhD dissertation, Carnegie Mellon University, 2001, 107–10.

59   *Der Pranger*, 1/4 (1920), 1–2, cit. and trans., Roos, 'Weimar's Crisis', 111.

from newly enfranchised women, be they prostitutes or National Assembly delegates, Schneider-Kainer trod a fine line between producing an erotically satisfying composition that would appeal to an envisaged male audience whilst simultaneously undermining this by hinting at the quotidian realities of state-regulated prostitution. Those who chose not to acknowledge those realities could, however, wilfully turn a blind eye to them. Whilst Schneider-Kainer refused to foist contempt and shame on women, her critique of what *Der Pranger* had that same year described as the 'shameless exploitation of the female body' was hardly an overt one.[60]

Conclusion

Against a backdrop of heightened fears pertaining to venereal disease (a contagion with which the prostitute was in the postwar public imaginary irrevocably associated) and with increased calls for the reform of state-regulated prostitution, the lesbian was a less challenging prospect for print and an altogether more marketable erotic commodity in 1920. Bard was surely fully conscious of this marketability but he entirely brushed over the boldness of Schneider-Kainer's foray into the production of lesbian fine art prints. He did so by packaging Schneider-Kainer's ambitious suite of coloured lithographs in reassuringly feminized language. If the woman artist managed to negotiate the numerous obstacles put in her path and assume masculine privileges, be it in terms of her education or career choices, as Schneider-Kainer did, she was routinely kept in check by a patriarchal art world.

Demonstrating little deference to the authority of the printed word, Schneider-Kainer refused to subserviently provide a visual translation of Lucian's ancient dialogues. Making only scant overt reference to prostitution and refraining from vilifying, caricaturing or hyper-sexualizing her female subjects, Schneider-Kainer put lesbianism centre-stage when

---

60 *Der Pranger*, 1:4 (1920), 3, cit. and trans., Roos, 'Weimar's crisis', 109.

illustrating a text that was not primarily concerned with female same-sex desire. The apparent subject matter of the text (prostitution) and the actual subject matter of the images (lesbianism) might have suggested the possibility of salacious content but there was little that could be described as such in Schneider-Kainer's tender portrayals of lesbian women. The exclusion of an explicit male presence might have created an entirely female world but that world, populated solely by nude and scantily clad women, existed for the pleasure of an implicit male presence (the spectator) and was commissioned at the bidding of a male publisher. Women may, as Tuchmann noted, have dominated the forty-seven pages of this large-format book, but they certainly did not dominate the networks of the Weimar Germany's patriarchal print erotica trade.

JESSICA GLASER

11 Beatrice Warde, May Lamberton Becker and 'Books Across the Sea'

Beatrice Warde (1900–69) was an advocate for the printing industry and is best known as publicity manager of the Monotype Corporation. As a typographic scholar, educator and theoretician with an international reputation, she devoted herself to 'spreading ideas about good typography … to the widest possible audiences' which she did with 'astonishing results'.[1] Referred to as the 'First Lady of Typography', Warde understood the workings of communications, which was manifest in her interest in typography, language, public relations and her commitment to education.[2] This chapter considers a little-known aspect of Warde's work, 'Books Across the Sea' (BAS), an Anglo-American book exchange that she founded during the Second World War with her mother, May Lamberton Becker (1873–1958). Created in order to foster cultural understanding between America and Britain and to counter complacent attitudes towards the Nazi threat, BAS is a significant area of Warde's work.

Born and brought up in New York, Warde was raised by her divorced mother, May Lamberton Becker, a well-connected literary figure and journalist with an influence overseas.[3] Lamberton Becker's writing appeared in publications including the *New York Evening Post*, *Times Literary*

---

1   S. A. Morley, 'Ambassadress of Fine Typography', *Print Review*, 12 (1957). 510–1.
2   John Dreyfus, 'Mrs Beatrice Warde the First Lady of Typography', *The Times*, September 1969, 16.
3   May Lamberton Becker, *Adventures in Reading: Introducing Books to Children* (New York: Frederick A. Stokes, 1936); May Lamberton Becker, *Choosing Books For Children* (London: Oxford University Press, 1937); May Lamberton Becker, *Introducing Charles Dickens* (New York: Dodd Mead and Co, 1940).

Supplement and *New York Herald Tribune* where, for forty years, her column 'Reader's Guide' provided book reviews and reading recommendations. Warde's career began as a librarian at the American Type Founders Library in New Jersey and brought her into contact with important figures in the printing industry including the American printer Daniel Berkeley Updike (1860–1941) and the influential British typographer, Stanley Morison (1889–1967). In January 1925 she moved to London and, in 1929, became publicity manager for the Monotype Corporation, an American company promoting and selling a patented type composition system associated with high standards and quality.[4] Her connections were extensive and her links with significant individuals from printing and publishing included the sculptor and typeface designer Eric Gill (1882–1940).[5] By the 1930s she had become a respected commentator on the printing industry and was synonymous with the Monotype Corporation.[6] During the Second World War, however, Monotype's engineering expertise was redirected to armament manufacture at the expense of products for the printing industry and, as a result, Warde's work for the Corporation reduced. Having decided to remain in Britain, she refocused her talents on causes she saw as important to the war effort.[7]

Shelley Gruendler has written the most comprehensive account of Warde's life and work, beginning with her upbringing in New York and progressing through the context and achievements of Warde's professional life, until her death in 1969.[8] However, scant reference is made to Warde's

[4] Judy Slinn, Sebastian Carter and Richard Southall, *History of the Monotype Corporation*, (Woodstock: Vanbrugh Press, 2014).

[5] Slinn, *History of the Monotype Corporation*, 70; Fiona MacCarthy, *Eric Gill* (London: Faber and Faber, 1989), 232–36; Nicolas Barker, *Stanley Morison* (London: Macmillan, 1972), 159–63, 169–70, 221; H. Carter, 'Morison, Stanley Arthur (1889-1967), typographer', *Oxford Dictionary of National Biography* [online].

[6] Jessica Glaser, 'Warde (*née* Becker), Beatrice Lamberton Becker (1900–69)', *Oxford Dictionary of National Biography* [online].

[7] Slinn, *History of the Monotype Corporation*, 89–103. Beatrice Warde and Paul Standard, *Bombed But Unbeaten* ... (New York: The Typophiles, 1941)

[8] Shelley Gruendler, *The Life and Work of Beatrice Warde*, PhD thesis, University of Reading March 2005.

wartime work.[9] Brief references to Warde's involvement with BAS appear in both Hollman and in Poore but again detail is lacking.[10] In 2010, however, a large collection of Warde's personal papers were presented to the Cadbury Research Library, University of Birmingham.[11] Through this collection, it has been possible to establish the details of Warde's wartime activities and the creation of BAS: an important element of her life made possible through her knowledge of, and connections within, the printing and publishing industry. Through BAS, Warde encouraged both printers and the public to value books as important weapons in the fight against Germany.[12]

Warde's Circumstances during Second World War

With her interest in politics, culture and society, Warde has been described as an Anti-Fascist activist, although her political beliefs are ambiguous. At the outbreak of Second World War she joined the London-based, American ex-patriot organization, the American Outpost, a bipartisan branch of the Committee to Defend America by Aiding the Allies (CDAAA). Formed in 1940 by William Allen White, the editor of the Kansas City *Emporia Gazette*, and Clark M. Eichelburger of the League of Nations Association, the role of the CDAAA was to convince the

---

[9] Gruendler, *The Life and Work of Beatrice Warde*, 182–97.
[10] Valerie Holman, *Print for Victory* (London: The British Library, 2008), 41–53; Benjamin Poore, 'Notes from the archive: T. S. Eliot and the Second World War', *Times Literary Supplement* (2015).
[11] This donation created the Beatrice Warde Archive, Cadbury Research Library Special Collections, University of Birmingham. MS823. Hereafter 'Warde Archive'.
[12] Beatrice Warde, 'United We Stand: …', *Scholastic Magazine* (c.1941); Beatrice Warde, 'Books as Ammunition', *Wilson Library Bulletin* (October 1943). The *Wilson Library Bulletin* was an American magazine for librarians and was published from 1914–95.

American public to support the allies' cause in order to protect America.[13] It gained support throughout America and across the world. By July 1940, 350 branches had been established in America and two million signatures had been attached to a declaration urging 'stop Hitler now'.[14] In Britain, the Outpost was a lively and vocal branch of the CDAAA, and Warde was an early and active member addressing a public meeting of the Outpost in London on 12 July 1940. By 1940, 500 Americans in London, including Warde, had signed a declaration supporting the aims of the CDAAA. The declaration emphasized America as a world power that could not ignore the Fascist threat without sacrificing its own security, economy and liberty:

> Events compel us to recognise now, and act upon our recognition, that the intent of any aggressive military power or group of such powers to dominate the world aims at the foundations of American democracy and threatens the future of every home in the land.

To help defend America, the Outpost called upon citizens to lobby their Congressional representatives, declaring, 'we must act as a united nation immediately. We must give to those who are fighting our cause all the material and moral support of which the American nation is capable – short of nothing' and went on to explain that wars in Europe and the Far East were a threat to American patriotism.

As an American in London, Warde had first-hand experience of war in Europe, but saw that misinformation in both countries was creating distrust between the two nations, which the Outpost was well-placed to challenge. Her anglophile mother had encouraged her appreciation of Britain and its literature, which Warde wanted to share with other Americans to counter that distrust.[15] Through her talks and articles for the Outpost,

---

13   The League of Nations Association was founded in 1920 as the first international organization promoting world peace, being eventually replaced by the United Nations.
14   CDAAA, *Declarations by Americans-In-Britain* (London: Outpost of the Committee to Defend America by Aiding the Allies, 1940). 'American Support for Britain: Growing Numbers of Adherents', *The Times* (Saturday 13 July 1940), 7.
15   May Lamberton Becker declared herself an Anglophile in the introduction to *Bombed But Unbeaten: Excerpts from the 'War Commentary of Beatrice L. Warde*. Warde and Standard, *Bombed But Unbeaten ...*, v–vi.

Warde gained prominence with both British and American audiences.[16] The Outpost also positioned Warde at the centre of a significant group of influential individuals who became close friends, including professor of international relations, Arthur Newell (1885–1976); the author and lecturer Alicia Street; and the poet T. S. Eliot (1888–1965).

When America joined the war in December 1941, the CDAAA ceased but the Outpost continued, announcing its solidarity with Americans in its January 1942 newsletter and continuing to report from Britain on America's role in the war and links with the British.[17] In search of mutual understanding and collaboration, the 'Outposters', as members were known, also wanted their readers in America to contribute to the newsletter with their reflections on America's role in the conflict, and by asking questions about life in Britain.

Books Across the Sea, UK

Three factors led to the formation of BAS in 1941. Firstly, Warde was concerned that 'new books in commercial quantities will not be allowed shipping between Britain and America'.[18] She worried that readers would be denied the opportunity to learn about each other, or spread goodwill, and that Nazi propaganda would gain influence.[19] Secondly, the Nazi Party understood the 'importance of the printed word' in the spread of ideas and began to control publication of books through censorship and book burnings, in order that German culture should be cleansed of liberalism,

---

16   Warde, 'United We Stand: …', *Scholastic Magazine* (c.1941). An example of Warde's writing for the Outpost newsletter is: Beatrice Warde, 'Shopping Hint', *News from the Outpost* (15 November 1940), 4.
17   'The English-Speaking People Must …', *News from the Outpost* (January 1942), 1, MS823/23, Warde Archive.
18   Arthur Newell, 'Mrs Beatrice Warde', *The Times* (25 September 1969), 12.
19   Beatrice Warde and Alicia Street, 'How BAS Started' [typescript] (London: Books Across the Sea, 1951), 1, MS823/17, Warde Archive.

Marxism and Jewish influence.[20] Thirdly, Warde was concerned that Nazi radio propaganda, particularly that of William Joyce, otherwise known as 'Lord Haw-Haw', an English Fascist and broadcaster at the German radio corporation, would influence the British public.[21]

Books were significant to Warde: they were central to her education and a factor in her choice of career. She saw books as the answer to spreading goodwill and knowledge of other cultures, dispelling misconceptions and countering Nazi propaganda.[22] In 1940, when Warde set up BAS, America had not joined the war but wartime conditions were felt in Britain: children were evacuated, rationing was introduced, blackouts were in place and British servicemen overseas had been killed, wounded or captured.[23] The 'Battle of the Atlantic' saw Germany attempt to stop the supply of goods to Britain in an effort to impact morale and fighting ability.[24] German U-boats stalked allied ships, and shipping lanes along the US east coast were also targeted, sustaining heavy losses.[25] This created challenges in the transportation of books, which Warde had to overcome. In addition, in Britain, many raw materials were restricted in order to free up supplies for the production of munitions. Paper became a controlled material on 2 September 1939 when manufacturers were licensed and only allowed to sell paper in reduced quantities.[26] Just at the time that paper was becoming a scarce and valued commodity books were in great demand by both the public and the military. British reading appetites increased while paper availability reduced, and the commercial trade in newly published American titles came to a halt.[27] These were the circumstances to which

20 Guenter Lewy, *Harmful and Undesirable* ... (New York: Oxford University Press, 2016), ix.
21 Lewy, *Harmful and Undesirable*, 2–3.
22 Warde and Street, 'How BAS Started'.
23 Juliet Gardiner, *The Blitz* ... (London: Harper Press, 2011), 25–48.
    Philip Zeigler, *London At War 1938–1945* (London: BCA, 2002), 81–142.
24 Gardiner, *The Blitz* ..., 1–24; Spencer Dunmore, *The Epic Story* ... (Toronto: McClelland & Stewart, 1999).
25 Dunmore, *The Epic Story*; Richard Freeman, *Atlantic Nightmare* ... (independently published, 2019), 32–48.
26 Slinn, *History of the Monotype Corporation*, 94.
27 Holman, *Print for Victory*, 41–53.

Warde responded when she decided to remain in Britain, join the Outpost and establish BAS.

The original BAS collection was founded on a gift of seventy new American books, hitherto unpublished in Britain, chosen, purchased and despatched by Lamberton Becker as a gesture of encouragement to a group of American and British friends wanting to enrich knowledge of 'real' America.[28] For many British people, views of America were conditioned by Hollywood stereotypes.[29] To redress the balance, Lamberton Becker recommended books that provided insights into American life, history and culture and which acted as ambassadors for those working for improved Anglo-American understanding. Although the titles of the initial collection are not known, each volume was inscribed with the phrase 'let's read about each other'.[30] Lamberton Becker reported on the project in her newspaper column and received 600 suggestions for books from readers throughout America, from which she and Frederic G. Melcher (1879–1963), editor of *Publisher's Weekly* selected seventy titles.[31] The arrival of the books in London was mentioned in a letter to *The Times*, and attracted widespread interest.[32] In December 1941, in the ballroom of the Waldorf Hotel, London, the Outpost held a book reception where members of the public, librarians and publishers were encouraged to examine the American books and arrange loans.[33] At the same event it was suggested that a reciprocal gift of British books be made to America. By the end of the reception BAS had been formed and by December 1941, the first BAS

---

28 Warde and Street, 'How BAS Started'.
29 Siân Nicholas, 'American Commentaries …', *Culture and Social History*, 4 (2007), 461–79; Guinn, Bennett, *British Naval Aviation* …,(London: I. B Tauris), 50–1.
30 Warde and Street, 'How BAS Started'.
31 In 1941 readers of Lamberton Becker's Column in the *New York Herald Tribune* were asked to 'name 20 first rate books about America that had appeared since 1939'; seventy titles were chosen and sent to Britain. Beatrice Warde, 'Books That "Mean England …"', *John O'London's Weekly*, (19 May 1944), 63, MS823/9, Warde Archive. Warde and Street, 'How BAS Started'; Frederic G. Melcher (1879–1963), *Harvard Square Library* [online].
32 Arthur Newell, 'Studying America …', *The Times* (9 June 1941), 5; John Hedlam, 'Anglo American Contacts', *The Times* (3 July 1941), 5.
33 Warde and Street, 'How BAS Started'.

group, known as a 'circle' was established in London. The BAS collection comprised American books on diverse subjects including history, poetry, politics, art, education and books for children. A reading room and loans centre were opened in the BAS offices at Aldwych House, London which was inundated with requests for loans from a collection which amounted to 700 items.[34] Warde probably used her professional contacts and public relations skills to help grow BAS and keep it in the public eye through the support of the press.[35] To ensure the Society had the backing of the book trade, BAS consulted publishing professionals, stayed within copyright and averted any adverse impact on the commercial activity of literary agents and booksellers.

After its success in London, a corresponding BAS circle was established in New York, with what became known as 'Ambassador Books' exchanged across the Atlantic. As private transatlantic shipping was impossible, each book was carried in the limited luggage of BAS members sailing between the two countries, or single copies were sent through the post. The Society was wholly run by volunteers. In a pamphlet 'Books Across the Sea: a Transatlantic Circle to Promote Better Understanding Through Books' (c.1941), BAS lists its councillors as Professor Arthur Newell (President), Warde (Chairman) and Alicia Street (Secretary). Keen to attract members who would contribute both financially and practically, there were three classes of membership: firstly, a 'corresponding member', for five shillings per year, would be sent book lists and the Society's news bulletin, and have the option of being put in touch with a member of the society in America to exchange letters; secondly, a 'sustaining member', for an unspecified donation, contributed towards the establishment and running of a reading room; and thirdly, 'member of the team' – rather than paying membership fees they undertook voluntary work for the society.

---

34 Warde, 'Books as Ammunition'; Newell, 'Studying America', 5.
35 'Books Across the Sea', *The Daily Telegraph* (12 June, 1944), 4; 'Books Across the Sea', *The Manchester Guardian* (12 April, 1947), 6; 'Index' [advertisement of BAS event], *The Times* (5 May 1943), 5. Beatrice Warde, 'Books Across the Sea: "Ambassadors of Good Will"' *The Times* (2 January 1942), 5.

In the same pamphlet the five original aims of the society were set out, reflecting Warde's interest in typography, printing and publishing. Using upper-case for emphasis, BAS's aims were: firstly, to increase goodwill and understanding between American and British people through 'PRINTED BOOKS'. Secondly, to encourage and ease the exchange of books between Britain and America, books were seen as 'GOODWILL EMISSARIES' and 'WARRIORS'. Thirdly, to establish a 'COMMON REALM' – a term used by BAS to describe itself as a 'meeting place' for like-minded Americans and Britons to exchange ideas through reading. Fourthly, to bring together printers, publishers, educators and book lovers to defend their shared heritage of literature. Fifthly, to defend and restore the reputation of books and supporting projects in order to repair the denigration of the written word.[36]

It is not known who wrote these aims, but in tone and content they had echoes of Warde's other writings including 'Inscription for a Printing Office' (1932). Produced for a broadside promoting Eric Gill's typeface Perpetua, the 'Inscription' emphasized the importance of printing to a free society and to history, and compared the printing office to sacred ground.[37] In 1940 she produced two variants of the 'Inscription' responding directly to Nazi persecution and linking the role of the printing office to the fight against tyranny.[38] Similarly BAS's aims presented printed books as 'weapons' to be used against an enemy, and book lovers were urged to defend, and protect their heritage through the exchange of books.[39] BAS saw this as a fight against moral, intellectual and physical damage and contempt for the written word, and evoked the same sentiments expressed in 'Inscription for a Printing Office'.[40]

---

36   'Books Across the Sea ...' [pamphlet] (London: Books Across the Sea, c.1941), MS823/17, Warde Archive.
37   Beatrice Warde, 'Inscription for a Printing Office' (London: The Monotype Corporation, 1932).
38   Beatrice Warde, 'Inscription for a Printing Office' [First variant], (privately published, June, 1940); Beatrice Warde, 'Inscription for a Printing Office' [Second variant], (London: Newspaper World, July 1940).
39   Warde, 'United We Stand ...'; Warde, 'Books as Ammunition'.
40   Books Across the Sea ...' [pamphlet].

In 1943 T. S. Eliot replaced Newell as president of BAS. Eliot, an internationally acclaimed poet, critic and publisher, was American by birth and British by citizenship. He was made president because of his high profile and professional links with publishing and, like Warde, his Anglo-American status.[41] Eliot's presidency of BAS was 'one of the most material expressions of his trans-Atlanticism'.[42] Although generally unacknowledged, Warde and Eliot developed a friendship through their work for BAS. Eliot's respect for Warde and Lamberton Becker is evident in his speech at the opening of the May Lamberton Becker Reading Room at the National Book League in January 1960, when he expressed his regard for both mother and daughter and their dedication to BAS.[43] Coinciding with Eliot assuming the presidency, BAS in London published revised aims. It is not known who authored these aims but the language was plainer and less theatrical than the original, no longer referencing 'fighting', but focusing on creating a lasting peace through books.[44] The aims re-emphasized promoting understanding between Britons and Americans and using the book exchange to spread goodwill, as well as supporting the work of educators and writers. The importance of the 'COMMON GROUND' as a physical or spiritual meeting place to exchange ideas was highlighted: a respectful location where books were valued as critical to civilization and goodwill; a place for shared pride in a common heritage of English literature; and which recognized mutual understanding as the only way to achieve lasting peace. The shift in focus from fighting in defence of democracy to promoting mutual understanding and long-lasting peace was the most noticeable difference between the original and revised aims but is, perhaps, understandable after four years of conflict and wartime restrictions.

The pamphlet also lists the names of twenty-nine honorary councillors, selected for their knowledge, contacts and their respected positions. Six of these individuals were, like Warde, American-born anglophiles; many

---

41 Ronald Bush, 'Eliot, Thomas Stearns (1888–1965)', *Oxford Dictionary of National Biography* [online].
42 Benjamin, 'Notes from the archive: T. S. Eliot and the Second World War' [online].
43 T. S. Eliot, [unpublished] 'Speech 28 January 1960 …'. MS823/9, Warde Archive.
44 'This is How You Can Help …' [pamphlet], (London: Books Across the Sea, c.1943), MS823/18, Warde Archive.

were linked to libraries or publishing, and were probably already part of Warde's professional and personal networks. Some, like Warde, were converts to Roman Catholicism. A number had links to universities, particularly Oxford and Cambridge. The group also included five MPs, appointed for their influential positions, to assist advocacy and promotion of the society.[45]

Simultaneously, in America BAS published a similar pamphlet *Books Across the Sea: A Transatlantic 'Common Ground'*, urging Americans to join: 'you will be doing something to manifest your faith in books as instruments of goodwill'.[46] It also claimed that BAS in America was approved by official circles: 'Join our "Books Across the Sea" Circle: help forward this pioneer work, which has been warmly commended in official circles and by eminent workers for United Nations solidarity. We are doing something *new*: we need your help'.

Choosing Books

BAS fulfilled what Warde and Lamberton Becker saw as a longstanding need and they believed the society would have been valuable before the war and would continue to be important afterwards in the education for the new world order.[47] Booklists and newly arrived titles were first circulated among members who reported on the ambassadorial value of the volumes and their suitability to become part of the collection.[48] The Society held

---

45   'This is How You Can Help ...' [pamphlet], 2.
46   *Books Across the Sea* ... (New York: Books Across the Sea, c.1943), MS823/17, Warde Archive.
47   'Books Across the Sea Post-War Policy [report], (Books Across the Sea, c.1944), MS823/17, Warde Archive.
      Beatrice Warde and Alicia Street, 'How Books Across the Sea Started' [typescript] c.1966, 7, MS823/17, Warde Archive.
48   Beatrice Warde, 'Extracts from an Address ...' (London: Books Across the Sea, April 1944), 2, MS823/9, Warde Archive.

'book receptions' where talks on the books were given by guests including librarians and publishers, and informal reader-panels evaluated titles for their contribution to cultural understanding. These panels were originally limited to twelve people, with each member giving a three-minute report on a newly arrived book and also suggesting an equivalent title in exchange. Discussions were lively and attendance increased through 'word of mouth'. Book receptions took place quarterly and in March 1946 the London circle of BAS debated ninety-two titles on themes as diverse as art and politics. Publications included *Death and Entrances* by Dylan Thomas; *The Lid Lifts* by Patrick Gordon Walker; George Orwell's *Critical Essays;* *The Little White Bear* by Enid Marx; *Victor Passmore* by Clive Bell; *Press, Parliament and People* by Francis Williams; and *Juvenile Delinquency and the Law* by A. N. Jones. Government and local authority reports and publications were also texts under consideration, such as *The Education Act 1944,* and *Report on Luton* by Fred Grundy.[49]

By 1945 the BAS collections had increased significantly. In America the collection was housed within Columbia University Library and comprised in excess of 2,000 British books. The London collection contained over 2,750 American books, 500 of which were for children. In both countries these were the only available copies of each title.[50] The combined British and American membership in 1945 was 2,000, including members of the public, librarians, authors and publishers.[51] By 1978, nine years after Warde's death, the society possessed 12,000 books which were made available to 70,000 members from 160 branches in Britain, America and other countries

---

49 'British Books for March ...' [booklist] (London: Books Across the Sea, March 1942), MS823/9, Warde Archive. Francis Williams, *Press, Parliament and People* (London: William Heinemann Ltd, 1946); A. N. Jones, *Juvenile Delinquency and the Law,* (London: Pelican, 1945); Fred Grundy, *Report on Luton* (Hertfordshire: Gibbs Bamforth, 1945); Enid Marx, *The Little White Bear* (London: Faber and Faber, 1945).

50 'The Latest From ...' (London: Books Across the Sea, October 1945), MS823/9, Warde Archive.

51 'British Books for March ...' [booklist] (London: Books Across the Sea, March 1942).

including Canada and India.[52] Newspaper and radio coverage promoted BAS, as did the Outpost, particularly through *News from the Outpost* and other public presentations. In America, newspapers, including the *New York Herald Tribune*, where Lamberton Becker was a regular contributor, the *Wilmington Morning Star* and the Washington D. C. *Evening Star* also published articles on the work of BAS.[53] Despite paper shortages reducing British newspapers to an average four pages, BAS was reported in the national papers including *The Daily Telegraph*, *The Manchester Guardian* and *The Times* reaching 16,000,000 readers by 1949.[54] Radio too was an increasingly popular way to access news; between 1942 and 1944 Warde made a series of twenty-five radio broadcasts, for the British War Relief Society which aired across America to promote the work and ideas of BAS.[55] Members often corresponded with Warde expressing an interest in learning about life in Britain, commenting on the progress and consequences of the war,[56] as well as offering predictions of Nazi conquests, doubts about the legitimacy of refugee status, and pessimistic outlooks on the war – information which was potentially demoralizing for Warde at a time when her work confidently predicted the British and their allies winning the war.[57]

52 "International Exchange …' (Un-named newspaper cutting, 1978), MS823/17, Warde Archive.
53 Willa Martin, 'Quizzical English …' *Wilmington Morning Star* [North Carolina], (6 March 1945), 6. Phillip H. Love, 'Just Between Ourselves', *The Evening Star* [Washington] (4 May1947), section B8.
54 'Books Across the Sea', The *Daily Telegraph* (12 June 1944), 4; 'Books Across the Sea', The *Manchester Guardian* (12 April 1947), 6; 'Index'[advertisement of BAS event], *The Times*, 5; Beatrice Warde, 'Books Across the Sea …', *The Times* (2 January 1942), 5.
55 Kevin Williams, *Read All About It* … (Abingdon: Routledge, 2009), 5; Barbara Bonner, *Books Across the Sea: Bulletin to Members* (London: Books Across the Sea, 1944), 1, MS823/9, Warde Archive. 'Books Across the Sea' The *Manchester Guardian*. 'Index'[advertisement of BAS event] *The Times*. Beatrice Warde, 'Books Across the Sea: "Ambassadors of Good Will"', *The Times*.
56 Warde kept correspondence from members of the society which is located in MS823/19, Warde Archive.
57 Letter to Miss Warde from T. Russ Hill, Detroit, MS823/19, Warde Archive. Letter to Beatrice Warde from Dorothy A. Kamen-Kaye, Caracas, MS823/19, Warde Archive.

Figure 11.1. Photograph of 'Books Across the Sea' scrapbooks, *Outpost*, April 1944, p. 4. Image courtesy of the Cadbury Research Library, University of Birmingham.

The BAS Scrapbook Exchange

In 1941, Warde and Lamberton Becker established the BAS scrapbook exchange for children (see Figure 11.1). The scrapbooks, also referred to as 'handmade' books, 'vividly portrayed the day-by-day scenes of life at home and at school and national holidays'.[58] For fear of overstretching the transatlantic post, announcement of the scrapbook exchange was delayed until Sunday 11 July 1943 when it was noted in the *New York Herald*

---

58   Beatrice Warde, 'Books Across the Sea' [Presentation], (Association of Special Libraries and Information Bureaux, 1945), MS823/17, Warde Archive.

Tribune.[59] The first book, made by a Vermont resident, showed the lives of British evacuee children in America, including details such as making maple sugar and Sunday School picnics. The scrapbook scheme was extended to include books made by school groups indicating life in each country, through the eyes of children of the same ages. Writing in *The Scholastic*, an American high school weekly magazine, Warde explained the importance of the scrapbook exchange in the fight against Nazi Germany. Writing in a child friendly, reassuring manner, Warde encouraged every American citizen over the age of seven to help fight Goebbels's propagandizing aims and Nazi attempts to divide allegiances and foster distrust. Fighting back encouraged understanding, communication and respect and would help derail Nazi ambition. Her idea of making scrapbooks for exchange explained that books were weapons, but also ambassadors of goodwill and understanding, bringing each nation to life for the other:

> ... he [Goebbels] wouldn't be so glad to hear that your school, and some similar school in England had each formed a 'Books Across the Sea' group and were exchanging goodwill gifts of books that explain America to Britain and *vice versa*.[60]

The Scholastic was circulated to 400,000 students and was used as an aid to classroom study. Lamberton Becker wrote regularly for the magazine and also became editor.

By 1943, forty schools across America were involved in the scrapbook scheme including North Central High School, Spokane Washington; West Seattle High School; and Newton High School, Queens, New York. By 1945, news of the scrapbook exchange had spread and become popular. In conjunction with Roy Publishers, New York, BAS held an annual competition for the best school scrapbook with the winning entry being published. There were also plans to exhibit the scrapbooks in the Metropolitan Museum of Art in New York.[61] These publications and exhibitions were made possible through the help of friends and colleagues of both Warde

59 'Schools Show American Life ...', *New York Herald Tribune* (11 July 1943), MS823/17, Warde Archive.
60 Warde, 'United We Stand'.
61 Barbara Bonner, *The Latest from* ... (London: Books Across the Sea, 1946), 2, MS823/9, Warde Archive.

and Lamberton Becker. In addition to their educational value, the children's scrapbooks helped Warde publicize BAS, using quotations from the scrapbook to stir emotions and elicit support:

> Boys and girls of England: we the pupils of Junior High School 45 send you this book. We know that even if England is 3,500 miles away from the United States in distance, it is not more than a few inches from our hearts.[62]

The pupils of Junior High School 45 described their scrapbook as token of a love and friendship, wanting their book and new friendships to have a permanent place and value in England. They also asked for a scrapbook in return.

Mental Mobilization

Engaging audiences on both sides of the Atlantic in an intellectual war effort to help counter Nazi propaganda was, for Warde, a vital 'mental mobilization'.[63] In a letter to Newell, written in 1942 from New York, she explained this term and her ideas for a central authority to take responsibility for 'mental mobilization.' She referred to a conversation with an 'important American official' on whether the US Government thought 'mental mobilization' was considered important enough for a term to be developed for this activity. The official, although supportive of her term, did not think it could be used until a co-ordinated organization was formed: 'that may come. We all hope so. [...] a "United Nations Commission" which would do what no one Government can (in the nature of things) do to create "United National" unity of minds, "we"-consciousness based on better understanding.' Warde believed that an organization like this would fight the Nazis and was urgently required. She also emphasized that while many were considering this issue, the Outpost and BAS were actively undertaking 'aggressive good will'.[64]

62   'The Latest From …', 2.
63   Warde, 'Books as Ammunition'.
64   Beatrice Warde, Letter to Professor Arthur Newell, MS823/17, Warde Archive.

From 1942 to 1944 Warde was in America promoting the work of the Outpost and BAS, giving presentations, staging exhibitions and making radio broadcasts. She also communicated with American politicians and officials, thereby raising the profile of BAS and also her own reputation.[65] Although Warde acknowledged that other forms of 'war work' were important, she asked 'how often do you come across a work party of literates who are determined to wrestle with certain dangerous misconceptions that are causing trouble ... between one Allied people and another?'[66] She saw books as the answer, at a time when they were scarce and people were turning to reading to escape the strains of war. In 1942, acknowledging 'a book famine', Warde described the British book in wartime as 'a story of heroism and gallant resourcefulness of quiet people of the "book world" at the time of the slaughter of twenty million books, and amid the worries of the paper famine'.[67] For Warde books were defence weapons against the enemy's efforts to 'divide and conquer'.[68]

To highlight the consequences of book destruction in wartime Britain, Warde helped organize an exhibition showcasing the bomb damage inflicted on London's printing companies, publishing offices, bookshops and libraries. Opened by Warde on 30 March 1942, the event exhibited charred remains of books and documents dating back to the fourteenth century, thereby reinforcing the impact of bomb damage on world history and knowledge.[69] The artefacts were clustered in themes: civilian population, warriors, children's books, artists and craftsmen and HMSO publications. Examples included *Acts of the Privy Council in England 1597*

---

[65] Warde does not give the names of the important individuals in her correspondence. However, she kept a record of quotes received from Government officials in Britain and America, including Elmer Davis, Director of The Office of War Information, Washington D.C., Brenden Bracken, Director Ministry of Information, William Nelson, British Division Office of War information and Hamish Hamilton American Division Ministry of Information. 'Extracts from Supportive Letters ...' (c.1943), MS823/17, Warde Archive.

[66] Warde, 'Books as Ammunition'.

[67] Warde, 'Books That "Mean England"', 63.

[68] Warde, 'Books as Ammunition'.

[69] Invitation to 'Books Under Fire' MS823/16, Warde Archive.

and a burnt copy of the *Congressional Record 1876*, which was selected as a reminder that the democracy of both countries was under attack. The exhibition also reported on preparations for the centenary celebrations of American independence and looked forward to the presence of delegates from Britain and Russia.[70]

Warde described BAS's activities as 'a game of good will tennis with the Atlantic as the net'. On the other hand she saw propaganda as the art of sending ideas along a one-way street. The energies of private citizens were 'better reserved for exchanging knowledge for knowledge, curiosity for curiosity, ignorance for ignorance, with other human beings in other friendly countries: in other words, sending ideas back and forth along a two-way street'.[71] As well as utilizing their contacts from the publishing world, Lamberton Becker and Warde's networks also extended to politics and government officials. Through her role at the *New York Herald Tribune*, Lamberton Becker circulated amongst these groups and forged links with the Head of the British Ministry of Information, American Division, Mary Agnes Hamilton (1882–1966), a former Labour member of parliament for Blackburn, who endorsed BAS and attended their first annual general meeting in London.[72] Formed in 1939, the ministry was a British government department with responsibilities including news, press censorship and wartime publicity in Britain and allied and neutral countries, including America. BAS supported the ministry's objectives and dispatched regular updates on its activities. The ministry was concerned that the conflict would become a 'war of nerves' involving the general public, concerns that were also expressed by Warde, the Outpost and BAS.[73] The British government understood it would need to use every means to

---

[70] Beatrice Warde, 'Bombed books of significance …', MS823/19, Warde Archive.

[71] 'Extracts from an Address Given by Mrs Beatrice Warde …' (London: Books Across the Sea, April 1944), 2. MS823/9, Warde Archive.

[72] Beatrice Warde, Letter to May Lamberton Becker (20 November 1941), MS823/5, Warde Archive; Janet, E. Grenier, 'Hamilton, [née Adamson], Mary Agnes (1882–1966), Politician and Broadcaster', *Oxford Dictionary of National Biography* [online]; Holman, *Print for Victory* … (London: British Library, 2008).

[73] 'The Art of War…', [online] *The National Archives* (2018). Holman, *Print for Victory* ….

counter this threat and as result, the ministry responded well to Warde and BAS. Warde kept written records of comments from prominent ministry individuals, including Mary Agnes Hamilton, Brenden Braken (1901–58)[74] and Hamish Hamilton (1900–88)[75] which confirmed the Ministry's approval of BAS and acted as an affirmation of the quality and value of books recommended.[76] Warde and Lamberton Becker also dealt with the American Office of War Information, an equivalent of the British Ministry of Information.[77] Similarly charged with imparting information and propaganda at home and overseas, the Office of War Information was equally supportive of BAS. Warde and Lamberton Becker had high-level contacts in the office and corresponded with its director, Elmer Davis (1890–1958), who also saw the postwar potential of BAS in establishing a new world order involving an influential America.[78]

Books Across the Sea after the War

Warde believed that BAS had a valuable role in a postwar society when the education of citizens in mutual understanding and respect would continue to be of value. With this in mind, BAS developed a postwar policy, outlining the role for the organization in fostering parallel book exchanges as a 'working demonstration of cultural reciprocity across national frontiers, by private citizens in the interest of MUTUAL better-understanding; one in which the spirit of fair give-and-take replaces the

---

74 Braken was a publisher and Minister of Information 1941–44; Charles Lysaght, 'The Irish spoofer …', *The Irish Times*, July 2016.
75 American born Hamish Hamilton founded Hamish Hamilton Ltd in 1931. Christopher Sinclair-Stevenson, Hamilton, Hamish [formerly James: Jamie], (publisher) [online] *Oxford Dictionary of National Biography*, Oxford University Press, 2010.
76 Extracts from supportive letters on the activities of BAS, c.1943.
77 The Office of War Information is Created, [online] National WWII Museum New Orleans, 2012.
78 Extracts from supportive letters on the activities of BAS, c1943.

"one-way thrust" of national propaganda'.[79] It was to remain a voluntary society and planned to extend its activities to other countries.

Throughout Second World War, BAS was part of the Outpost but in 1946 the Outpost closed and BAS looked to partner with a new organization, the English-Speaking Union, which had aims and a structure analogous with BAS.[80] With branches in Britain and America, the English-Speaking Union was an international charity which brought together individuals from different cultures to increase communication and understanding through the English language. As a consequence of the closure of the Outpost, the BAS collection in London became part of Westminster Libraries, and was located in a specially created reading room in South Audley Street Library, Mayfair. Using her connections, Warde engaged Eleanor Roosevelt (1884–1962) to speak at the opening of the reading room in January 1946.[81] Warde and Lamberton Becker had links with Roosevelt through her support for child evacuees to America, an area in which they were also involved. Roosevelt's presence at the opening of the BAS reading room was detailed in the press, creating valuable promotion for BAS and its aims.[82] In her speech, Roosevelt highlighted the value of learning about different cultures and countries through books and connected the merit of this activity with the aims of the United Nations Organization, providing a public validation for Warde and Lamberton Becker of the international importance of the organization they had created.

Warde and Lamberton Becker also established and ran the New York and Boston circles of BAS.[83] Although the Society had been a significant part of their wartime work, both Warde and Lamberton Becker maintained other professional and charitable interests, all of which were linked

---

79   'BAS Post-War Policy' [report] (London: Books Across the Sea, c.1944), MS823/17, Warde Archive.
80   The English-Speaking Union was founded in 1918 by Sir Evelyn Leslie Wrench (1882–1966). Alex May, Wrench, Sir (John) Evelyn Leslie [online] *Oxford Dictionary of National Biography,* Oxford University Press, 2009.
81   Beatrice Warde, 'Dear Colleagues in America' [letter] (4 January 1946), MS823/17, Warde Archive.
82   'BAS: Mrs. Roosevelt …', *The Times* (1 February 1946), 7.
83   'BAS Bulletin …', 1944, 1.

to Anglo-American understanding through cultural exchange. One such endeavour was the establishment of the Kinsmen, an organization founded in 1941, from an idea of Mrs Lucy Bemrose, wife of the printer William Bemrose.[84] The Kinsmen represented the parents of British evacuee children sent to America. Its objective was the strengthening of connections between parents and American foster families. The organization also shared news of evacuee children in its newsletter, the *Seagull Post* and, after the war, to thank Americans for providing sanctuary for British children, arranged educational scholarships for American students in Britain. In addition, Warde also became involved with the British-American-Canadian-Associates [BMCA], an organization supporting educational links through cultural exchanges. Established in 1931 by Professor Arthur Newell as a lecture fellowship programme, the BMCA initially focused on four areas: world citizenship, women's work, trade and commerce and interreligious relationships. Also responsible for distributing Fulbright scholarships, by 1950 the BMCA described its aims as furthering mutual understanding between peoples of the British Commonwealth and America and as educating public opinion in the institutions of these countries, their cultures, civil, domestic and business life. The work of this organization continued until it was disbanded in 1997.

Conclusion

This chapter has provided an overview of an uncharted area of Beatrice Warde's professional activity during Second World War. In founding BAS Warde used the skills and contacts she had gained in the pre-war printing industry to foster cultural understanding and challenge complacency towards Fascism. Through this work she established an enduring legacy in the form of a respected society that continued beyond her lifetime. It is

---

84 Joseph S. Evans, 'British Parents Unite …' *New York Herald Tribune* (20 March 1941), 1, MS823/19, Warde Archive. Lamberton Becker was a journalist for the *New York Herald Tribune,* and probably had connections with this piece.

hoped that this research will stimulate awareness of and interest in Warde's work during this period, as well as encouraging future study. Areas which warrant further investigation include the impact of her networks on the creation and development of BAS as well as the influence of her wartime work on her postwar ambition and activities in the printing industry. In addition, this work creates opportunity for future research into Warde's use of publishing to promote Anglo-American understanding.

Notes on Contributors

ARTEMIS ALEXIOU is a Senior Lecturer in Design Studies and Design History at York St John University, UK. She has taught at Manchester School of Art and other HE institutions since 2013. She studied architecture at Oxford Brookes University and graphic design at London Metropolitan University. She holds an AHRC-funded PhD in design, media and women's history by the Manchester Institute for Research and Innovation in Art & Design, Manchester Metropolitan University. Her research concentrates on late nineteenth-century feminist periodicals, especially to the manner in which texts and paratexts (mainly design, visual and material) co-functioned in relation to gender politics, and other intersecting concepts such as class and ethnicity. She is a member of the Royal Historical Society, and a Fellow of the HEA.

ANIL AYKAN BARNBROOK is a Graphic Designer and educator from Instabul, Turkey. She graduated from the Graphic Design Department of Mimar Sinan Fine Arts University in 2005 and completed her PhD on Typography at the same university in 2014. Between 2005 and 2014 she was a teaching assistant and tutor in several universities in Istanbul; since 2014 she has been working as a graphic designer at Barnbrook in London, UK.

JESSICA GLASER is Senior Lecturer in Graphic Design and Typography at the University of Wolverhampton, and a part-time PhD student at Birmingham City University in the UK. Her thesis examines the identification and presentation of Beatrice Warde as 'First Lady of Typography'.

ANGELA GRIFFITH is an Assistant Professor with the Department of the History of Art and Architecture, Trinity College Dublin, Ireland. She is co-author of *Making their Mark: Irish Painter-Etchers* (Hodge and Griffith, 2019) and co-editor of *Harry Clarke and Artistic Visions of the*

New Irish State (Griffith, Helmers and Kennedy, 2018). She is on the board of the National Print Museum, Ireland.

REESE ALEXANDRA IRWIN is a Consultant Librarian and independent researcher. She holds a Master of Library and Information Science from the University of British Columbia, and a Master of Arts in English from Simon Fraser University in Canada. Her MA project, 'Compiling *Sanditon*' (2018), analysed the earliest print iterations of Jane Austen's last manuscript, *Sanditon*. She is co-author, with Michelle Levy, of 'The Female Authors of Cadell and Davies', in *Women's Literary Networks and Romanticism: 'A Tribe of Authoresses'* edited by Andrew Winckles and Angela Rehbein (2017).

ERIKA LEDERMAN is a Cataloguer of Photographs at the Victoria & Albert Museum, UK, which she joined in 2008. She is currently studying for a PhD at the Photographic History Research Centre at De Montfort University and the V&A, through the AHRC Collaborative Doctoral Award scheme. Her thesis examines nineteenth-century female institutional photographers, assessing the socio-political contexts that shaped their careers and subsequently perpetuated their exclusion from prevailing photographic histories.

HANNAH LYONS is a Curator at Royal Museums Greenwich, UK. Her AHRC-funded PhD with Birkbeck, University of London and the V&A, examined the role, status and output of professional women printmakers, c.1750–1830. Previously she has worked in curatorial roles at Tate and Christ Church Picture Gallery, University of Oxford.

ABBEY REES-HALES is an AHRC Midlands4Cities-funded PhD Student and a Postgraduate Teaching Assistant in the Department of Art History, Curating and Visual Studies at the University of Birmingham, UK. Her thesis examines the largely overlooked contribution made by female artists to the erotic and homoerotic visual cultures of interwar France and Germany.

ROSE ROBERTO is a part-time Lecturer in the School of Humanities and Teaching Resources Librarian at Bishop Grosseteste University, Lincoln, UK. She studied Library and Information Science at the University of California, Los Angeles, and history of the book at the University of Reading. Her current research examines the intersection of visual culture and educational publishing, and the hidden histories related to race, gender and class embedded in the material culture of the transnational book trade during the nineteenth and twentieth centuries. She was series editor for the *Art Researchers' Guides* to different cities in the UK and Ireland (2011–2017), and a contributor to the award-winning *Edinburgh History of the British and Irish Press, Vol. 2* (Finkelstein, 2020), and *Circulation and Control: Artistic Culture and Intellectual Property in the Nineteenth Century* (Delamaire and Slauter, 2021). She is a Fellow of the HEA.

DIANNE ROMAN is a retired Fine Arts and Design Professor. Her MFA is in Media Arts and her doctorate from Virginia Commonwealth University, USA is in Media, Art and Text. As an independent scholar she researches the American woman in the nineteenth-century print shop. Her recently published article 'Early Newspapering in Jefferson County: John S. Gallaher and his *The Ladies' Garland*' (2019) examines the contributions that printers' wives made to an early nineteenth-century women's magazine. She maintains a visual studio practice and is currently investigating the female involvement in the development and growth of printing across her home state of West Virginia.

ROSA SMURRA is Associate Professor of Medieval History at the University of Bologna, Italy, where she teaches Comparative History of European Cities. She is co-author of *Storia delle Città Italiane: Dal Tardoantico al Primo Rinascimento* (Bocchi, Ghizzoni, Smurra, 2002) and co-editor of *Imago Urbis: L'Immagine della Città nella Storia d'Italia* (Bocchi and Smurra, 2003), *The Far-sighted Gaze of Capital Cities: Essays in Honour of Francesca Bocchi* (Smurra et al., 2014), and *Bologna's Porticos in the European Context* (Bocchi and Smurra, 2015).

Besides urban history, her research interests include gender history, and manuscript book history.

PATRICIA THOMAS is an Honorary Research Associate in the School of Design at Massey University in New Zealand. Originally a print designer, she now researches the history of print with a special interest in ephemera and advertising. Her recent publications include *Colonising Te Whanganui ā Tara and Marketing Wellington 1840–1849: Displaying [Dis]Possession* (2019); *The Other Side of History: Underground Literature and the 1951 Waterfront Dispute* (2017), *Iconoclastic Effrontery: Rex Fairburn, Bob Lowry and the Printing of Polemics* (2017) and *Emigration and Imperial Business: The New Zealand Company Brand 1839–1841* (2016).

Index

advertising
    jobbing 119–33
    periodical press 183–91
    shock 233–9
Alcott, Louisa May 104–5, 109
Anglo-America 273–94
Anti-Fascist activism 273–94
apprentice/s 21, 53, 63, 70, 81, 87, 95, 149
art criticism 245–71
arts and crafts movement, the 205
Arundel Society for Promoting the Knowledge of Art, the 141–66

book trade
    Bologna, thirteen- and fourteenth-century 9–31
    Books Across the Sea 273–94
    illustrated, the 72–8
Boscawen Street 112, 134, 136
Boston, Massachusetts 85–109
branding 219–43

children's books 35, 40–2, 55, 289
Cole, Henry 142
corsets 184–8
Courtney Library, Royal Institution of Cornwall 112, 115, 120
Cowper, Isabel Agnes 141–66
Cuala
    Industries 199–200
    Press 195–218

Dialogues of the Courtesans see *Hetairikoi Dialogoi*
decorated letters 120, 124, 129
Denison, Mary A. 104, 106–7

Dixie, Lady Florence 180–3
dress, alternative see Dixie, Lady Florence
Dun Emer
    Industries 198–9, 207
    Press 195–218
design
    editorial 167–93
    history of 1–4, 8
    poster see posters, propaganda
    protest 219–43

Eliot, T. S. 277, 282
engravings 42, 62–3, 67–9, 78, 80–1, 138, 147–8, 166, 215, 217
ephemera 115, 119–20, 135, 211
eroticism 253, 258, 260, 264
etching 57, 59, 63–5, 67–9, 73
Examples of Art Workmanship 141–66

family
    Byrne, the 58–83
    Cowper, the 141–66
    Heard, the 116–7
    Newbery, the 33–56
    Yeats, the 195–218
Fenwick Miller, Florence 178–80
Fern, Fanny 97, 102, 104
    see also Willis Eldridge, Sara Payson
First World War 248–9, 251
force-feeding 235–6
format 15, 92, 93, 96, 129, 152, 175
founts 111–40, 172–3

Genette, Gérard 167, 169
guerrilla marketing 221, 240–1

Hetairikoi Dialogoi 245–71
Hetärengespräche des Lukian see *Hetairikoi Dialogoi*
hand-colouring 214, 257
Heard
    Goodridge, Edward 117, 140
    Goodridge, Elizabeth 111, 113, 115–6, 118–9, 133, 140
    John 111, 116
    MacFarlane, John 117
Hopkins, Eliza Ann Woodruff 106–7

illustration, book 57–83, 141–66, 195–218, 245–71
interview, periodical (newspaper) 176–83
Irish art printing 195–218
Irish Revival movement, the 195–218

landscape
    painters 57, 240
    painting 59, 62, 64–6, 69, 71, 80, 211
lesbianism 245–71
Lucian of Samosata see *Hetairikoi Dialogoi*

manuscript book production 9–31
mastheads, periodical 167–93
Morris
    William 196, 201, 203–6
    May 199
Müller, Henrietta 167, 170, 174, 176

National Press Agency 172
Newbery
    Elizabeth 33–56
    John 33–5, 41, 48–9, 51–3
newspapers, weekly 85–109
nineteenth-century
    American newspapers 85–109
    British feminist periodicals 167–93
    British provincial printing 111–40

typeface/s 93, 111–40, 172–6, 274, 281
Norris, Reverend Thomas Folsom 90, 92–3, 108

Olive Branch, The 85–109

Pankhurst
    Christabel 228–9, 236
    Emmeline 221, 235
    Sylvia 224–6, 229, 232, 241
paratexts 167–93
Pethick-Lawrence, Emmeline 224, 231, 235
photomechanical reproduction 206–7
posters, propaganda 219–43
Pouchée, Louis John 114
prostitution, heterosexual 245–71

Royal Academy of Arts, the 58, 59, 65–7

Schneider-Kaine, Lene 245–71
Second World War 273–5, 292
South Kensington Museum (SKM) 141–66
Suffragette, The 222, 234, 236
Suffragettes, the 219–43

Thompson, Charles Thurston 142, 147
Thompson, John 147

Victoria & Albert Museum see South Kensington Museum (SKM)
Votes for Women 225–6, 229, 232–4, 236, 238, 240–1

Walker, Emery 196, 199, 212
Weimar Republic 245, 259, 264
West Briton and Cornwall Advertiser, the 111, 115–7, 129, 131–3, 140
Willis Eldridge, Sara Payson 101–2, 104, 109

Index

see also Fern, Fanny
Woman, New 167–93, 259
Woman's Herald see *Women's Penny Paper*
women
    artists 245–71
    compositors 85–109
    editors 85–109, 167–93
    engravers 57–83
    photographers 141–66
    printers 33–56, 85–109, 111–40, 167–93, 245–71
    publishers 33–56, 57–83, 85–109, 111–40
    scribes 9–31
    stationers 9–31
    typesetters 85–109
    widows in business 57–83, 111–40
    writers 85–109

women's (or Women's)
    hair 177–8, 180, 182–4, 188–91
    movement, the 167–93, 219–43
    Penny Paper 167–93
    portraits 167–93
    Press, the 231–4
    Print History Project (WPHP) 33–56
    Printing Society 167, 170
    sexuality 245–71
    Social and Political Union (WSPU) 219–43
wood-engraving 147, 151

Yeats
    Elizabeth Corbet 195–218
    Jack Butler 206, 216
    William Butler 195, 199

Printing History and Culture

Series Editors

Caroline Archer-Parré, Malcolm Dick and John Hinks

This series unites the allied fields of printing history and print culture, and is therefore concerned not only with the design, production and distribution of printed material but also its consumption, reception and impact. It includes the histories of the machinery and equipment, of the industry and its personnel, of the printing processes, the design of its artefacts (books, newspapers, journals, fine prints, and ephemera) and with the related arts and crafts, including calligraphy, type-founding, typography, papermaking, bookbinding, illustration, and publishing. It also covers the cultural context and environment in which print was produced and consumed.

This series is issued by the Centre for Printing History and Culture, a joint initiative between Birmingham City University and the University of Birmingham that seeks to encourage research into all aspects and periods of printing history and culture, as well as education and training into the art and practice of printing.

Published Volumes

Vol. 1   Ian Cawood and Lisa Peters (eds): *Print, Politics and the Provincial Press in Modern Britain*.
2019. 260 pages. ISBN 978-1-78874-430-0

Vol. 2   Artemis Alexiou and Rose Roberto (eds): *Women in Print 1: Design and Identities*.
2022. 320 pages. ISBN 978-1-78997-978-7

Printed by
CPI books GmbH, Leck